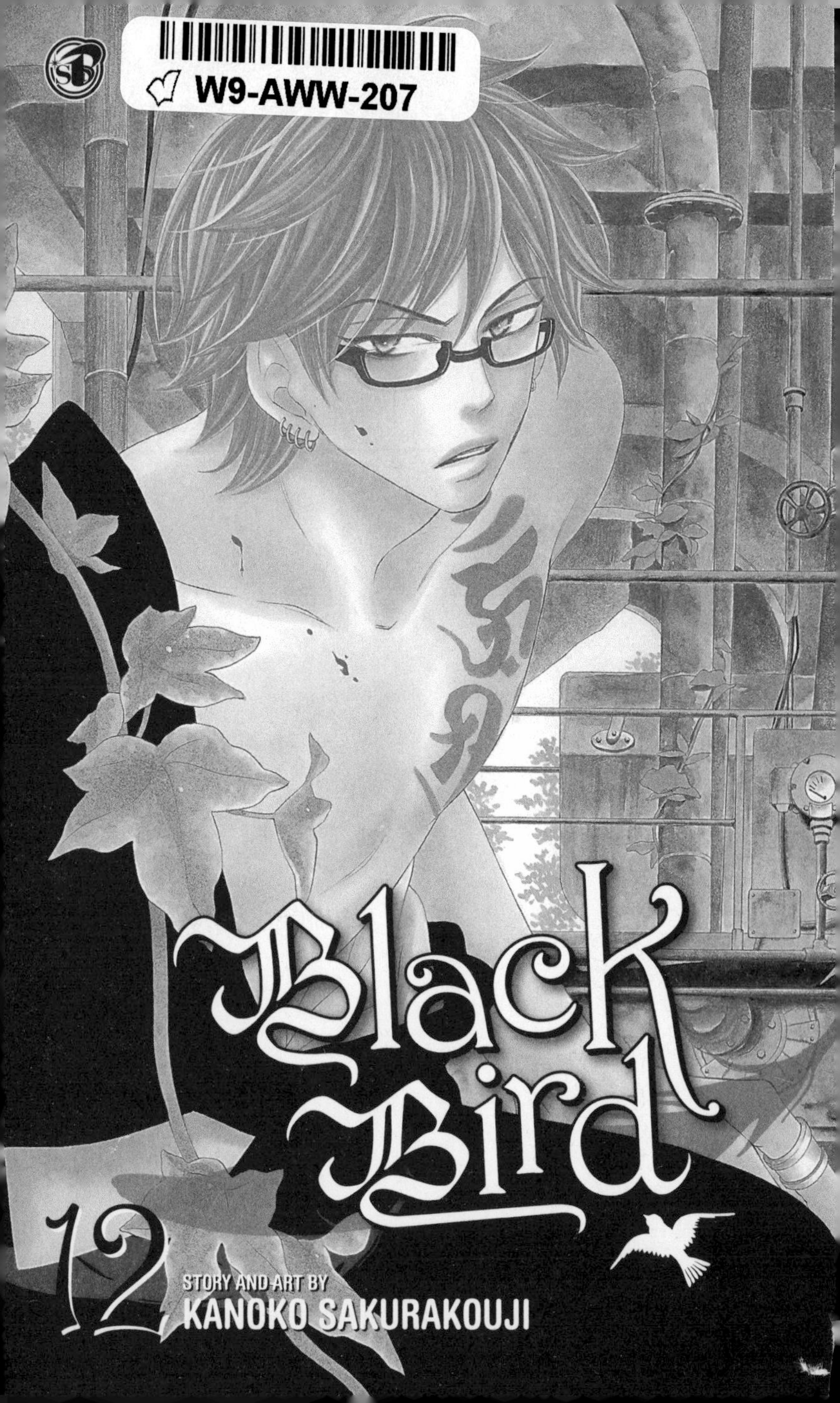
Black Bird
12
STORY AND ART BY
KANOKO SAKURAKOUJI

Black Bird

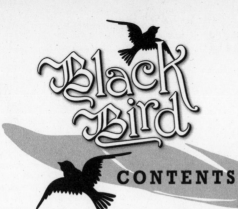

CONTENTS

CHARACTERS

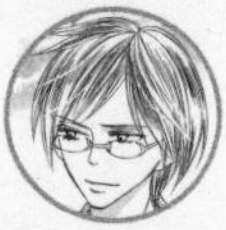

TADANOBU KUZUNOHA
Kyo's close friend since childhood. Current leader of the Kitsune clan.

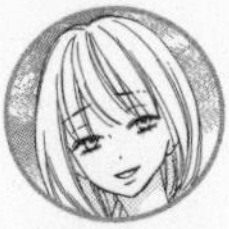

KAEDE
Her father Roh supported Sho's ambitions to seize the clan leadership. She is Sho's attendant.

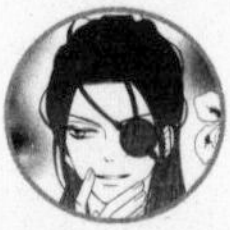

SHO USUI
Kyo's older brother and a ex-member of the Eight Daitengu. He is also know as Sojo. His attempted cou failed and his whereabou are currently unknown.

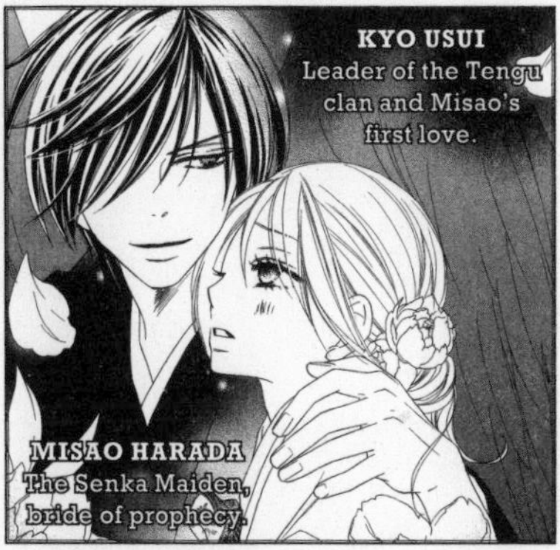
KYO USUI
Leader of the Tengu clan and Misao's first love.
MISAO HARADA
The Senka Maiden, bride of prophecy.

THE EIGHT DAITENGU
Kyo's bodyguards. Their names designate their official posts.

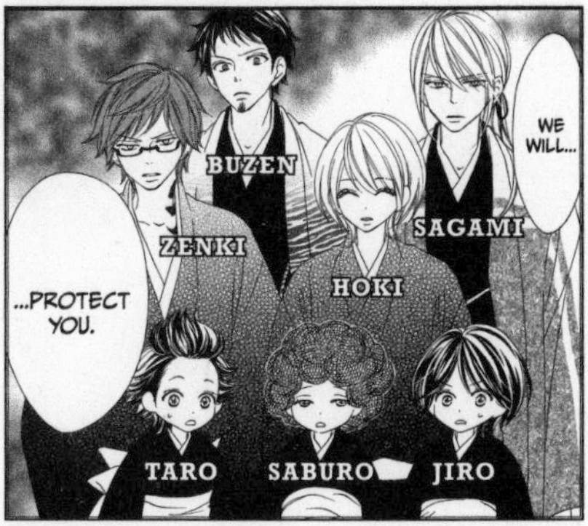
WE WILL...
...PROTECT YOU.
BUZEN
SAGAMI
ZENKI
HOKI
TARO
SABURO
JIRO

STORY THUS FAR
Misao can see spirits and demons, and her childhood sweetheart Kyo has been protecting her since she was little.

"Someday, I'll come for you, I promise." Kyo reappears the day before Misao's 16th birthday to tell her, "Your 16th birthday marks 'open season' on you." She is the Senka Maiden, and if a demon drinks her blood, he is granted a long life. If he eats her flesh, he gains eternal youth. And if he makes her his bride, his clan will prosper...And Kyo is a *tengu*, a crow demon, with his sights firmly set on her.

So far, Kyo has avoided sleeping with Misao because he knows that sex with a demon is somehow dangerous for the Senka Maiden, but when poison nearly kills him, he finally gives in and takes Misao.

Now that Kyo's powers have no equal, his older brother Sho, presumed dead, reappears. Sho plans to use the might he obtained through his resurrection, Misao's blood, and his domination of other demon clans to throw the tengu village into confusion and create a world of anarchy.

Fighting erupts that threatens to divide the village, and Sho tries to tear apart Kyo's loyal Daitengu by targeting their weakest points.

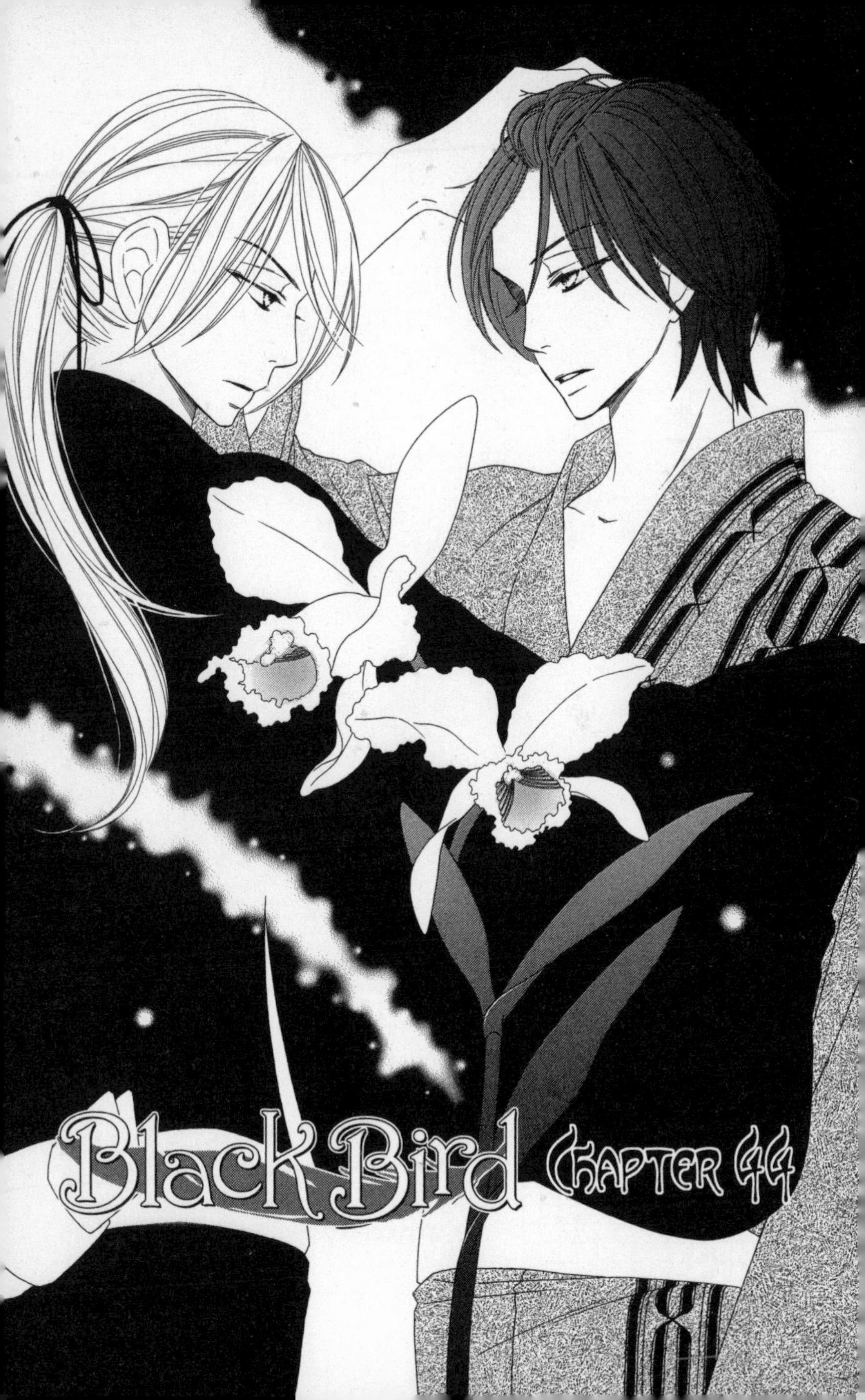
Black Bird
Chapter 44

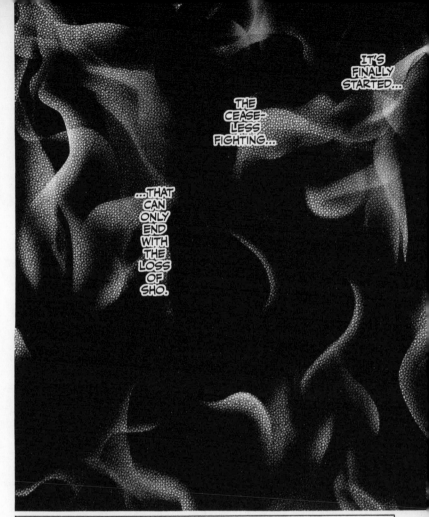

IT'S FINALLY STARTED...

THE CEASE-LESS FIGHTING...

...THAT CAN ONLY END WITH THE LOSS OF SHO.

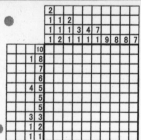

Hello. This is Kanako Sakurakouji. ♡
Finally, the long awaited Volume 12... ✦
I've gotten this far thanks
to all of you!

I've created a Picross puzzle.
← Who could be hiding here?

6

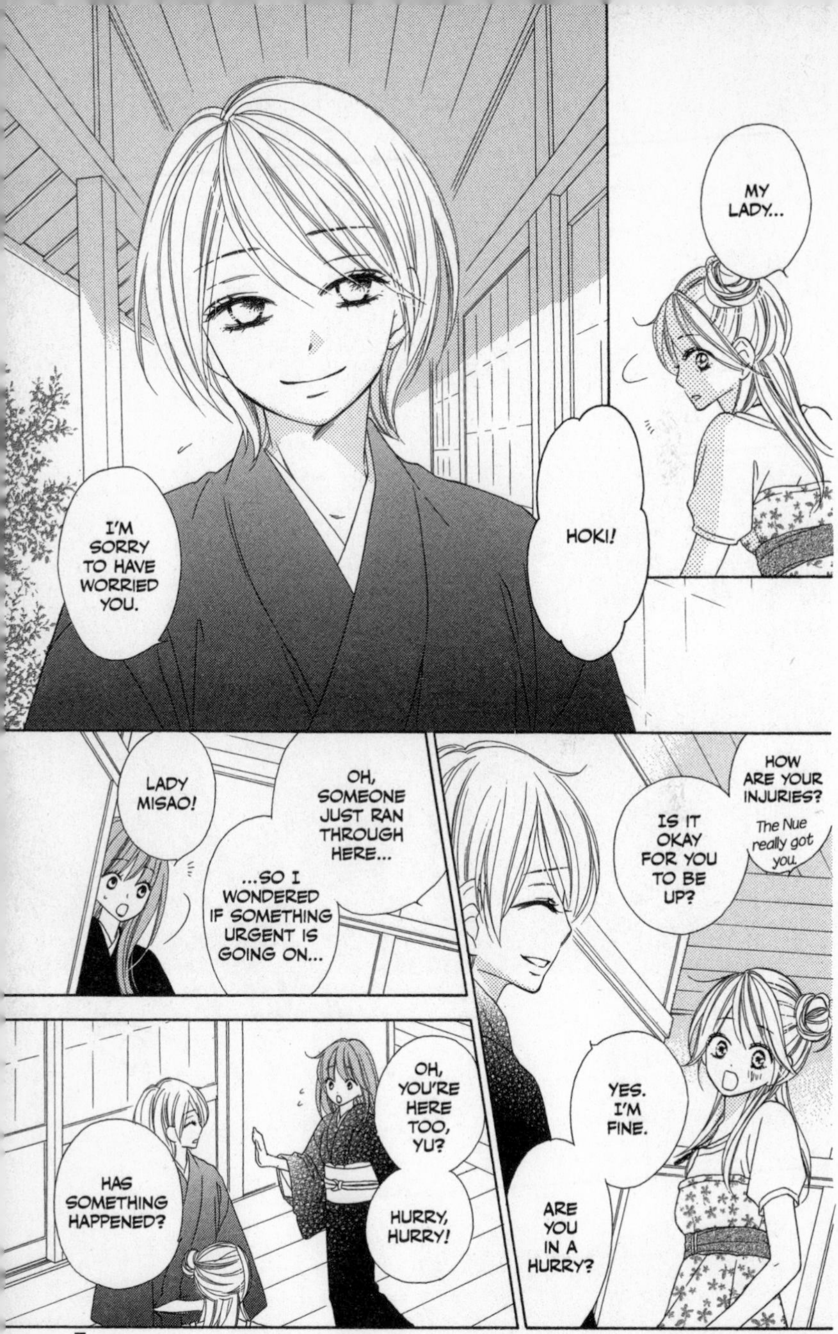
MY LADY...
HOKI!
I'M SORRY TO HAVE WORRIED YOU.
HOW ARE YOUR INJURIES?
The Nue really got you.
IS IT OKAY FOR YOU TO BE UP?
YES. I'M FINE.
ARE YOU IN A HURRY?
LADY MISAO!
OH, SOMEONE JUST RAN THROUGH HERE...
...SO I WONDERED IF SOMETHING URGENT IS GOING ON...
OH, YOU'RE HERE TOO, YU?
HURRY, HURRY!
HAS SOMETHING HAPPENED?

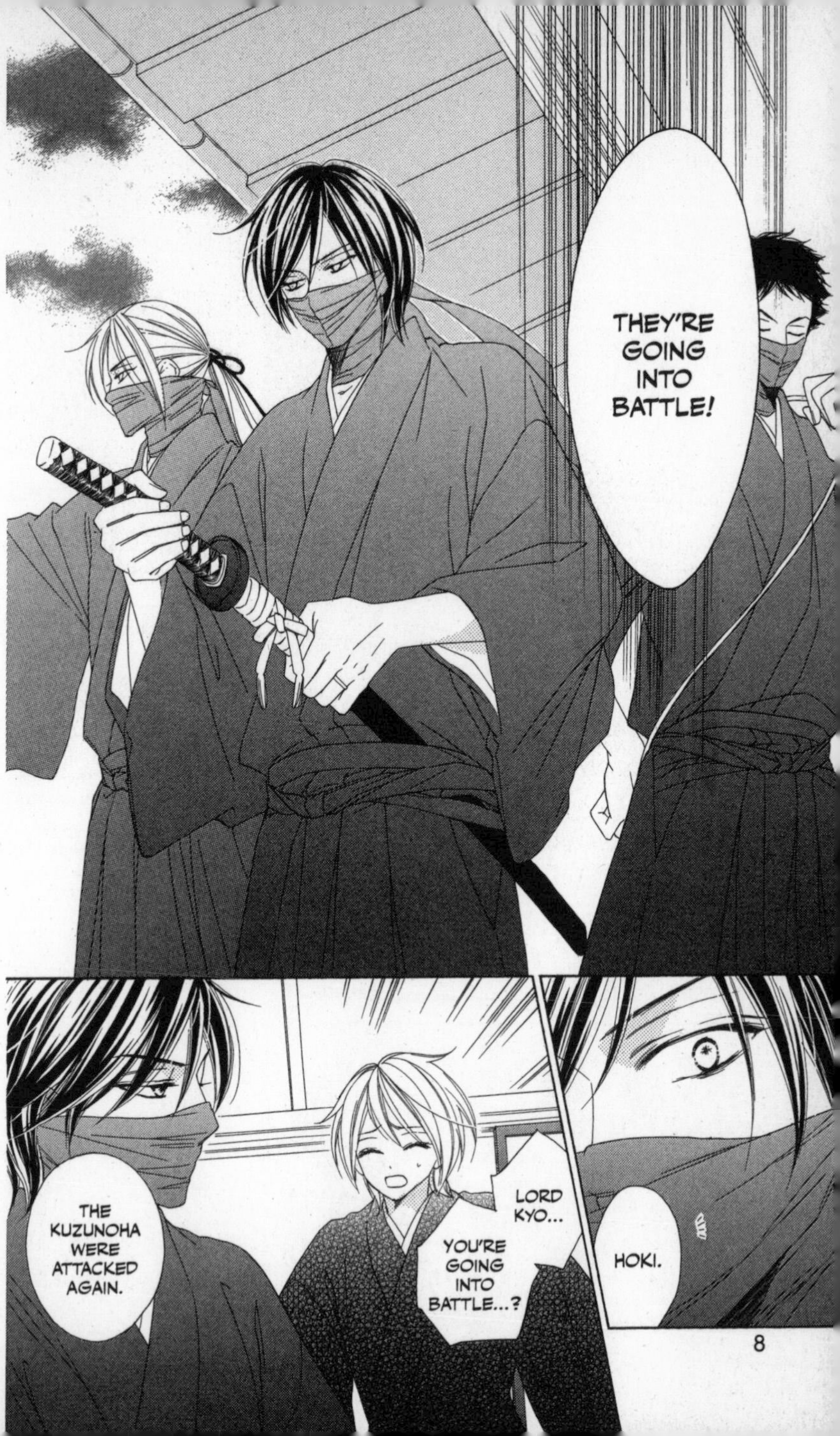
THEY'RE GOING INTO BATTLE!
HOKI.
LORD KYO...
YOU'RE GOING INTO BATTLE...?
THE KUZUNOHA WERE ATTACKED AGAIN.

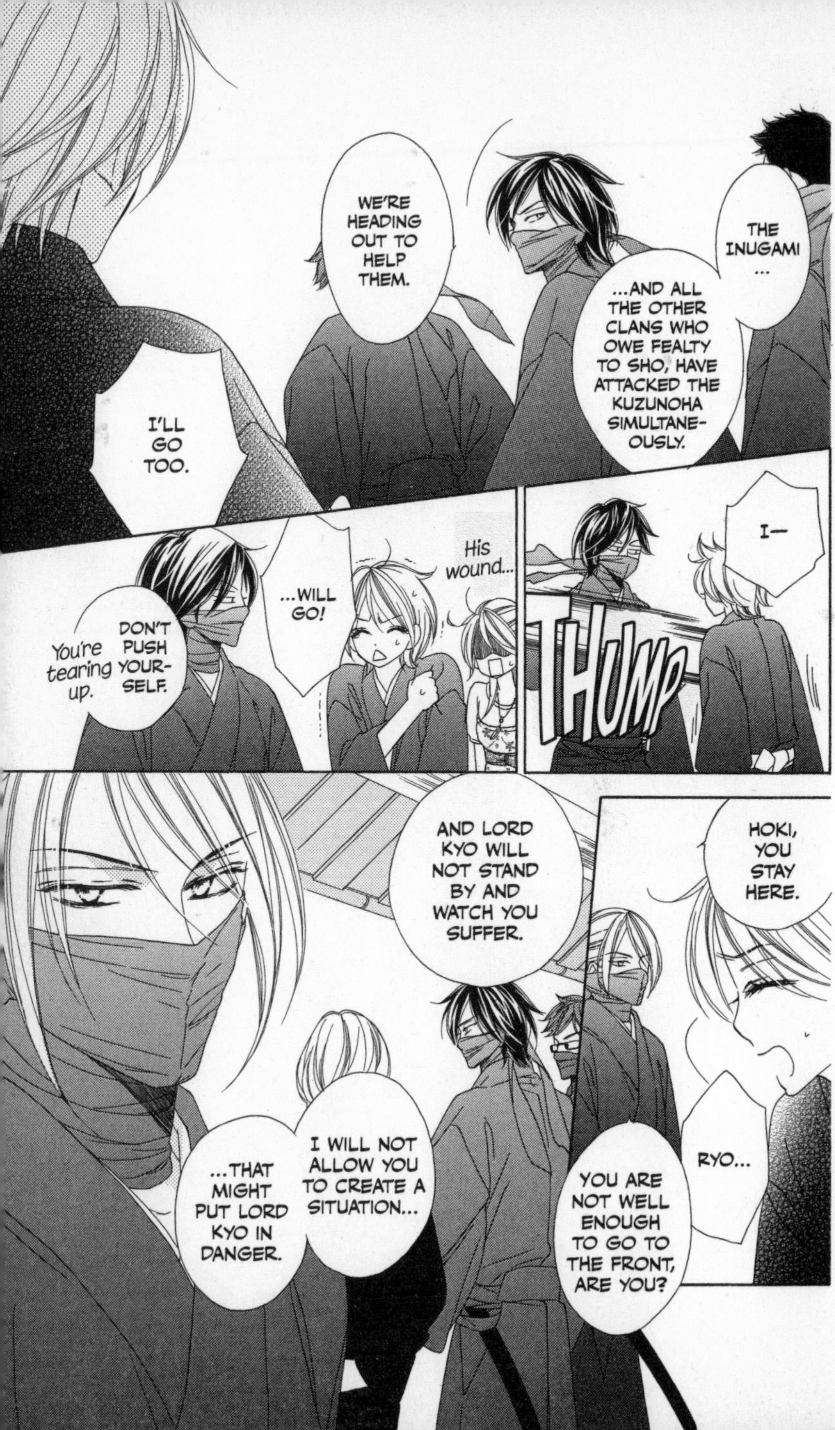
THE INUGAMI ...
...AND ALL THE OTHER CLANS WHO OWE FEALTY TO SHO, HAVE ATTACKED THE KUZUNOHA SIMULTANEOUSLY.
WE'RE HEADING OUT TO HELP THEM.
I'LL GO TOO.
I—
THUMP
His wound...
...WILL GO!
DON'T PUSH YOURSELF.
You're tearing up.
HOKI, YOU STAY HERE.
RYO...
YOU ARE NOT WELL ENOUGH TO GO TO THE FRONT, ARE YOU?
AND LORD KYO WILL NOT STAND BY AND WATCH YOU SUFFER.
I WILL NOT ALLOW YOU TO CREATE A SITUATION...
...THAT MIGHT PUT LORD KYO IN DANGER.

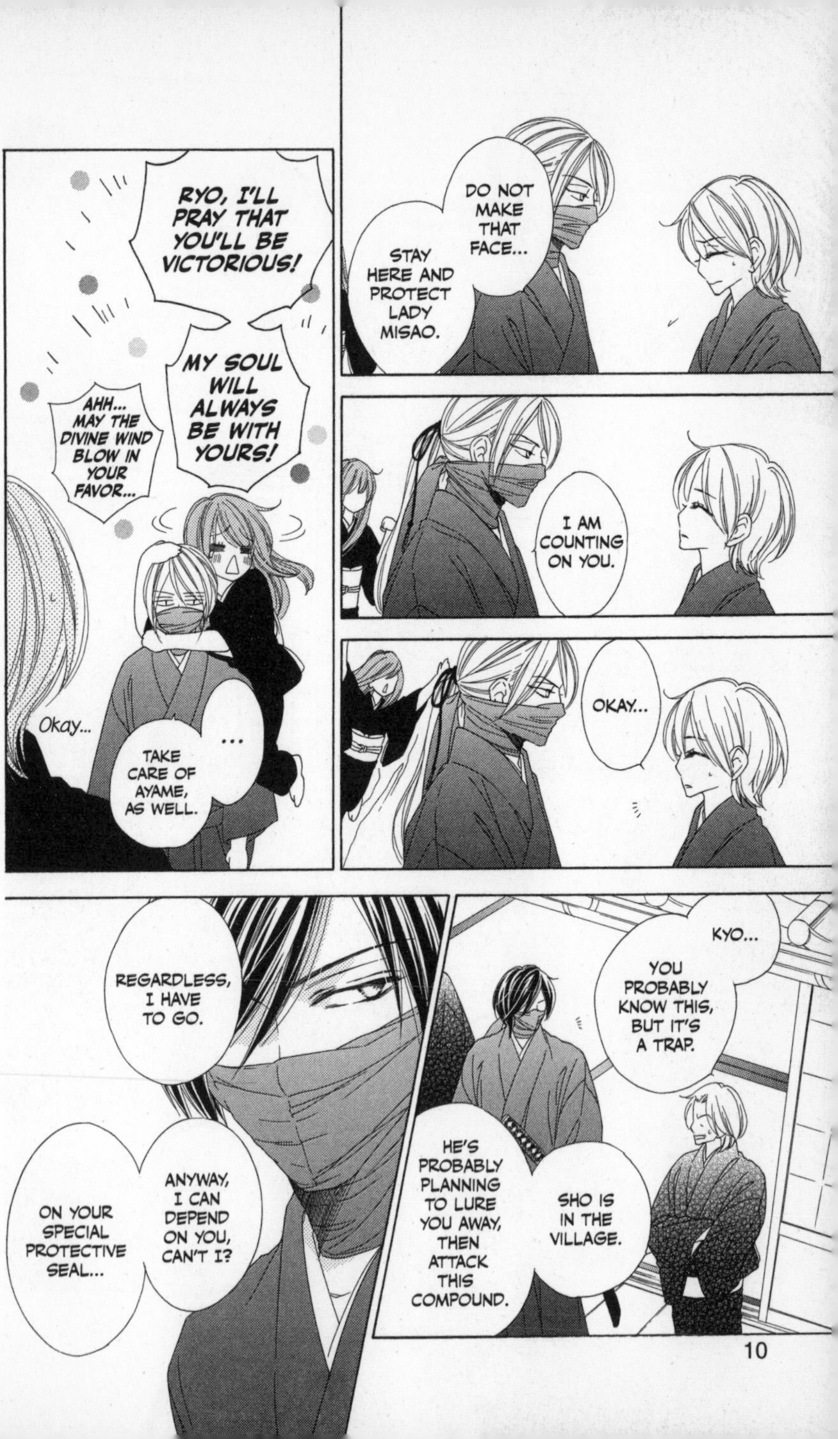
DO NOT MAKE THAT FACE...
STAY HERE AND PROTECT LADY MISAO.
I AM COUNTING ON YOU.
OKAY...
RYO, I'LL PRAY THAT YOU'LL BE VICTORIOUS!
MY SOUL WILL ALWAYS BE WITH YOURS!
AHH... MAY THE DIVINE WIND BLOW IN YOUR FAVOR...
...
TAKE CARE OF AYAME, AS WELL.
Okay...
KYO...
YOU PROBABLY KNOW THIS, BUT IT'S A TRAP.
SHO IS IN THE VILLAGE.
HE'S PROBABLY PLANNING TO LURE YOU AWAY, THEN ATTACK THIS COMPOUND.
REGARDLESS, I HAVE TO GO.
ANYWAY, I CAN DEPEND ON YOU, CAN'T I?
ON YOUR SPECIAL PROTECTIVE SEAL...

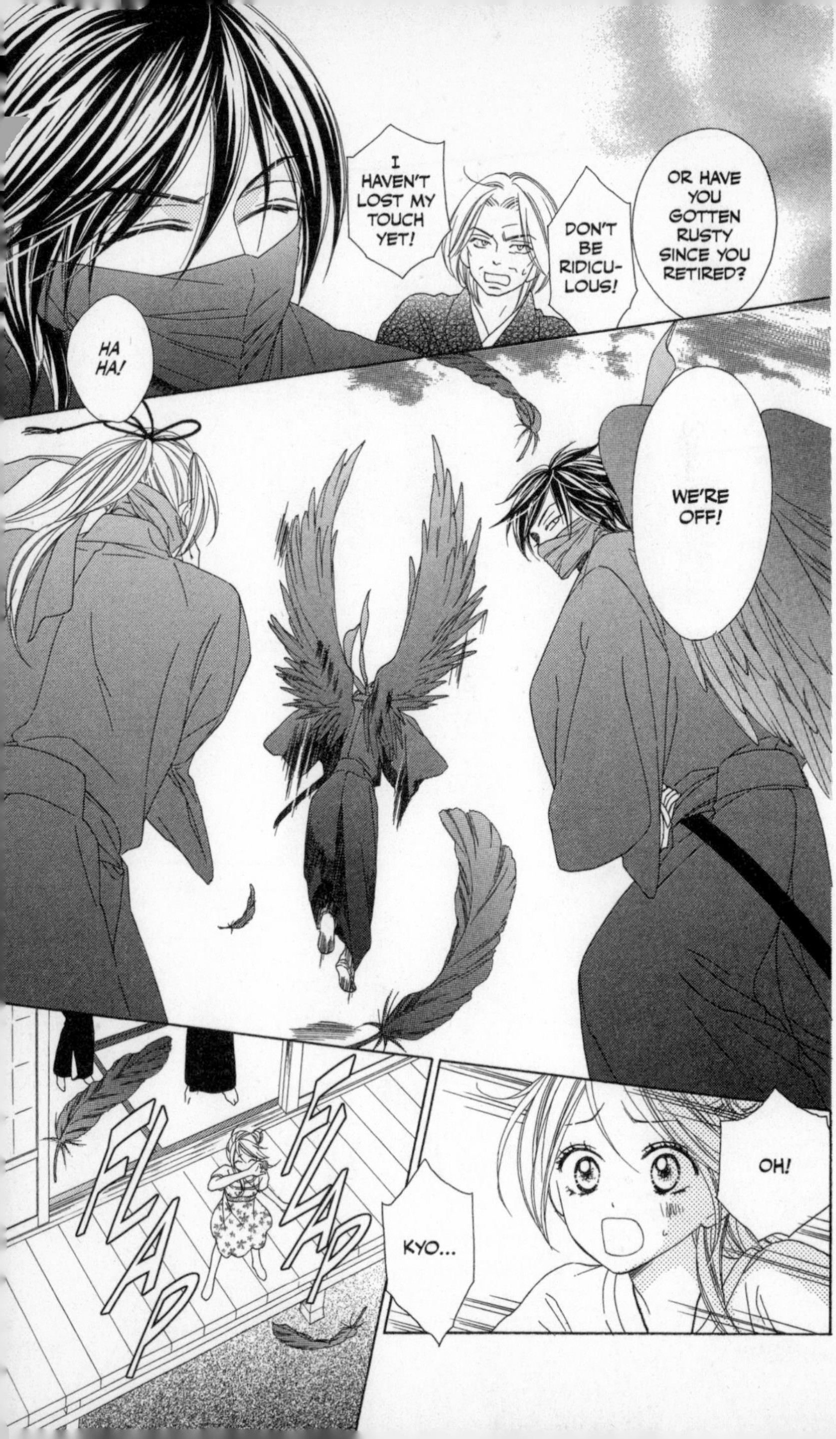
OR HAVE YOU GOTTEN RUSTY SINCE YOU RETIRED?
DON'T BE RIDICULOUS!
I HAVEN'T LOST MY TOUCH YET!
HA HA!
WE'RE OFF!
OH!
KYO...
FLAP
FLAP

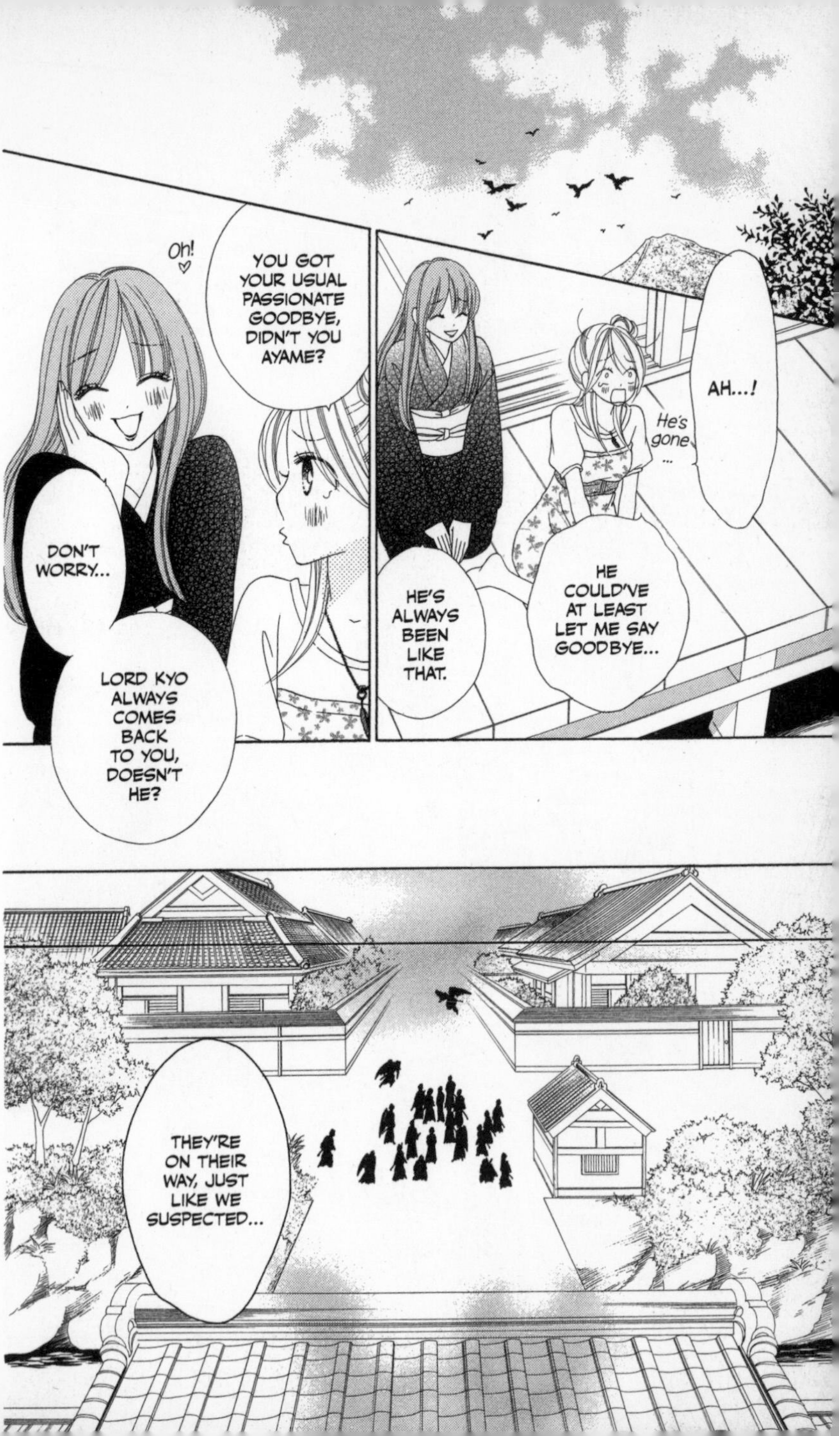
AH...!
He's gone...
HE COULD'VE AT LEAST LET ME SAY GOODBYE...
HE'S ALWAYS BEEN LIKE THAT.
YOU GOT YOUR USUAL PASSIONATE GOODBYE, DIDN'T YOU AYAME?
Oh! ♡
DON'T WORRY...
LORD KYO ALWAYS COMES BACK TO YOU, DOESN'T HE?
THEY'RE ON THEIR WAY, JUST LIKE WE SUSPECTED...

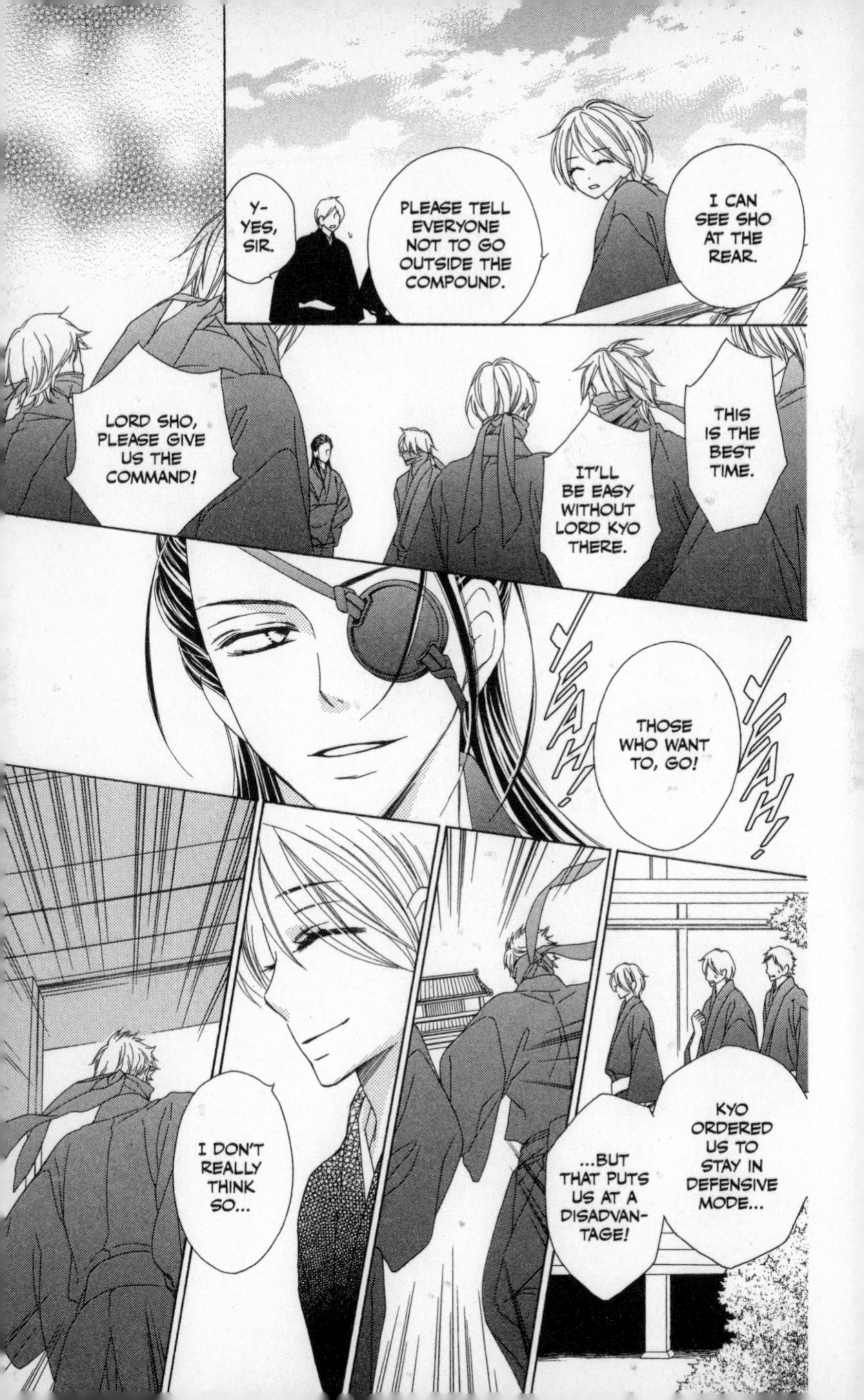
I CAN SEE SHO AT THE REAR.
PLEASE TELL EVERYONE NOT TO GO OUTSIDE THE COMPOUND.
Y-YES, SIR.
THIS IS THE BEST TIME.
IT'LL BE EASY WITHOUT LORD KYO THERE.
LORD SHO, PLEASE GIVE US THE COMMAND!
YEAH!
THOSE WHO WANT TO, GO!
YEAH!
KYO ORDERED US TO STAY IN DEFENSIVE MODE...
...BUT THAT PUTS US AT A DISADVANTAGE!
I DON'T REALLY THINK SO...

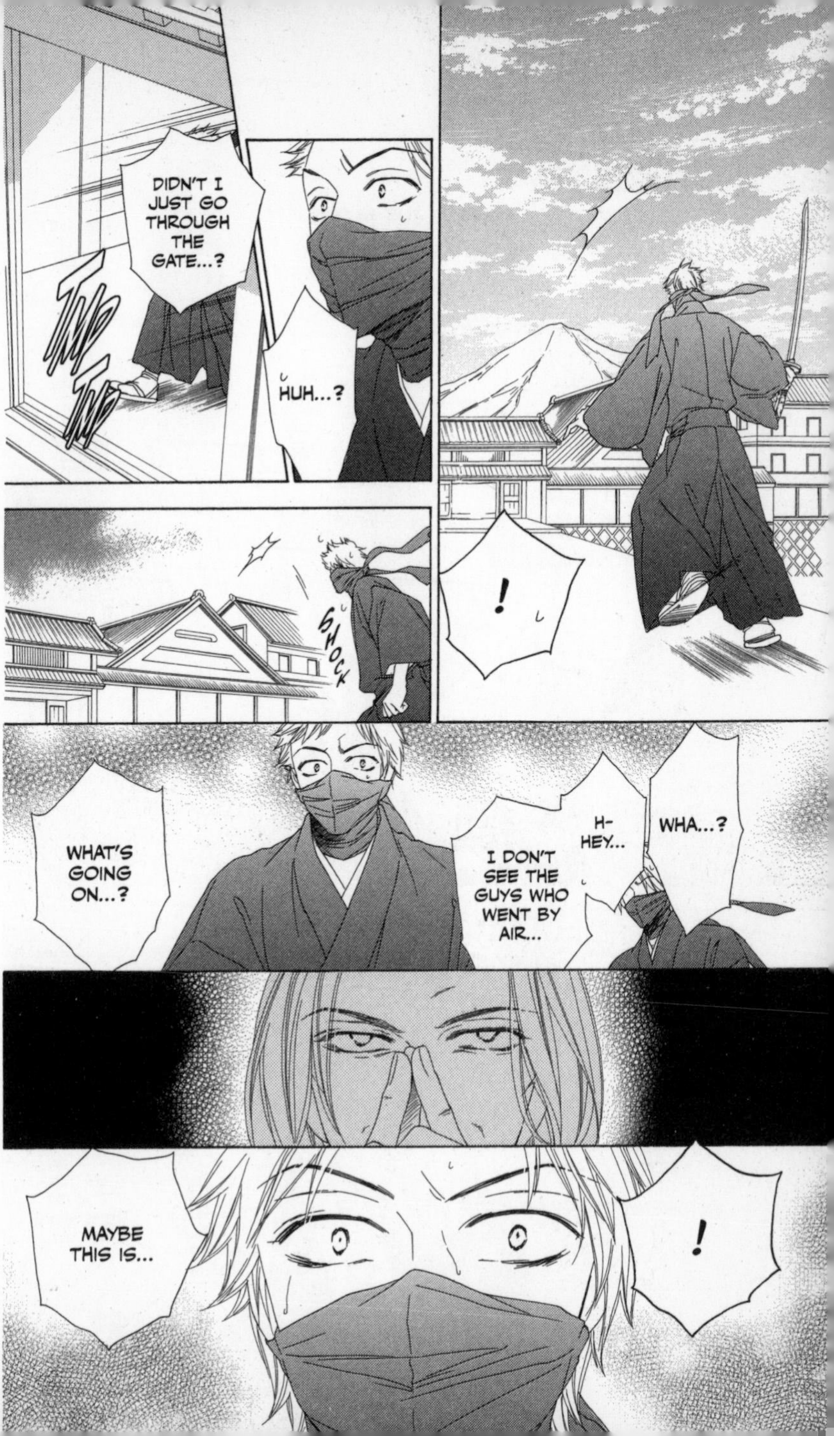
!
HUH...?
DIDN'T I JUST GO THROUGH THE GATE...?
SHOCK
WHA...?
H- HEY... I DON'T SEE THE GUYS WHO WENT BY AIR...
WHAT'S GOING ON...?
!
MAYBE THIS IS...

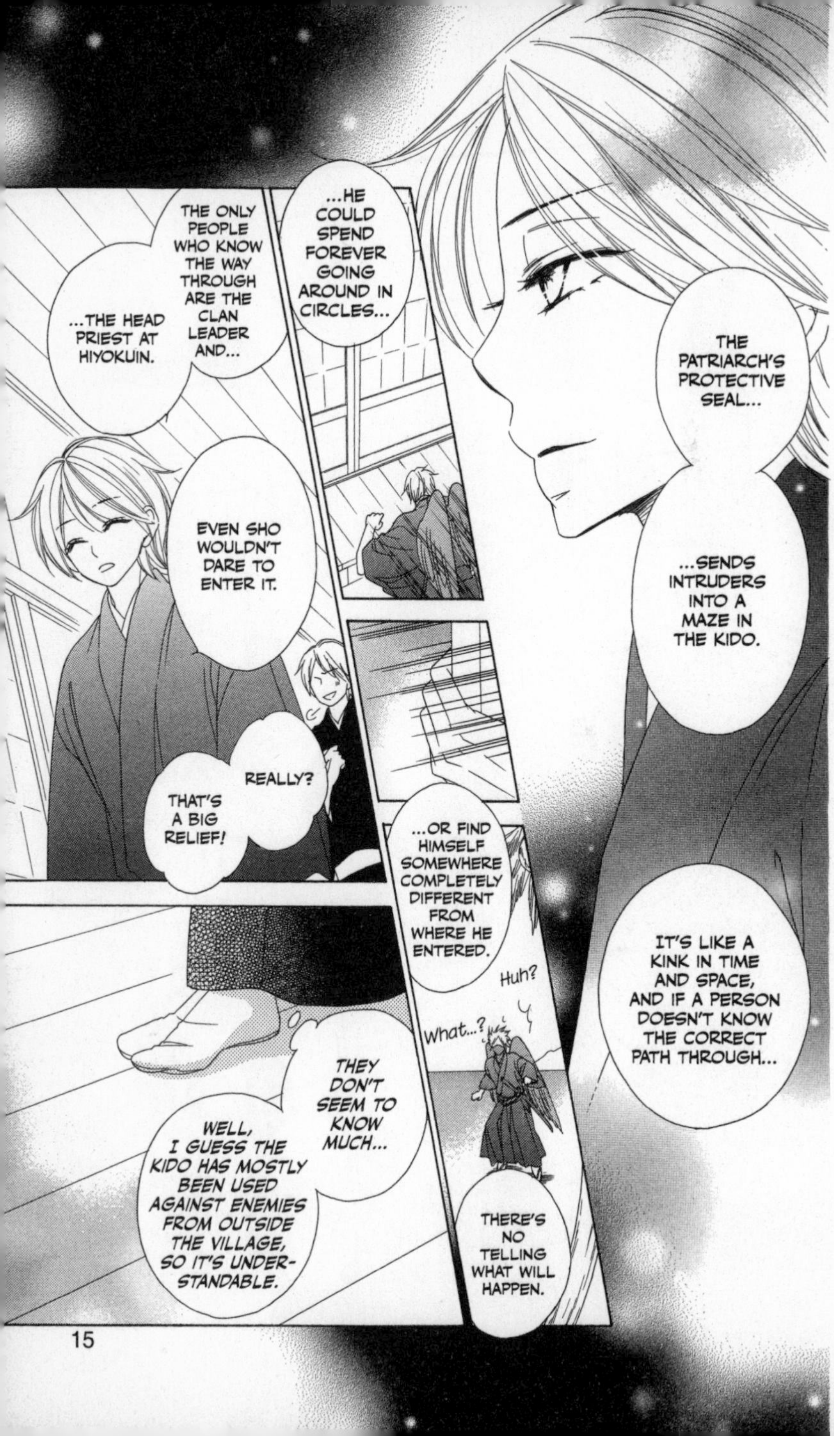
THE PATRIARCH'S PROTECTIVE SEAL...
...SENDS INTRUDERS INTO A MAZE IN THE KIDO.
IT'S LIKE A KINK IN TIME AND SPACE, AND IF A PERSON DOESN'T KNOW THE CORRECT PATH THROUGH...
...HE COULD SPEND FOREVER GOING AROUND IN CIRCLES...
...OR FIND HIMSELF SOMEWHERE COMPLETELY DIFFERENT FROM WHERE HE ENTERED.
Huh?
What...?
THERE'S NO TELLING WHAT WILL HAPPEN.
THE ONLY PEOPLE WHO KNOW THE WAY THROUGH ARE THE CLAN LEADER AND...
...THE HEAD PRIEST AT HIYOKUIN.
EVEN SHO WOULDN'T DARE TO ENTER IT.
REALLY?
THAT'S A BIG RELIEF!
THEY DON'T SEEM TO KNOW MUCH...
WELL, I GUESS THE KIDO HAS MOSTLY BEEN USED AGAINST ENEMIES FROM OUTSIDE THE VILLAGE, SO IT'S UNDER-STANDABLE.

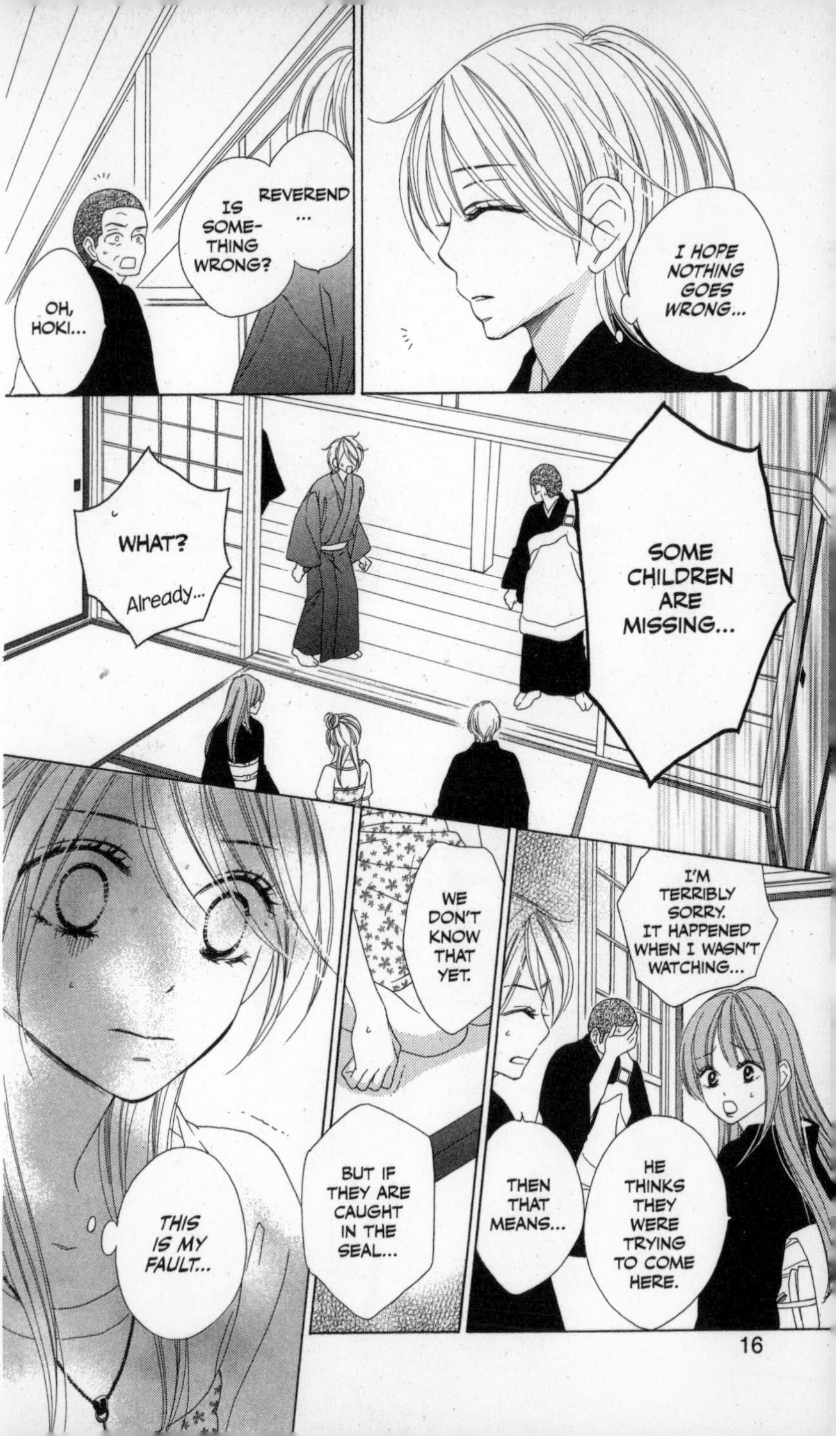
I HOPE NOTHING GOES WRONG...
REVEREND...
IS SOME-THING WRONG?
OH, HOKI...
SOME CHILDREN ARE MISSING...
WHAT? Already...
I'M TERRIBLY SORRY. IT HAPPENED WHEN I WASN'T WATCHING...
HE THINKS THEY WERE TRYING TO COME HERE.
THEN THAT MEANS...
WE DON'T KNOW THAT YET.
BUT IF THEY ARE CAUGHT IN THE SEAL...
THIS IS MY FAULT...

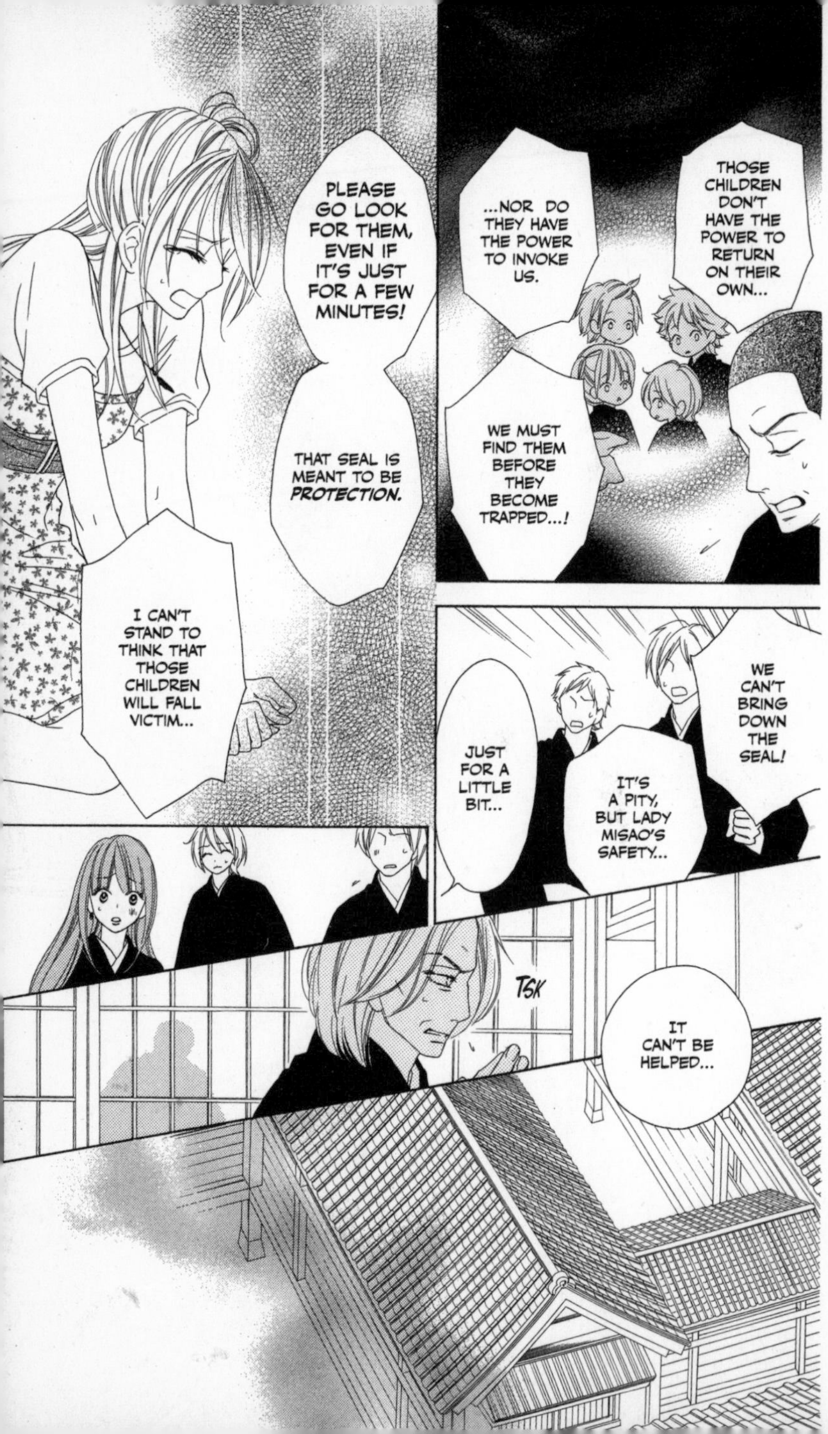
THOSE CHILDREN DON'T HAVE THE POWER TO RETURN ON THEIR OWN...
...NOR DO THEY HAVE THE POWER TO INVOKE US.
WE MUST FIND THEM BEFORE THEY BECOME TRAPPED...!
WE CAN'T BRING DOWN THE SEAL!
IT'S A PITY, BUT LADY MISAO'S SAFETY...
JUST FOR A LITTLE BIT...
PLEASE GO LOOK FOR THEM, EVEN IF IT'S JUST FOR A FEW MINUTES!
THAT SEAL IS MEANT TO BE *PROTECTION.*
I CAN'T STAND TO THINK THAT THOSE CHILDREN WILL FALL VICTIM...
IT CAN'T BE HELPED...
TSK

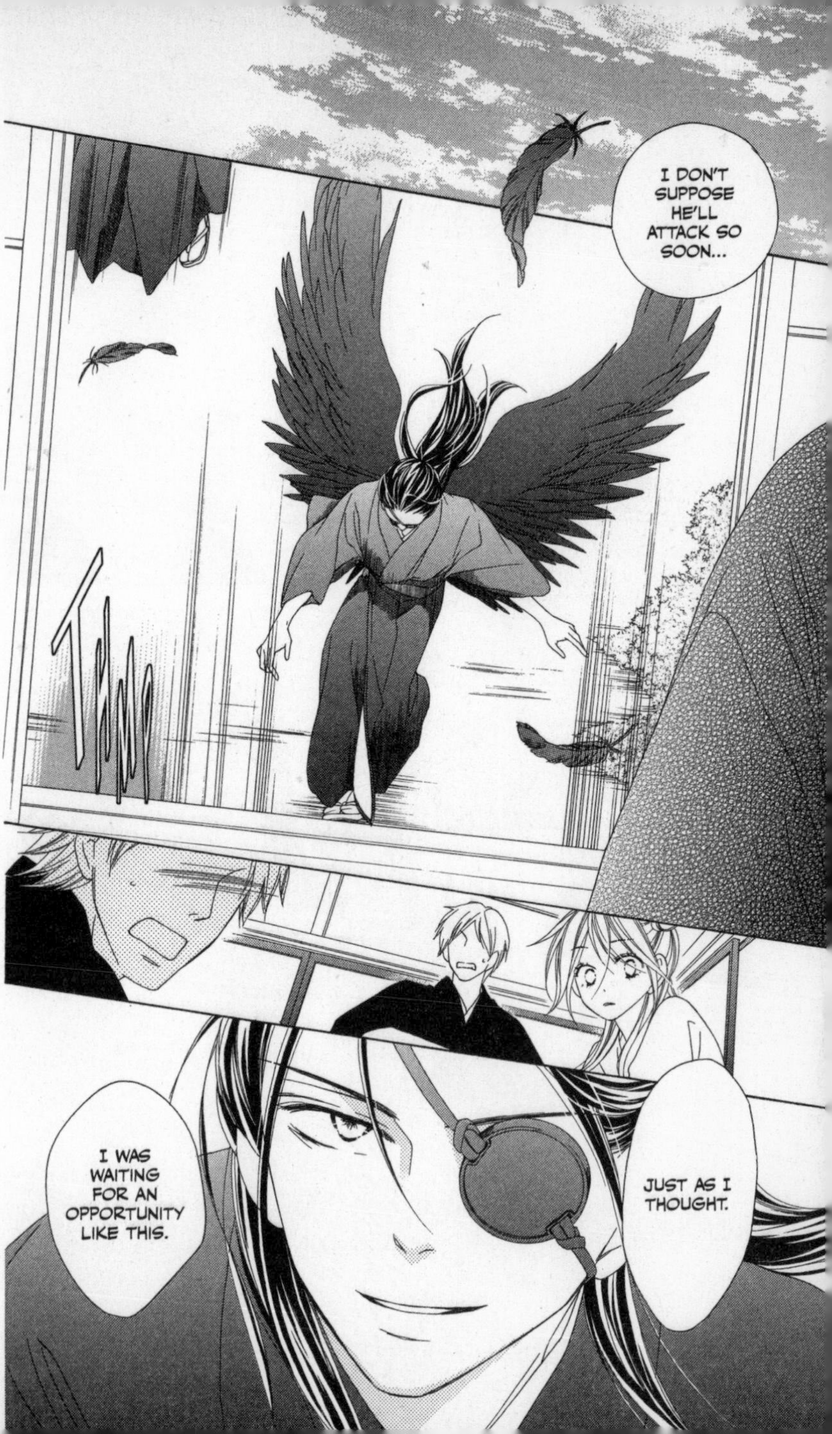
I DON'T SUPPOSE HE'LL ATTACK SO SOON...
JUST AS I THOUGHT.
I WAS WAITING FOR AN OPPORTUNITY LIKE THIS.

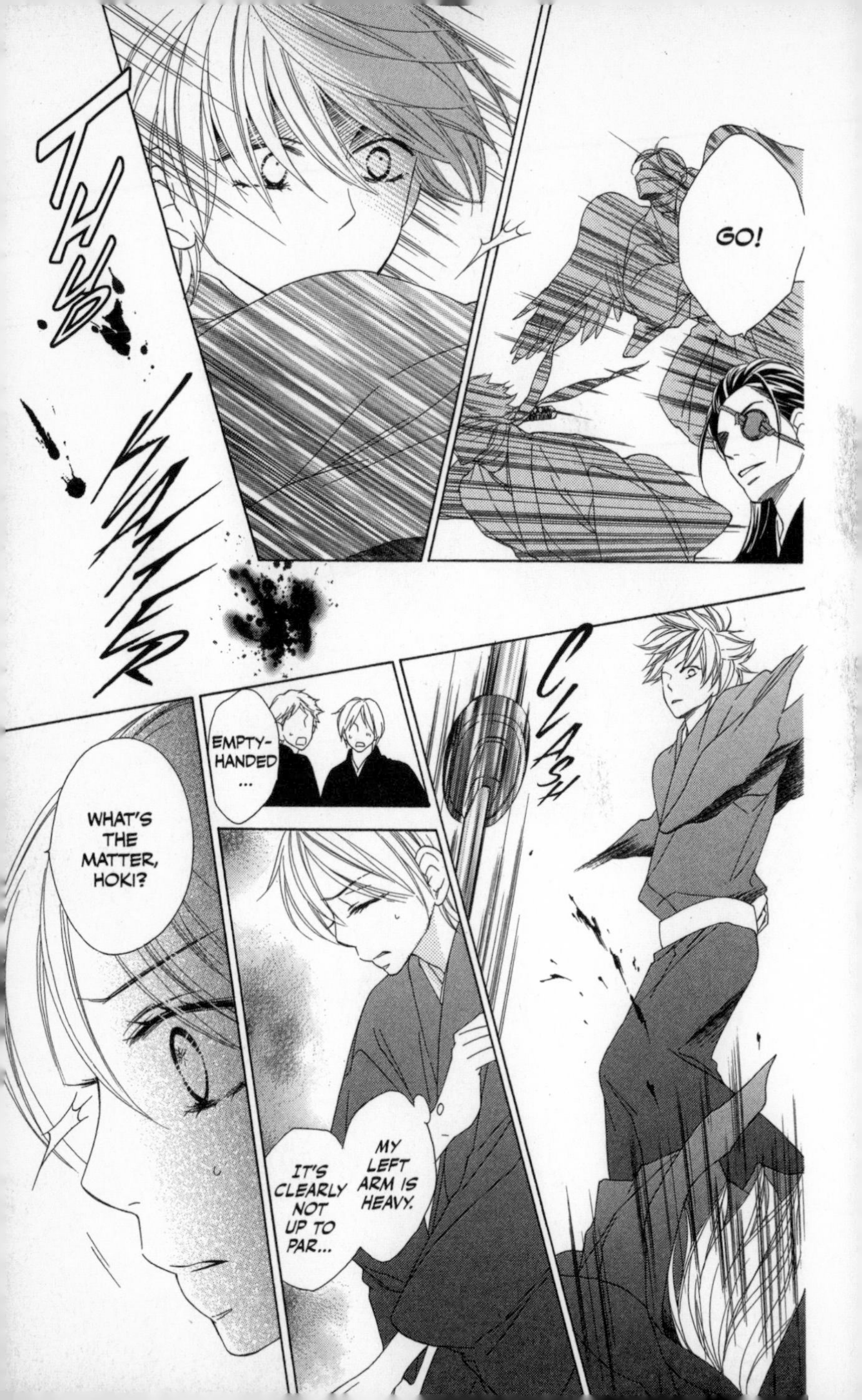
GO!
THUD
CLASH
EMPTY-HANDED...
MY LEFT ARM IS HEAVY.
IT'S CLEARLY NOT UP TO PAR...
WHAT'S THE MATTER, HOKI?

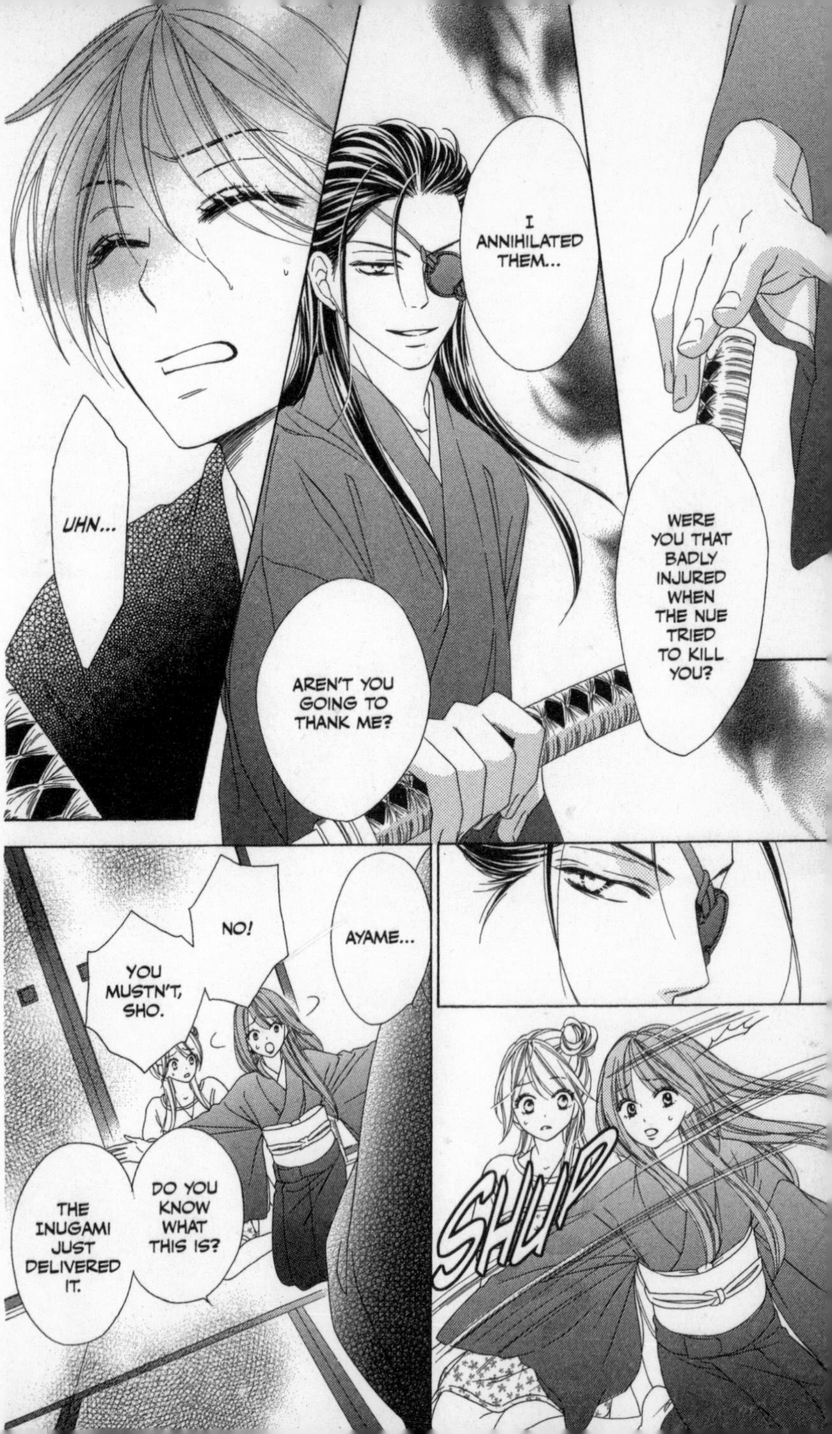
I ANNIHILATED THEM...
WERE YOU THAT BADLY INJURED WHEN THE NUE TRIED TO KILL YOU?
AREN'T YOU GOING TO THANK ME?
UHN...
SHUP
AYAME...
NO!
YOU MUSTN'T, SHO.
DO YOU KNOW WHAT THIS IS?
THE INUGAMI JUST DELIVERED IT.

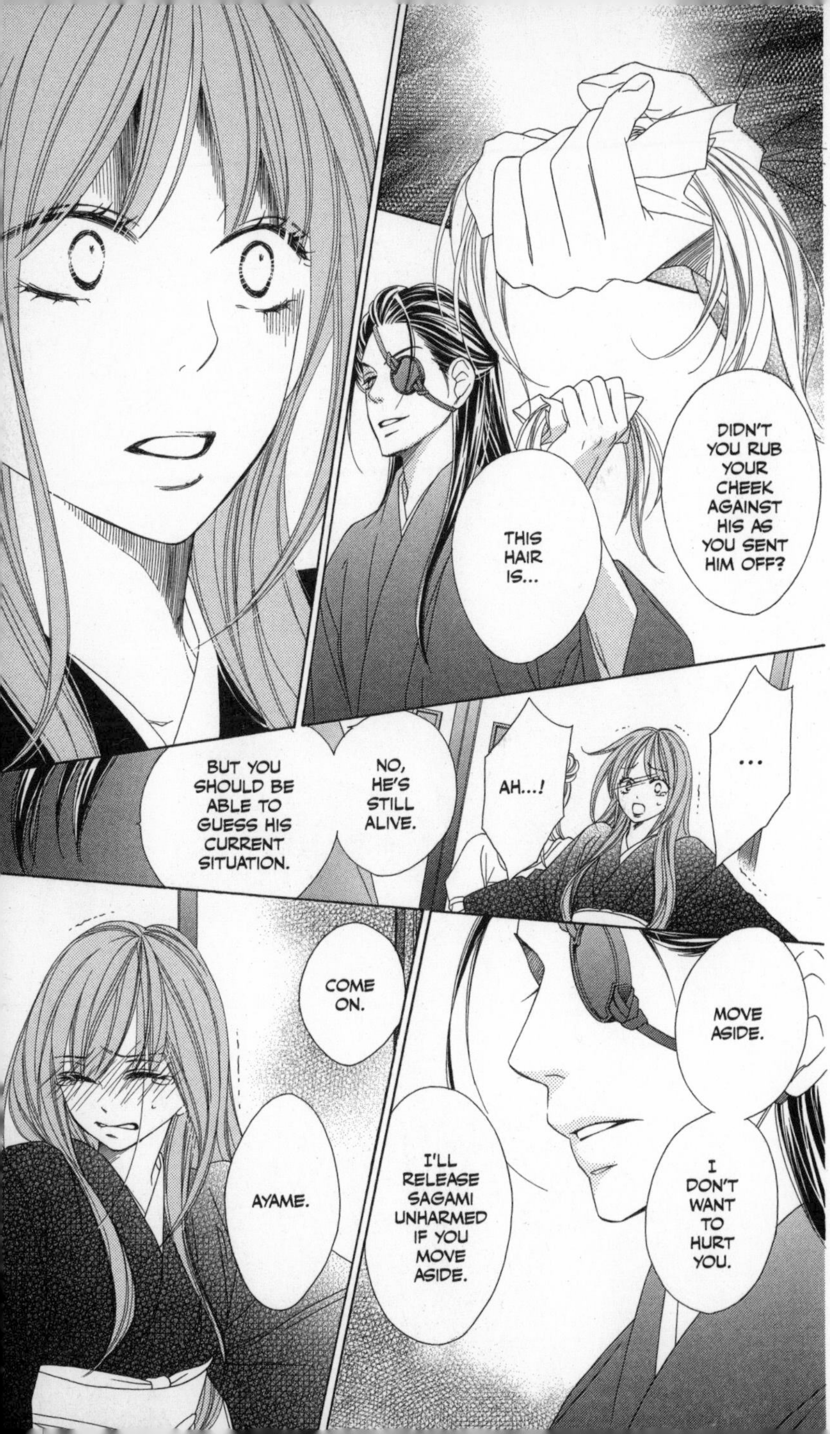
DIDN'T YOU RUB YOUR CHEEK AGAINST HIS AS YOU SENT HIM OFF?
THIS HAIR IS...
...
AH...!
NO, HE'S STILL ALIVE.
BUT YOU SHOULD BE ABLE TO GUESS HIS CURRENT SITUATION.
MOVE ASIDE.
I DON'T WANT TO HURT YOU.
I'LL RELEASE SAGAMI UNHARMED IF YOU MOVE ASIDE.
COME ON.
AYAME.

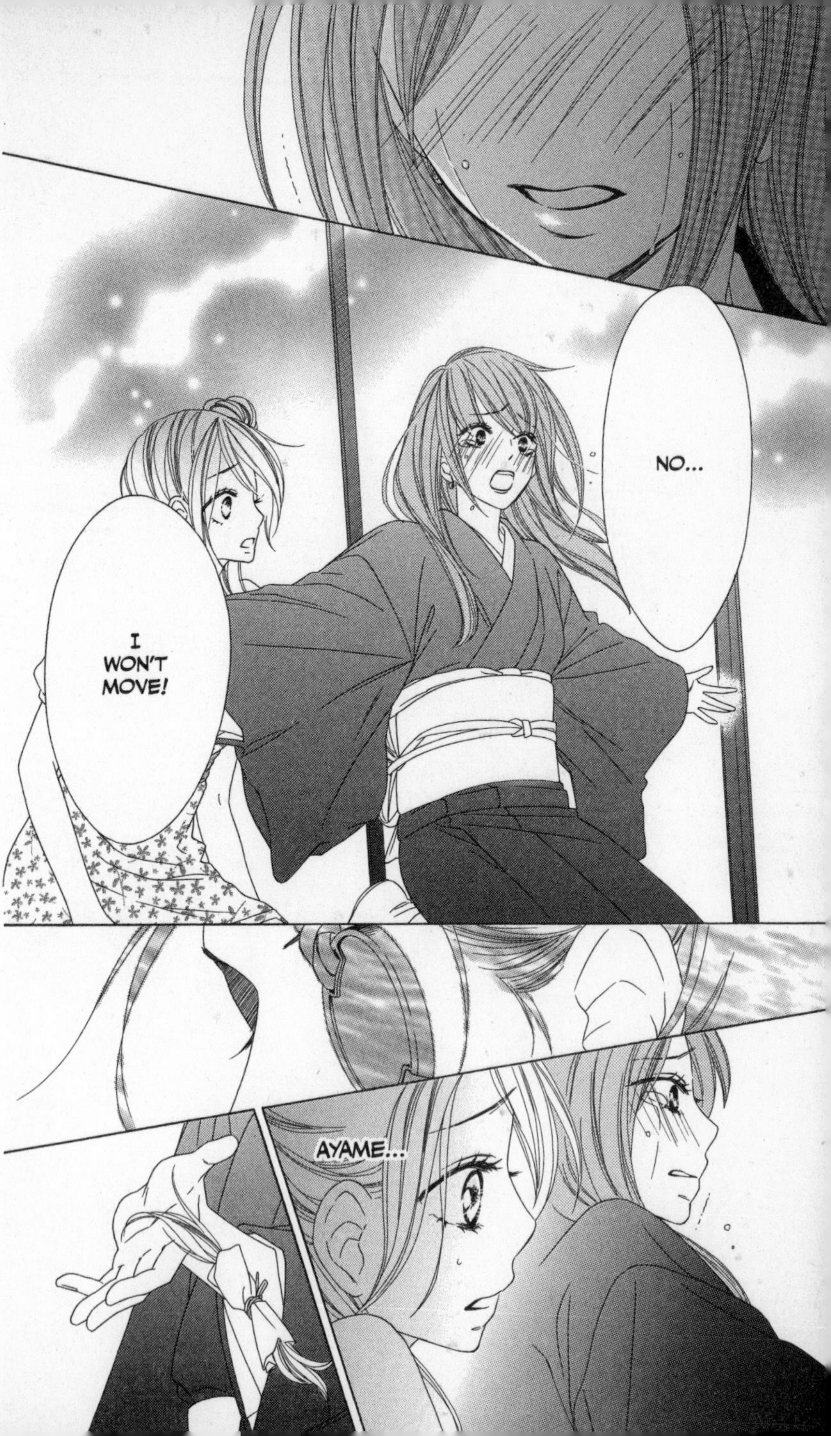
NO...
I WON'T MOVE!
AYAME...

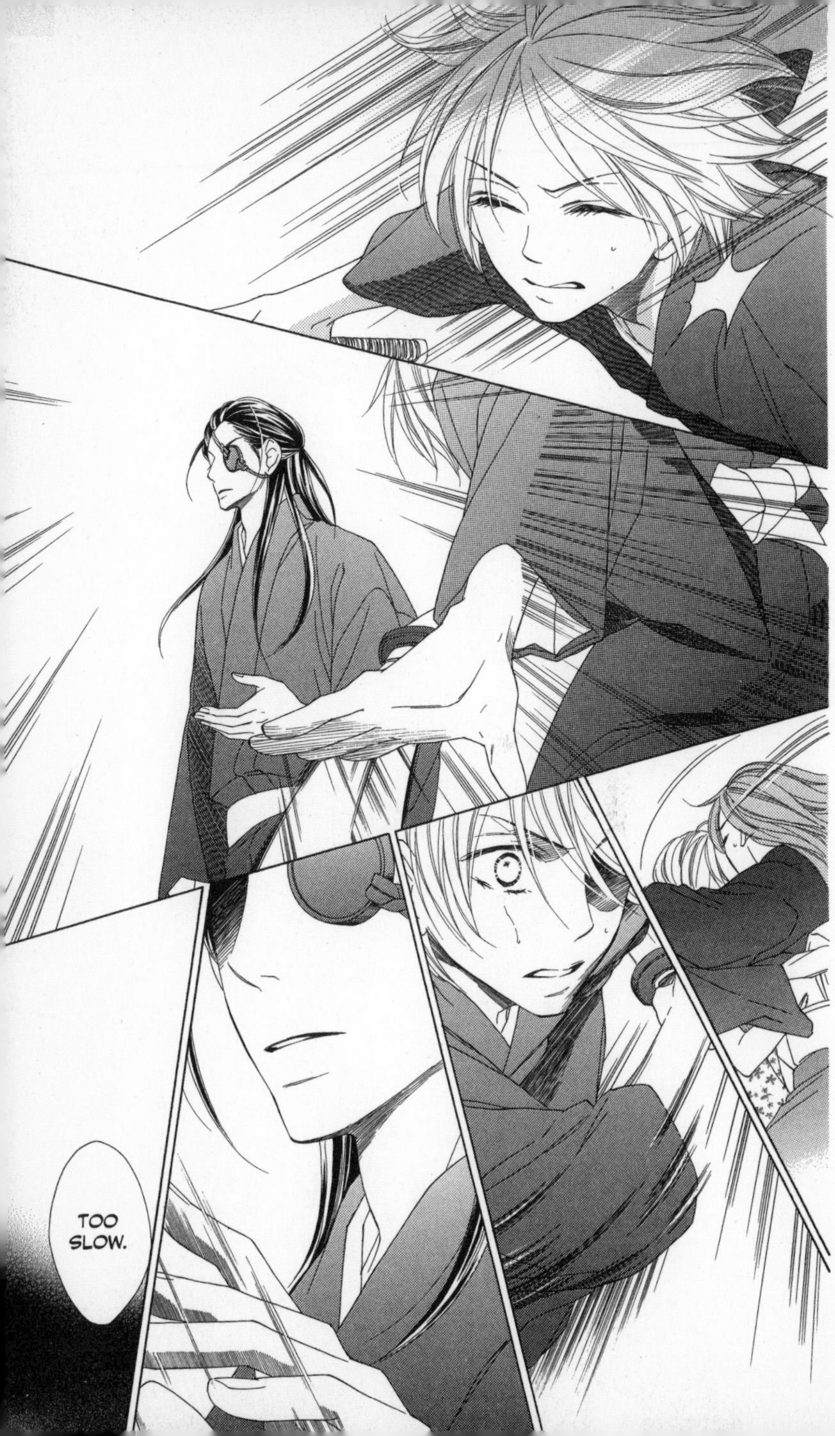
TOO SLOW.

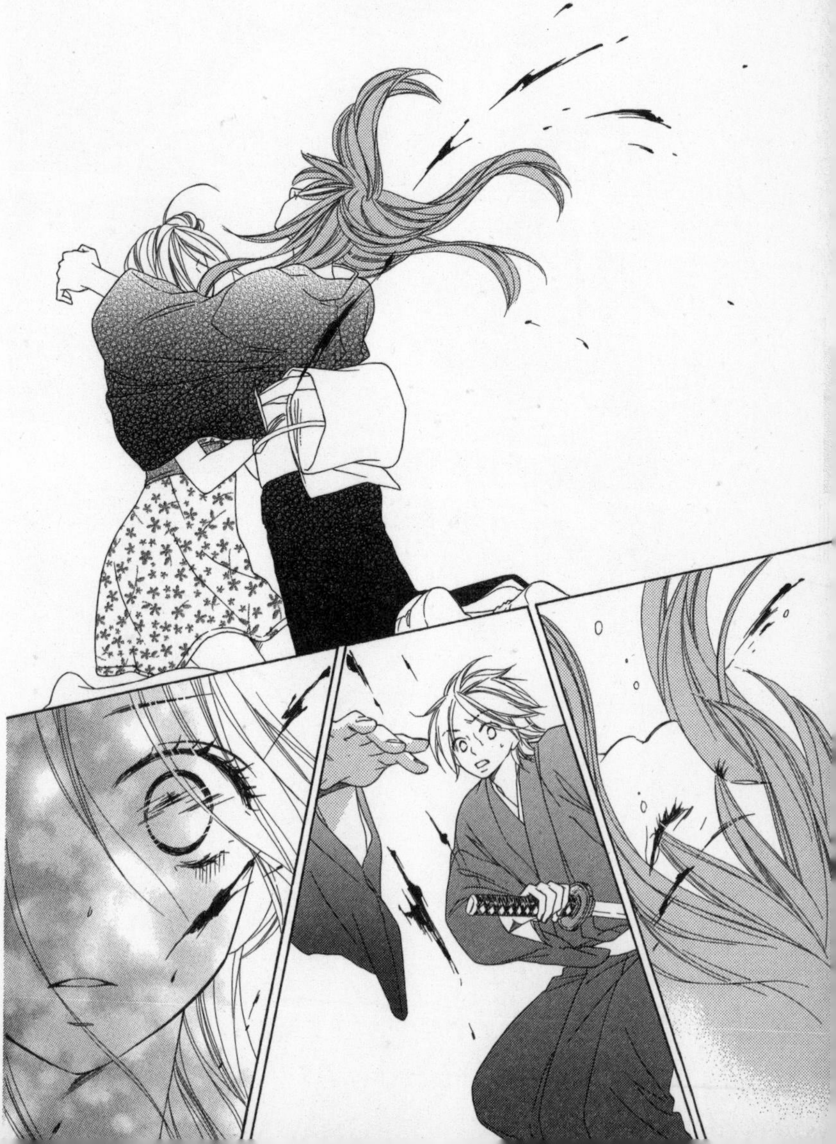

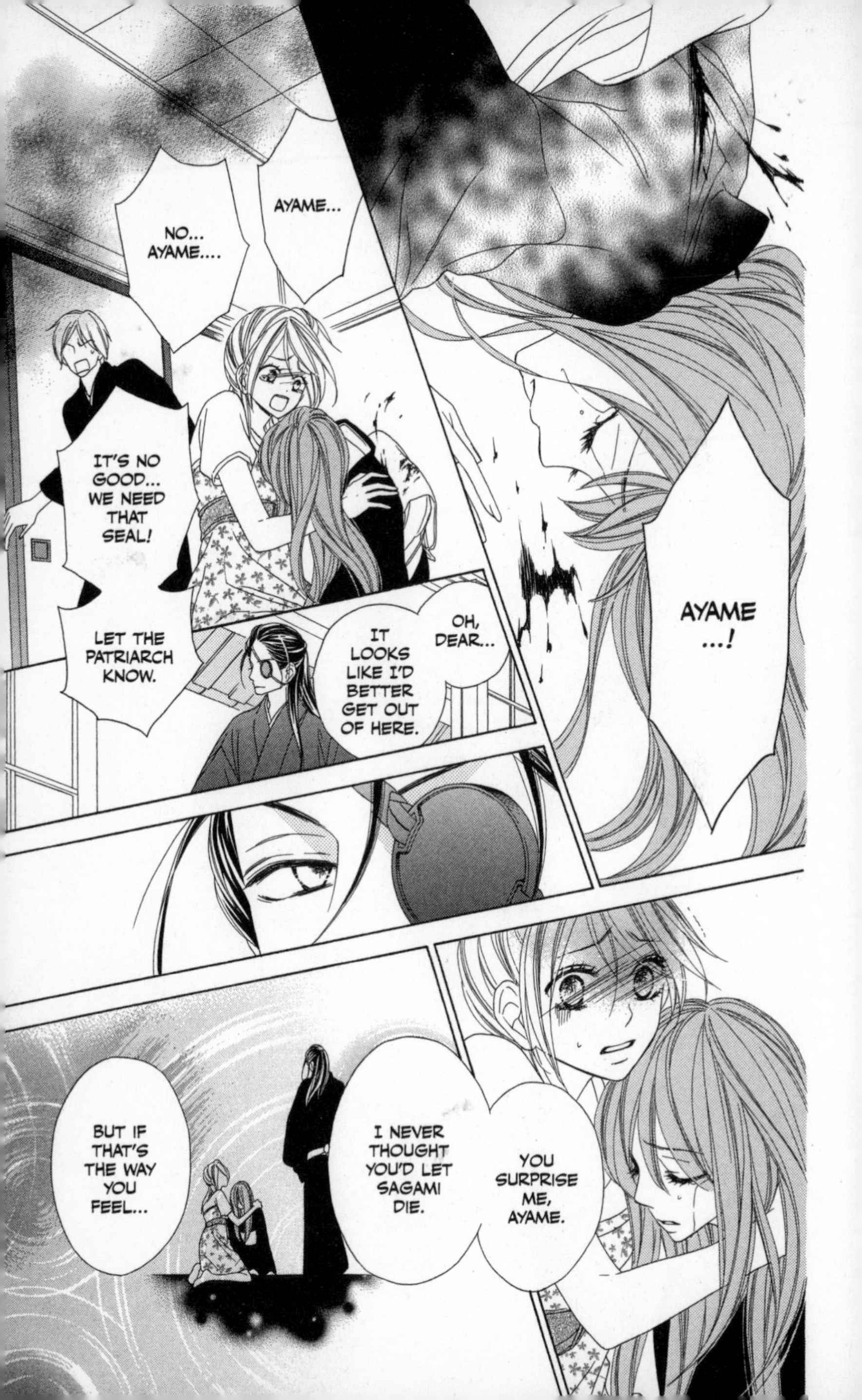
AYAME ...!
AYAME...
NO... AYAME....
IT'S NO GOOD... WE NEED THAT SEAL!
LET THE PATRIARCH KNOW.
OH, DEAR...
IT LOOKS LIKE I'D BETTER GET OUT OF HERE.
YOU SURPRISE ME, AYAME.
I NEVER THOUGHT YOU'D LET SAGAMI DIE.
BUT IF THAT'S THE WAY YOU FEEL...

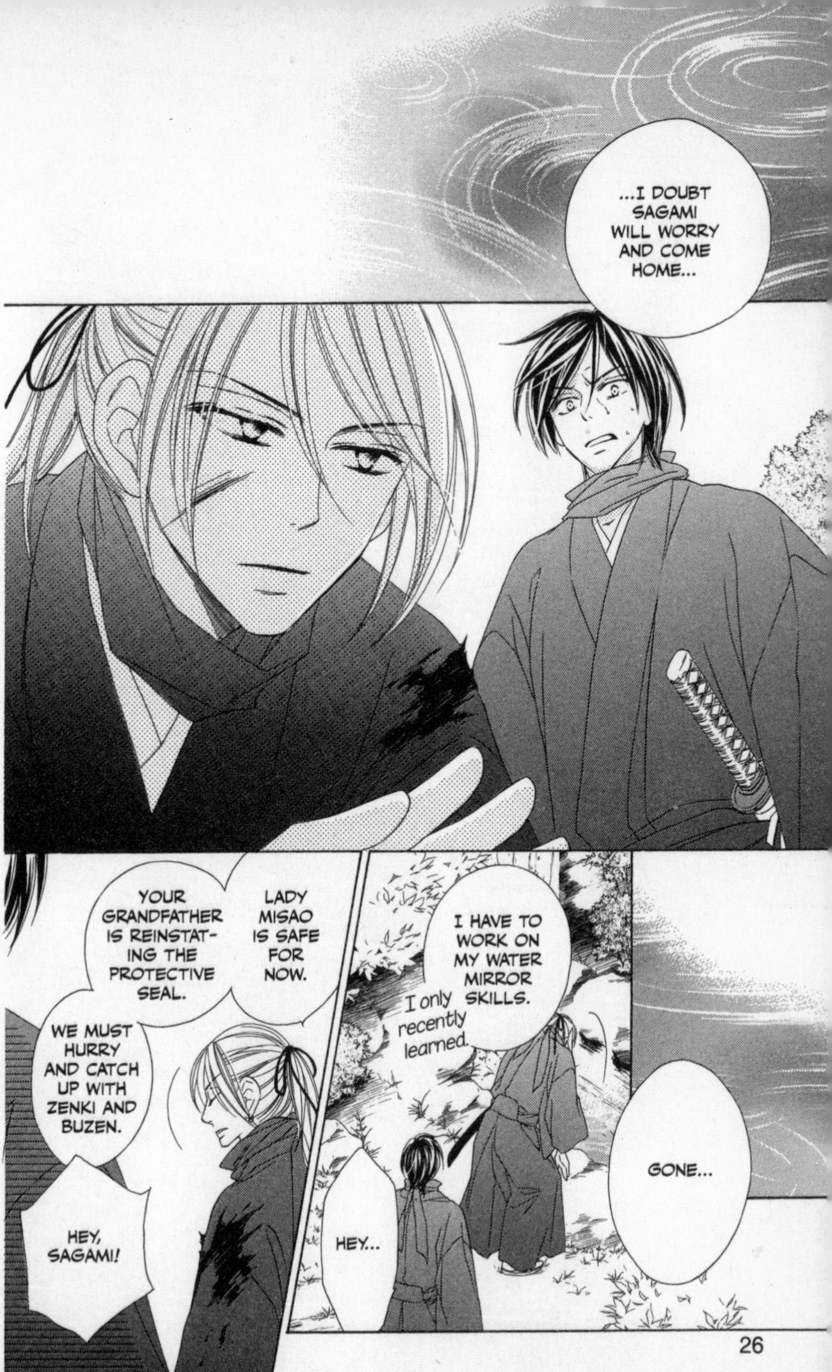
...I DOUBT SAGAMI WILL WORRY AND COME HOME...
GONE...
I HAVE TO WORK ON MY WATER MIRROR SKILLS.
I only recently learned.
HEY...
LADY MISAO IS SAFE FOR NOW.
YOUR GRANDFATHER IS REINSTATING THE PROTECTIVE SEAL.
WE MUST HURRY AND CATCH UP WITH ZENKI AND BUZEN.
HEY, SAGAMI!

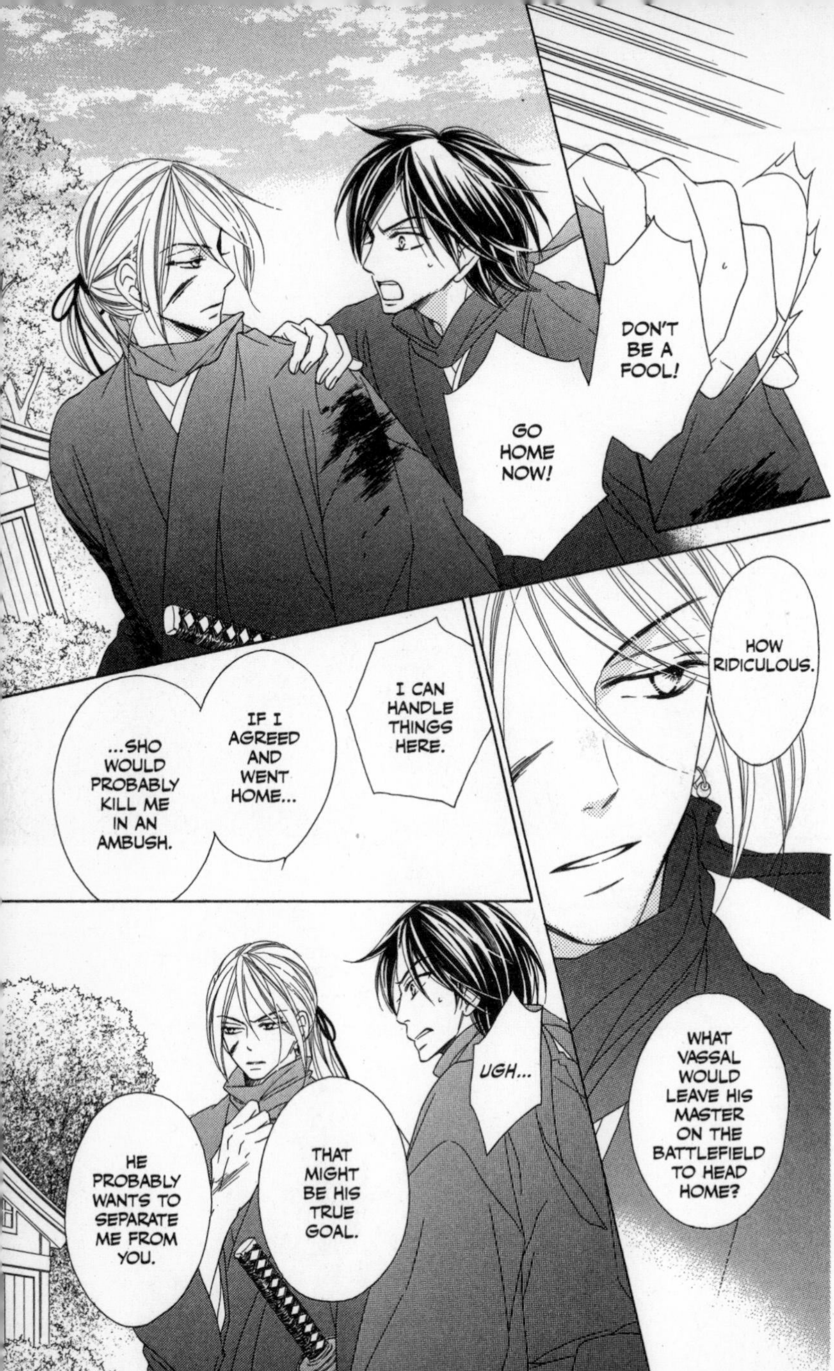
DON'T BE A FOOL!
GO HOME NOW!
HOW RIDICULOUS.
WHAT VASSAL WOULD LEAVE HIS MASTER ON THE BATTLEFIELD TO HEAD HOME?
I CAN HANDLE THINGS HERE.
IF I AGREED AND WENT HOME...
...SHO WOULD PROBABLY KILL ME IN AN AMBUSH.
UGH...
THAT MIGHT BE HIS TRUE GOAL.
HE PROBABLY WANTS TO SEPARATE ME FROM YOU.

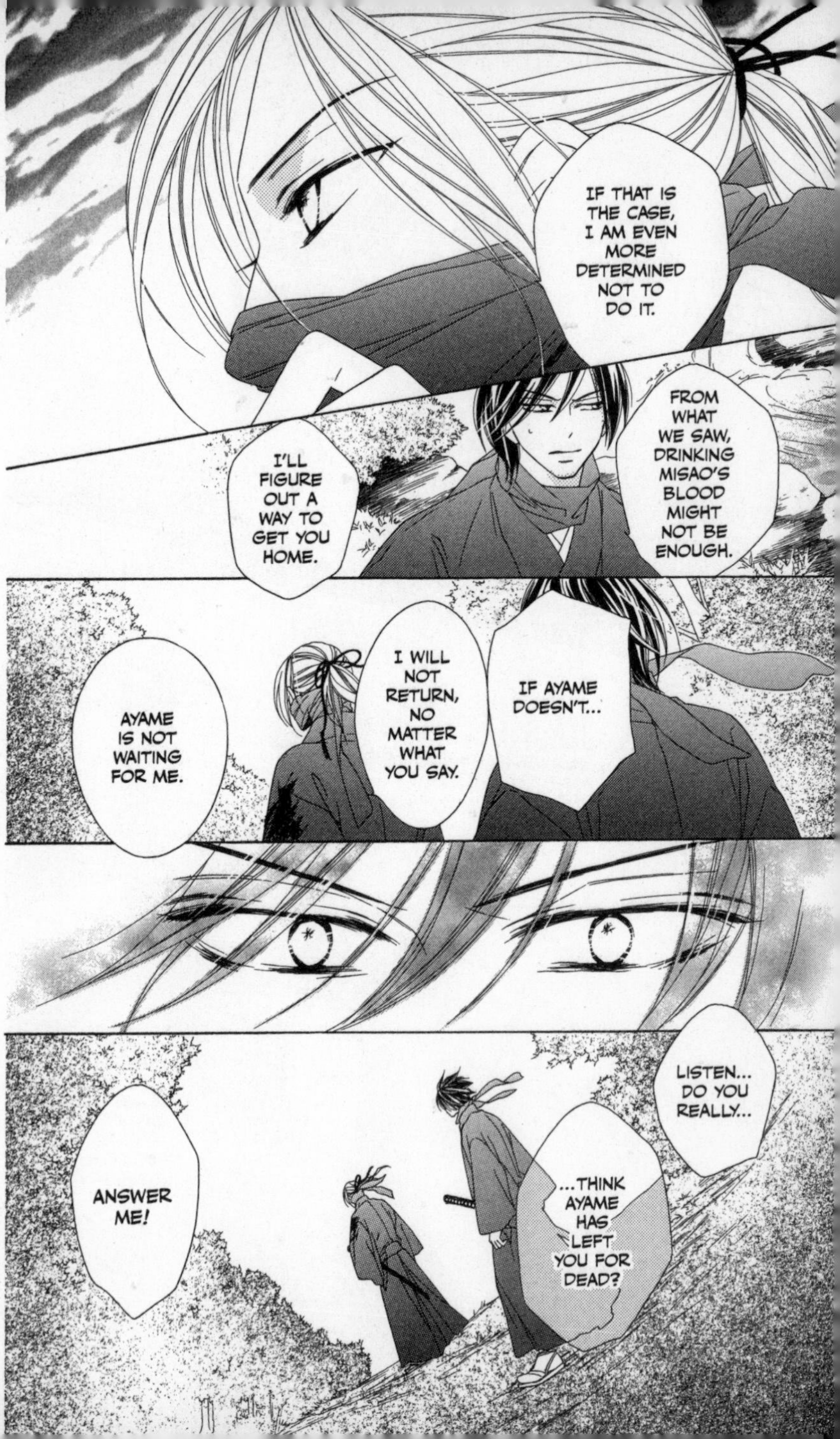
IF THAT IS THE CASE, I AM EVEN MORE DETERMINED NOT TO DO IT.
FROM WHAT WE SAW, DRINKING MISAO'S BLOOD MIGHT NOT BE ENOUGH.
I'LL FIGURE OUT A WAY TO GET YOU HOME.
IF AYAME DOESN'T...
I WILL NOT RETURN, NO MATTER WHAT YOU SAY.
AYAME IS NOT WAITING FOR ME.
LISTEN... DO YOU REALLY...
...THINK AYAME HAS LEFT YOU FOR DEAD?
ANSWER ME!

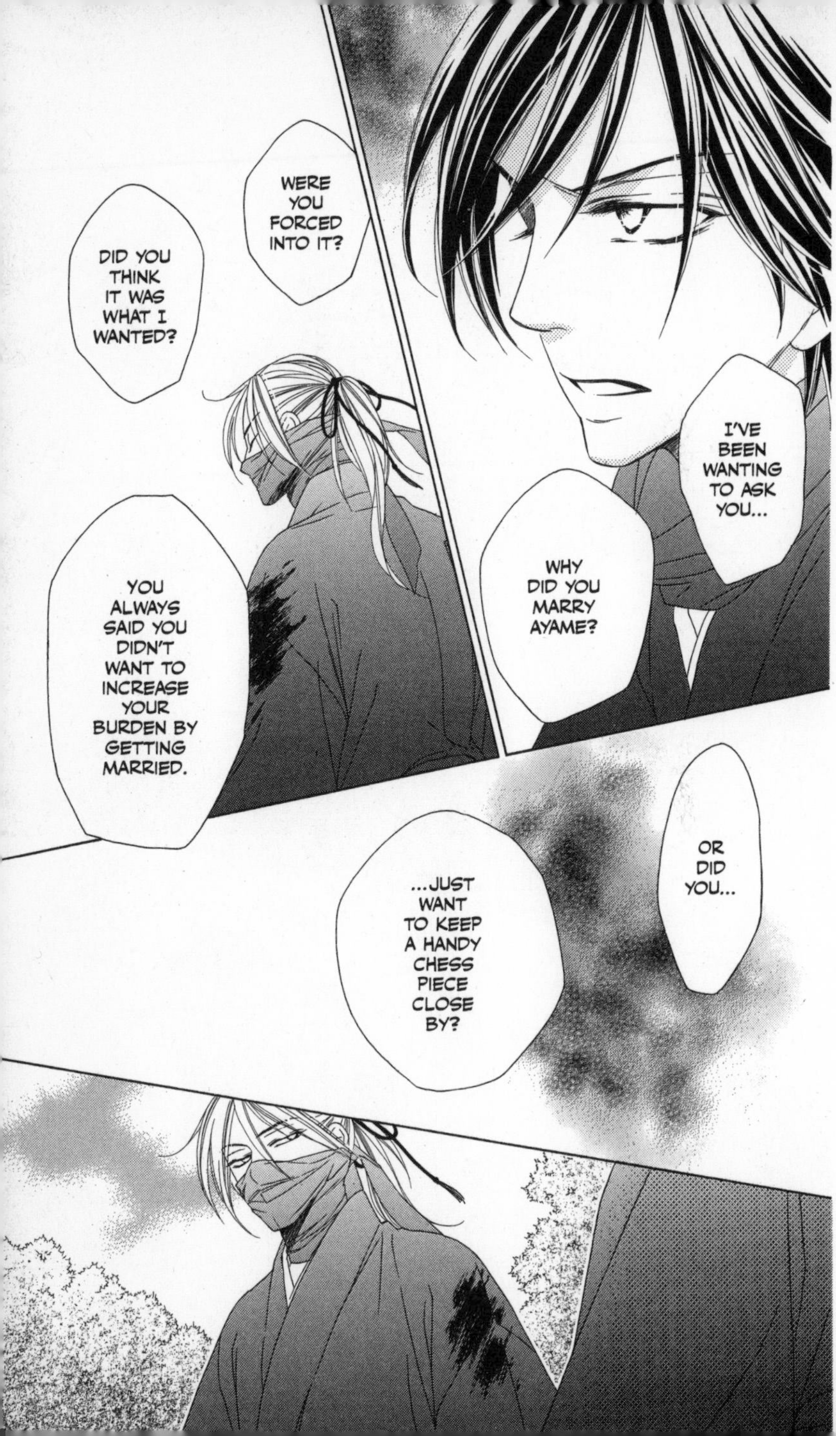
I'VE BEEN WANTING TO ASK YOU...
WHY DID YOU MARRY AYAME?
WERE YOU FORCED INTO IT?
DID YOU THINK IT WAS WHAT I WANTED?
YOU ALWAYS SAID YOU DIDN'T WANT TO INCREASE YOUR BURDEN BY GETTING MARRIED.
OR DID YOU...
...JUST WANT TO KEEP A HANDY CHESS PIECE CLOSE BY?

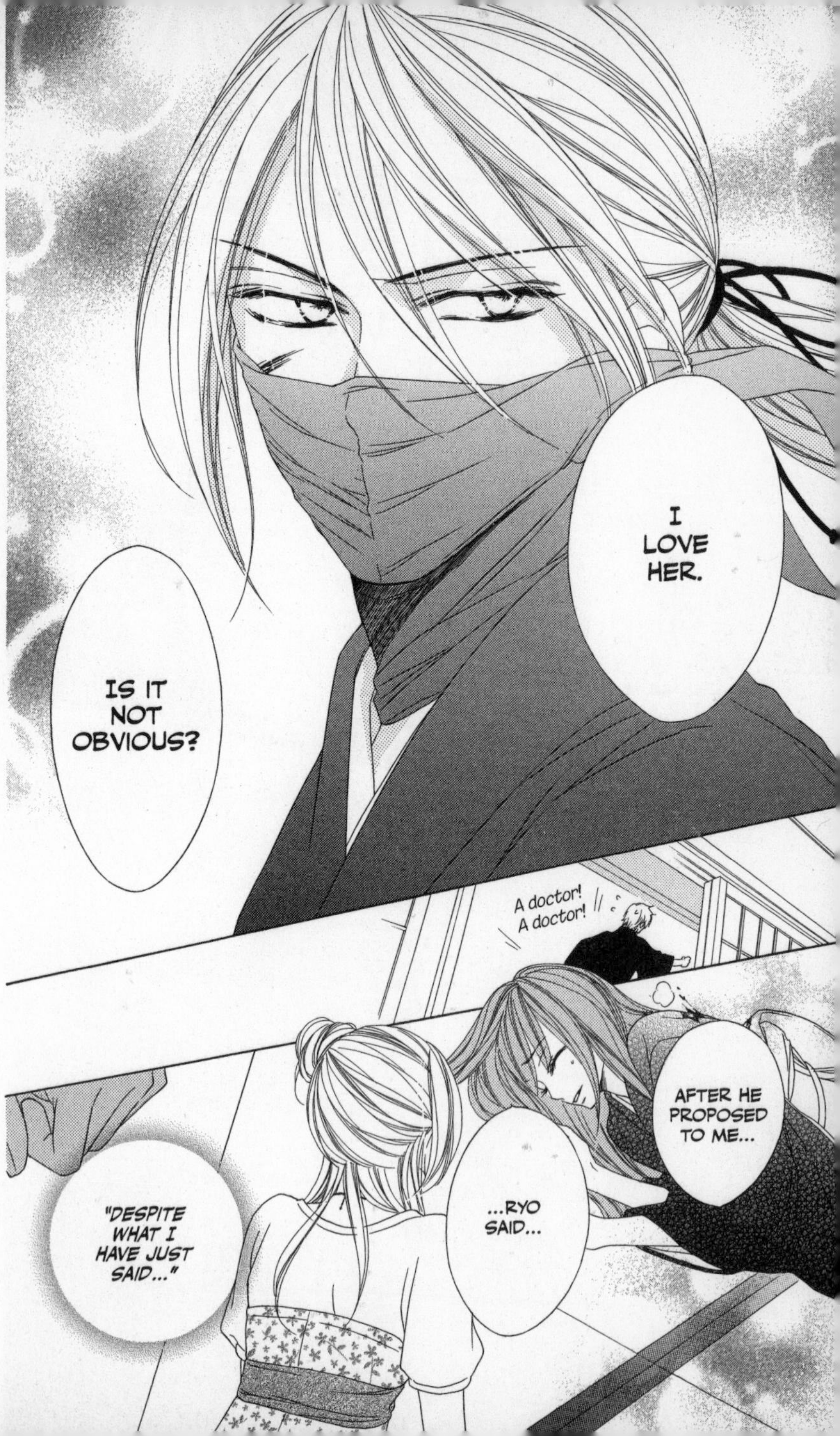
I LOVE HER.
IS IT NOT OBVIOUS?
A doctor! A doctor!
AFTER HE PROPOSED TO ME...
...RYO SAID...
"DESPITE WHAT I HAVE JUST SAID..."

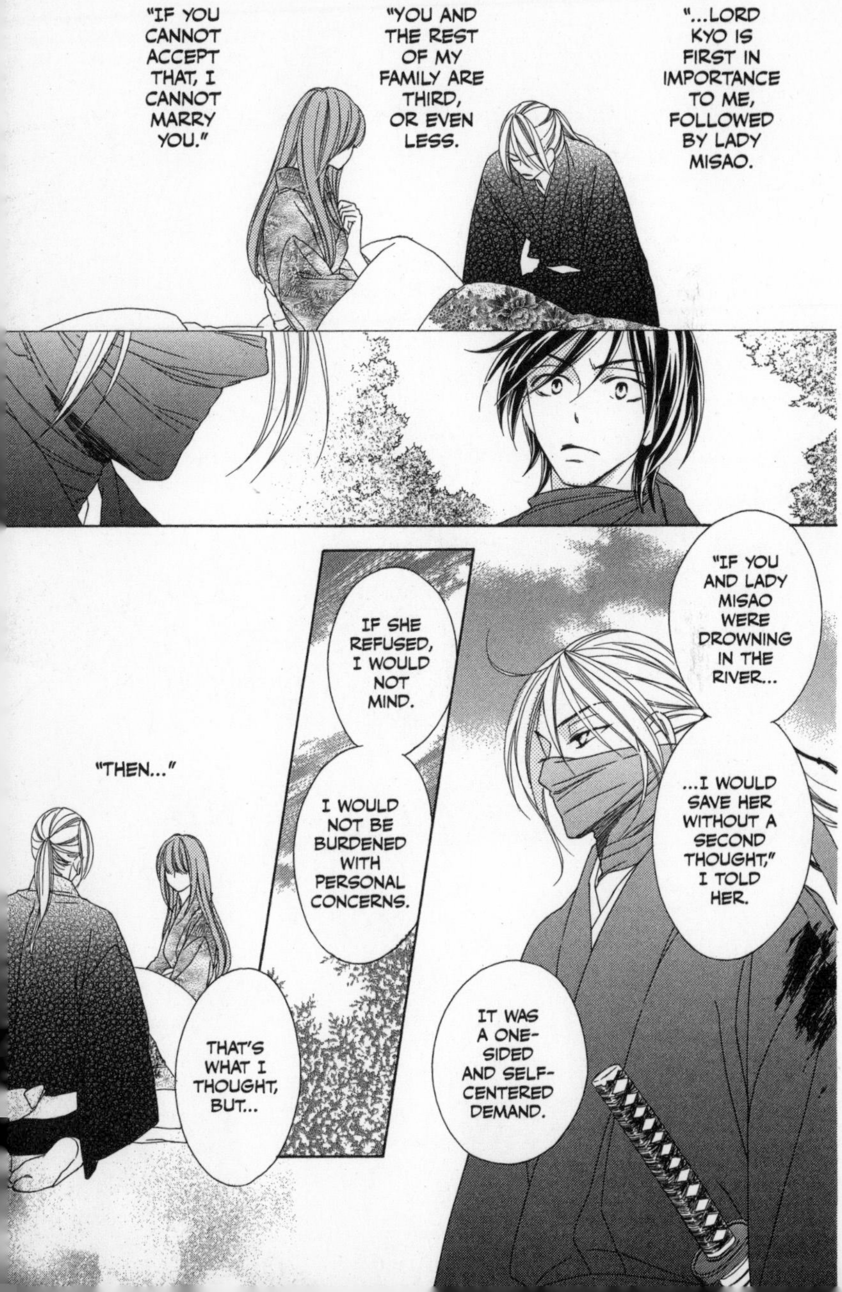
"...LORD KYO IS FIRST IN IMPORTANCE TO ME, FOLLOWED BY LADY MISAO.
"YOU AND THE REST OF MY FAMILY ARE THIRD, OR EVEN LESS.
"IF YOU CANNOT ACCEPT THAT, I CANNOT MARRY YOU."
"IF YOU AND LADY MISAO WERE DROWNING IN THE RIVER...
...I WOULD SAVE HER WITHOUT A SECOND THOUGHT," I TOLD HER.
IT WAS A ONE-SIDED AND SELF-CENTERED DEMAND.
IF SHE REFUSED, I WOULD NOT MIND.
I WOULD NOT BE BURDENED WITH PERSONAL CONCERNS.
"THEN..."
THAT'S WHAT I THOUGHT, BUT...

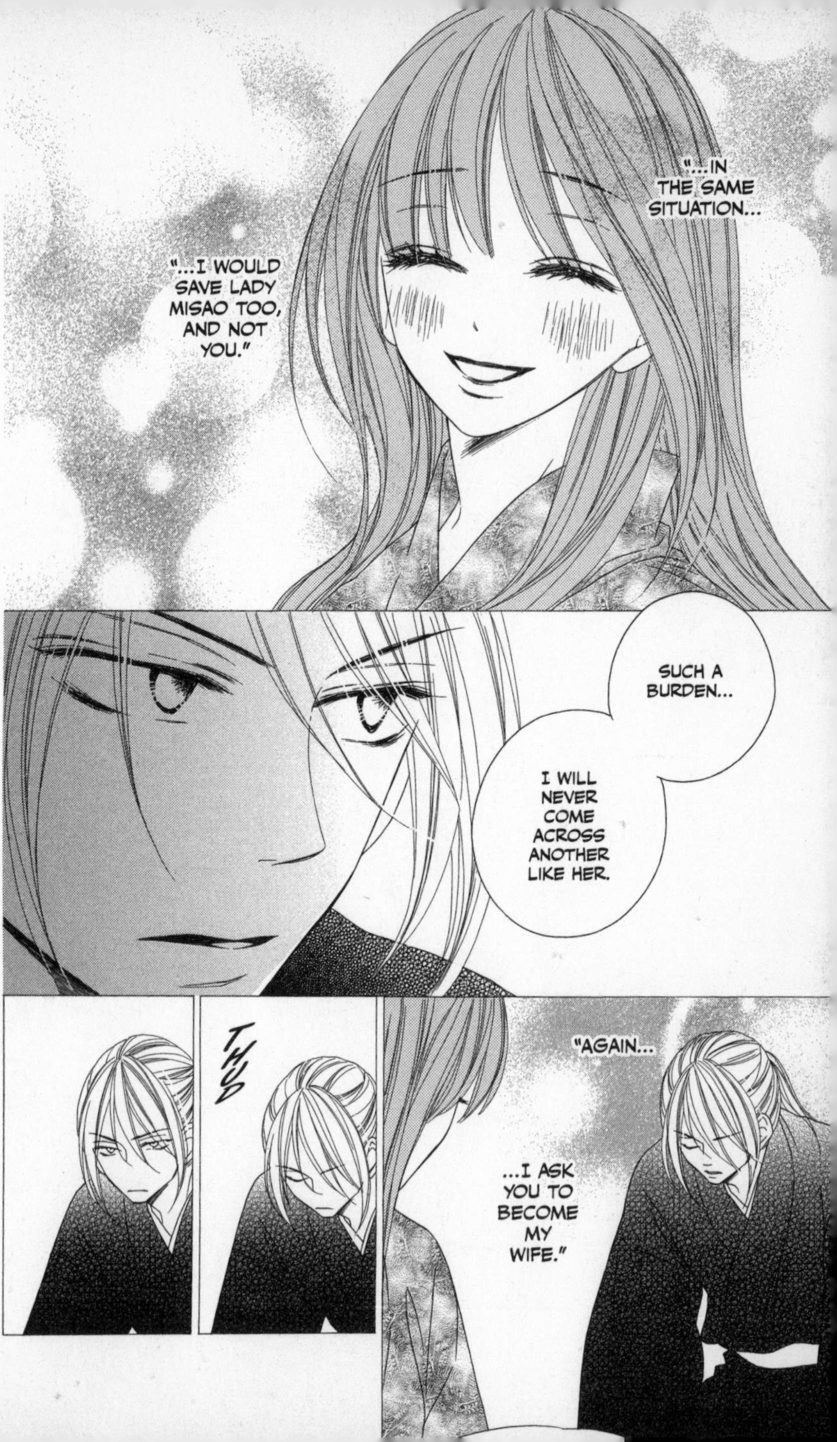
"...IN THE SAME SITUATION...
"...I WOULD SAVE LADY MISAO TOO, AND NOT YOU."
SUCH A BURDEN...
I WILL NEVER COME ACROSS ANOTHER LIKE HER.
"AGAIN...
...I ASK YOU TO BECOME MY WIFE."
THUD

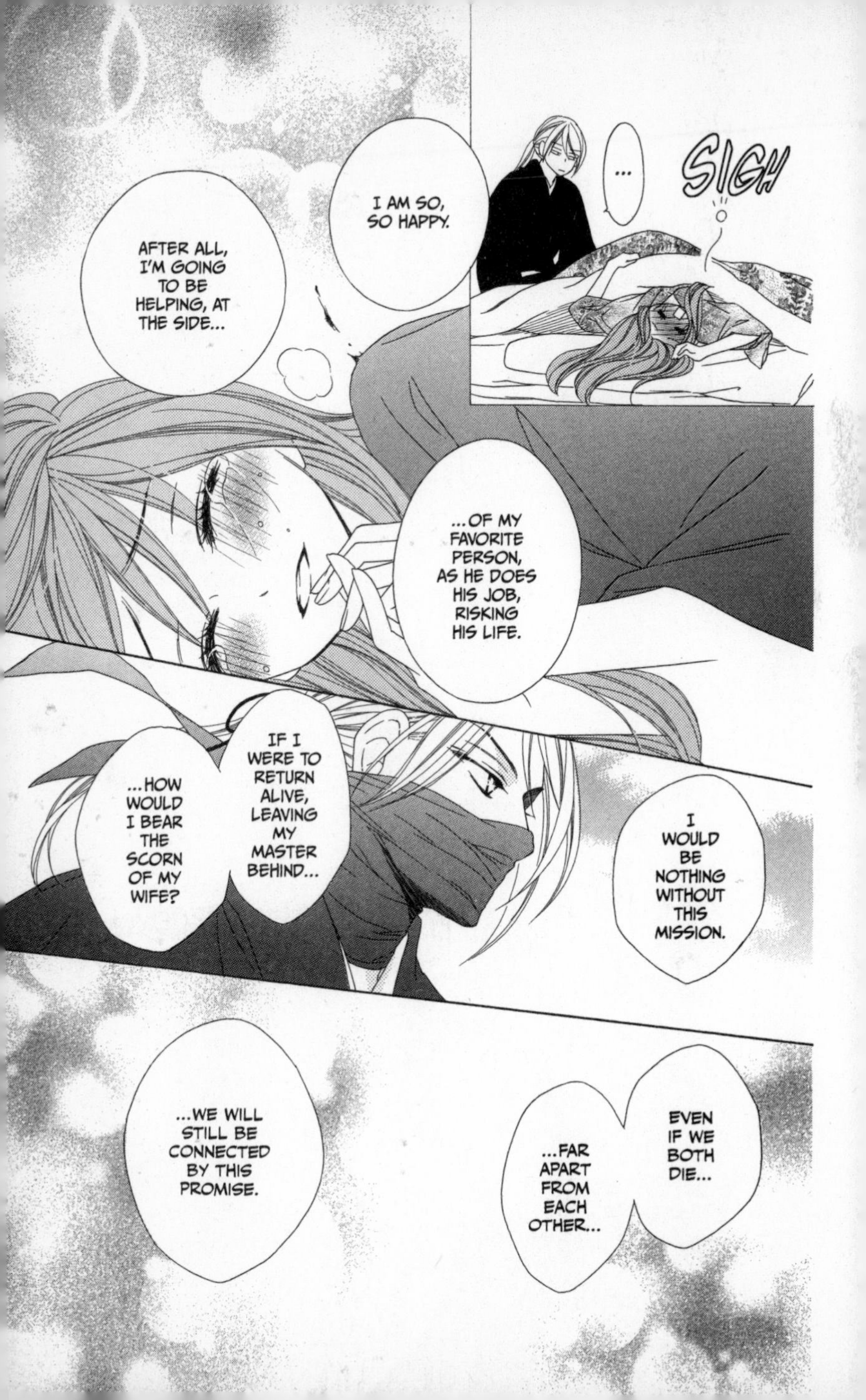
SIGH
...
I AM SO, SO HAPPY.
AFTER ALL, I'M GOING TO BE HELPING, AT THE SIDE...
...OF MY FAVORITE PERSON, AS HE DOES HIS JOB, RISKING HIS LIFE.
I WOULD BE NOTHING WITHOUT THIS MISSION.
IF I WERE TO RETURN ALIVE, LEAVING MY MASTER BEHIND...
...HOW WOULD I BEAR THE SCORN OF MY WIFE?
EVEN IF WE BOTH DIE...
...FAR APART FROM EACH OTHER...
...WE WILL STILL BE CONNECTED BY THIS PROMISE.

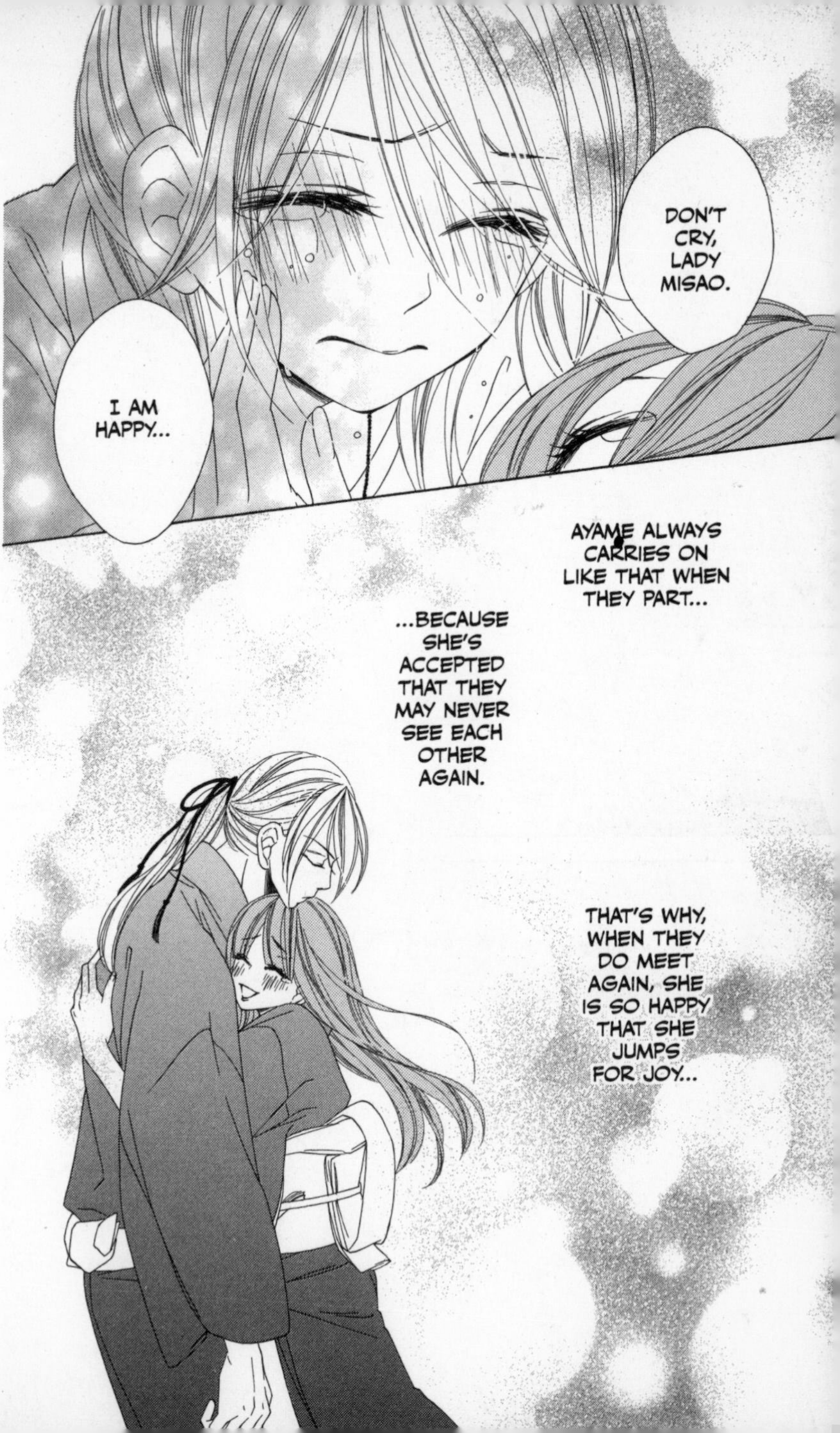
DON'T CRY, LADY MISAO.
I AM HAPPY...
AYAME ALWAYS CARRIES ON LIKE THAT WHEN THEY PART...
...BECAUSE SHE'S ACCEPTED THAT THEY MAY NEVER SEE EACH OTHER AGAIN.
THAT'S WHY, WHEN THEY DO MEET AGAIN, SHE IS SO HAPPY THAT SHE JUMPS FOR JOY...

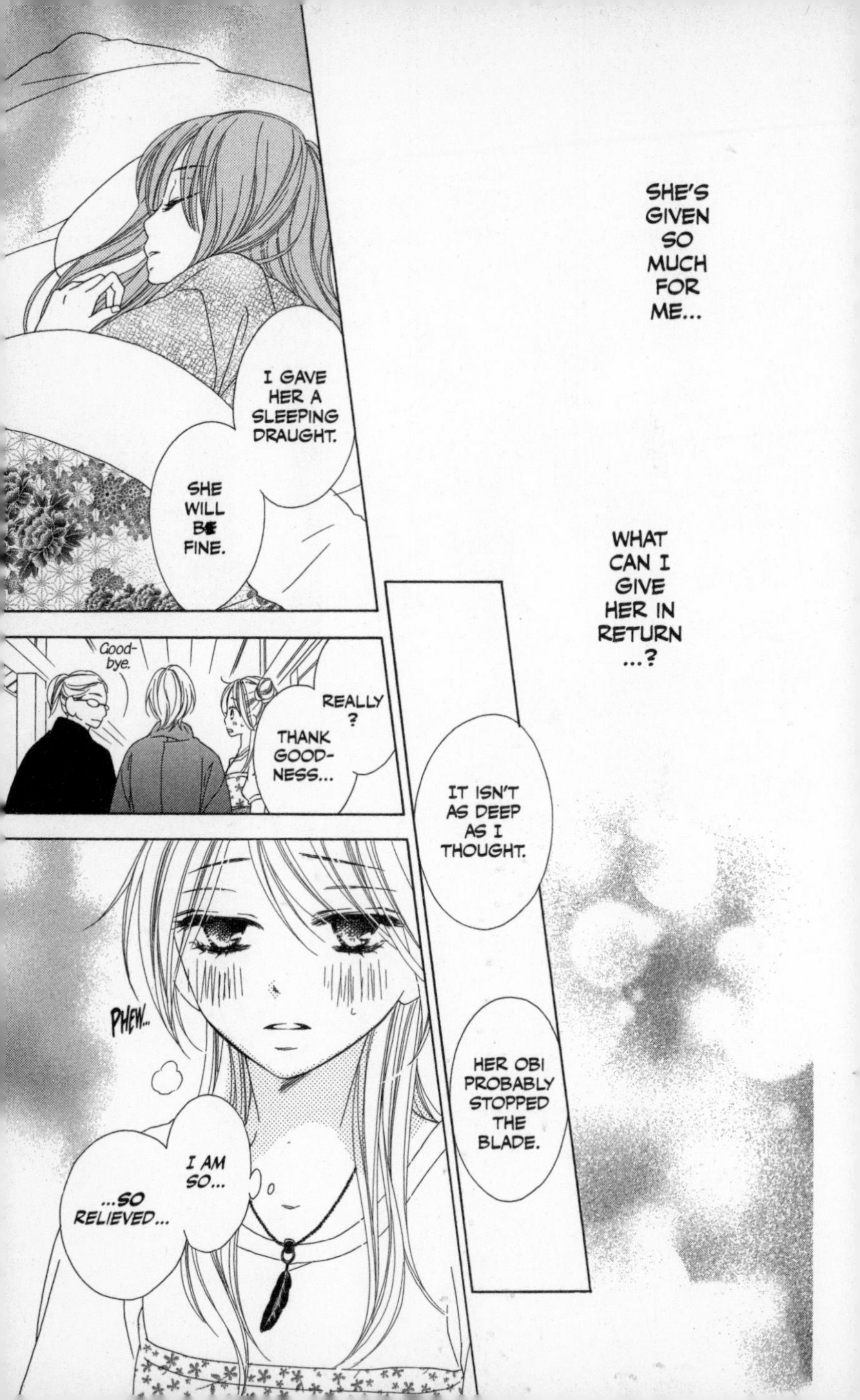
I GAVE HER A SLEEPING DRAUGHT.
SHE WILL BE FINE.
IT ISN'T AS DEEP AS I THOUGHT.
HER OBI PROBABLY STOPPED THE BLADE.
Good-bye.
REALLY?
THANK GOODNESS...
PHEW...
I AM SO...
...SO RELIEVED...
SHE'S GIVEN SO MUCH FOR ME...
WHAT CAN I GIVE HER IN RETURN...?

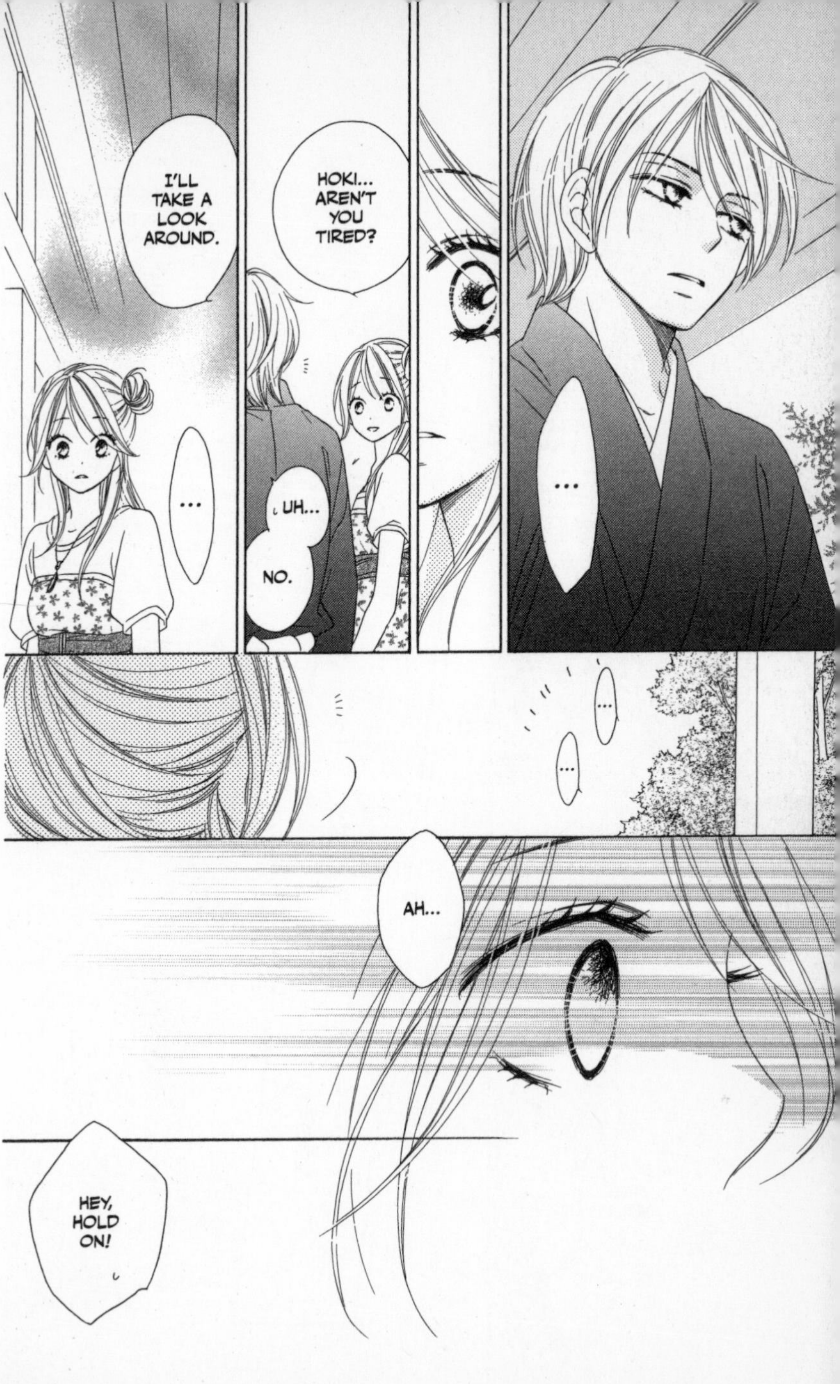
...
HOKI... AREN'T YOU TIRED?
UH...
NO.
I'LL TAKE A LOOK AROUND.
...
...
...
AH...
HEY, HOLD ON!

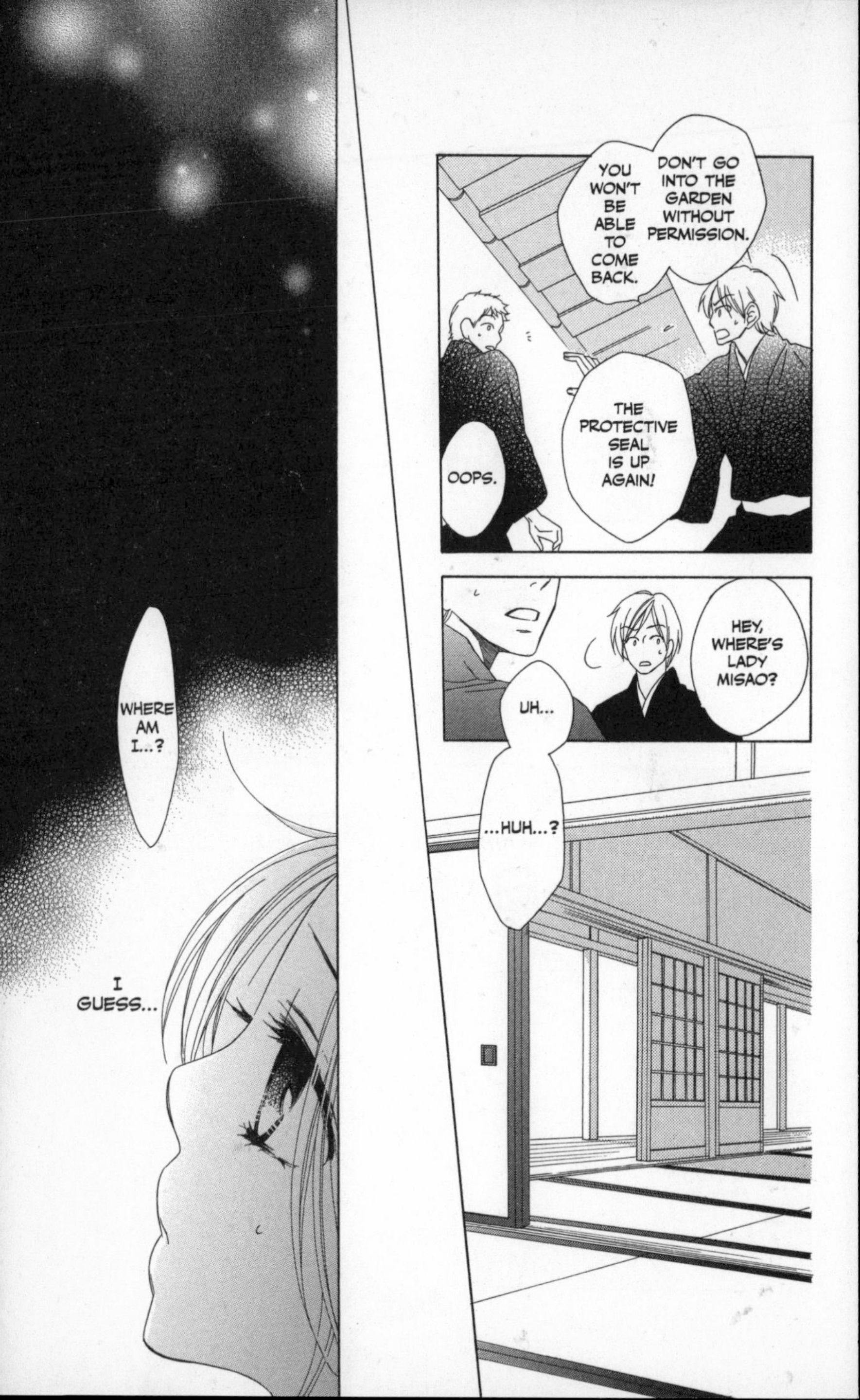
DON'T GO INTO THE GARDEN WITHOUT PERMISSION.
YOU WON'T BE ABLE TO COME BACK.
THE PROTECTIVE SEAL IS UP AGAIN!
OOPS.
HEY, WHERE'S LADY MISAO?
UH...
...HUH...?
WHERE AM I...?
I GUESS...

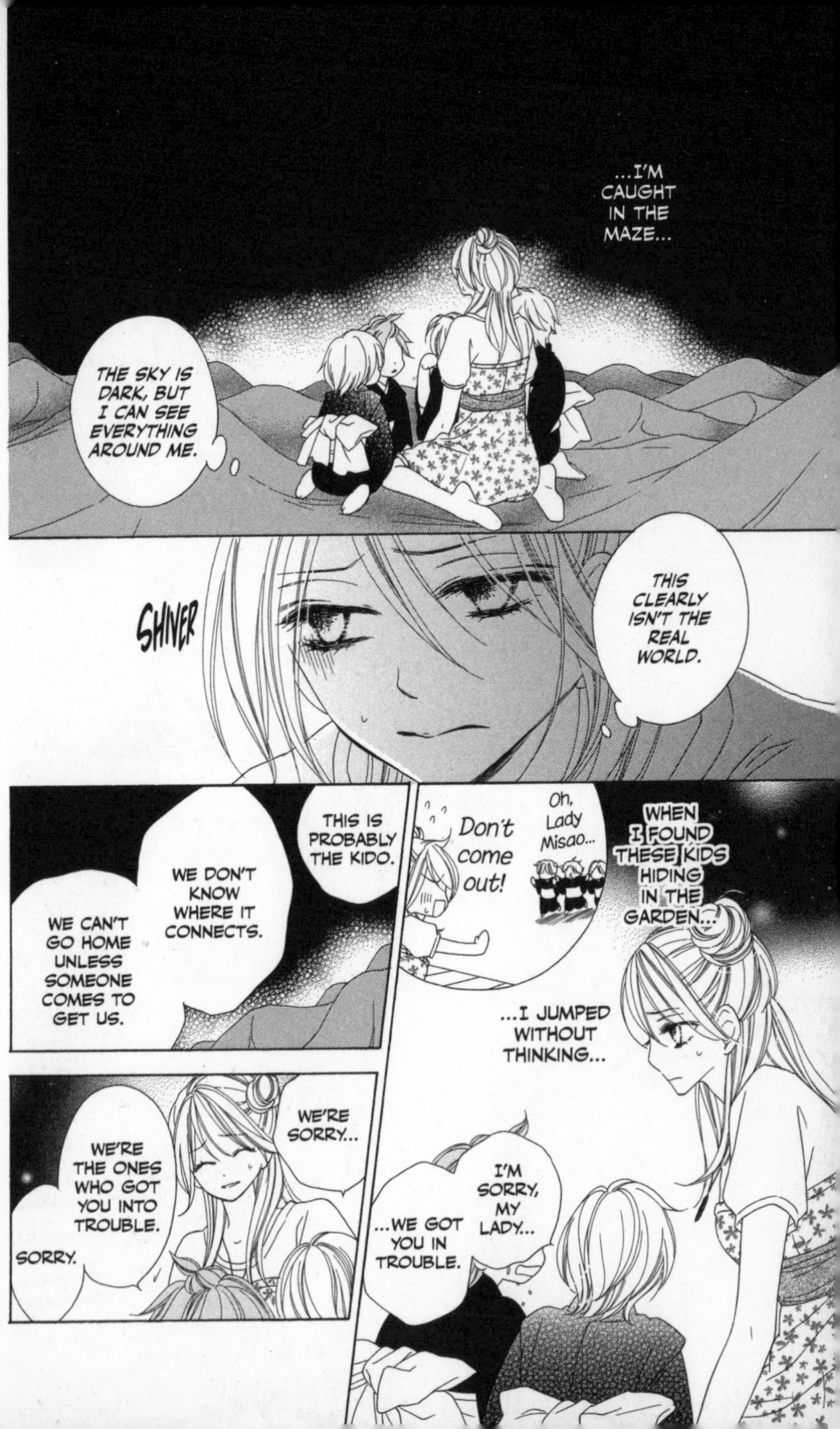
...I'M CAUGHT IN THE MAZE...
THE SKY IS DARK, BUT I CAN SEE EVERYTHING AROUND ME.
THIS CLEARLY ISN'T THE REAL WORLD.
SHIVER
WHEN I FOUND THESE KIDS HIDING IN THE GARDEN...
Oh, Lady Misao...
Don't come out!
...I JUMPED WITHOUT THINKING...
I'M SORRY, MY LADY...
...WE GOT YOU IN TROUBLE.
THIS IS PROBABLY THE KIDO.
WE DON'T KNOW WHERE IT CONNECTS.
WE CAN'T GO HOME UNLESS SOMEONE COMES TO GET US.
WE'RE SORRY...
WE'RE THE ONES WHO GOT YOU INTO TROUBLE.
SORRY.

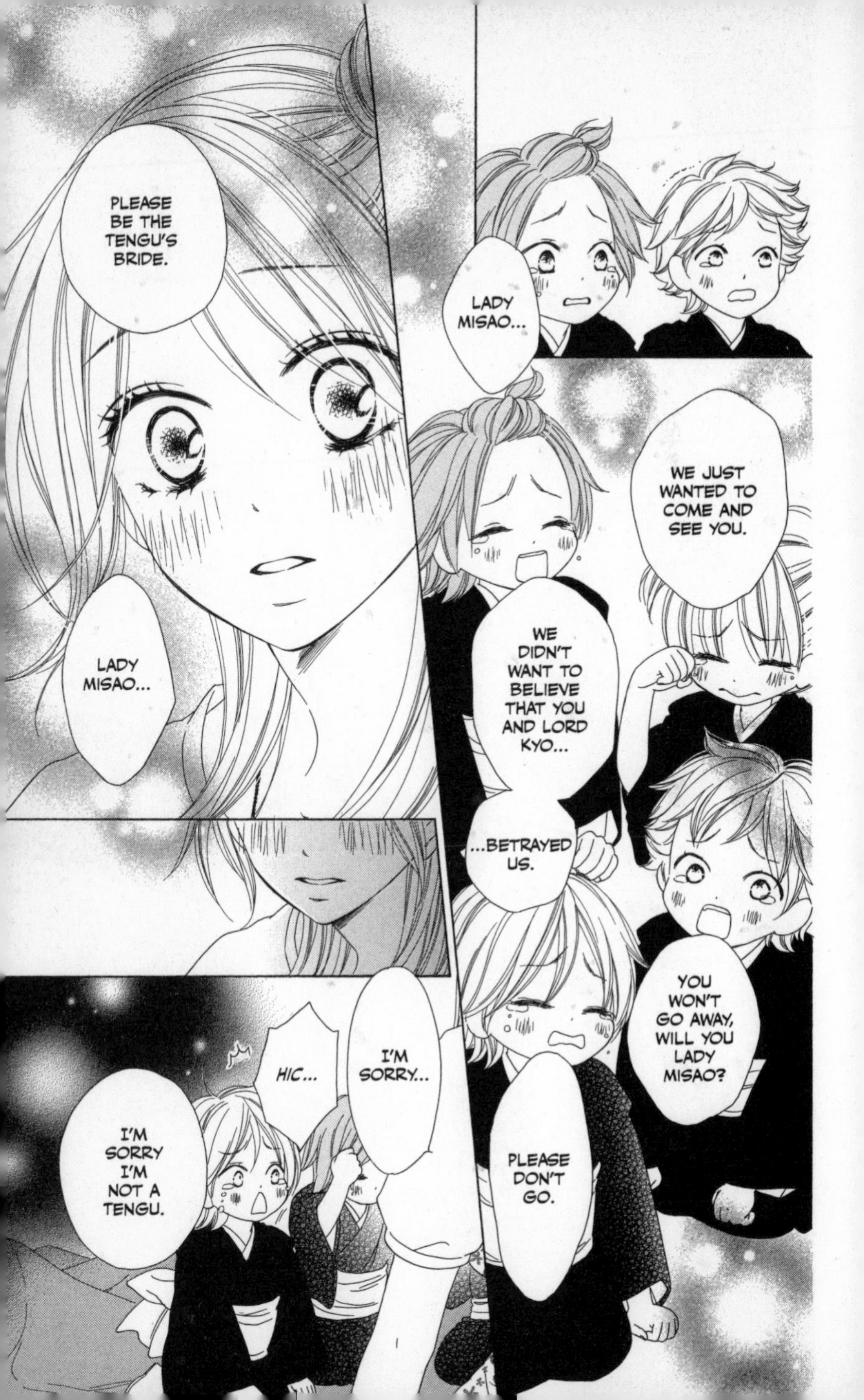
LADY MISAO...
WE JUST WANTED TO COME AND SEE YOU.
WE DIDN'T WANT TO BELIEVE THAT YOU AND LORD KYO...
...BETRAYED US.
YOU WON'T GO AWAY, WILL YOU LADY MISAO?
PLEASE DON'T GO.
PLEASE BE THE TENGU'S BRIDE.
LADY MISAO...
I'M SORRY...
HIC...
I'M SORRY I'M NOT A TENGU.

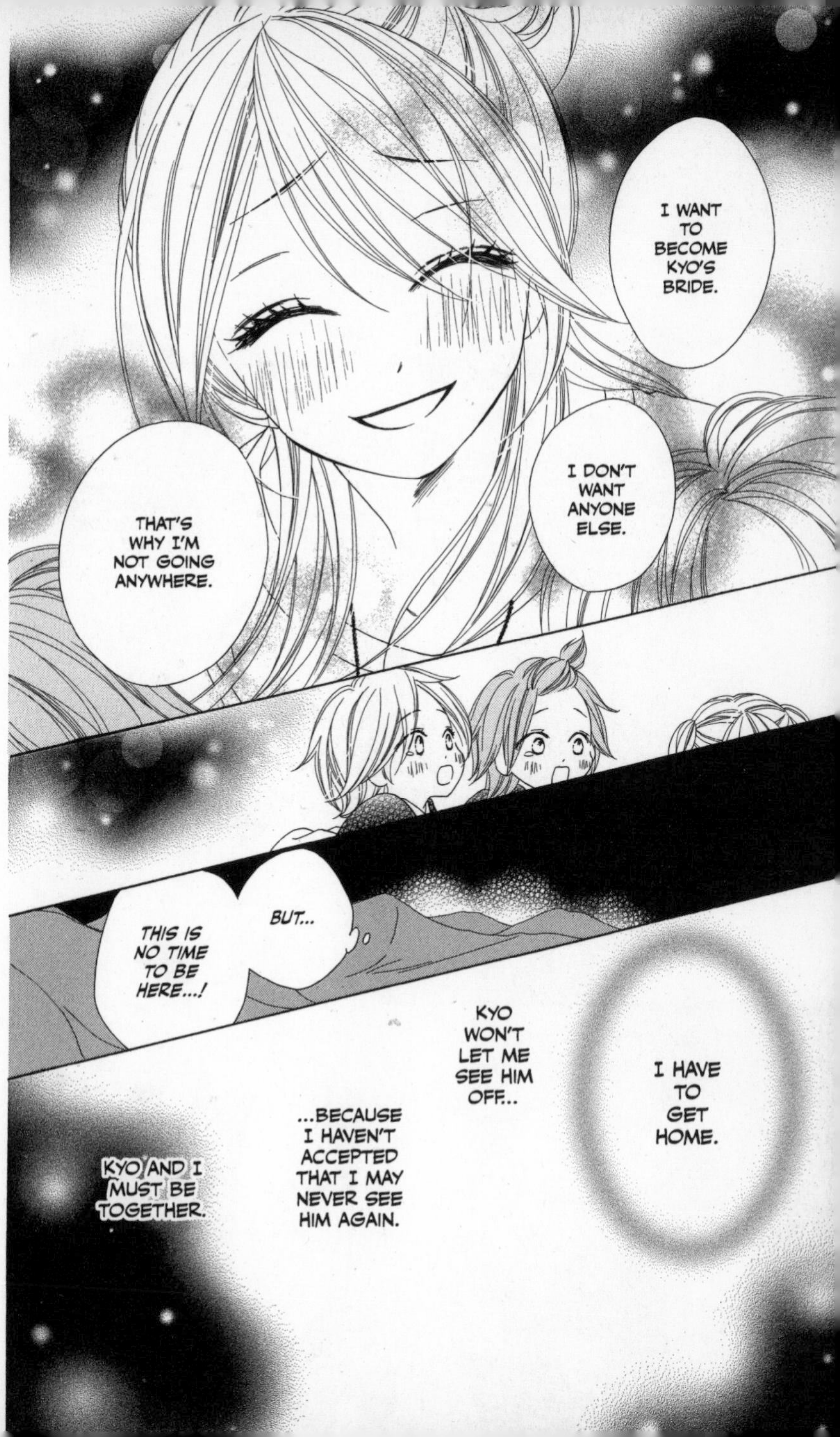
I WANT TO BECOME KYO'S BRIDE.
I DON'T WANT ANYONE ELSE.
THAT'S WHY I'M NOT GOING ANYWHERE.
BUT...
THIS IS NO TIME TO BE HERE...!
I HAVE TO GET HOME.
KYO WON'T LET ME SEE HIM OFF...
...BECAUSE I HAVEN'T ACCEPTED THAT I MAY NEVER SEE HIM AGAIN.
KYO AND I MUST BE TOGETHER.

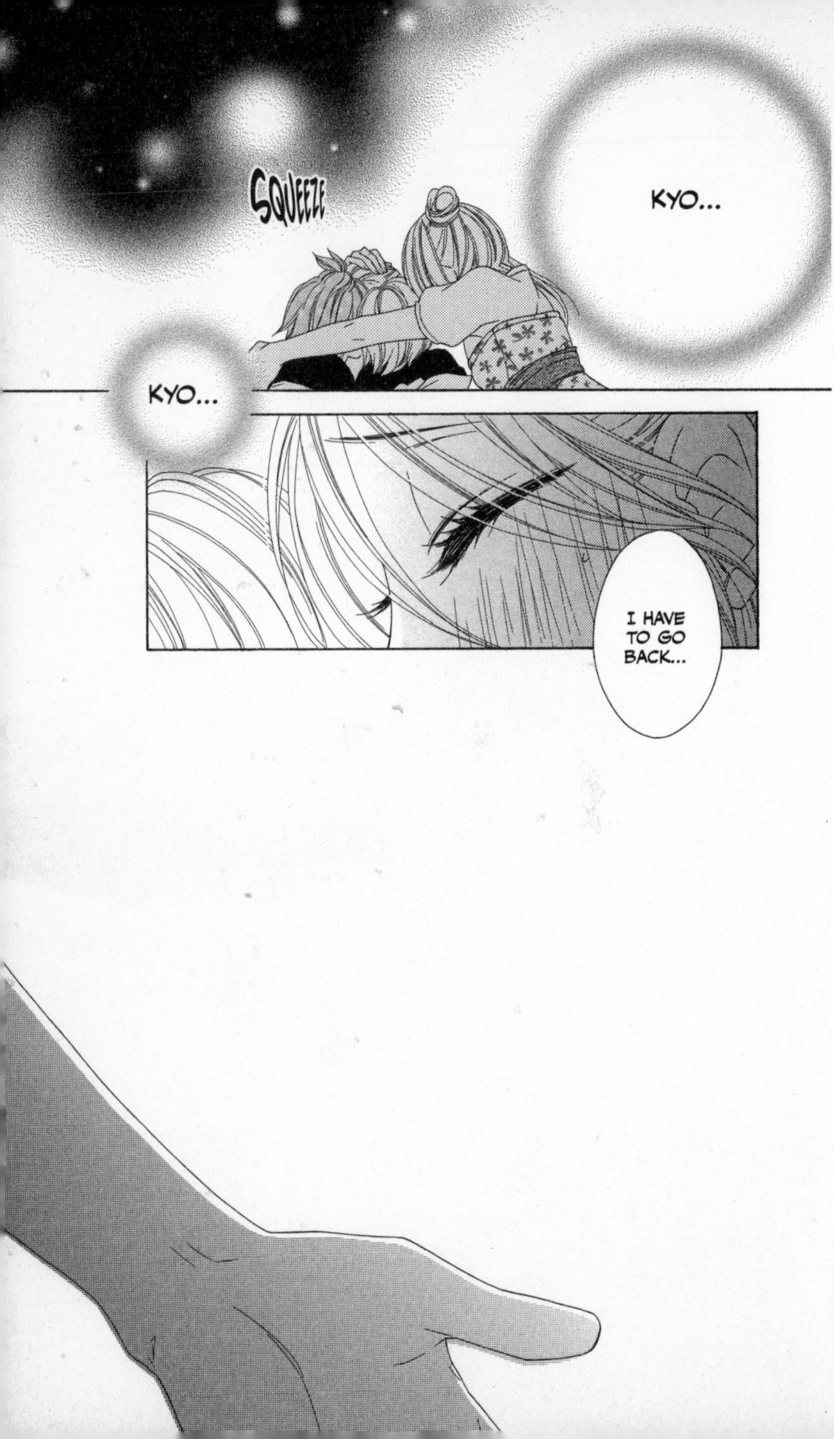
KYO...
SQUEEZE
KYO...
I HAVE TO GO BACK...

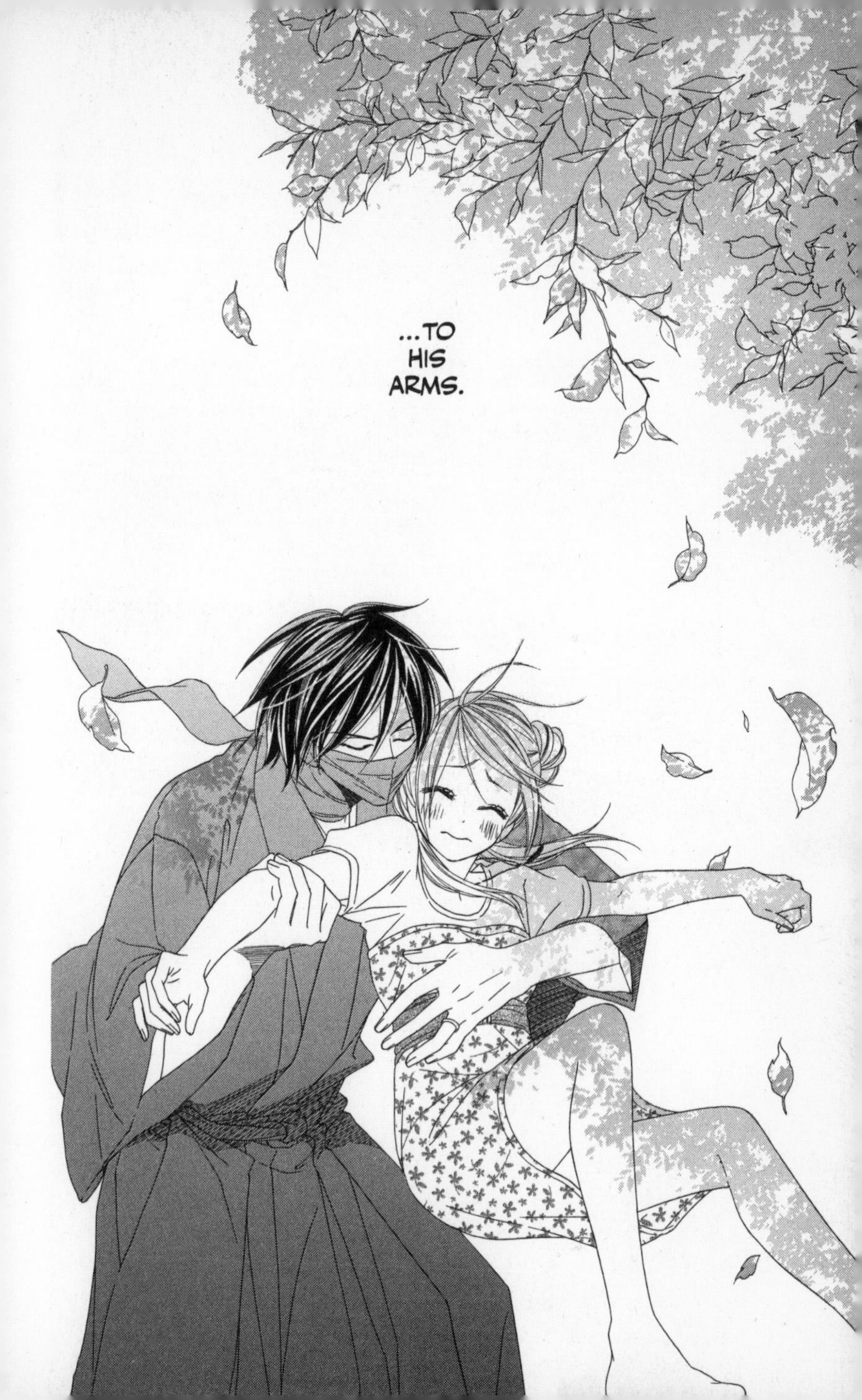
...TO HIS ARMS.

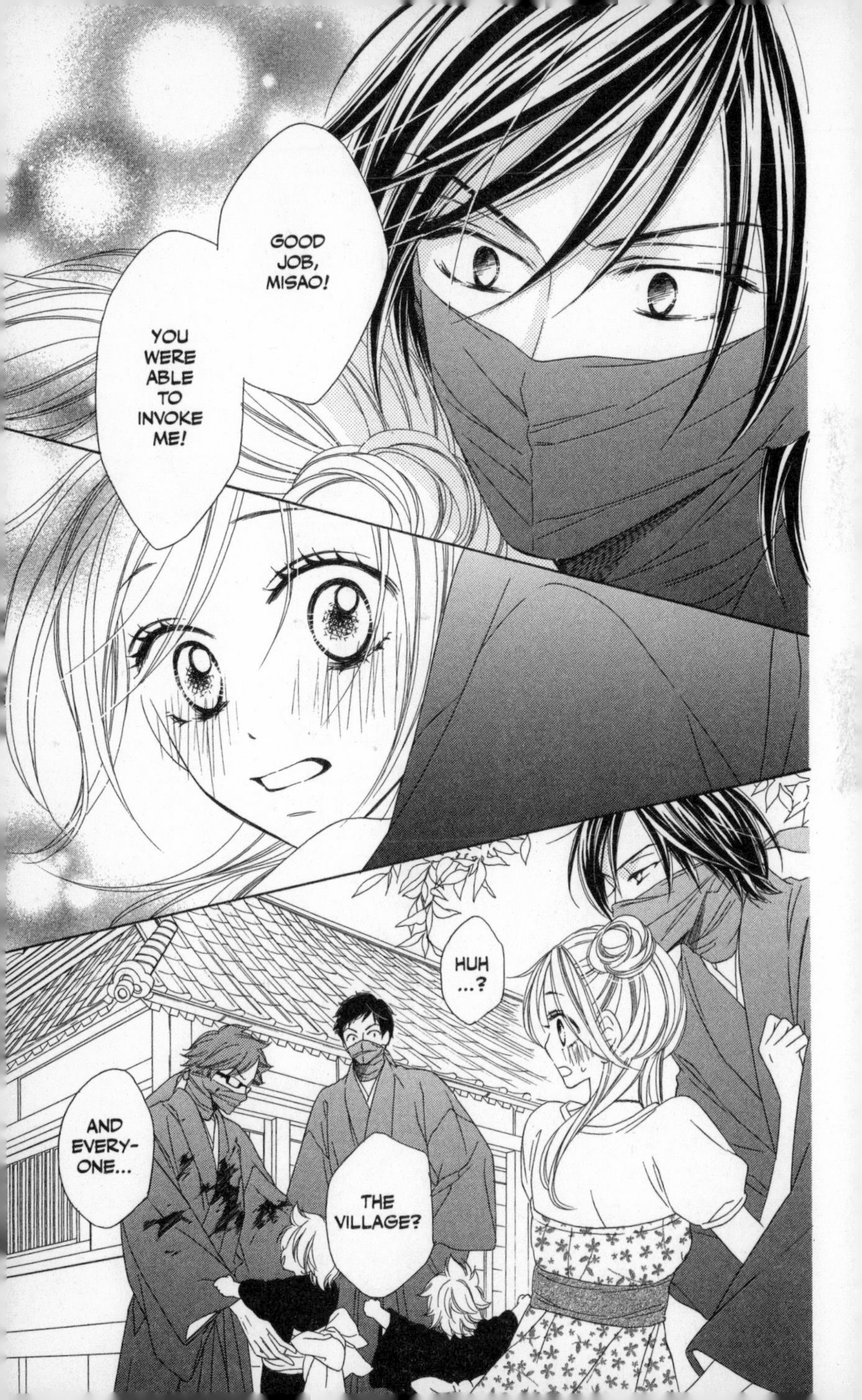
GOOD JOB, MISAO!
YOU WERE ABLE TO INVOKE ME!
HUH ...?
AND EVERY-ONE...
THE VILLAGE?

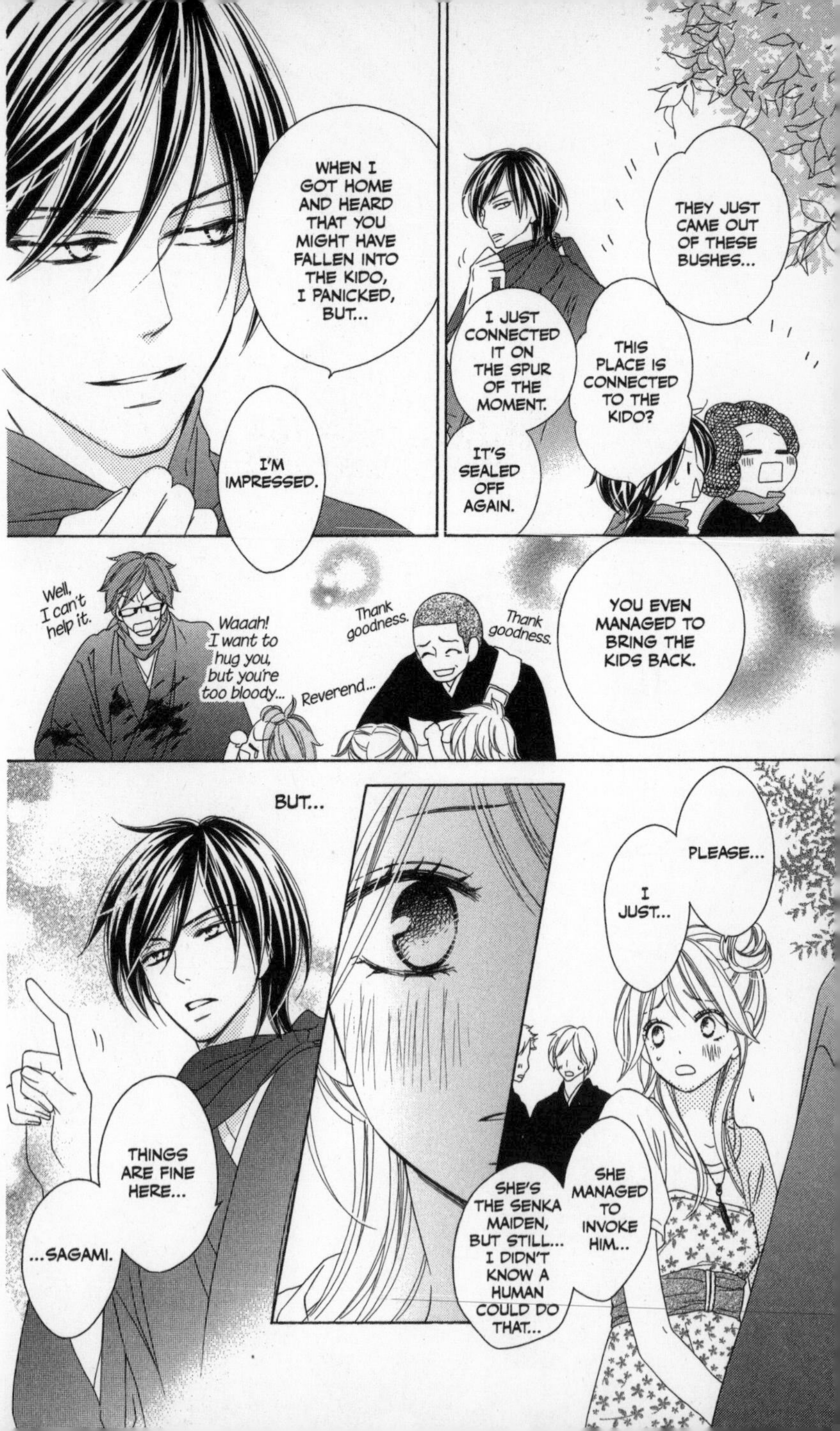
THEY JUST CAME OUT OF THESE BUSHES...
THIS PLACE IS CONNECTED TO THE KIDO?
I JUST CONNECTED IT ON THE SPUR OF THE MOMENT.
IT'S SEALED OFF AGAIN.
WHEN I GOT HOME AND HEARD THAT YOU MIGHT HAVE FALLEN INTO THE KIDO, I PANICKED, BUT...
I'M IMPRESSED.
YOU EVEN MANAGED TO BRING THE KIDS BACK.
Thank goodness.
Thank goodness.
Reverend...
Waaah! I want to hug you, but you're too bloody...
Well, I can't help it.
PLEASE...
I JUST...
SHE MANAGED TO INVOKE HIM...
SHE'S THE SENKA MAIDEN, BUT STILL... I DIDN'T KNOW A HUMAN COULD DO THAT...
BUT...
THINGS ARE FINE HERE...
...SAGAMI.

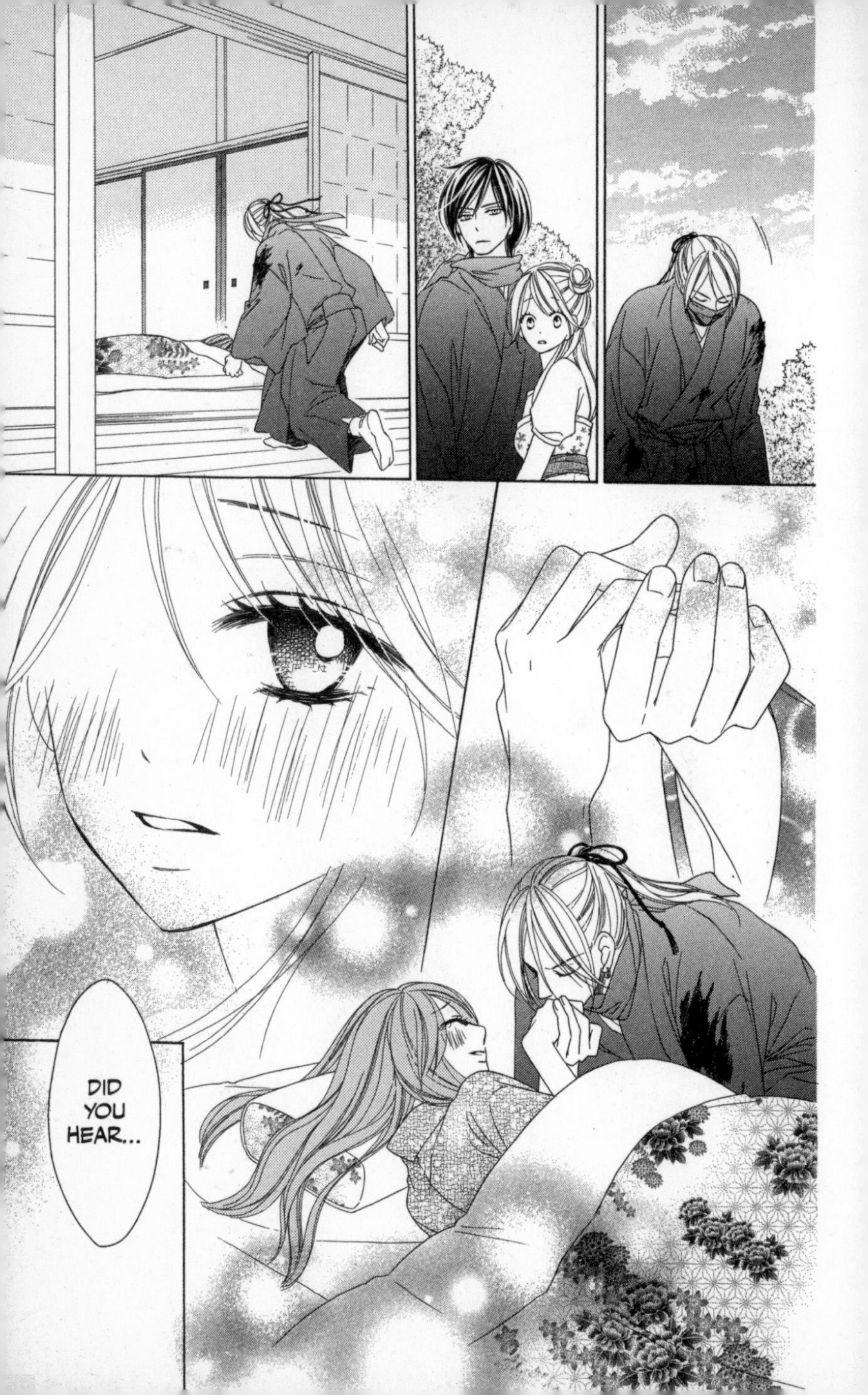
DID YOU HEAR...

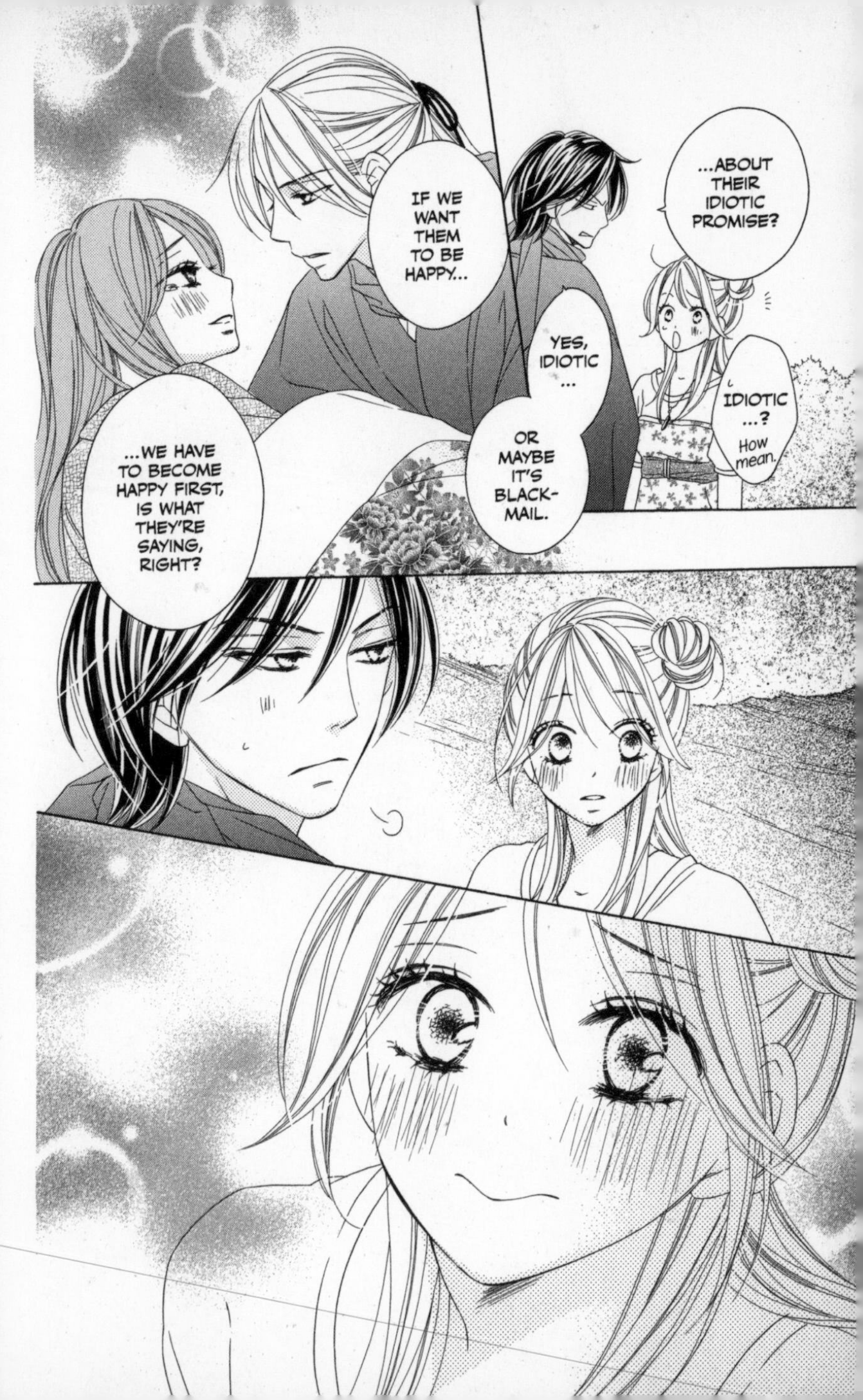
...ABOUT THEIR IDIOTIC PROMISE?
IDIOTIC ...? How mean.
YES, IDIOTIC ...
OR MAYBE IT'S BLACK-MAIL.
IF WE WANT THEM TO BE HAPPY...
...WE HAVE TO BECOME HAPPY FIRST, IS WHAT THEY'RE SAYING, RIGHT?

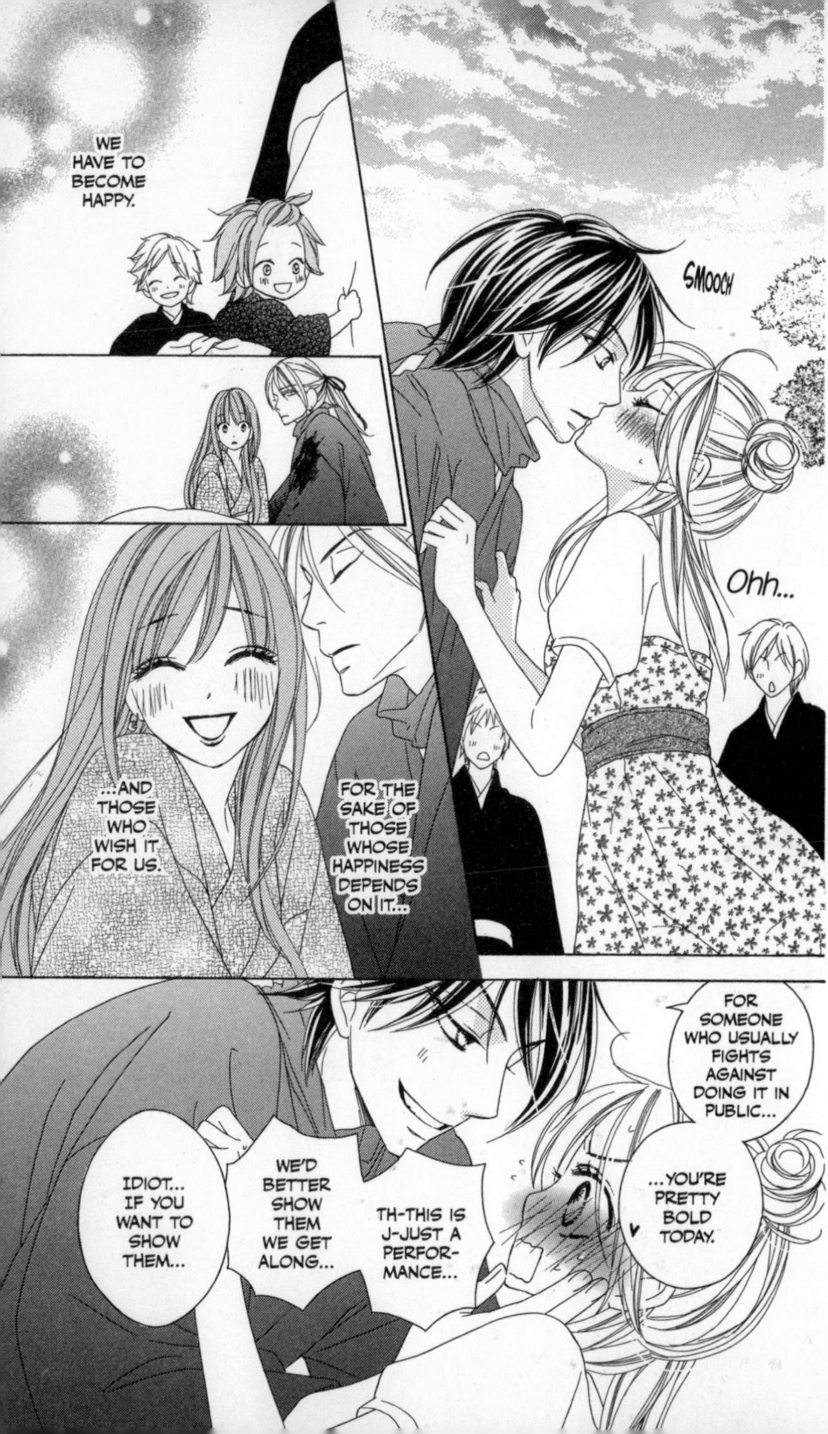
SMOOCH
Ohh...
WE HAVE TO BECOME HAPPY.
FOR THE SAKE OF THOSE WHOSE HAPPINESS DEPENDS ON IT...
...AND THOSE WHO WISH IT FOR US.
FOR SOMEONE WHO USUALLY FIGHTS AGAINST DOING IT IN PUBLIC...
...YOU'RE PRETTY BOLD TODAY.
TH-THIS IS J-JUST A PERFORMANCE...
WE'D BETTER SHOW THEM WE GET ALONG...
IDIOT... IF YOU WANT TO SHOW THEM...

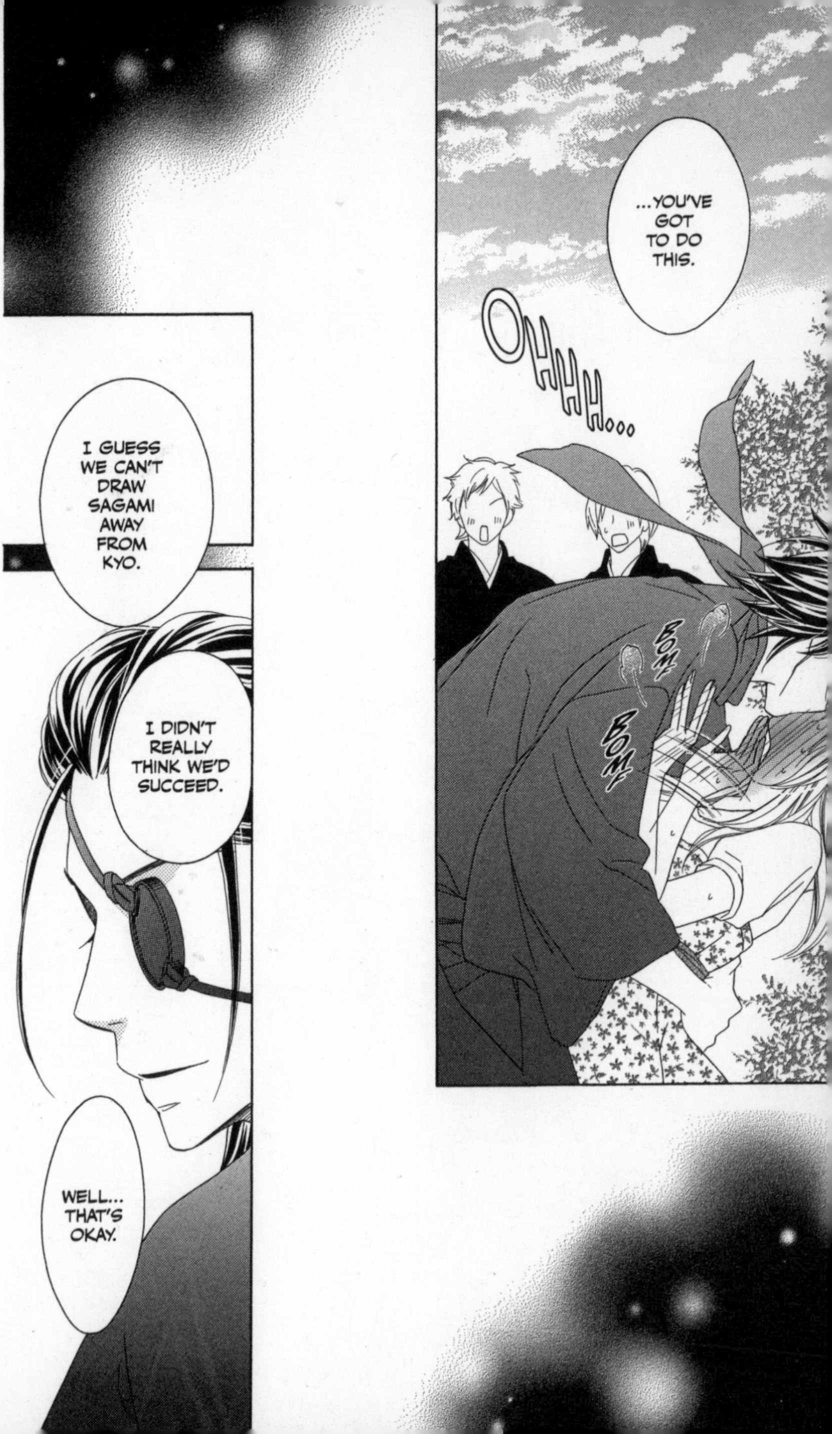
...YOU'VE GOT TO DO THIS.
OHHH...
BOM
BOM
I GUESS WE CAN'T DRAW SAGAMI AWAY FROM KYO.
I DIDN'T REALLY THINK WE'D SUCCEED.
WELL... THAT'S OKAY.

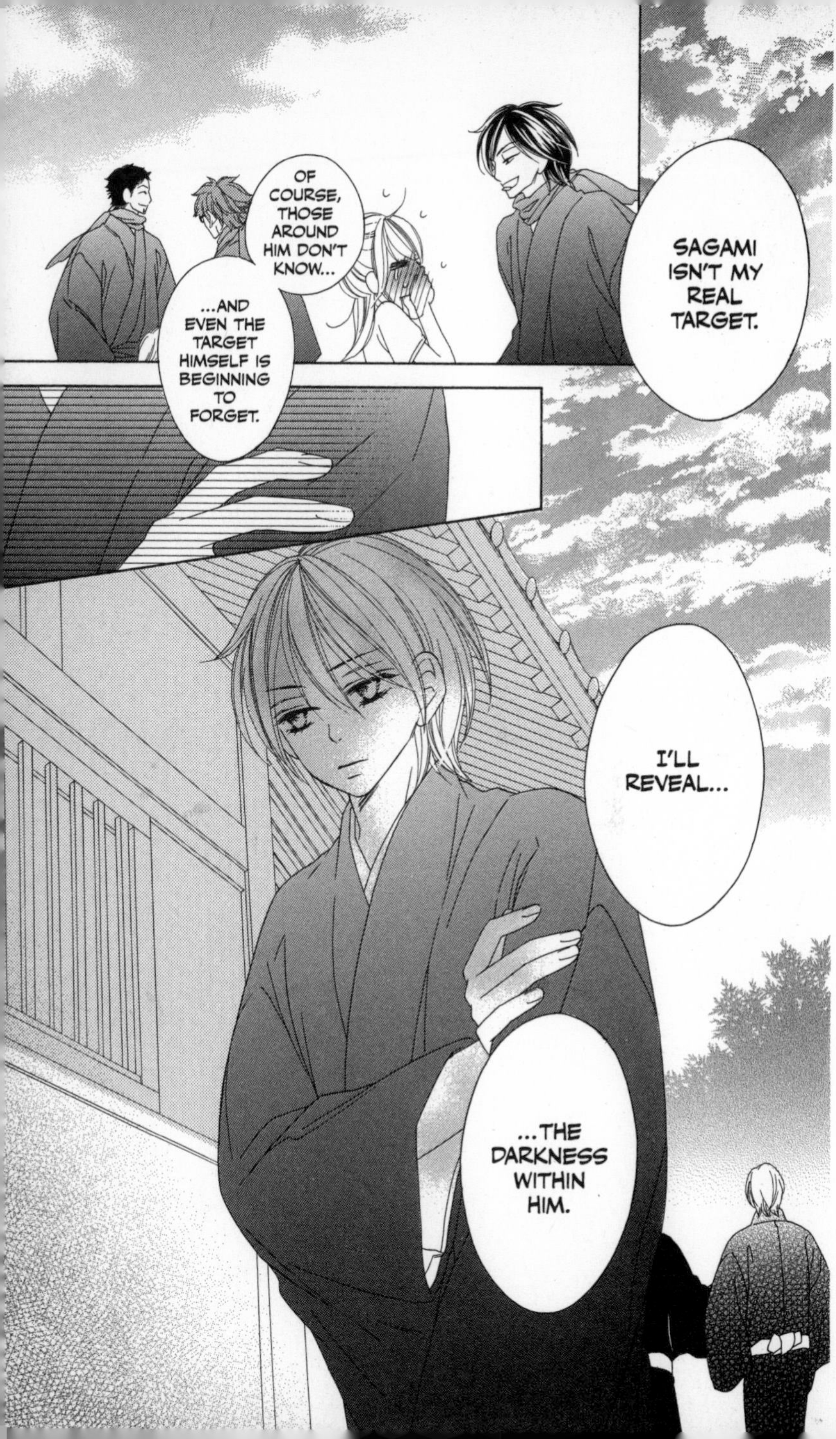
SAGAMI ISN'T MY REAL TARGET.
OF COURSE, THOSE AROUND HIM DON'T KNOW...
...AND EVEN THE TARGET HIMSELF IS BEGINNING TO FORGET.
I'LL REVEAL...
...THE DARKNESS WITHIN HIM.

Kyo has been turned into
all sorts of interesting
merchandise like body pillows,
"make a face" games, bath
towels, etc., but how about
something like this next?

A teacup. If you pour hot water
into it, surprise! Kyo's clothing
vanishes. ♡

Sorry
to
disap-
point
you!

Go ahead and have some fun with him...

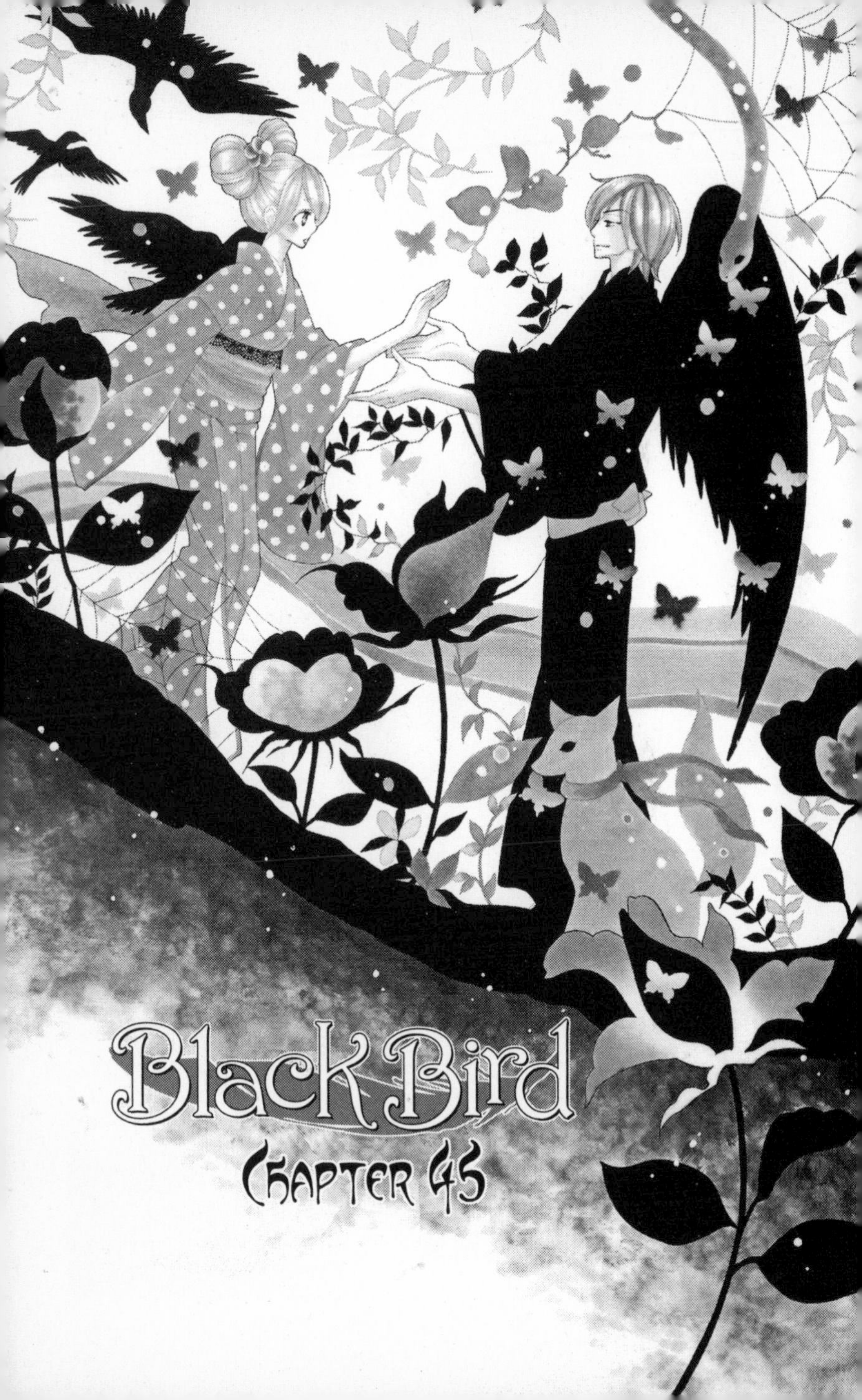
Black Bird
Chapter 45

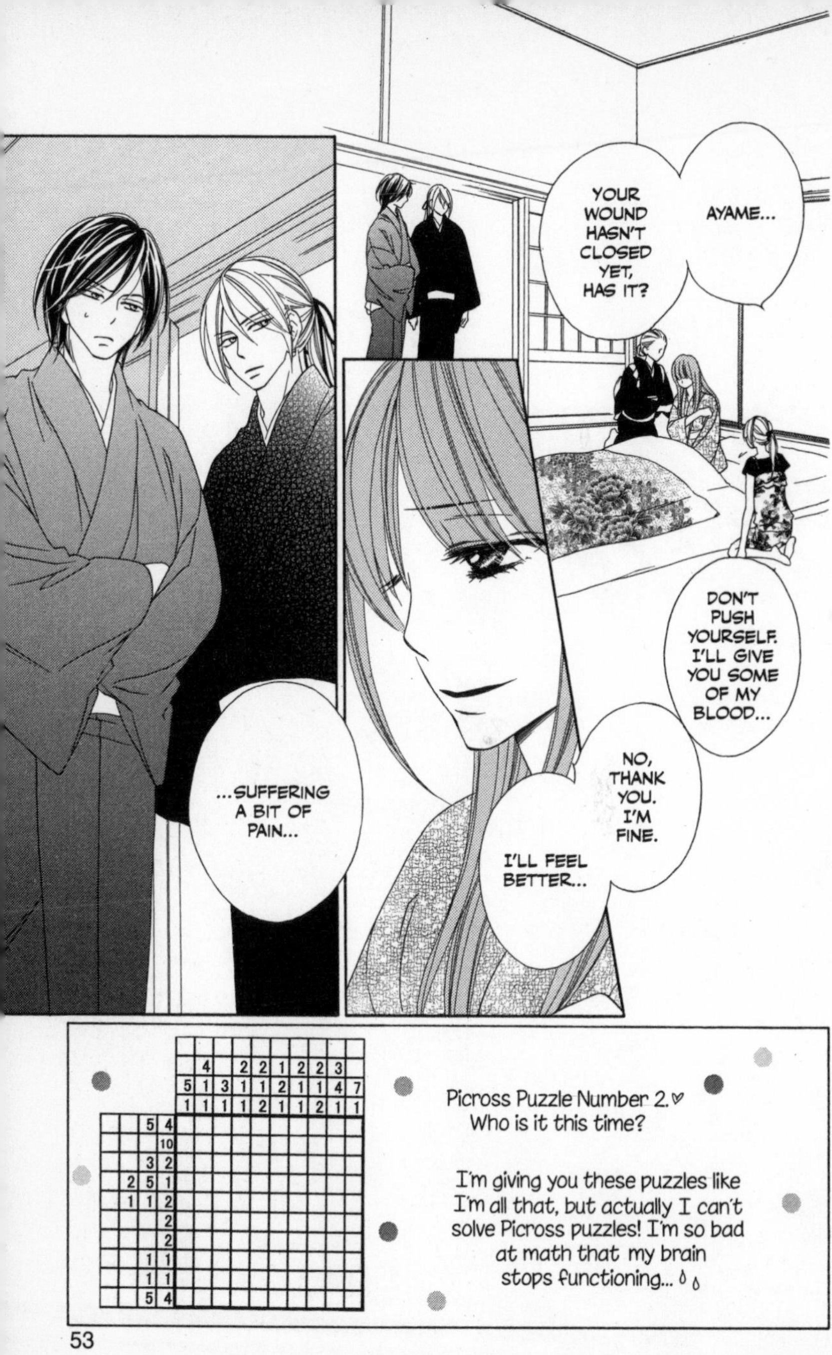
AYAME...
YOUR WOUND HASN'T CLOSED YET, HAS IT?
DON'T PUSH YOURSELF. I'LL GIVE YOU SOME OF MY BLOOD...
NO, THANK YOU. I'M FINE.
I'LL FEEL BETTER...
...SUFFERING A BIT OF PAIN...

				4		2	2	1	2	2	3	
			5	1	3	1	1	2	1	1	4	7
			1	1	1	1	2	1	1	2	1	1
	5	4										
		10										
	3	2										
2	5	1										
1	1	2										
		2										
		2										
	1	1										
	1	1										
	5	4										

Picross Puzzle Number 2.♡
Who is it this time?

I'm giving you these puzzles like I'm all that, but actually I can't solve Picross puzzles! I'm so bad at math that my brain stops functioning...

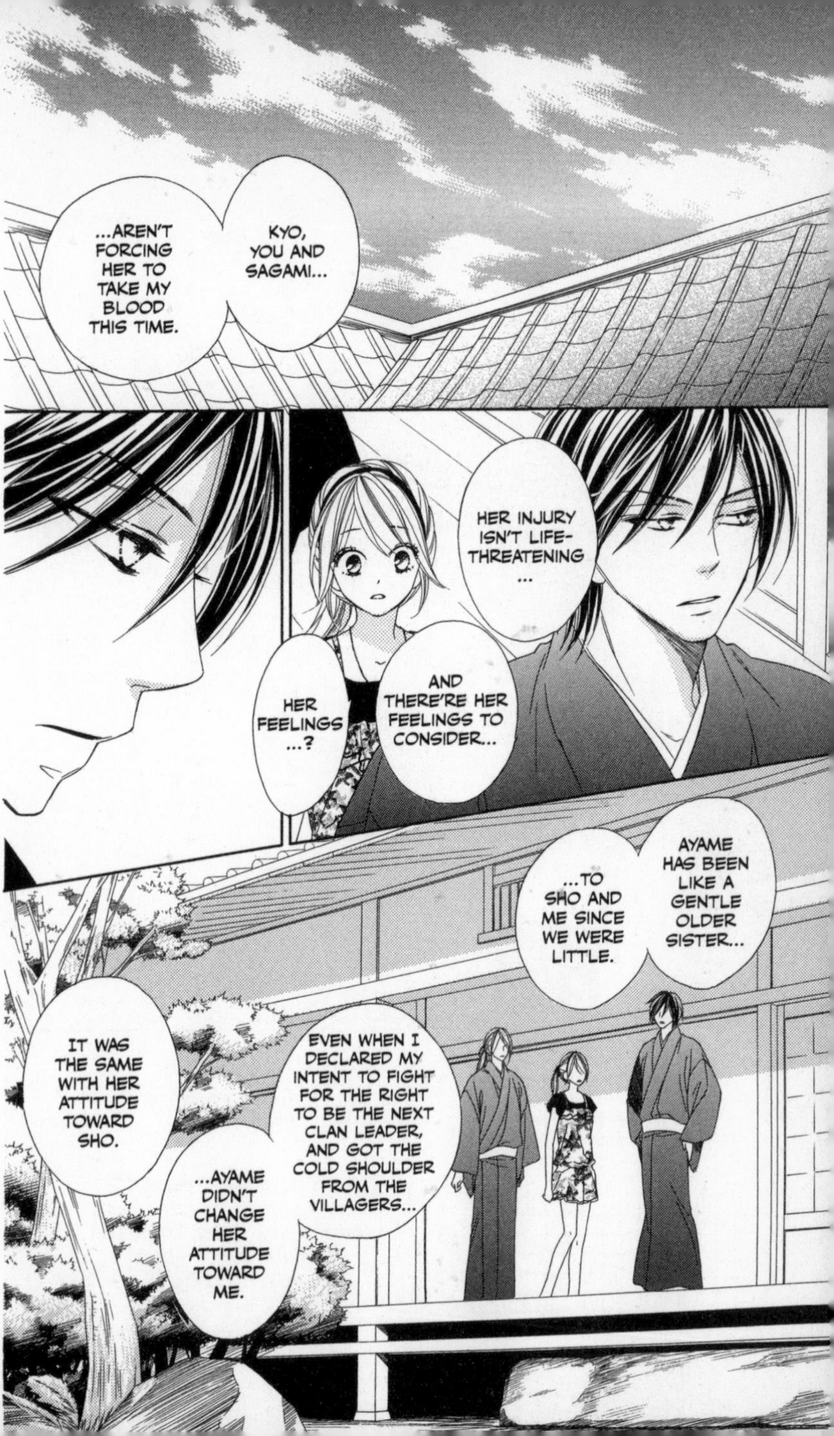
KYO, YOU AND SAGAMI...
...AREN'T FORCING HER TO TAKE MY BLOOD THIS TIME.
HER INJURY ISN'T LIFE-THREATENING ...
AND THERE'RE HER FEELINGS TO CONSIDER...
HER FEELINGS ...?
AYAME HAS BEEN LIKE A GENTLE OLDER SISTER...
...TO SHO AND ME SINCE WE WERE LITTLE.
EVEN WHEN I DECLARED MY INTENT TO FIGHT FOR THE RIGHT TO BE THE NEXT CLAN LEADER, AND GOT THE COLD SHOULDER FROM THE VILLAGERS...
...AYAME DIDN'T CHANGE HER ATTITUDE TOWARD ME.
IT WAS THE SAME WITH HER ATTITUDE TOWARD SHO.

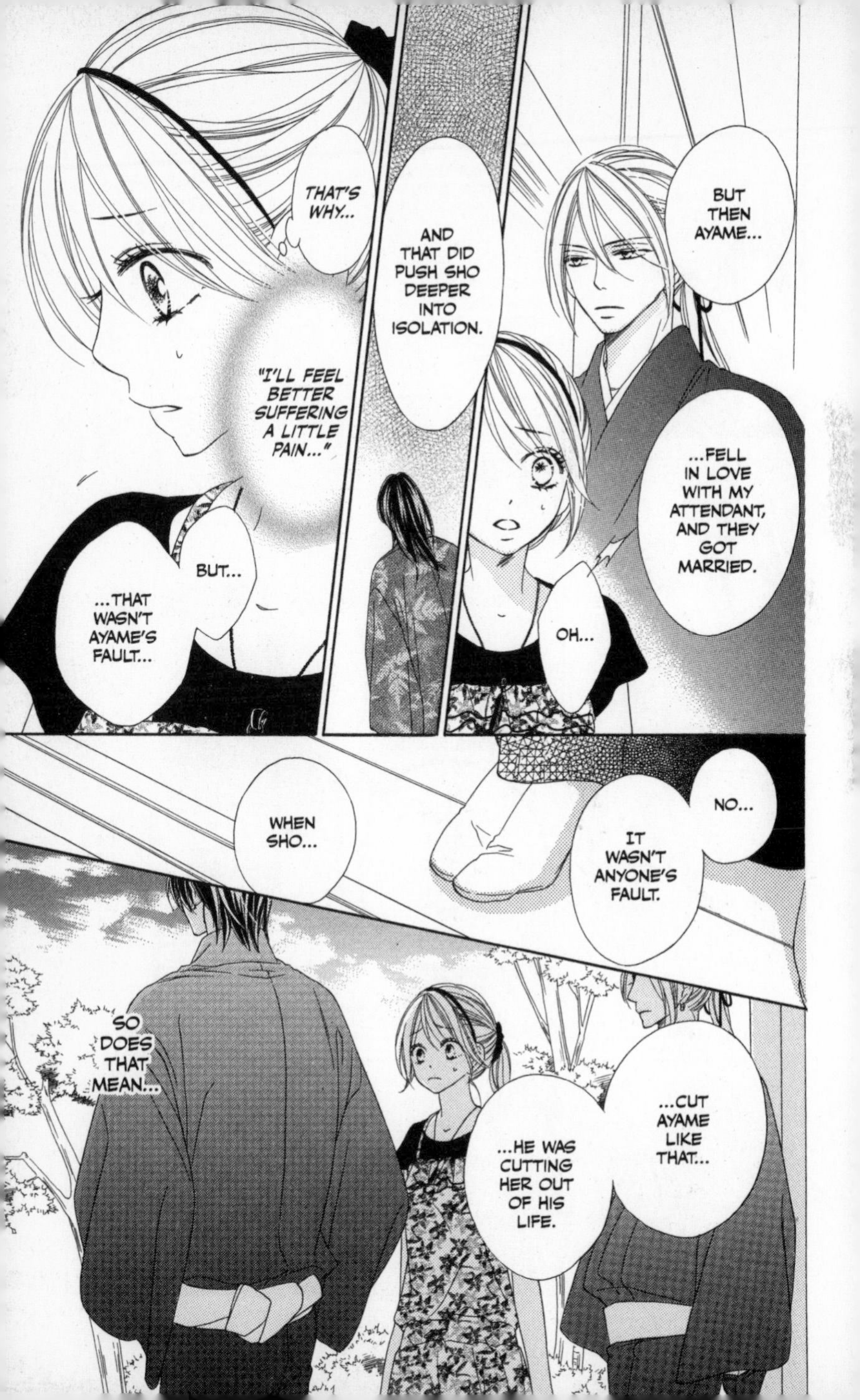
BUT THEN AYAME...
...FELL IN LOVE WITH MY ATTENDANT, AND THEY GOT MARRIED.
OH...
AND THAT DID PUSH SHO DEEPER INTO ISOLATION.
THAT'S WHY...
"I'LL FEEL BETTER SUFFERING A LITTLE PAIN..."
BUT...
...THAT WASN'T AYAME'S FAULT...
NO...
IT WASN'T ANYONE'S FAULT.
WHEN SHO...
...CUT AYAME LIKE THAT...
...HE WAS CUTTING HER OUT OF HIS LIFE.
SO DOES THAT MEAN...

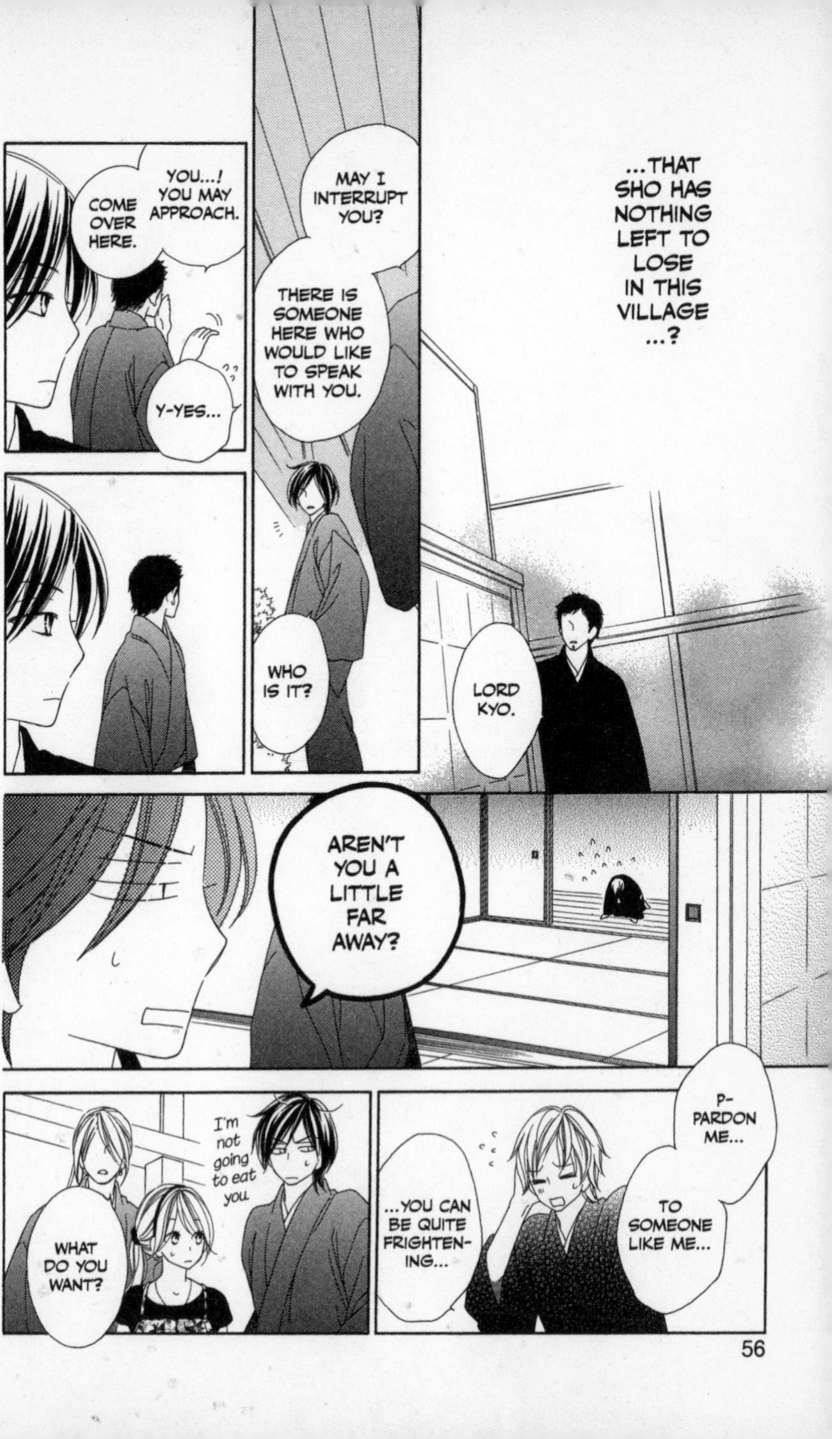
...THAT SHO HAS NOTHING LEFT TO LOSE IN THIS VILLAGE ...?
LORD KYO.
MAY I INTERRUPT YOU?
THERE IS SOMEONE HERE WHO WOULD LIKE TO SPEAK WITH YOU.
WHO IS IT?
YOU...! YOU MAY APPROACH.
COME OVER HERE.
Y-YES...
AREN'T YOU A LITTLE FAR AWAY?
P-PARDON ME...
TO SOMEONE LIKE ME...
...YOU CAN BE QUITE FRIGHTEN-ING...
I'm not going to eat you.
WHAT DO YOU WANT?

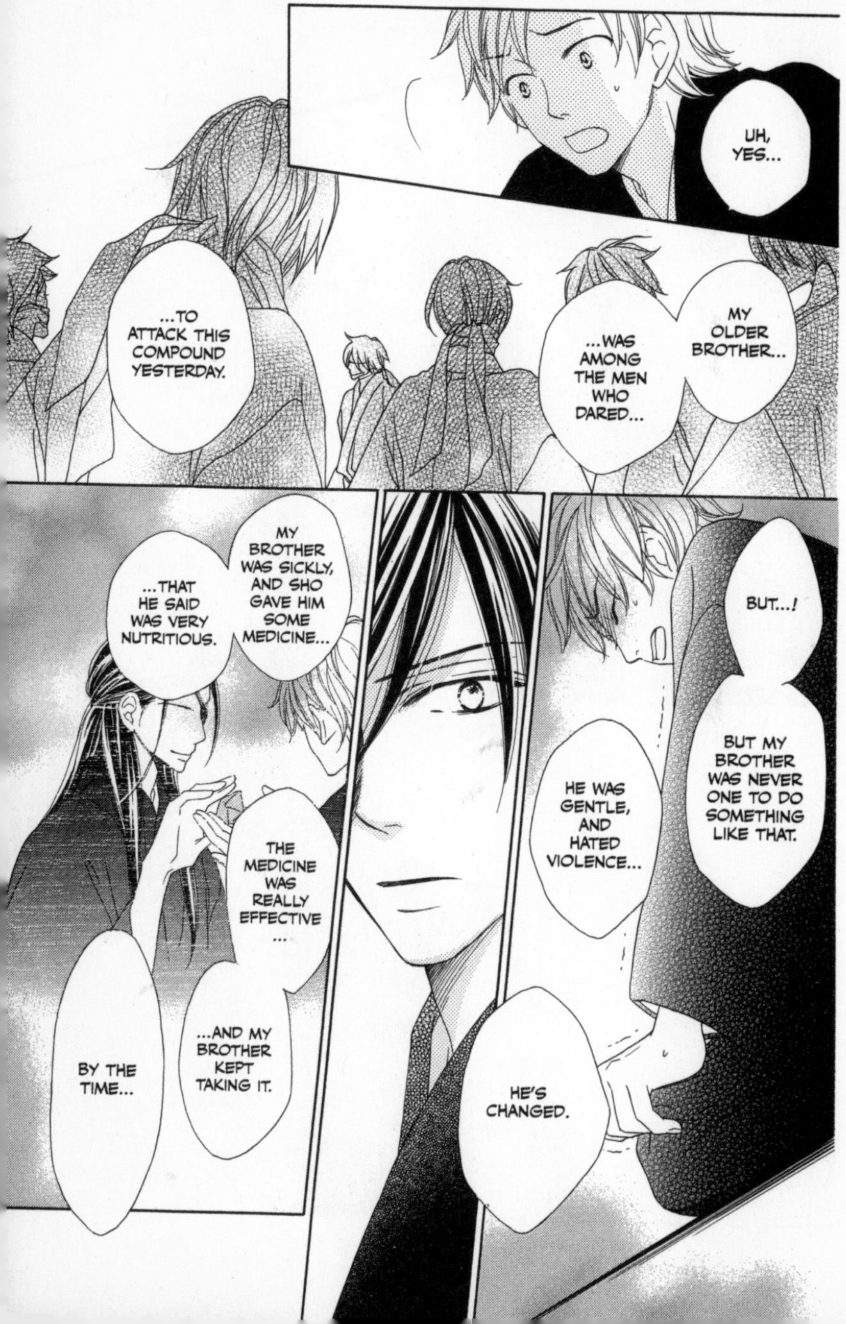
UH, YES...
MY OLDER BROTHER...
...WAS AMONG THE MEN WHO DARED...
...TO ATTACK THIS COMPOUND YESTERDAY.
BUT...!
BUT MY BROTHER WAS NEVER ONE TO DO SOMETHING LIKE THAT.
HE WAS GENTLE, AND HATED VIOLENCE...
HE'S CHANGED.
MY BROTHER WAS SICKLY, AND SHO GAVE HIM SOME MEDICINE...
...THAT HE SAID WAS VERY NUTRITIOUS.
THE MEDICINE WAS REALLY EFFECTIVE...
...AND MY BROTHER KEPT TAKING IT.
BY THE TIME...

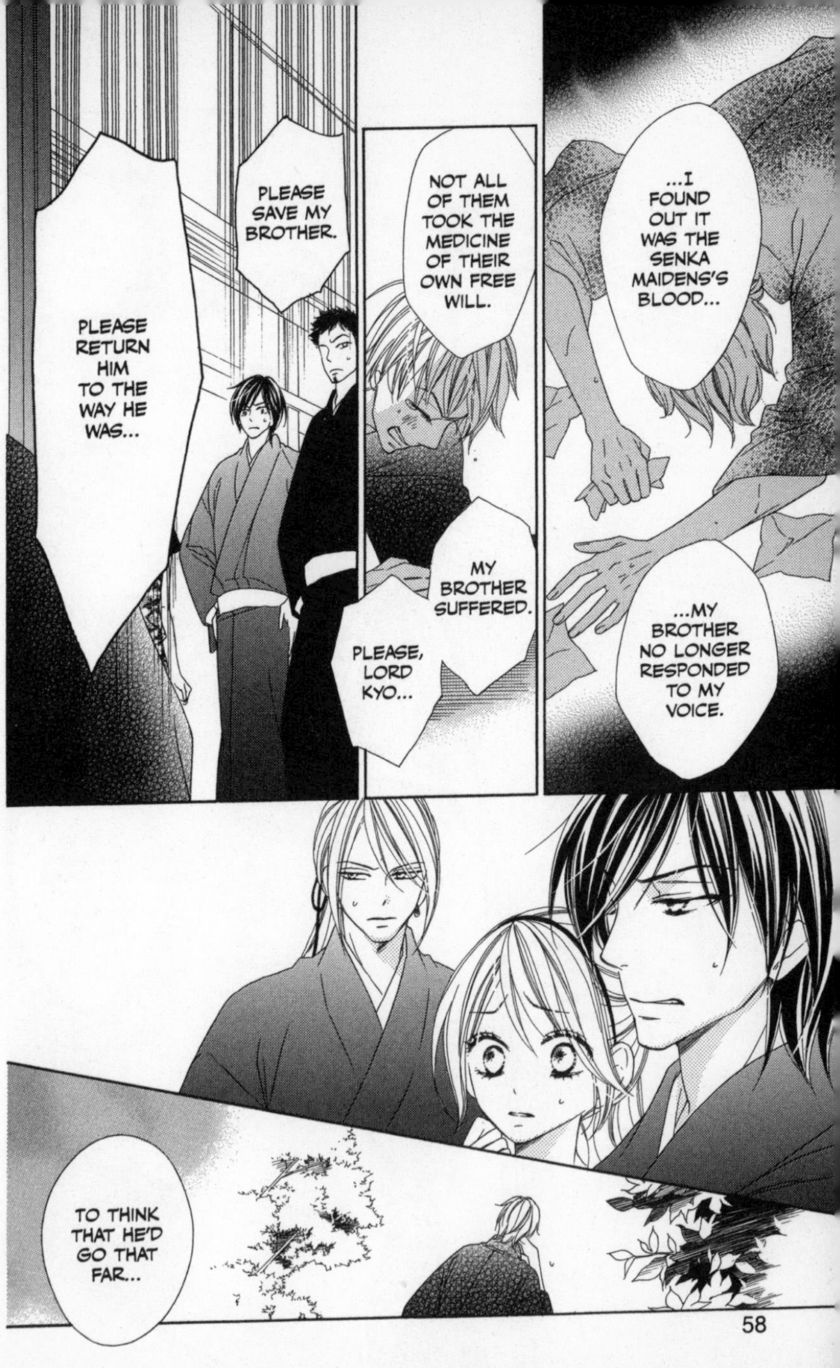
...I FOUND OUT IT WAS THE SENKA MAIDENS'S BLOOD...
...MY BROTHER NO LONGER RESPONDED TO MY VOICE.
NOT ALL OF THEM TOOK THE MEDICINE OF THEIR OWN FREE WILL.
MY BROTHER SUFFERED.
PLEASE, LORD KYO...
PLEASE SAVE MY BROTHER.
PLEASE RETURN HIM TO THE WAY HE WAS...
TO THINK THAT HE'D GO THAT FAR...

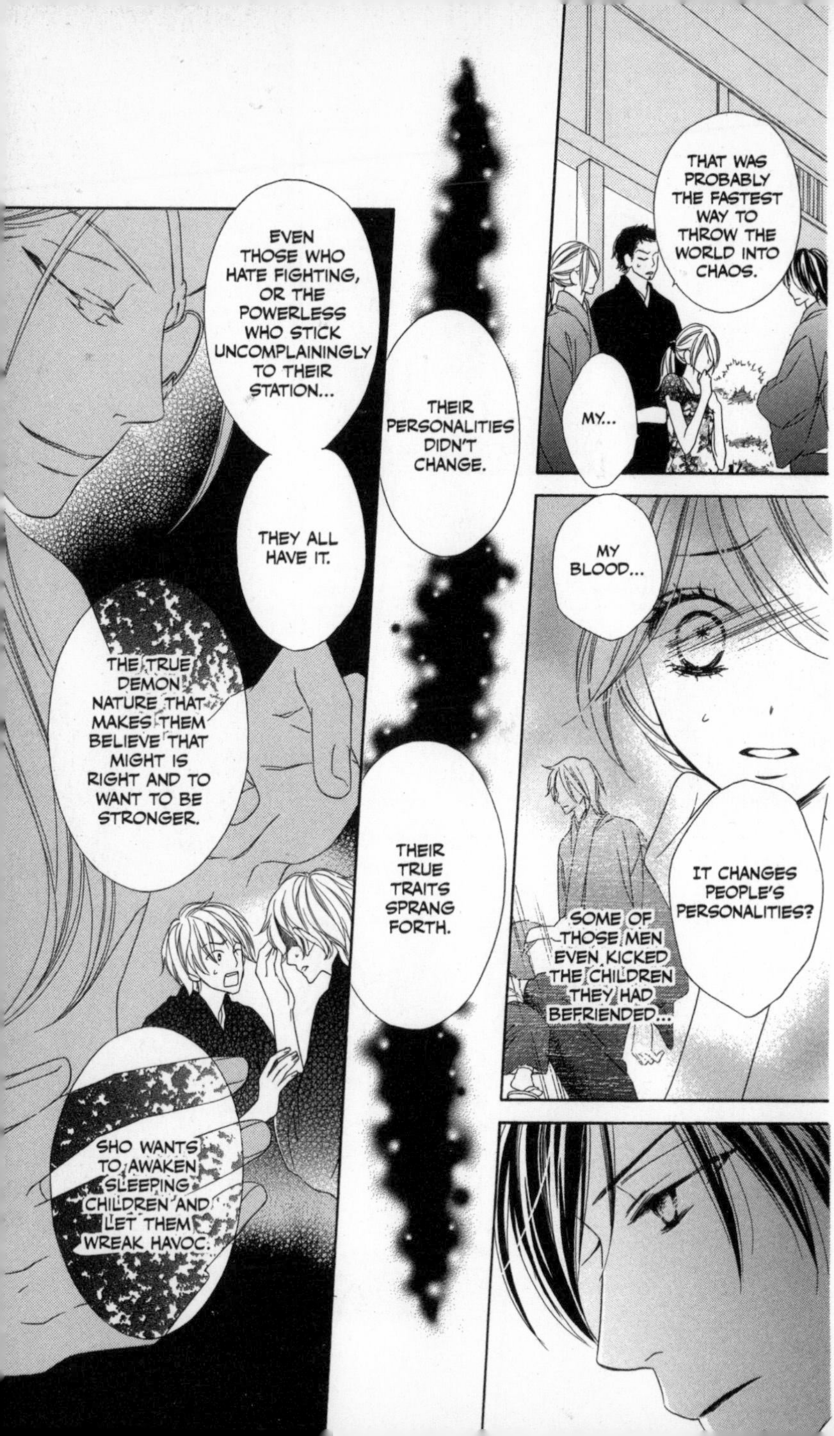
THAT WAS PROBABLY THE FASTEST WAY TO THROW THE WORLD INTO CHAOS.
MY...
MY BLOOD...
IT CHANGES PEOPLE'S PERSONALITIES?
SOME OF THOSE MEN EVEN KICKED THE CHILDREN THEY HAD BEFRIENDED...
THEIR PERSONALITIES DIDN'T CHANGE.
THEIR TRUE TRAITS SPRANG FORTH.
EVEN THOSE WHO HATE FIGHTING, OR THE POWERLESS WHO STICK UNCOMPLAININGLY TO THEIR STATION...
THEY ALL HAVE IT.
THE TRUE DEMON NATURE THAT MAKES THEM BELIEVE THAT MIGHT IS RIGHT AND TO WANT TO BE STRONGER.
SHO WANTS TO AWAKEN SLEEPING CHILDREN AND LET THEM WREAK HAVOC.

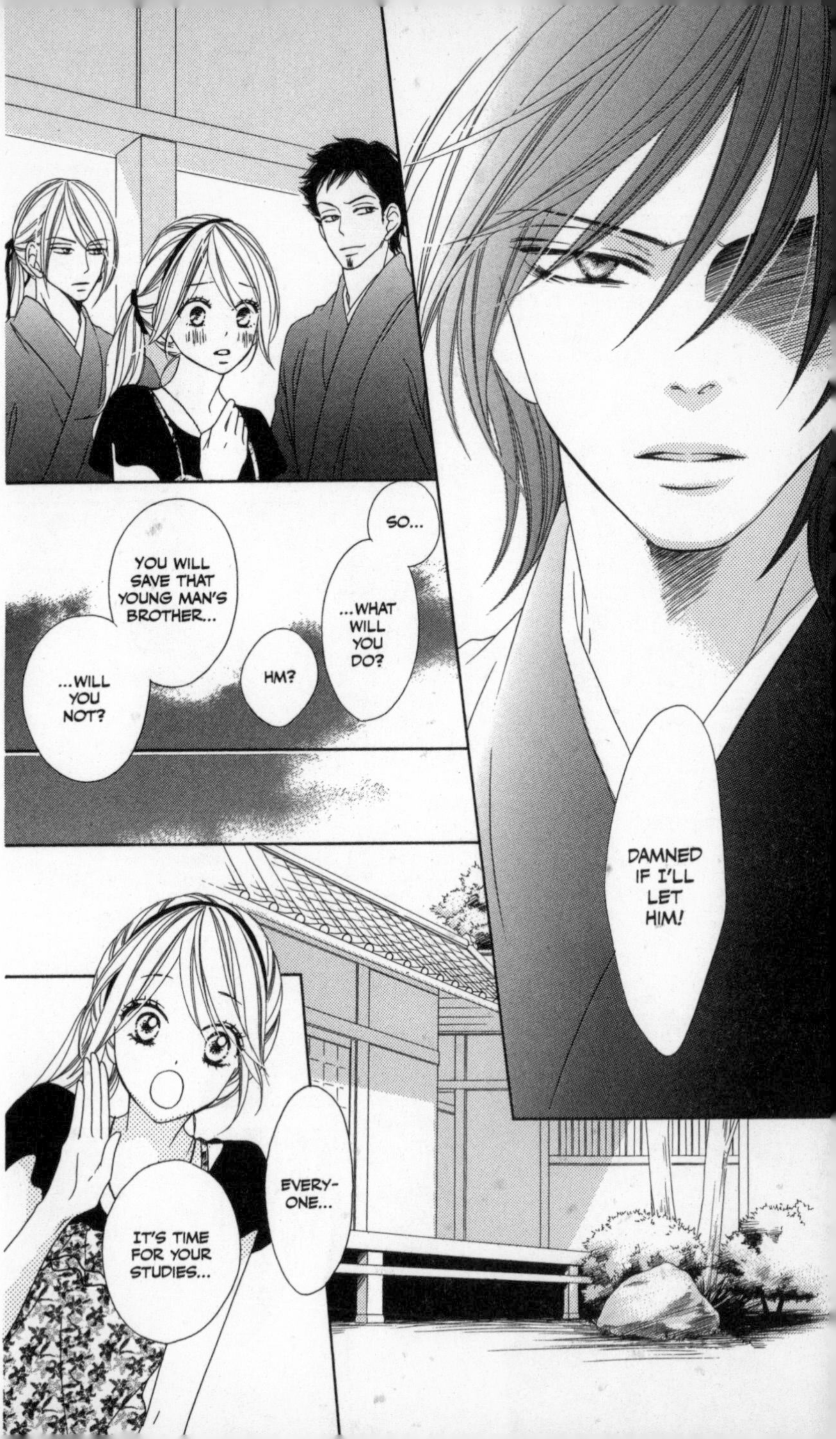
DAMNED IF I'LL LET HIM!
SO...
...WHAT WILL YOU DO?
HM?
YOU WILL SAVE THAT YOUNG MAN'S BROTHER...
...WILL YOU NOT?
EVERY-ONE...
IT'S TIME FOR YOUR STUDIES...

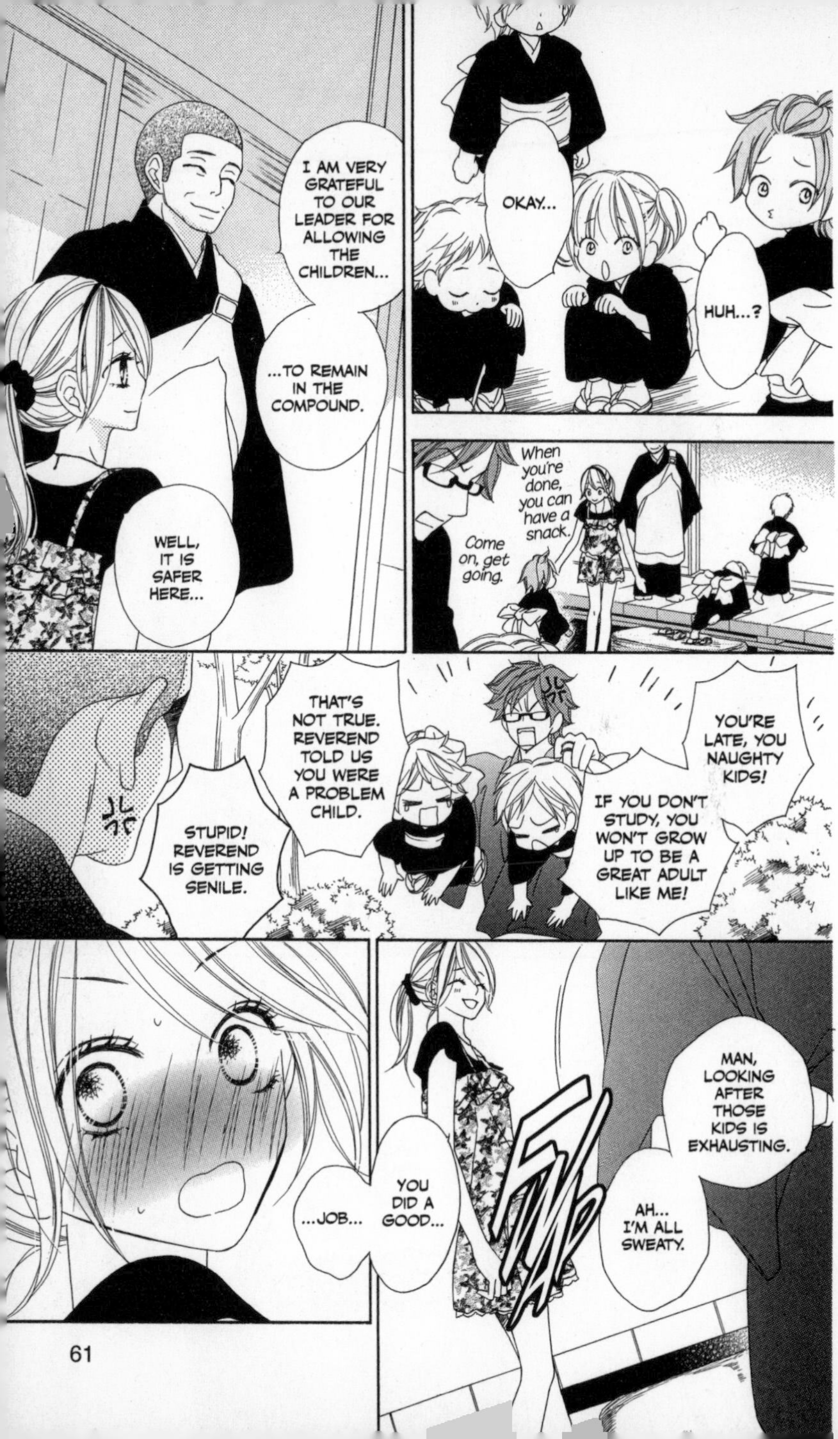
OKAY...
HUH...?
When you're done, you can have a snack.
Come on, get going.
I AM VERY GRATEFUL TO OUR LEADER FOR ALLOWING THE CHILDREN...
...TO REMAIN IN THE COMPOUND.
WELL, IT IS SAFER HERE...
YOU'RE LATE, YOU NAUGHTY KIDS!
IF YOU DON'T STUDY, YOU WON'T GROW UP TO BE A GREAT ADULT LIKE ME!
THAT'S NOT TRUE. REVEREND TOLD US YOU WERE A PROBLEM CHILD.
STUPID! REVEREND IS GETTING SENILE.
MAN, LOOKING AFTER THOSE KIDS IS EXHAUSTING.
AH... I'M ALL SWEATY.
YOU DID A GOOD...
...JOB...

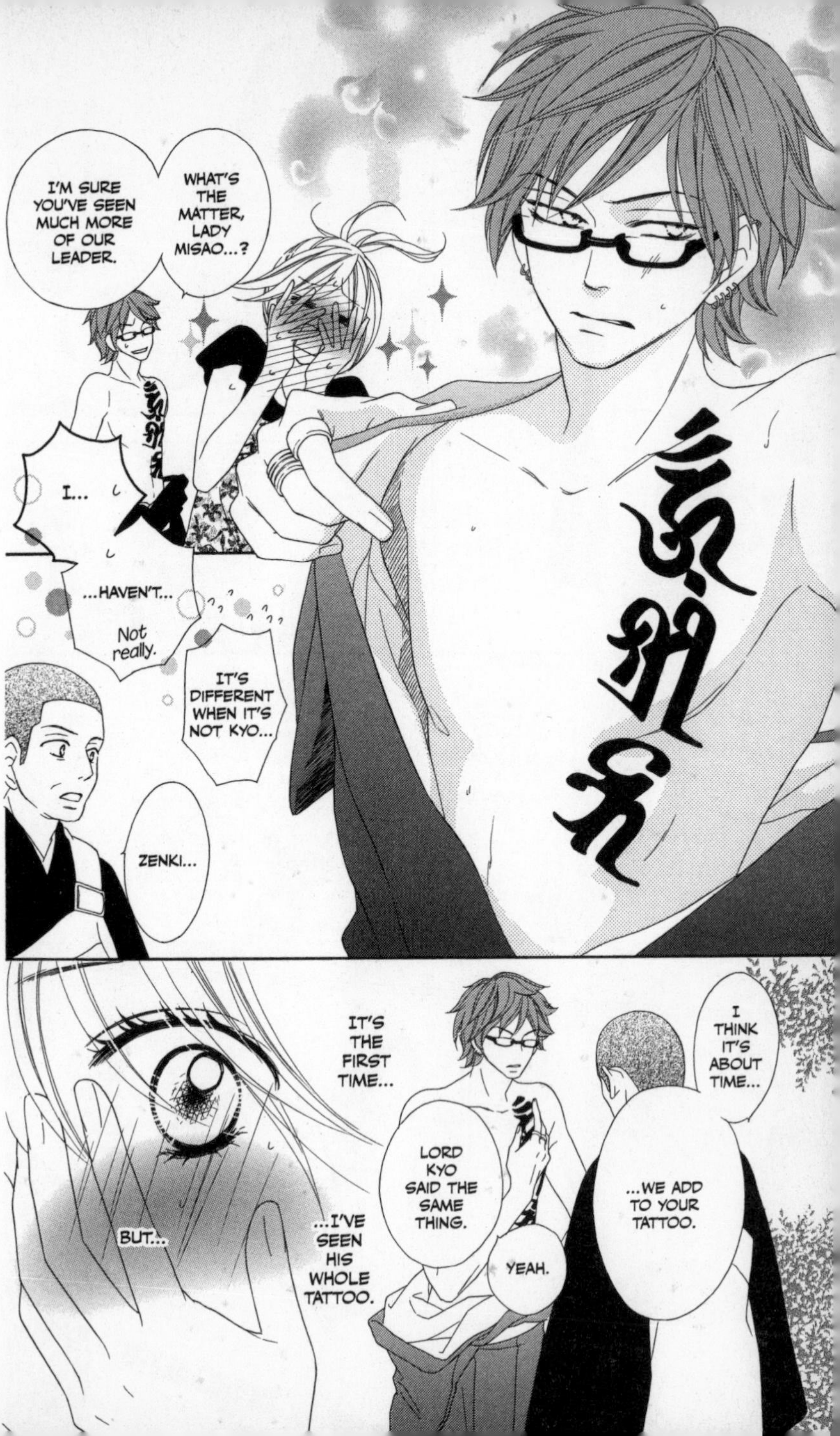
WHAT'S THE MATTER, LADY MISAO...?
I'M SURE YOU'VE SEEN MUCH MORE OF OUR LEADER.
I...
...HAVEN'T...
Not really.
IT'S DIFFERENT WHEN IT'S NOT KYO...
ZENKI...
I THINK IT'S ABOUT TIME...
...WE ADD TO YOUR TATTOO.
YEAH.
LORD KYO SAID THE SAME THING.
IT'S THE FIRST TIME...
...I'VE SEEN HIS WHOLE TATTOO.
BUT...

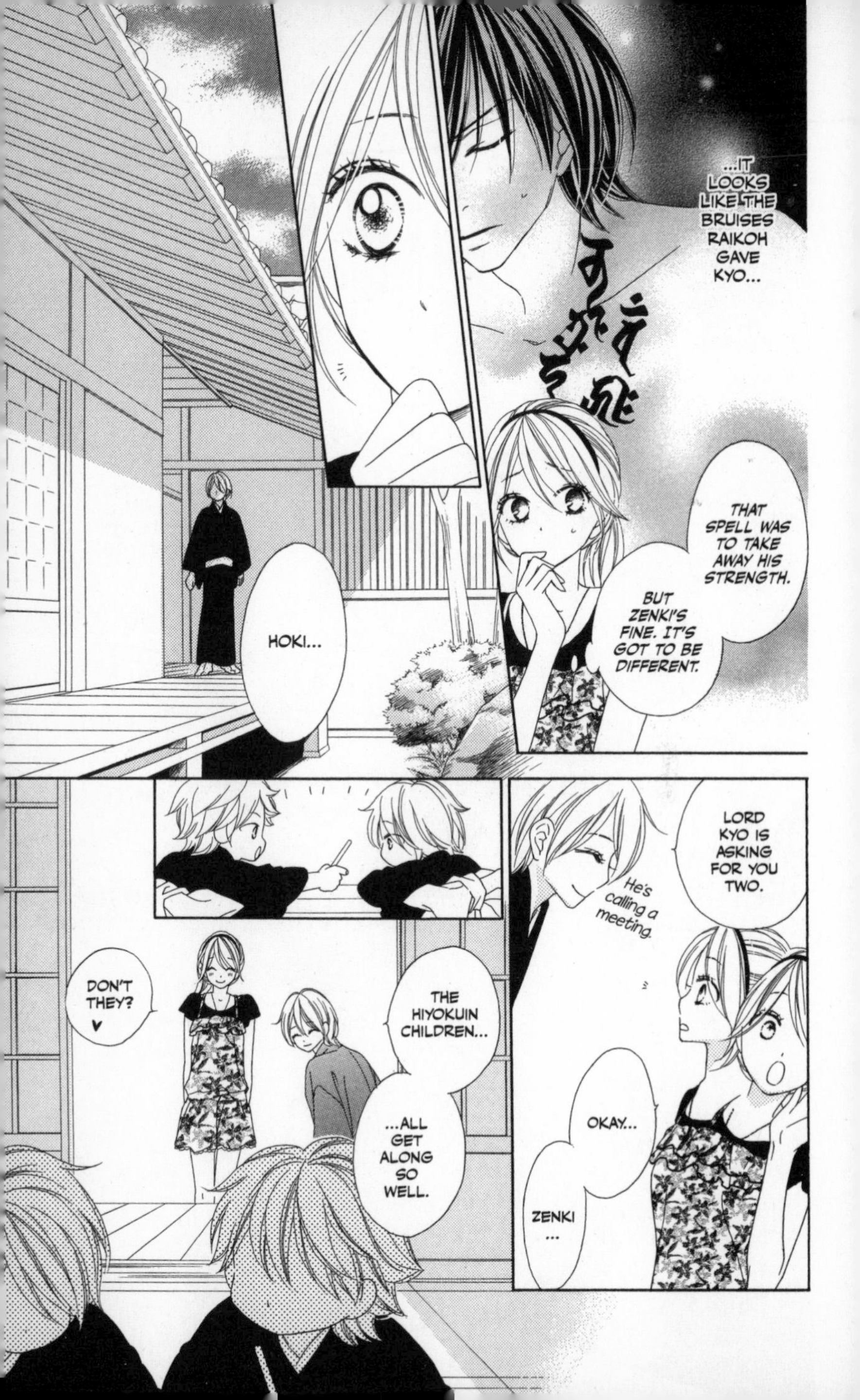
...IT LOOKS LIKE THE BRUISES RAIKOH GAVE KYO...
THAT SPELL WAS TO TAKE AWAY HIS STRENGTH.
BUT ZENKI'S FINE. IT'S GOT TO BE DIFFERENT.
HOKI...
LORD KYO IS ASKING FOR YOU TWO.
He's calling a meeting.
OKAY...
ZENKI ...
THE HIYOKUIN CHILDREN...
...ALL GET ALONG SO WELL.
DON'T THEY? ♥

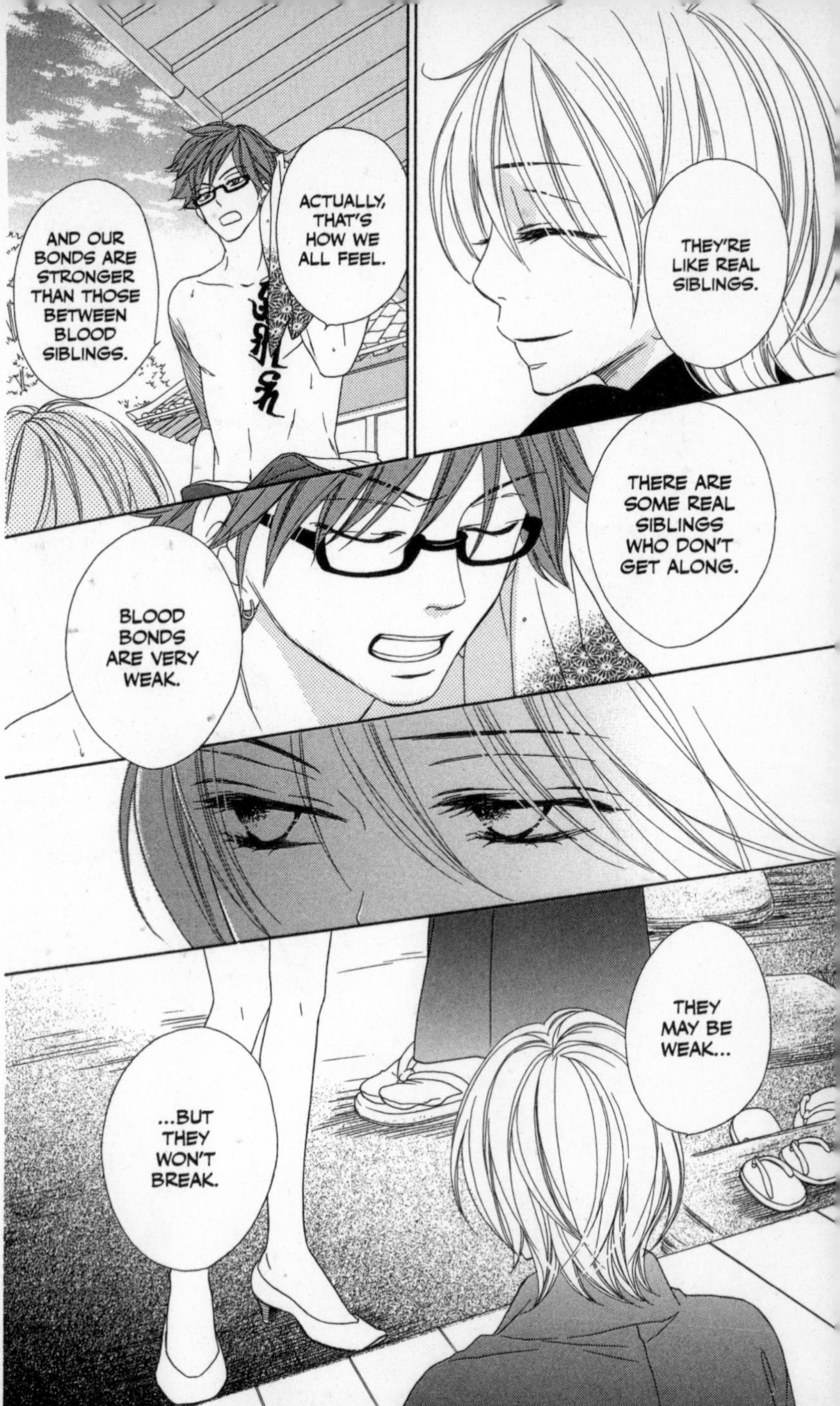
THEY'RE LIKE REAL SIBLINGS.
ACTUALLY, THAT'S HOW WE ALL FEEL.
AND OUR BONDS ARE STRONGER THAN THOSE BETWEEN BLOOD SIBLINGS.
THERE ARE SOME REAL SIBLINGS WHO DON'T GET ALONG.
BLOOD BONDS ARE VERY WEAK.
THEY MAY BE WEAK...
...BUT THEY WON'T BREAK.

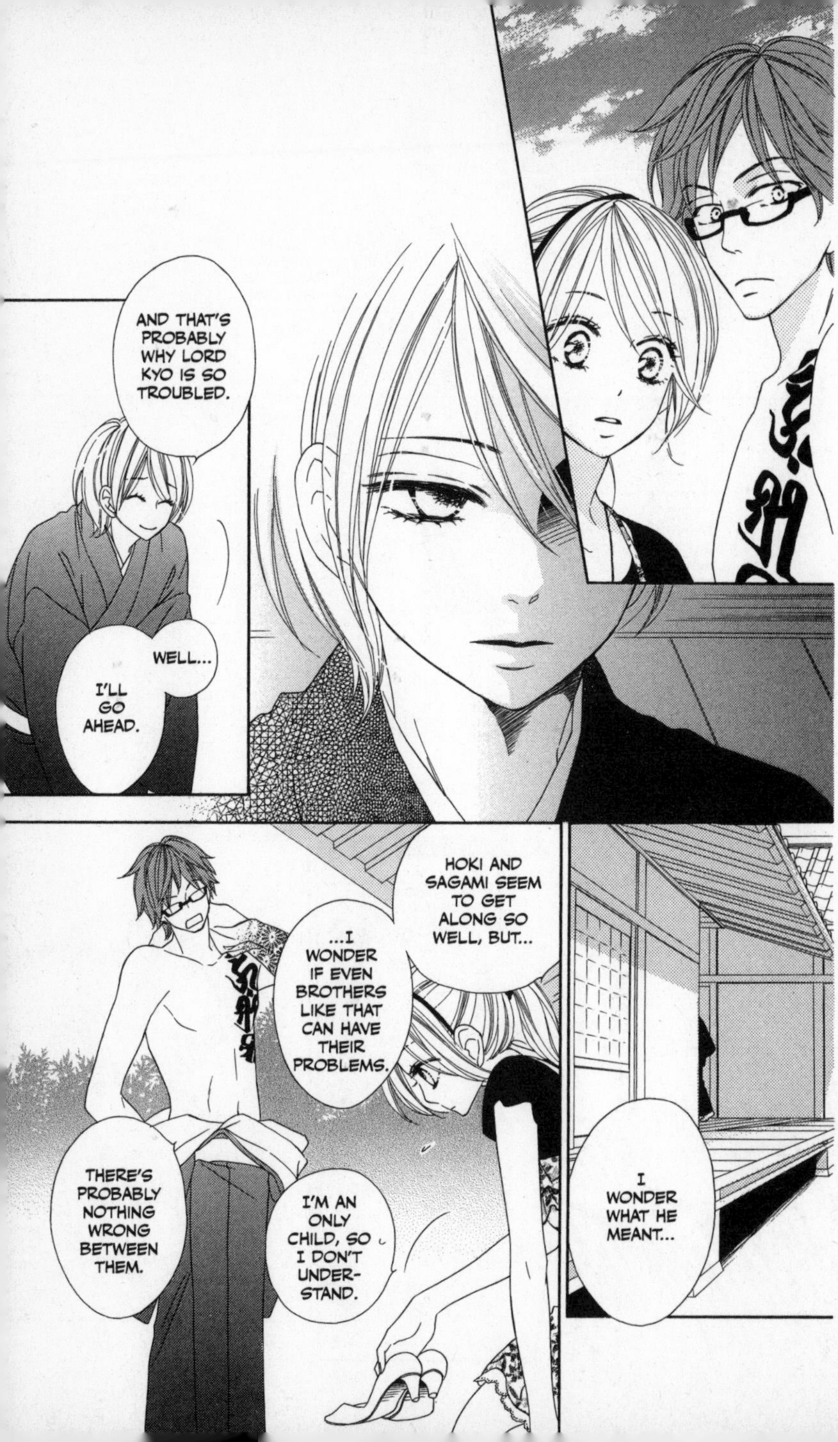

AND THAT'S PROBABLY WHY LORD KYO IS SO TROUBLED.
WELL... I'LL GO AHEAD.
I WONDER WHAT HE MEANT...
HOKI AND SAGAMI SEEM TO GET ALONG SO WELL, BUT...
...I WONDER IF EVEN BROTHERS LIKE THAT CAN HAVE THEIR PROBLEMS.
I'M AN ONLY CHILD, SO I DON'T UNDER-STAND.
THERE'S PROBABLY NOTHING WRONG BETWEEN THEM.

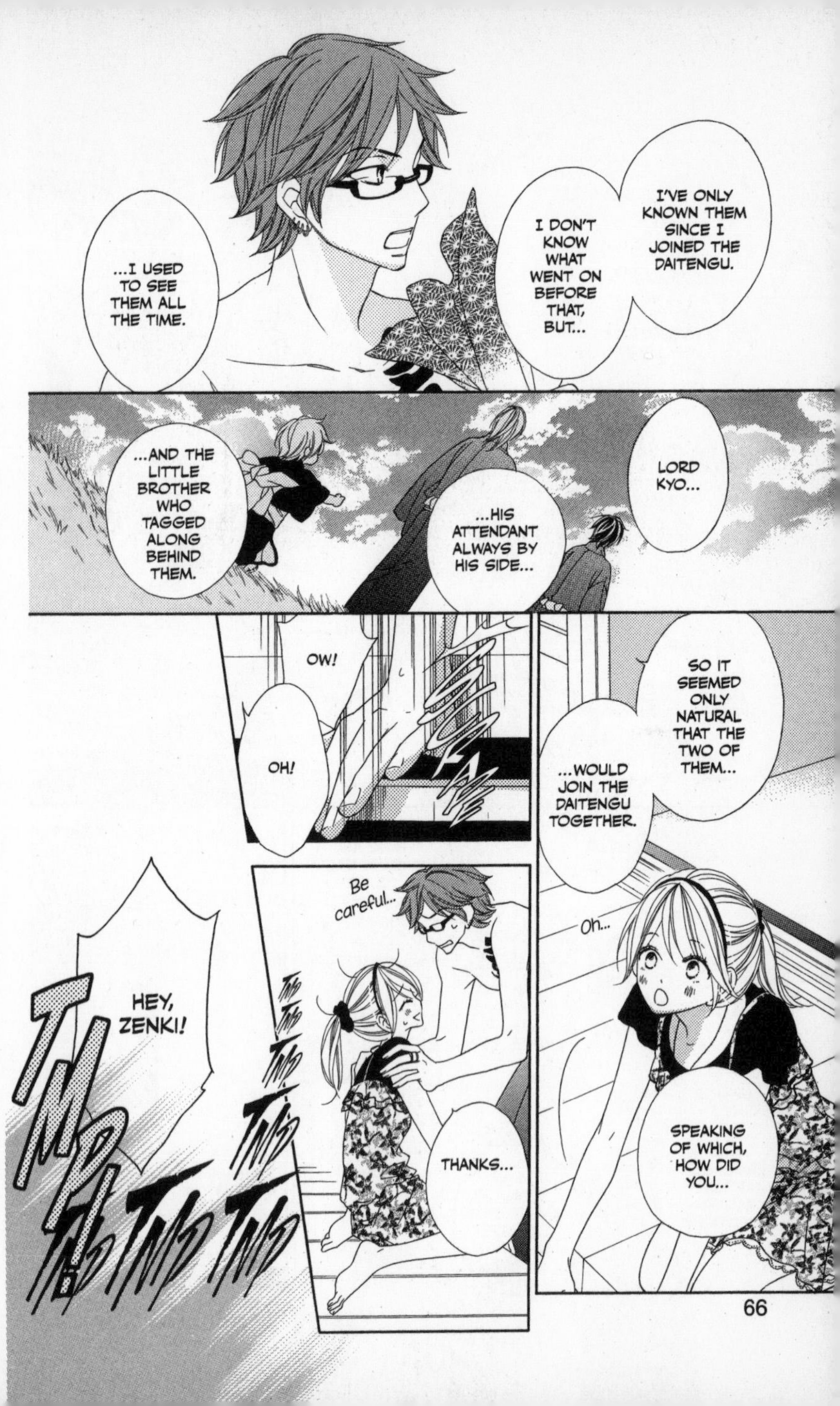
I'VE ONLY KNOWN THEM SINCE I JOINED THE DAITENGU.
I DON'T KNOW WHAT WENT ON BEFORE THAT, BUT...
...I USED TO SEE THEM ALL THE TIME.
LORD KYO...
...HIS ATTENDANT ALWAYS BY HIS SIDE...
...AND THE LITTLE BROTHER WHO TAGGED ALONG BEHIND THEM.
SO IT SEEMED ONLY NATURAL THAT THE TWO OF THEM...
...WOULD JOIN THE DAITENGU TOGETHER.
Oh...
SPEAKING OF WHICH, HOW DID YOU...
OW!
OH!
Be careful...
THANKS...
HEY, ZENKI!

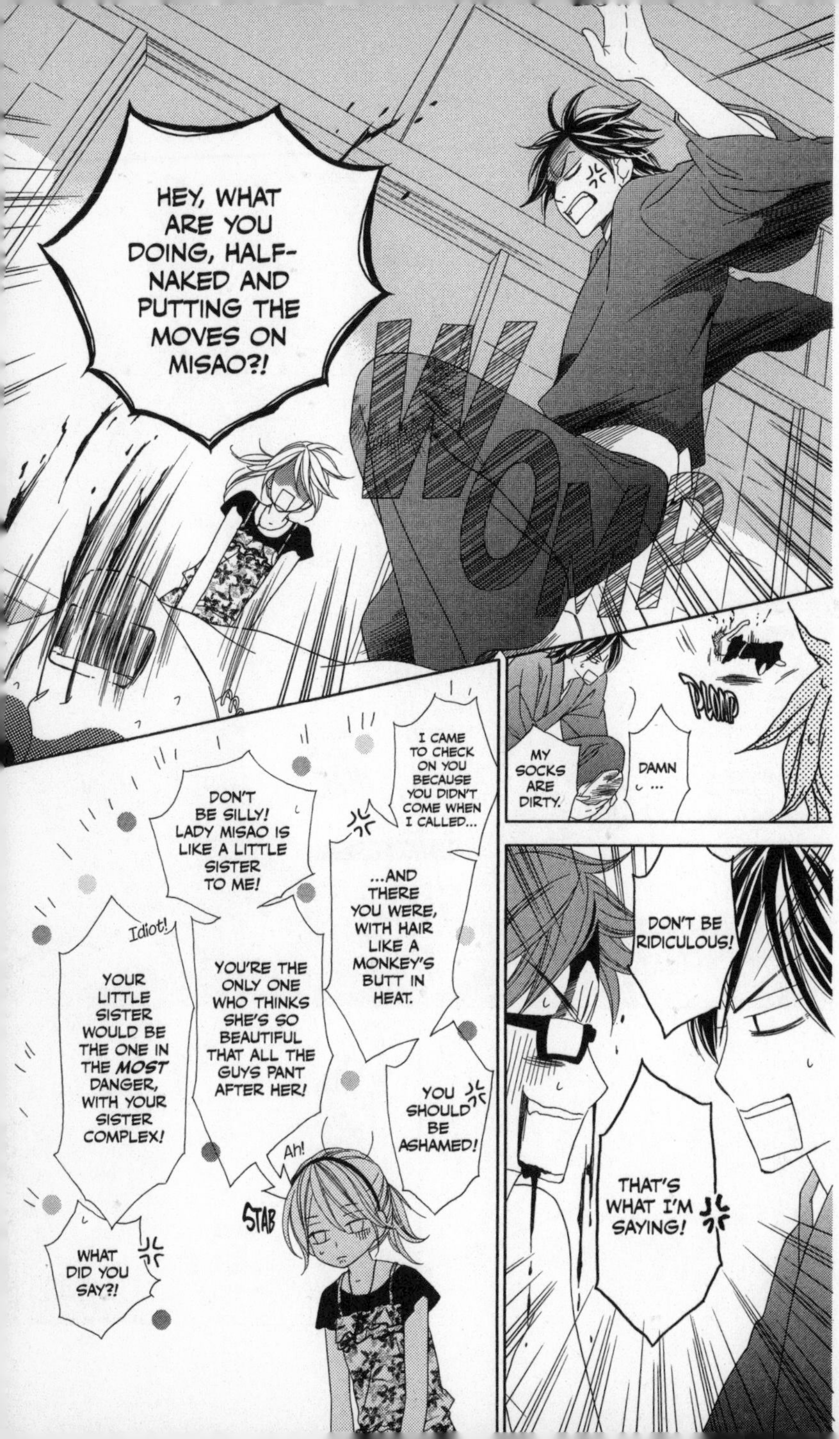
HEY, WHAT ARE YOU DOING, HALF-NAKED AND PUTTING THE MOVES ON MISAO?!
WOMP
PLOMP
DAMN ...
MY SOCKS ARE DIRTY.
DON'T BE RIDICULOUS!
THAT'S WHAT I'M SAYING!
I CAME TO CHECK ON YOU BECAUSE YOU DIDN'T COME WHEN I CALLED...
...AND THERE YOU WERE, WITH HAIR LIKE A MONKEY'S BUTT IN HEAT.
YOU SHOULD BE ASHAMED!
DON'T BE SILLY! LADY MISAO IS LIKE A LITTLE SISTER TO ME!
YOU'RE THE ONLY ONE WHO THINKS SHE'S SO BEAUTIFUL THAT ALL THE GUYS PANT AFTER HER!
Idiot!
YOUR LITTLE SISTER WOULD BE THE ONE IN THE *MOST* DANGER, WITH YOUR SISTER COMPLEX!
Ah!
STAB
WHAT DID YOU SAY?!

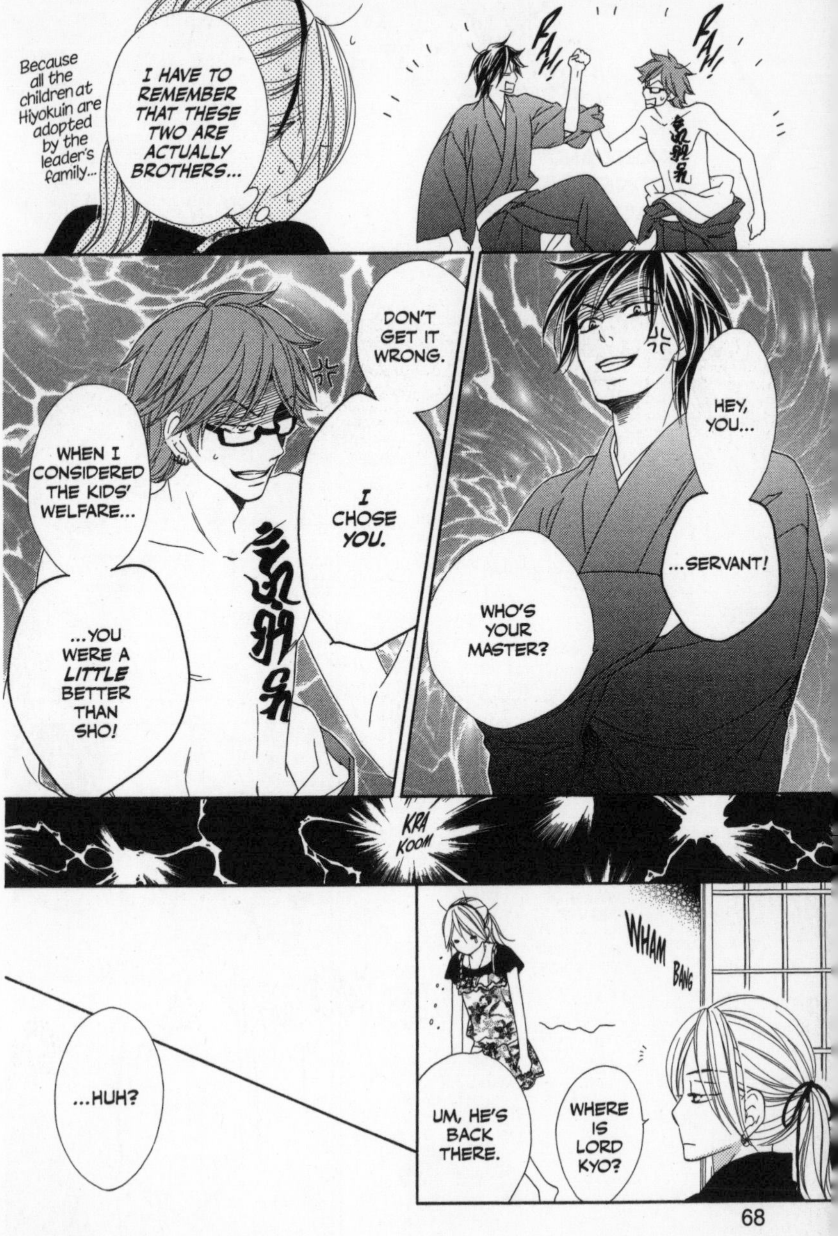
RAH!
RAH!
I HAVE TO REMEMBER THAT THESE TWO ARE ACTUALLY BROTHERS...
Because all the children at Hiyokuin are adopted by the leader's family...
HEY, YOU...
...SERVANT!
WHO'S YOUR MASTER?
DON'T GET IT WRONG.
I CHOSE YOU.
WHEN I CONSIDERED THE KIDS' WELFARE...
...YOU WERE A LITTLE BETTER THAN SHO!
KRA KOOM
WHAM BANG
WHERE IS LORD KYO?
UM, HE'S BACK THERE.
...HUH?

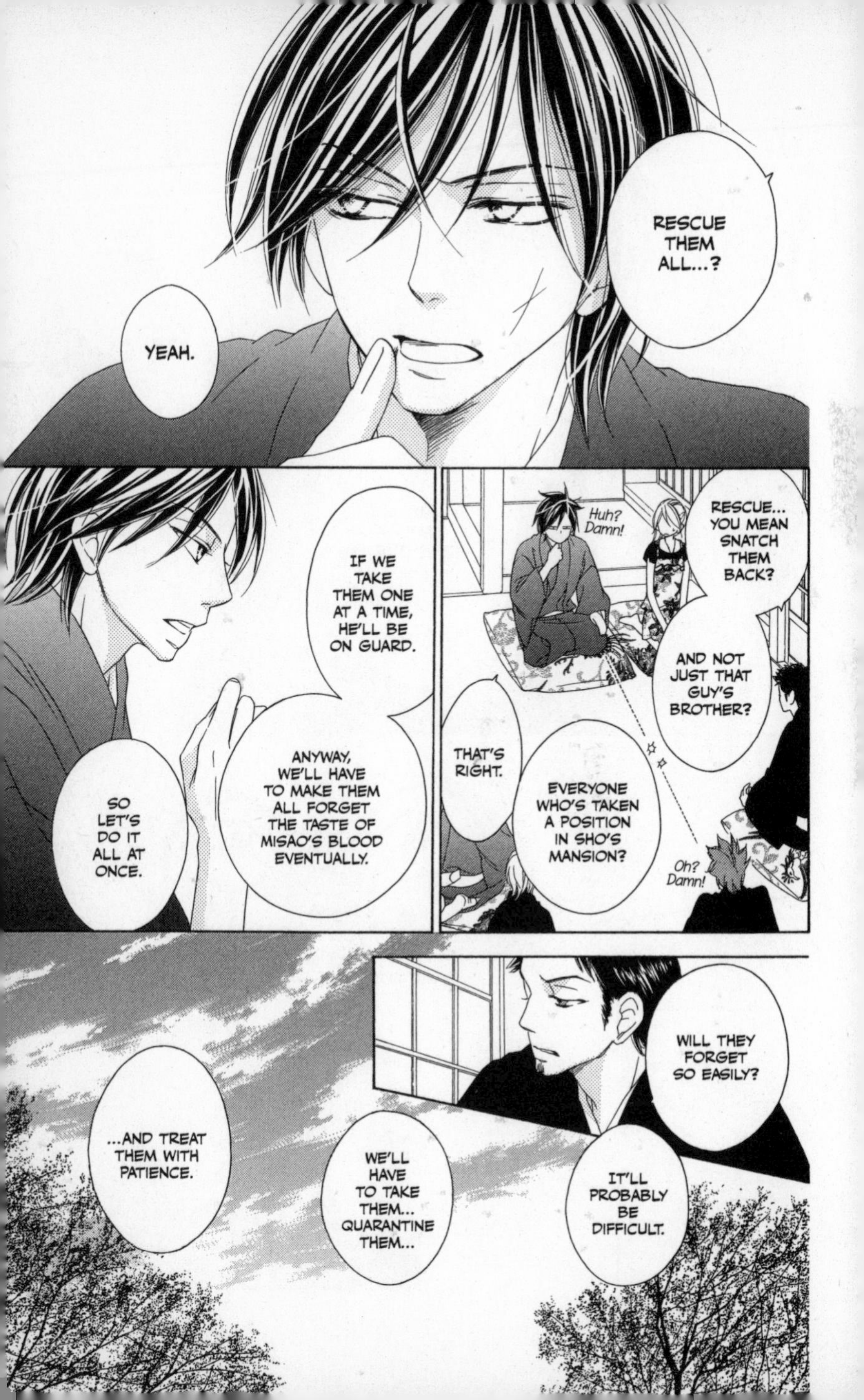
RESCUE THEM ALL...?
YEAH.
RESCUE... YOU MEAN SNATCH THEM BACK?
AND NOT JUST THAT GUY'S BROTHER?
Huh? Damn!
EVERYONE WHO'S TAKEN A POSITION IN SHO'S MANSION?
THAT'S RIGHT.
Oh? Damn!
IF WE TAKE THEM ONE AT A TIME, HE'LL BE ON GUARD.
SO LET'S DO IT ALL AT ONCE.
ANYWAY, WE'LL HAVE TO MAKE THEM ALL FORGET THE TASTE OF MISAO'S BLOOD EVENTUALLY.
WILL THEY FORGET SO EASILY?
IT'LL PROBABLY BE DIFFICULT.
WE'LL HAVE TO TAKE THEM... QUARANTINE THEM...
...AND TREAT THEM WITH PATIENCE.

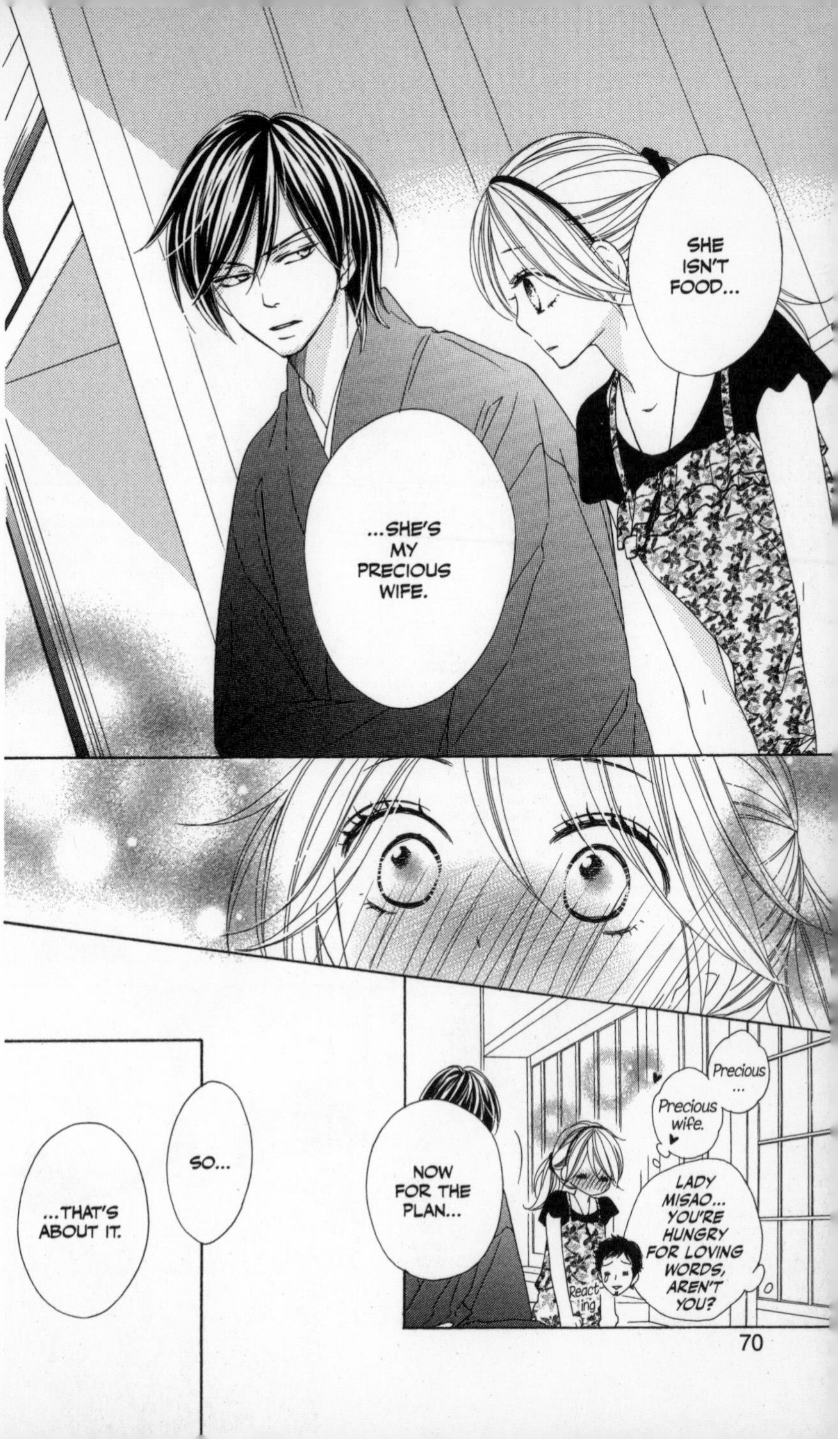
SHE ISN'T FOOD...
...SHE'S MY PRECIOUS WIFE.
Precious...
Precious wife.
LADY MISAO... YOU'RE HUNGRY FOR LOVING WORDS, AREN'T YOU?
NOW FOR THE PLAN...
React-ing
SO...
...THAT'S ABOUT IT.

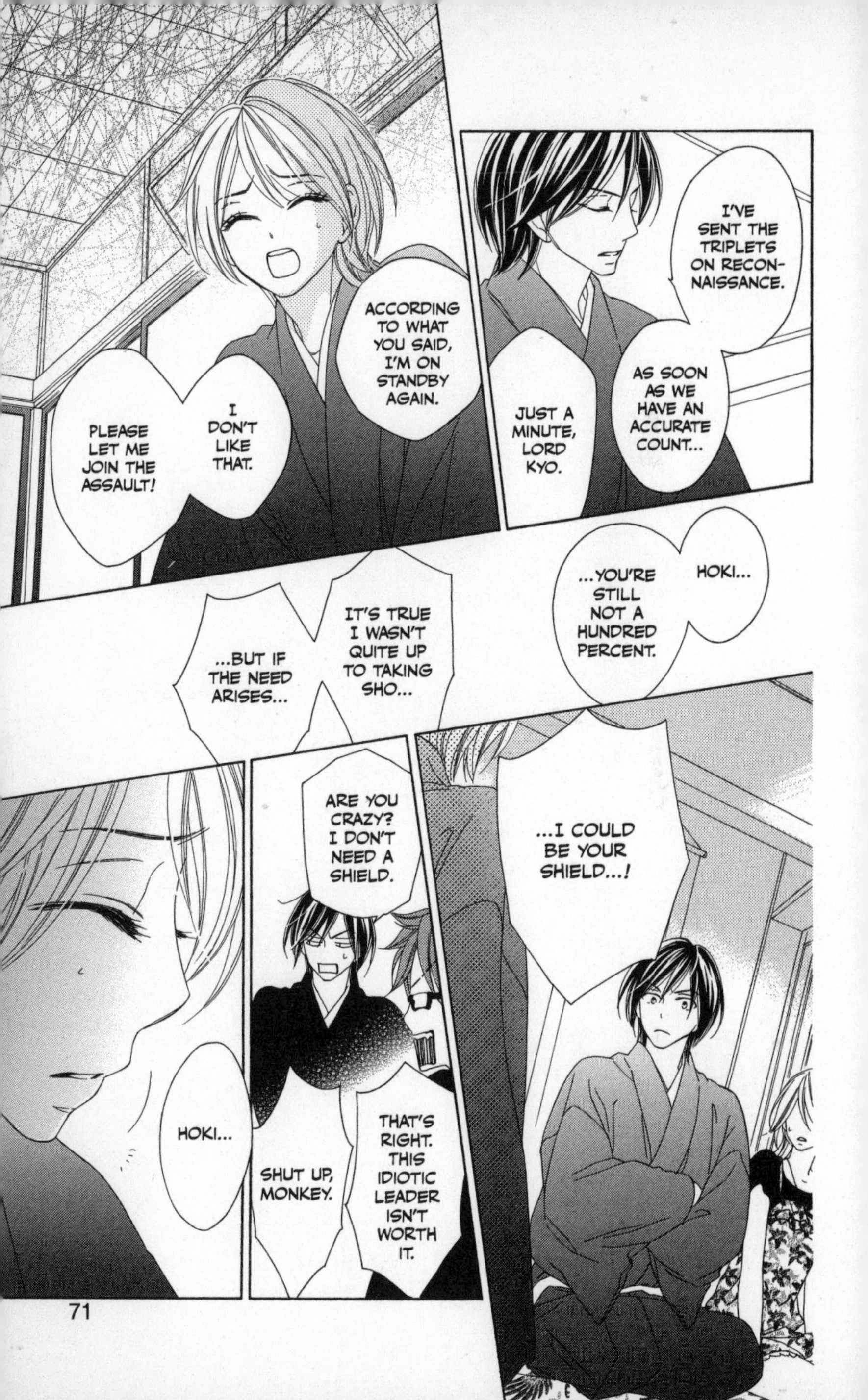
I'VE SENT THE TRIPLETS ON RECONNAISSANCE.
AS SOON AS WE HAVE AN ACCURATE COUNT...
JUST A MINUTE, LORD KYO.
ACCORDING TO WHAT YOU SAID, I'M ON STANDBY AGAIN.
I DON'T LIKE THAT.
PLEASE LET ME JOIN THE ASSAULT!
HOKI...
...YOU'RE STILL NOT A HUNDRED PERCENT.
IT'S TRUE I WASN'T QUITE UP TO TAKING SHO...
...BUT IF THE NEED ARISES...
...I COULD BE YOUR SHIELD...!
ARE YOU CRAZY? I DON'T NEED A SHIELD.
THAT'S RIGHT. THIS IDIOTIC LEADER ISN'T WORTH IT.
SHUT UP, MONKEY.
HOKI...

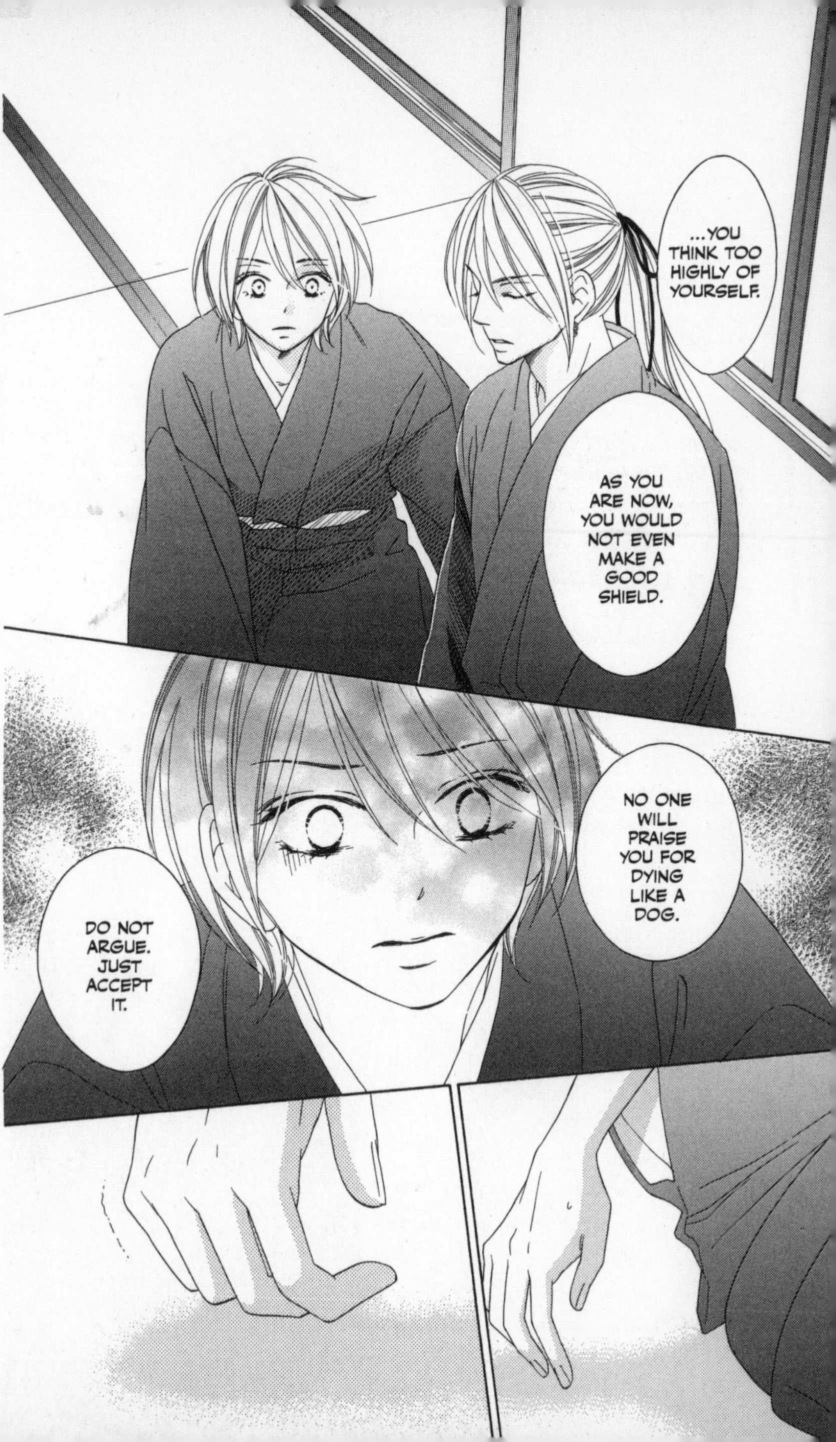
...YOU THINK TOO HIGHLY OF YOURSELF.
AS YOU ARE NOW, YOU WOULD NOT EVEN MAKE A GOOD SHIELD.
NO ONE WILL PRAISE YOU FOR DYING LIKE A DOG.
DO NOT ARGUE. JUST ACCEPT IT.

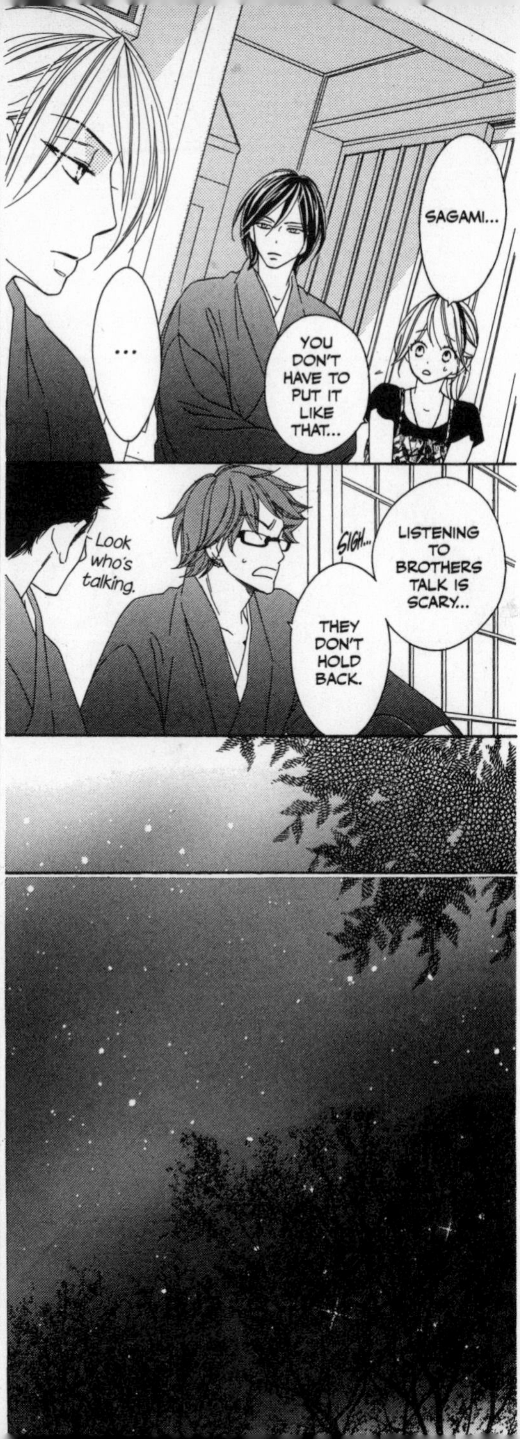
SAGAMI...
YOU DON'T HAVE TO PUT IT LIKE THAT...
...
LISTENING TO BROTHERS TALK IS SCARY...
SIGH...
THEY DON'T HOLD BACK.
Look who's talking.

When Volume 11 came out, I had a second book signing. Thank you to all who came! ♡

This was my hairstyle that day.

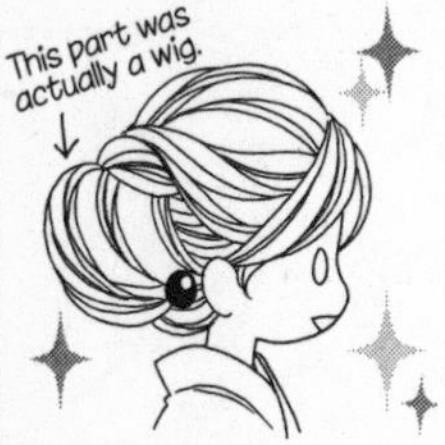
This part was actually a wig.

I looked like a madam.

Thank you also to the editorial staff who came with me, the sellers, and also to the Yurindo Fujisawa bookstore who asked me to come!

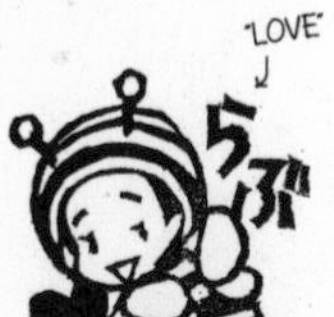
"LOVE"
らぶ

This is the stamp I put next to my signature.

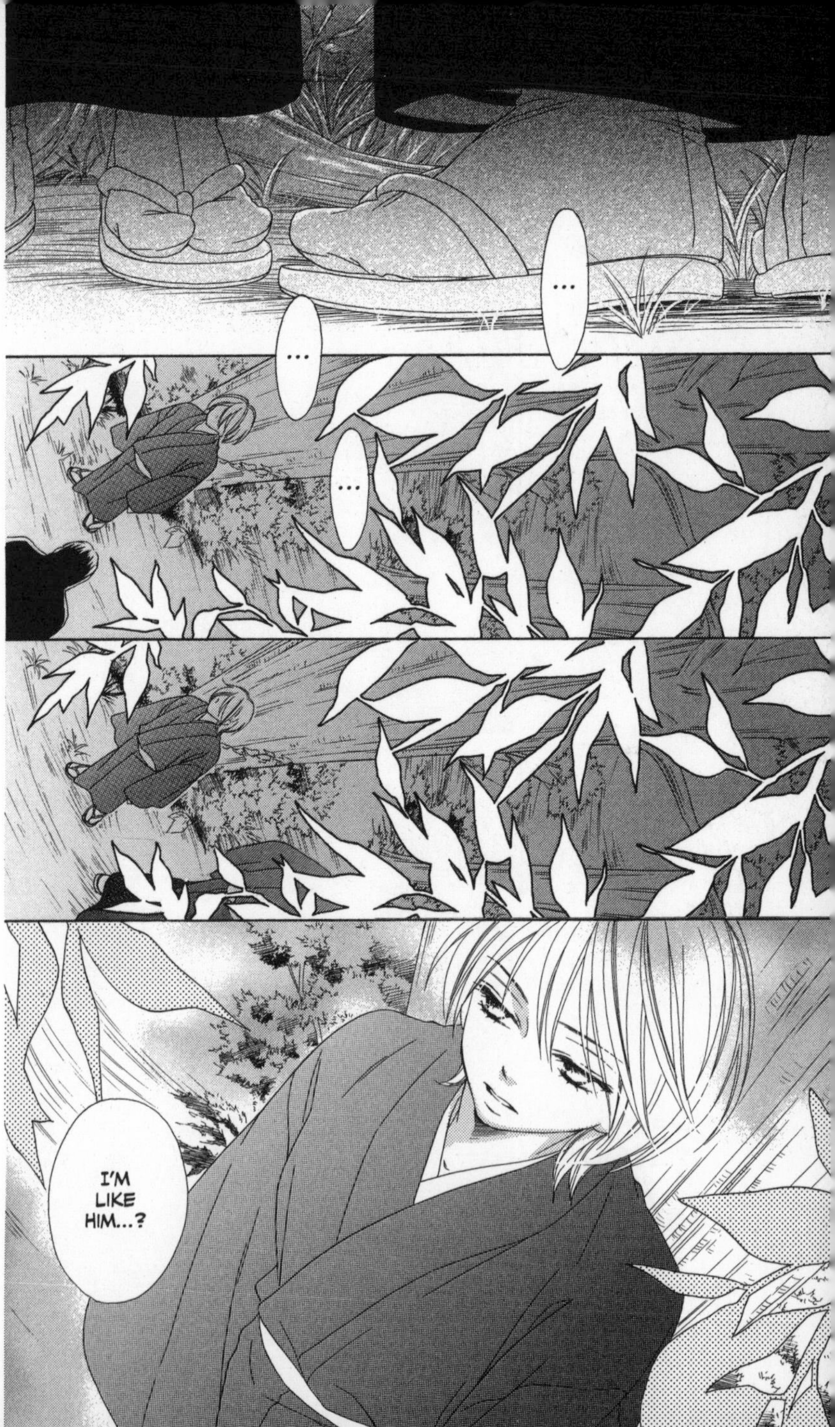
...
...
...
I'M LIKE HIM...?

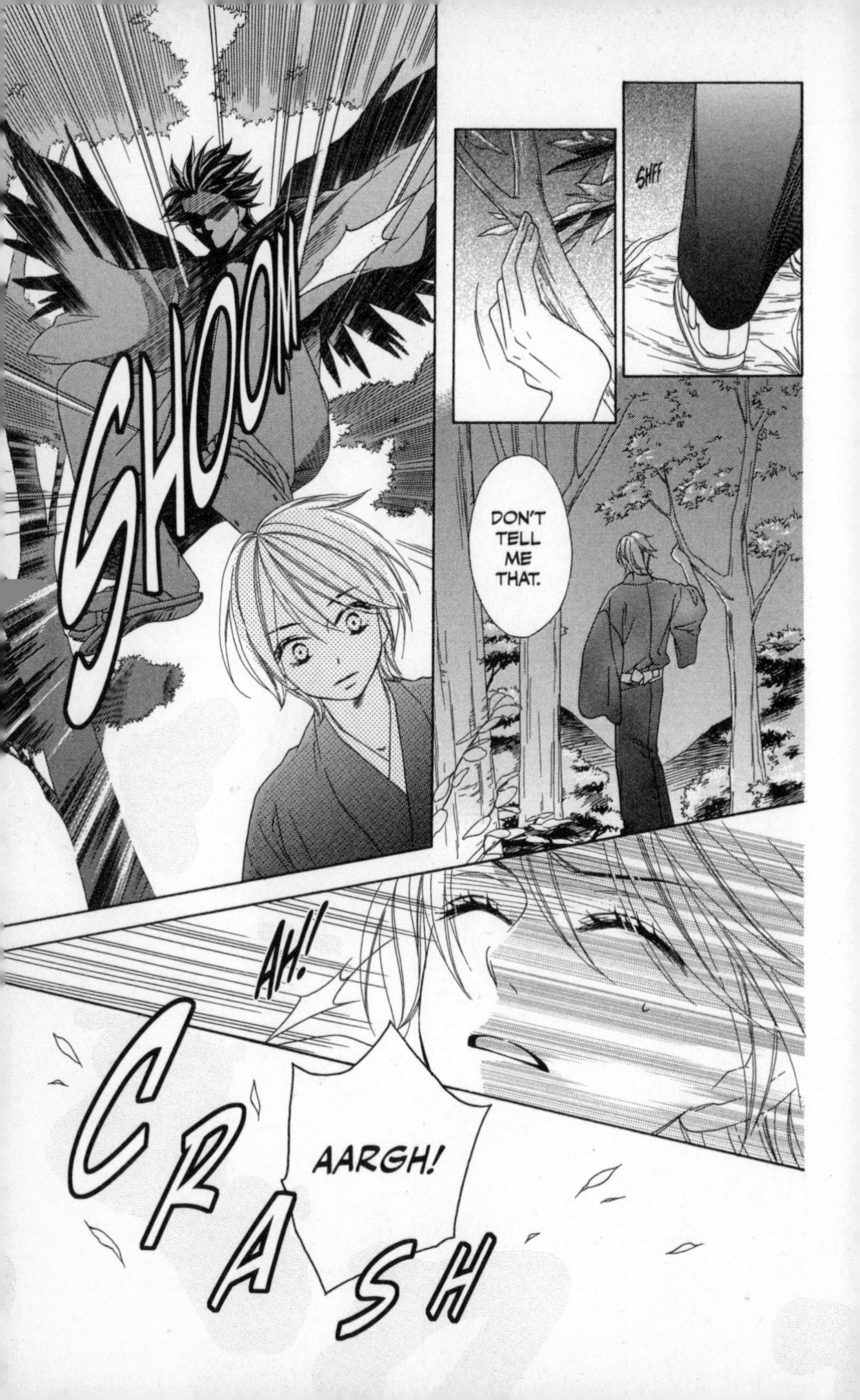
SHFF
DON'T TELL ME THAT.
SHOOM
AH!
AARGH!
CRASH

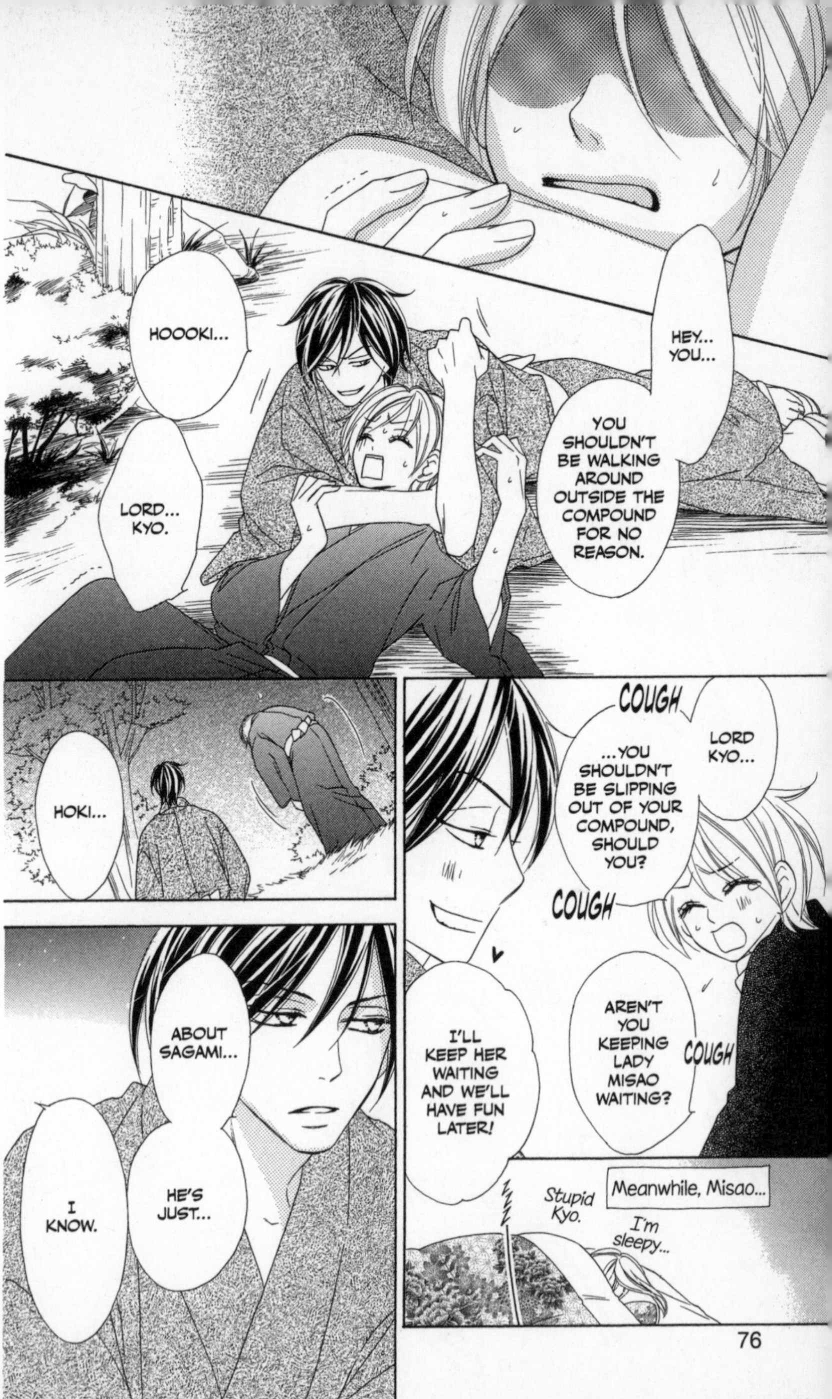

HEY... YOU...
YOU SHOULDN'T BE WALKING AROUND OUTSIDE THE COMPOUND FOR NO REASON.
HOOOKI...
LORD... KYO.
COUGH
LORD KYO...
...YOU SHOULDN'T BE SLIPPING OUT OF YOUR COMPOUND, SHOULD YOU?
COUGH
AREN'T YOU KEEPING LADY MISAO WAITING?
COUGH
I'LL KEEP HER WAITING AND WE'LL HAVE FUN LATER!
Meanwhile, Misao...
Stupid Kyo.
I'm sleepy...
HOKI...
ABOUT SAGAMI...
HE'S JUST...
I KNOW.

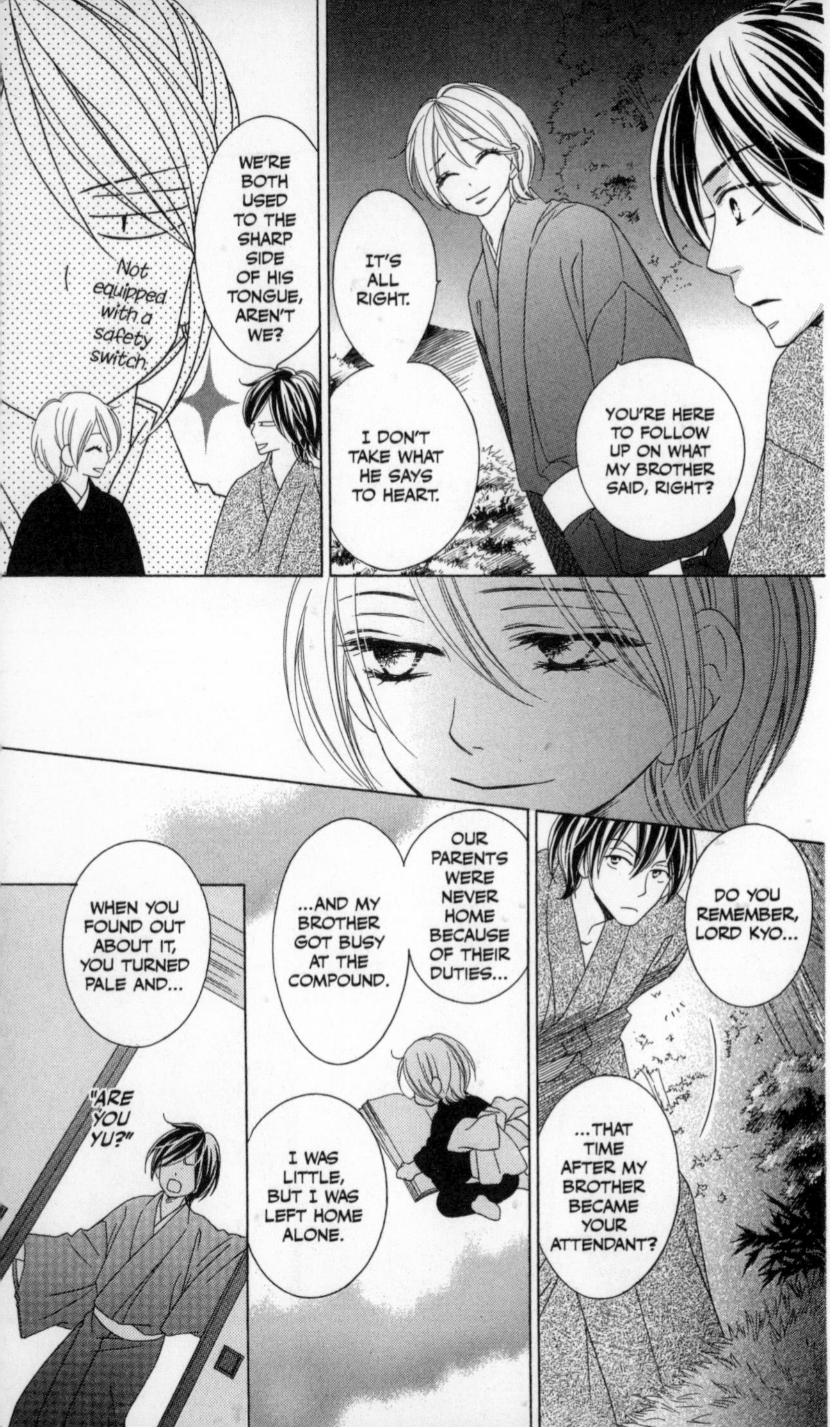
YOU'RE HERE TO FOLLOW UP ON WHAT MY BROTHER SAID, RIGHT?
IT'S ALL RIGHT.
I DON'T TAKE WHAT HE SAYS TO HEART.
WE'RE BOTH USED TO THE SHARP SIDE OF HIS TONGUE, AREN'T WE?
Not equipped with a safety switch.
DO YOU REMEMBER, LORD KYO...
...THAT TIME AFTER MY BROTHER BECAME YOUR ATTENDANT?
OUR PARENTS WERE NEVER HOME BECAUSE OF THEIR DUTIES...
...AND MY BROTHER GOT BUSY AT THE COMPOUND.
I WAS LITTLE, BUT I WAS LEFT HOME ALONE.
WHEN YOU FOUND OUT ABOUT IT, YOU TURNED PALE AND...
"ARE YOU YU?"

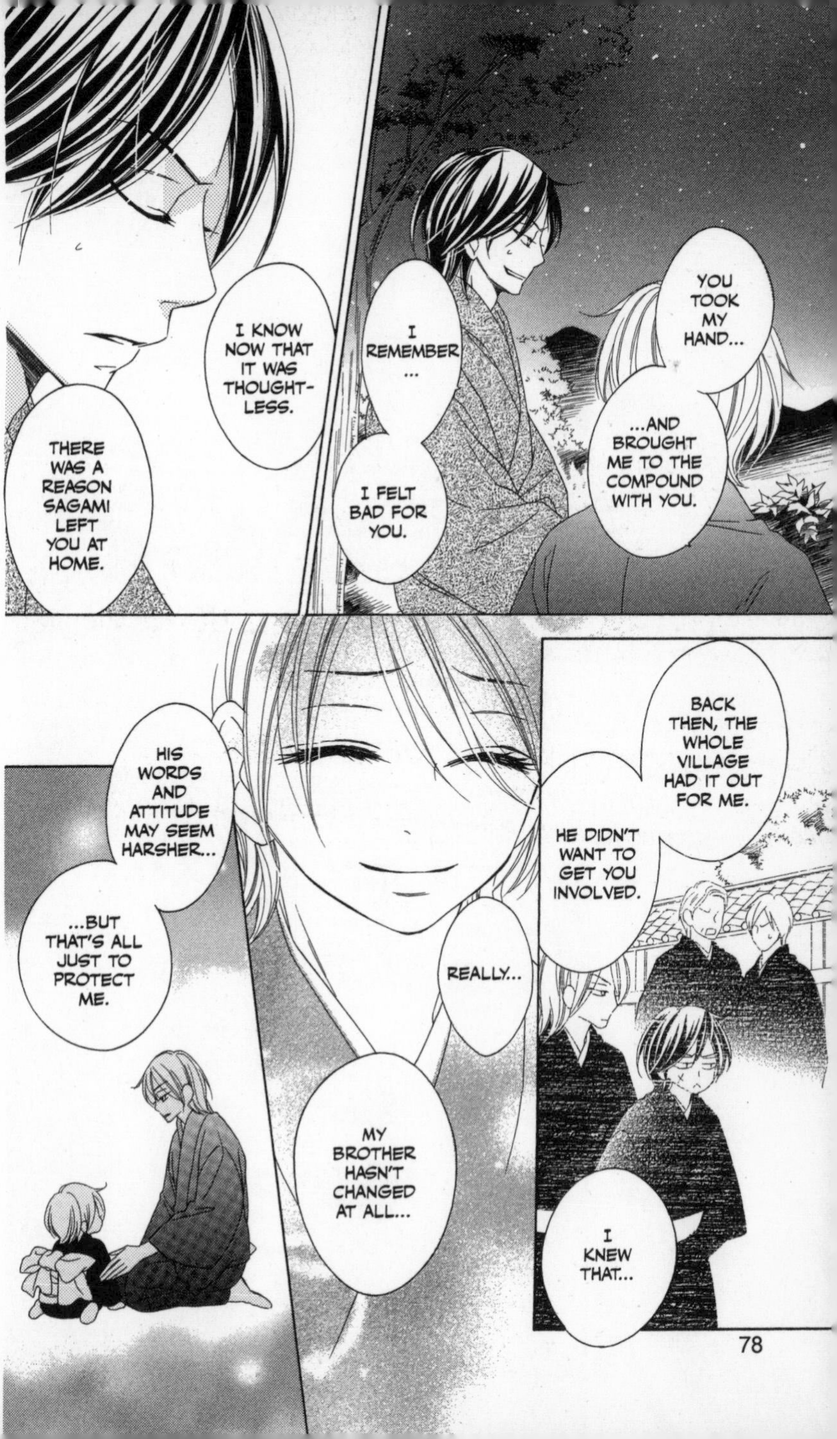
YOU TOOK MY HAND...
...AND BROUGHT ME TO THE COMPOUND WITH YOU.
I REMEMBER...
I FELT BAD FOR YOU.
I KNOW NOW THAT IT WAS THOUGHT-LESS.
THERE WAS A REASON SAGAMI LEFT YOU AT HOME.
BACK THEN, THE WHOLE VILLAGE HAD IT OUT FOR ME.
HE DIDN'T WANT TO GET YOU INVOLVED.
I KNEW THAT...
REALLY...
MY BROTHER HASN'T CHANGED AT ALL...
HIS WORDS AND ATTITUDE MAY SEEM HARSHER...
...BUT THAT'S ALL JUST TO PROTECT ME.

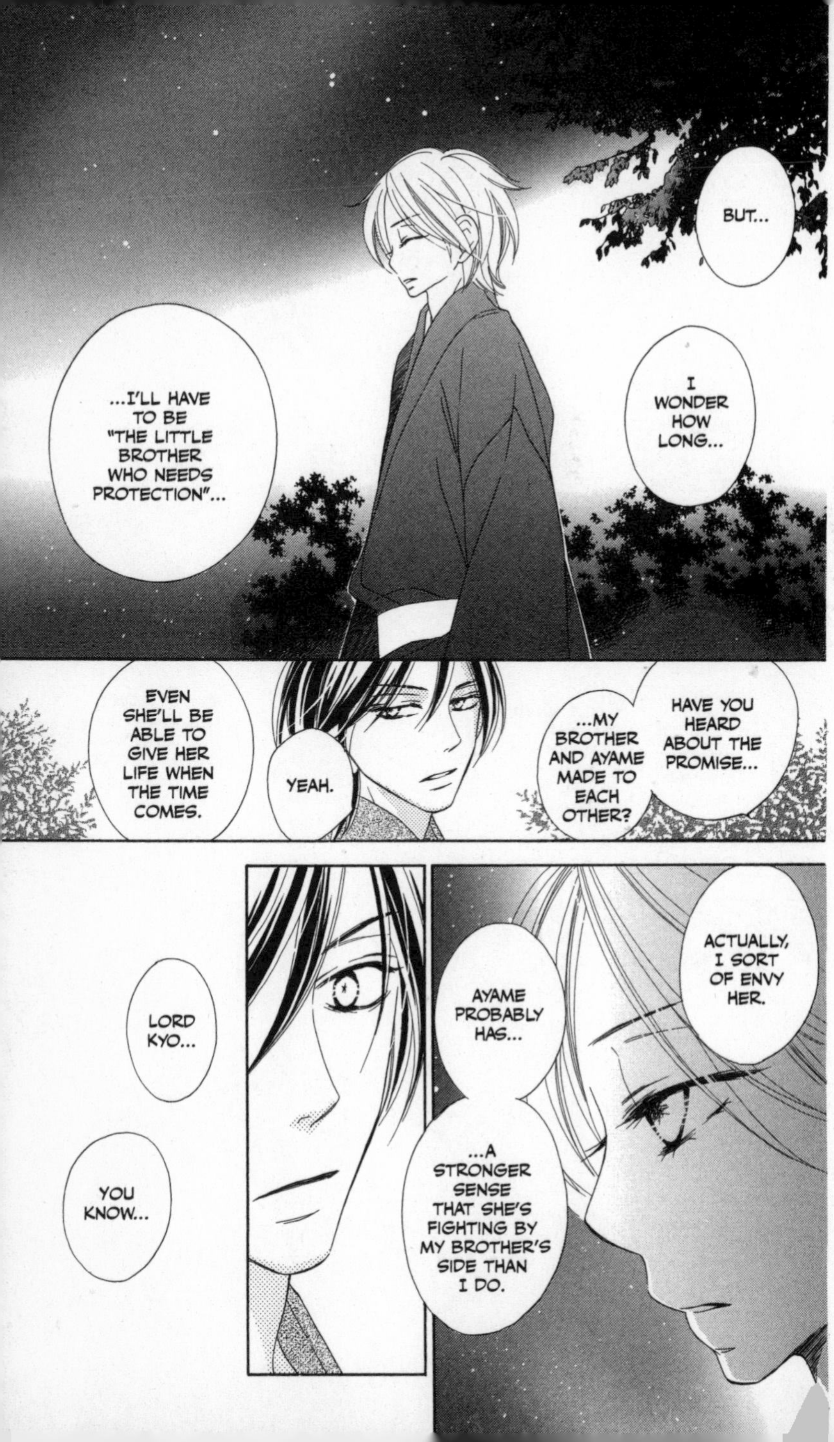
BUT...
I WONDER HOW LONG...
...I'LL HAVE TO BE "THE LITTLE BROTHER WHO NEEDS PROTECTION"...
HAVE YOU HEARD ABOUT THE PROMISE...
...MY BROTHER AND AYAME MADE TO EACH OTHER?
YEAH.
EVEN SHE'LL BE ABLE TO GIVE HER LIFE WHEN THE TIME COMES.
ACTUALLY, I SORT OF ENVY HER.
AYAME PROBABLY HAS...
...A STRONGER SENSE THAT SHE'S FIGHTING BY MY BROTHER'S SIDE THAN I DO.
LORD KYO...
YOU KNOW...

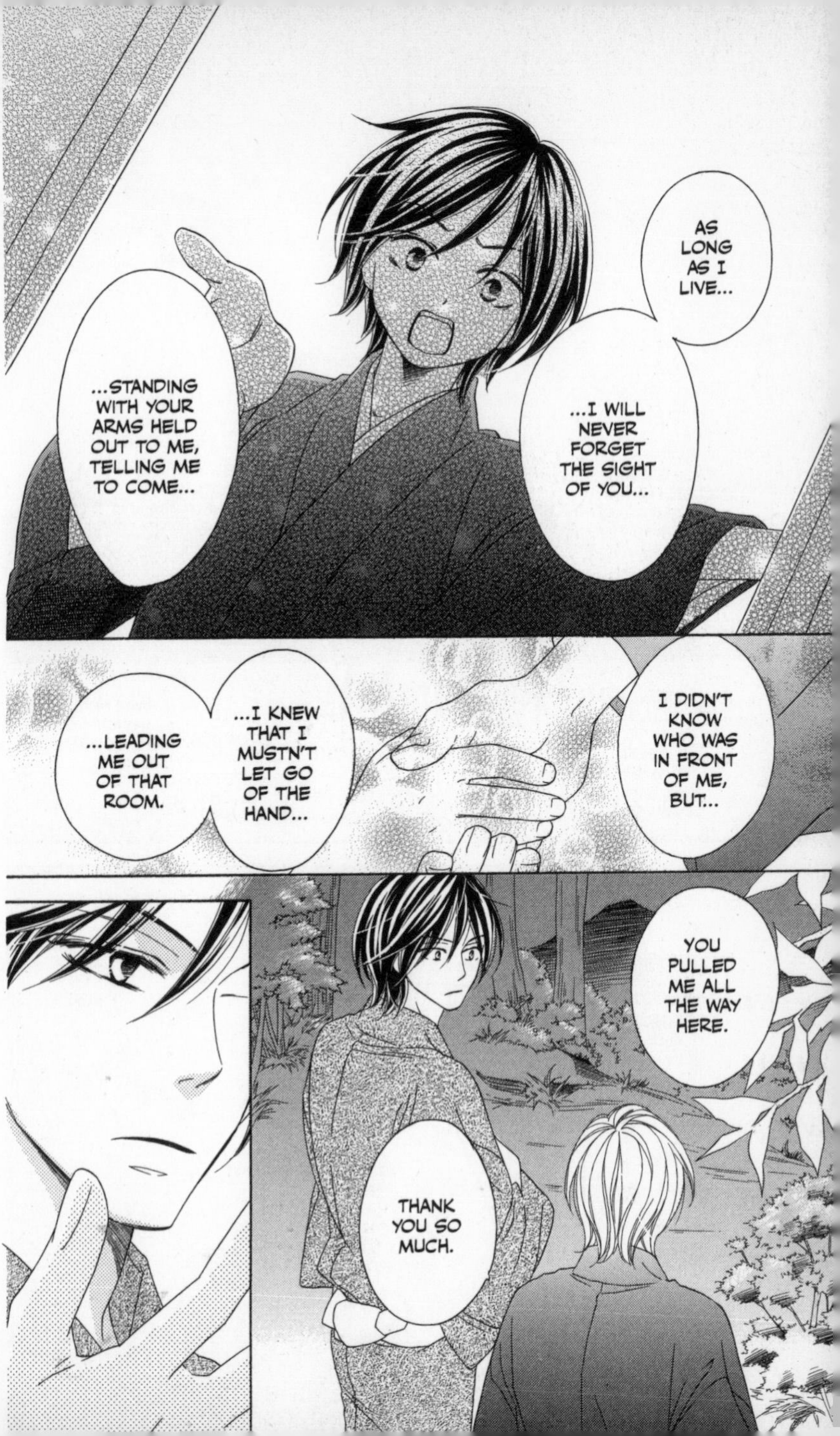
AS LONG AS I LIVE...
...I WILL NEVER FORGET THE SIGHT OF YOU...
...STANDING WITH YOUR ARMS HELD OUT TO ME, TELLING ME TO COME...
I DIDN'T KNOW WHO WAS IN FRONT OF ME, BUT...
...I KNEW THAT I MUSTN'T LET GO OF THE HAND...
...LEADING ME OUT OF THAT ROOM.
YOU PULLED ME ALL THE WAY HERE.
THANK YOU SO MUCH.

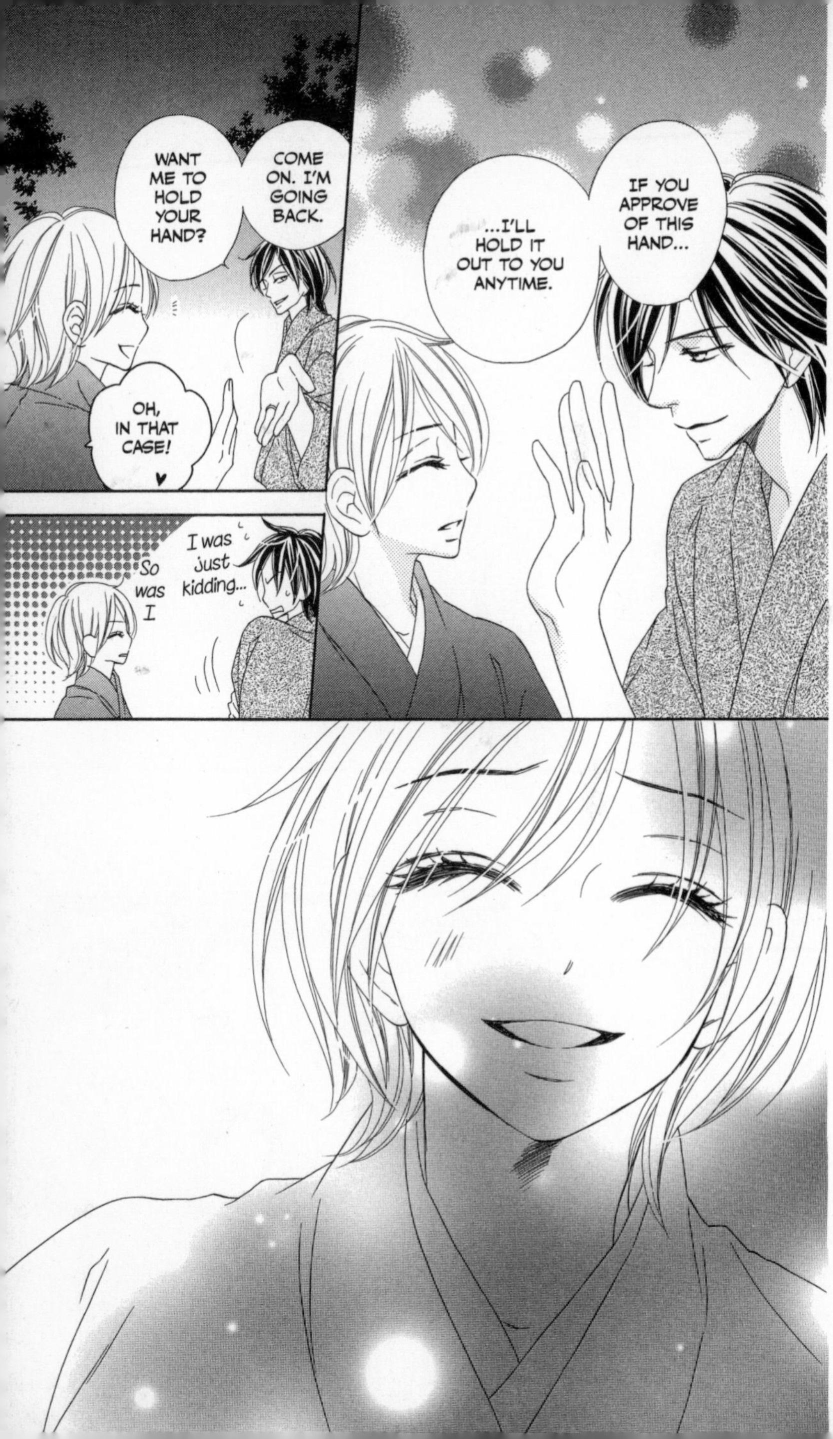
IF YOU APPROVE OF THIS HAND...
...I'LL HOLD IT OUT TO YOU ANYTIME.
COME ON. I'M GOING BACK.
WANT ME TO HOLD YOUR HAND?
OH, IN THAT CASE! ♥
I was just kidding...
So was I

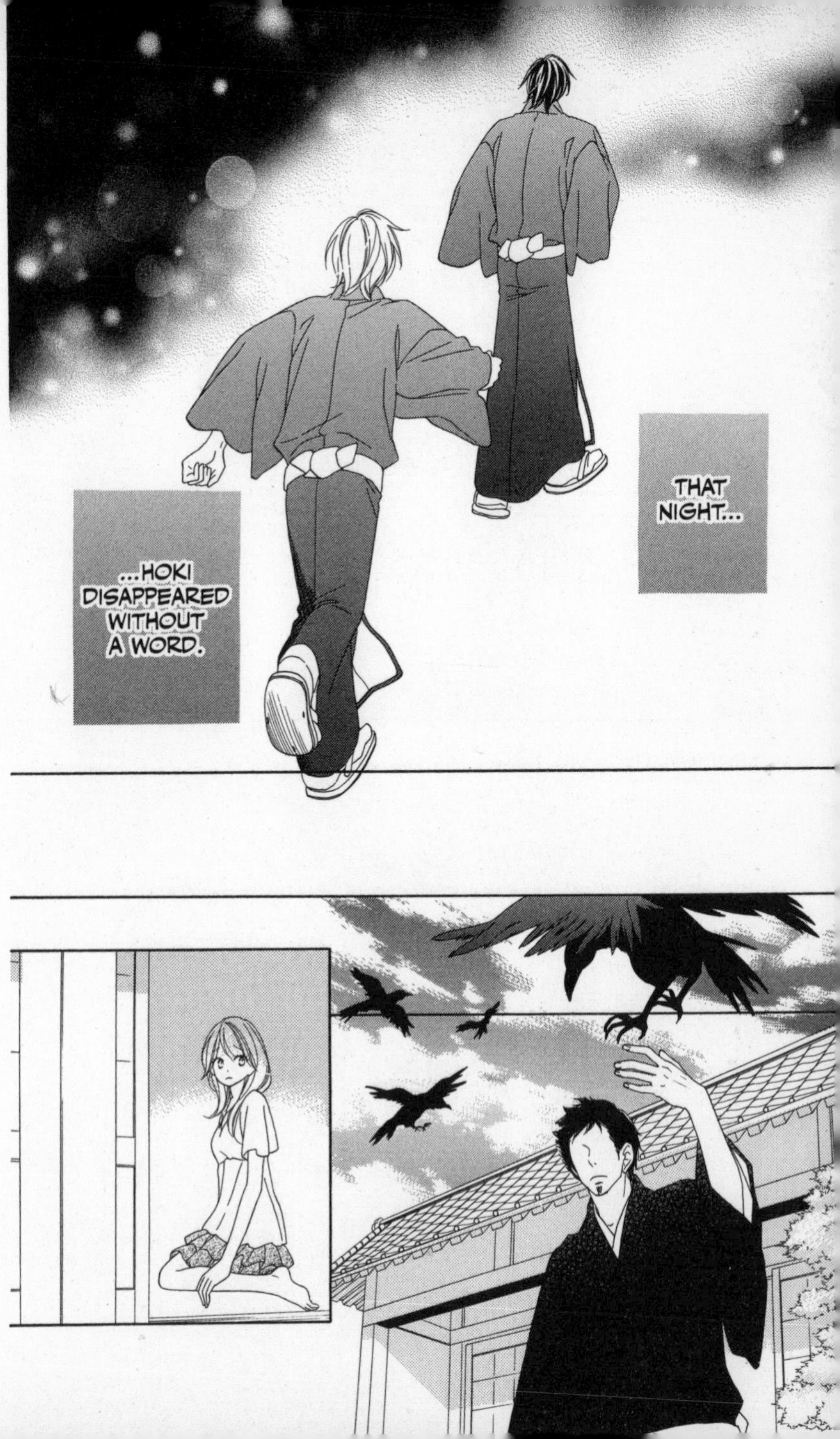
THAT NIGHT...
...HOKI DISAPPEARED WITHOUT A WORD.

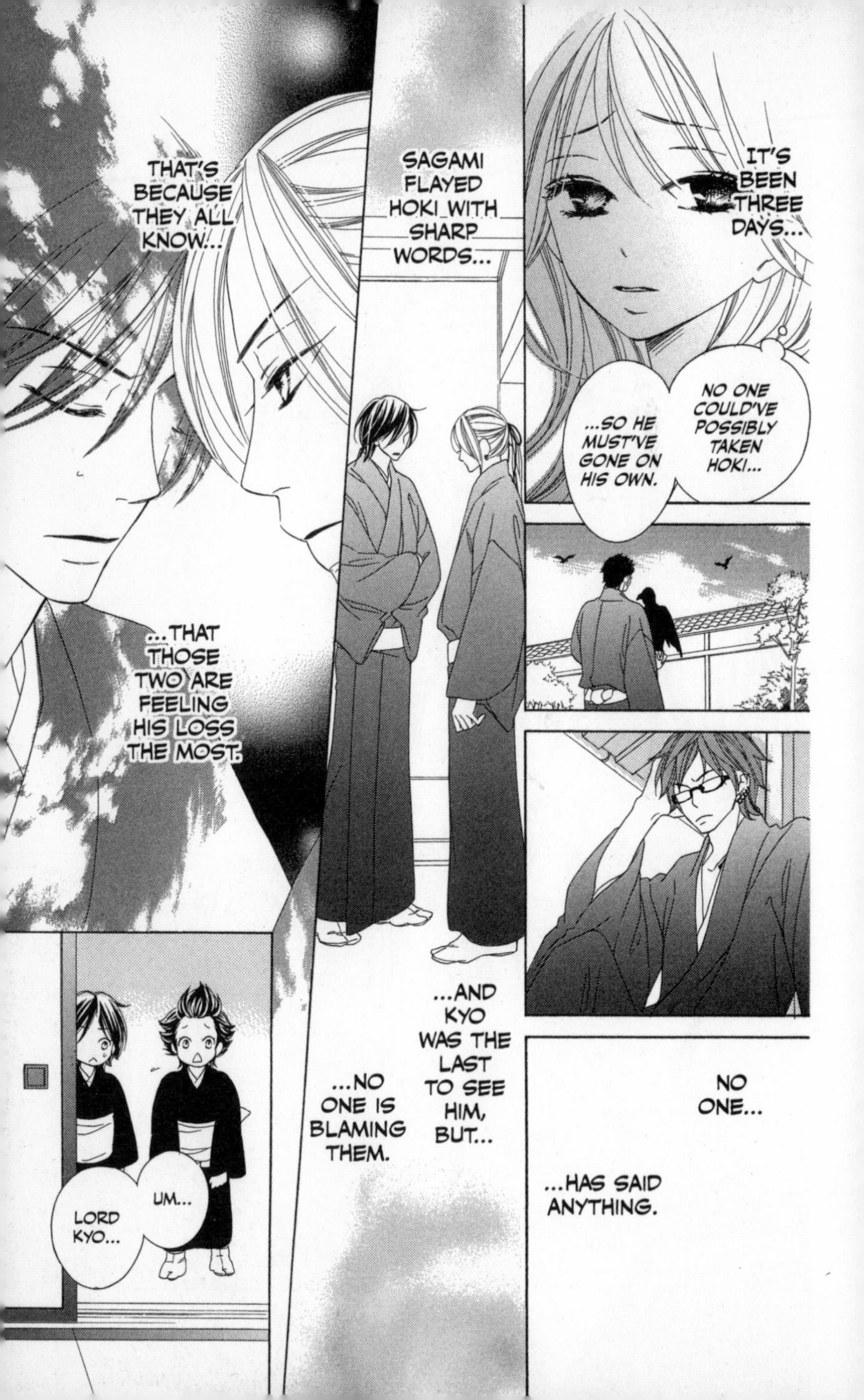
IT'S BEEN THREE DAYS...
NO ONE COULD'VE POSSIBLY TAKEN HOKI...
...SO HE MUST'VE GONE ON HIS OWN.
NO ONE...
...HAS SAID ANYTHING.
SAGAMI FLAYED HOKI WITH SHARP WORDS...
...AND KYO WAS THE LAST TO SEE HIM, BUT...
...NO ONE IS BLAMING THEM.
THAT'S BECAUSE THEY ALL KNOW...
...THAT THOSE TWO ARE FEELING HIS LOSS THE MOST.
UM...
LORD KYO...

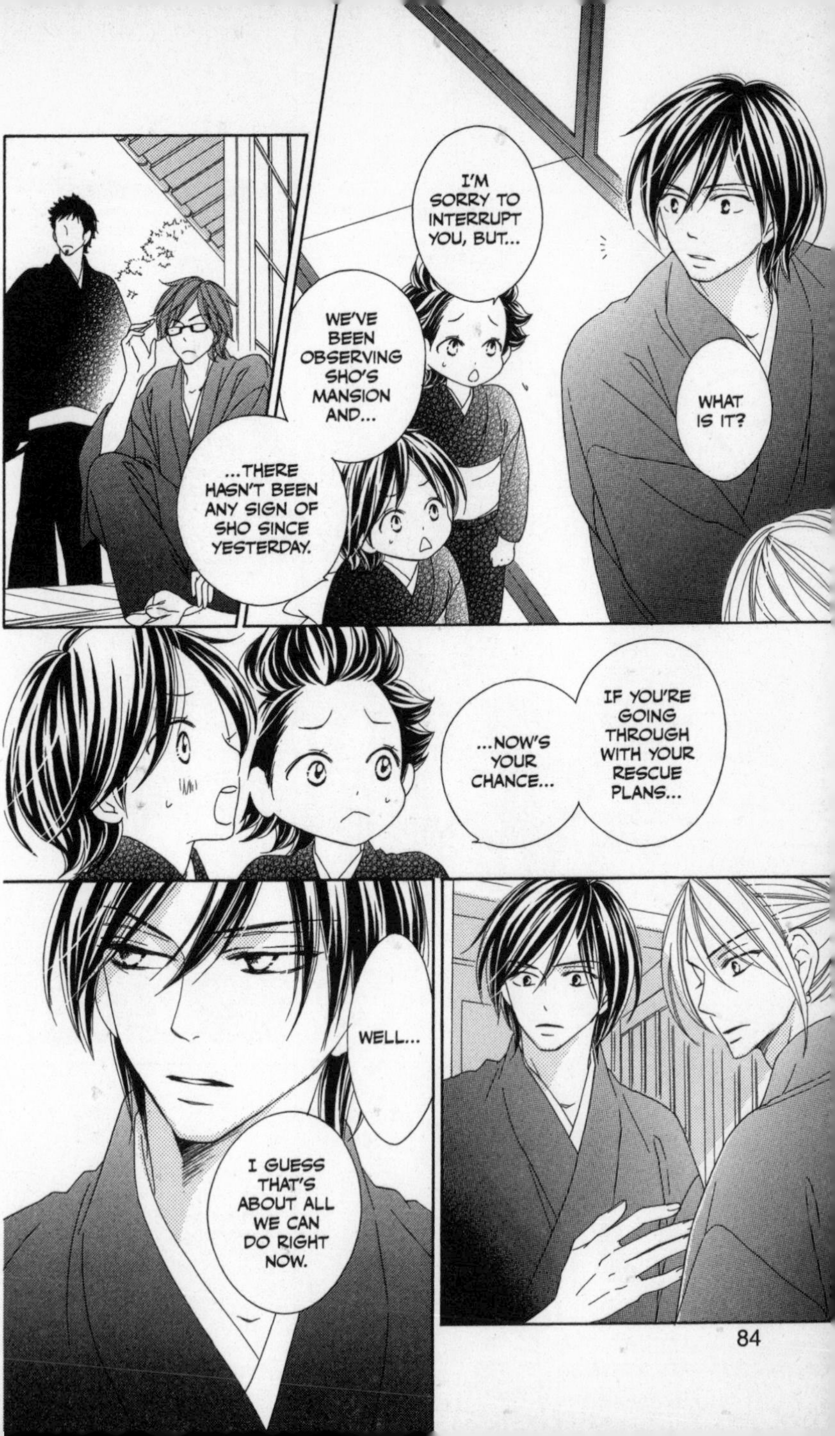
I'M SORRY TO INTERRUPT YOU, BUT...
WHAT IS IT?
WE'VE BEEN OBSERVING SHO'S MANSION AND...
...THERE HASN'T BEEN ANY SIGN OF SHO SINCE YESTERDAY.
IF YOU'RE GOING THROUGH WITH YOUR RESCUE PLANS...
...NOW'S YOUR CHANCE...
WELL...
I GUESS THAT'S ABOUT ALL WE CAN DO RIGHT NOW.

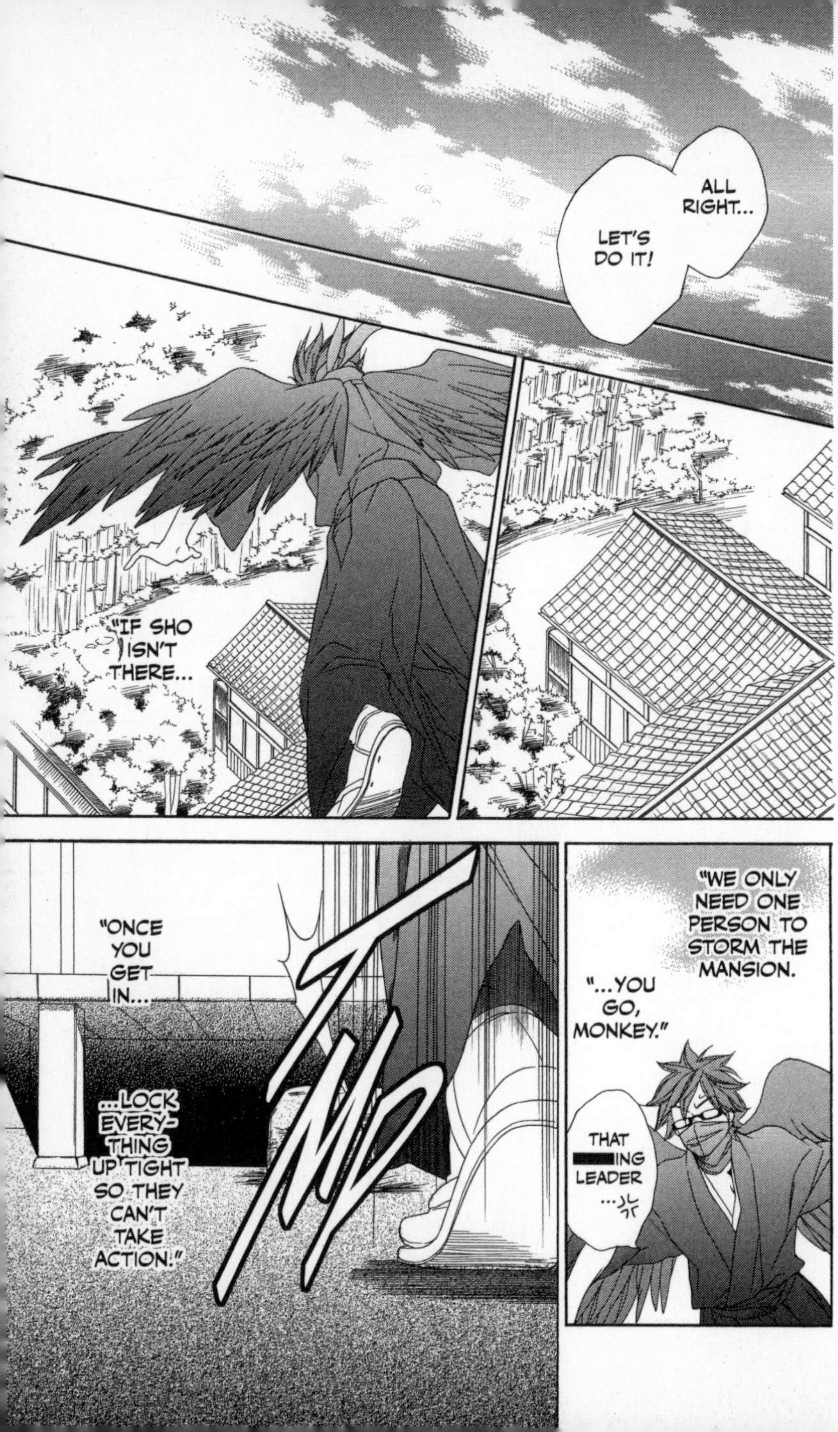
ALL RIGHT...
LET'S DO IT!
"IF SHO ISN'T THERE...
"WE ONLY NEED ONE PERSON TO STORM THE MANSION.
"...YOU GO, MONKEY."
THAT [redacted]ING LEADER ...
"ONCE YOU GET IN...
...LOCK EVERY-THING UP TIGHT SO THEY CAN'T TAKE ACTION."

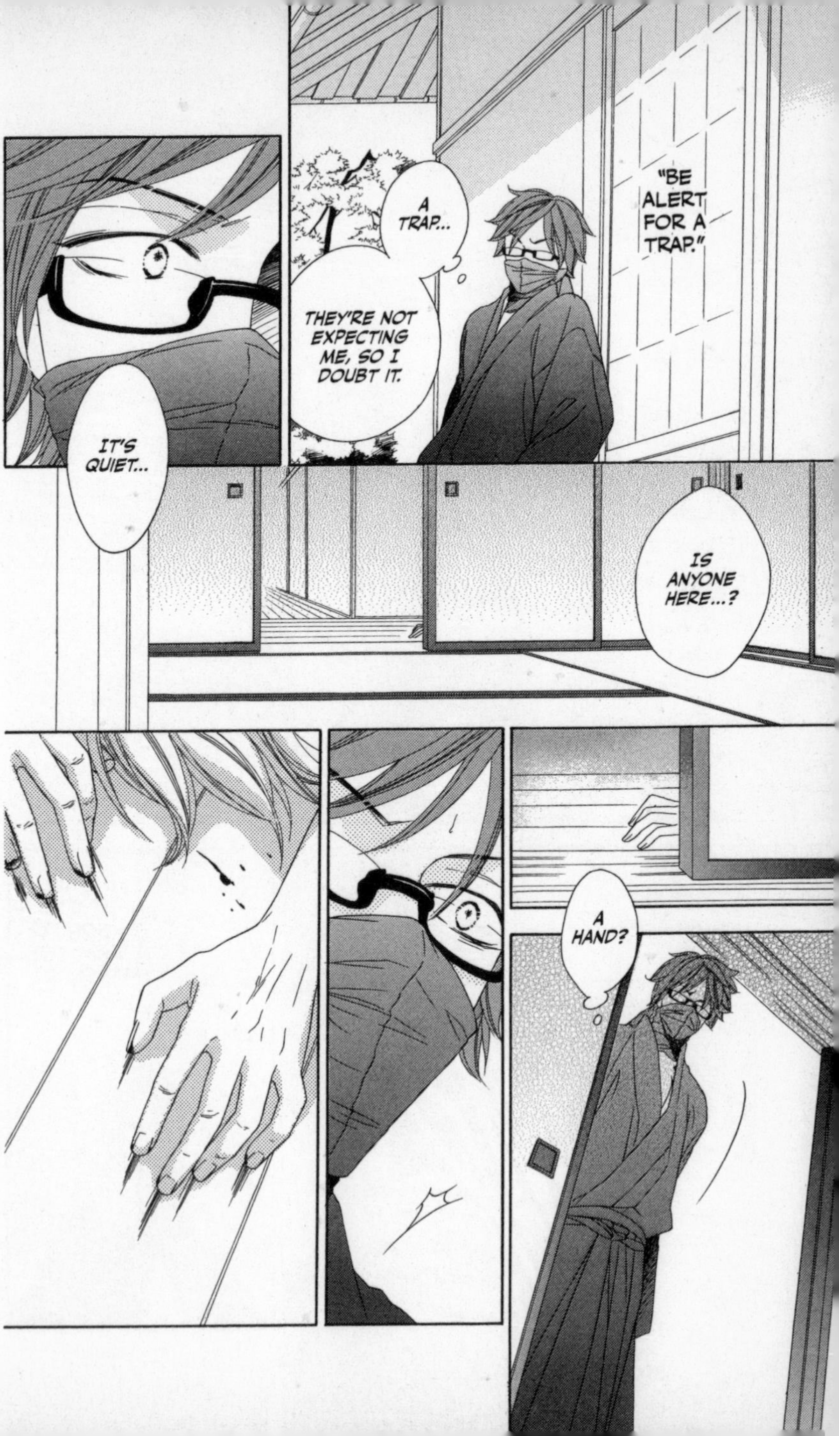
"BE ALERT FOR A TRAP."
A TRAP...
THEY'RE NOT EXPECTING ME, SO I DOUBT IT.
IT'S QUIET...
IS ANYONE HERE...?
A HAND?

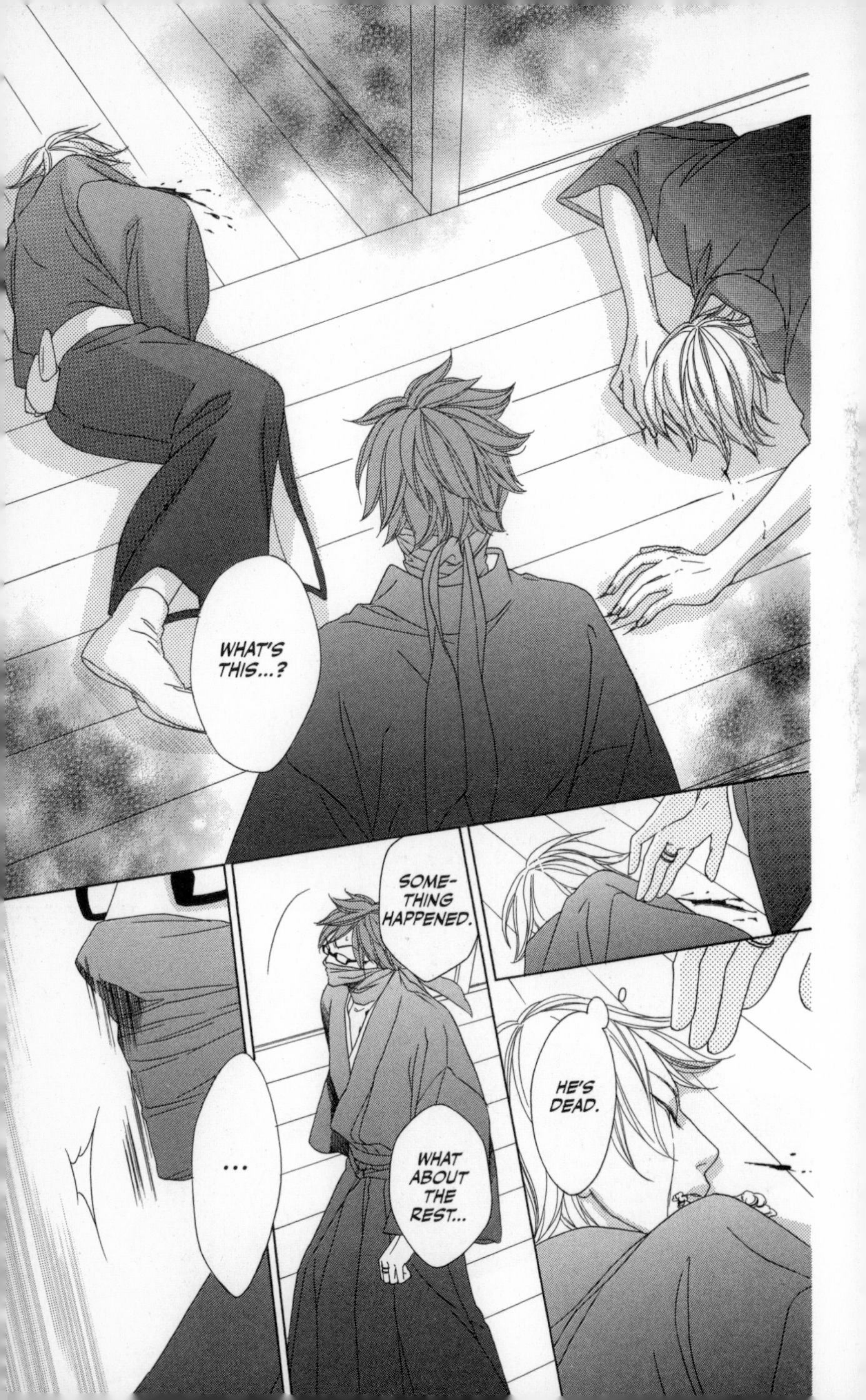
WHAT'S THIS...?
HE'S DEAD.
SOME-THING HAPPENED.
WHAT ABOUT THE REST...
...

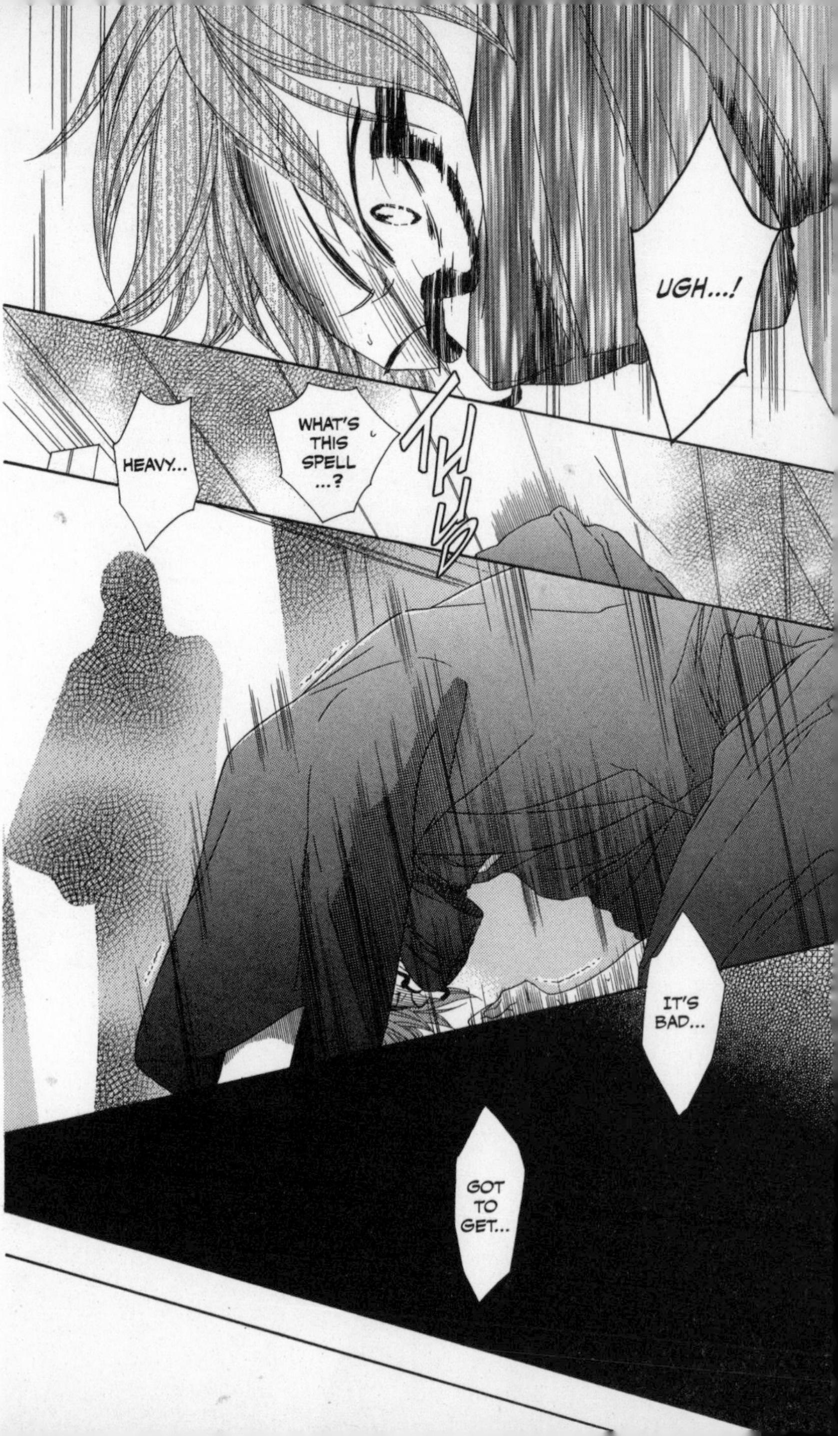
UGH...!
WHAT'S THIS SPELL ...?
HEAVY...
IT'S BAD...
GOT TO GET...

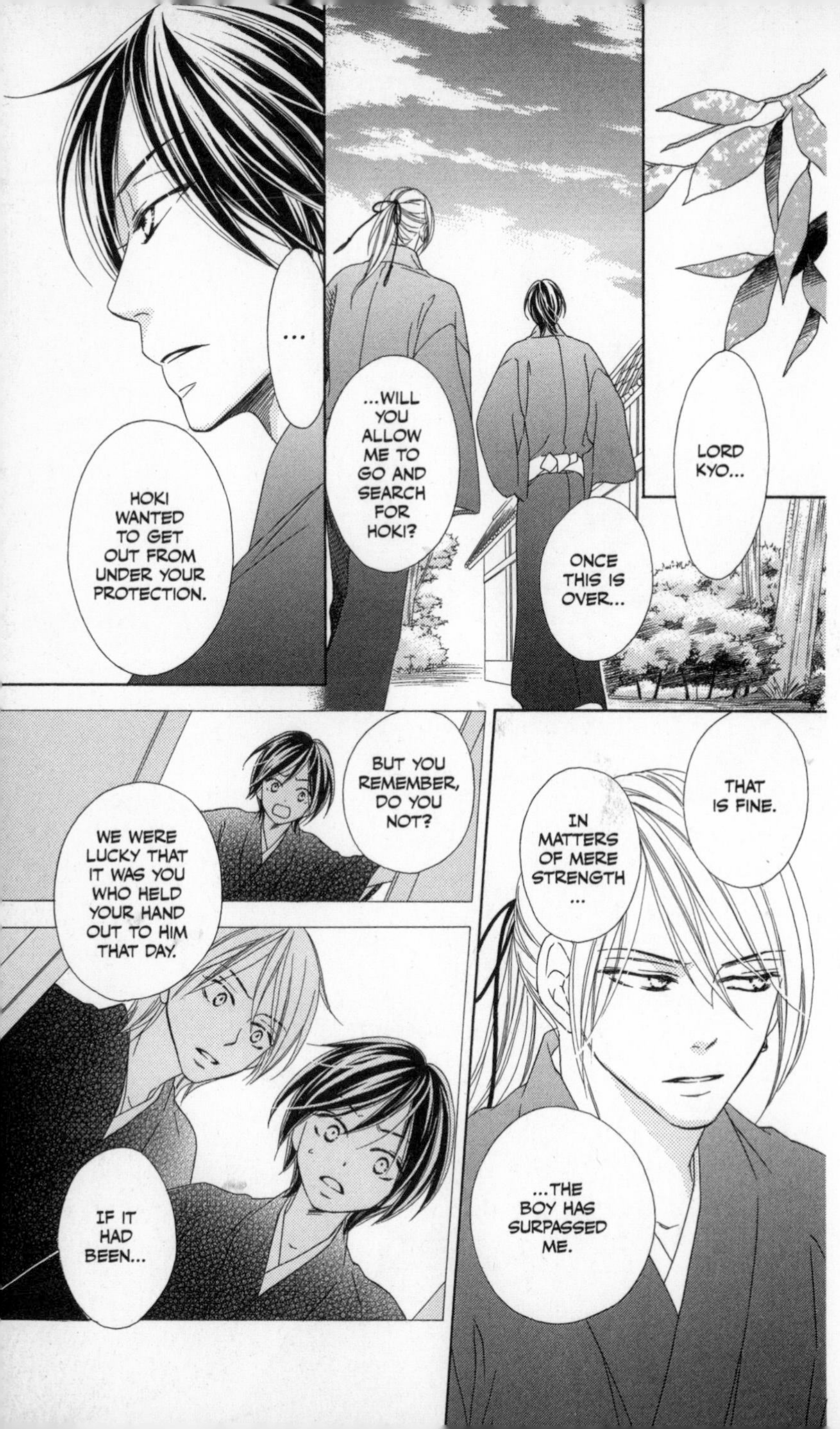
LORD KYO...
ONCE THIS IS OVER...
...WILL YOU ALLOW ME TO GO AND SEARCH FOR HOKI?
...
HOKI WANTED TO GET OUT FROM UNDER YOUR PROTECTION.
THAT IS FINE.
IN MATTERS OF MERE STRENGTH...
...THE BOY HAS SURPASSED ME.
BUT YOU REMEMBER, DO YOU NOT?
WE WERE LUCKY THAT IT WAS YOU WHO HELD YOUR HAND OUT TO HIM THAT DAY.
IF IT HAD BEEN...

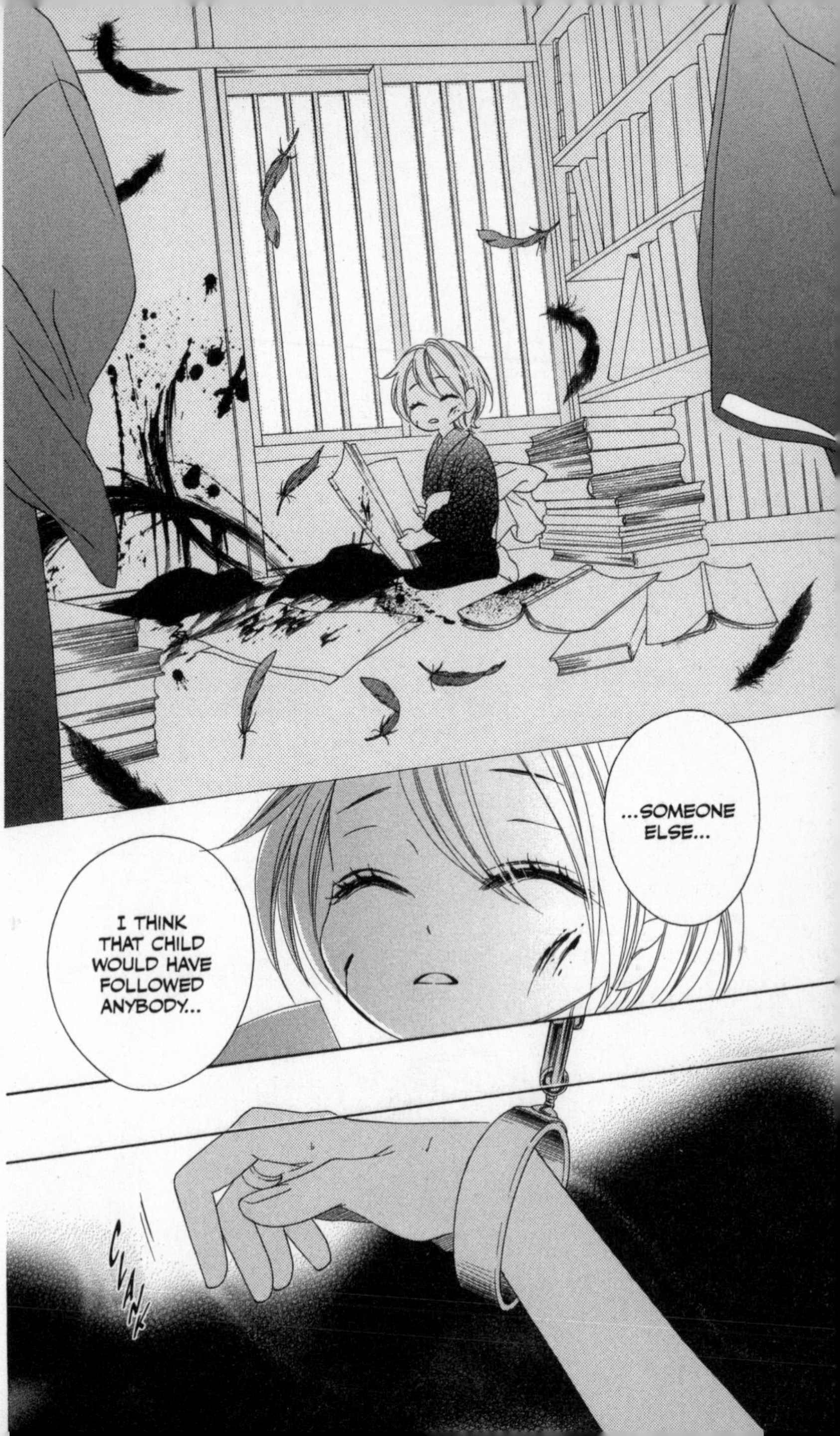
...SOMEONE ELSE...
I THINK THAT CHILD WOULD HAVE FOLLOWED ANYBODY...
CLANK

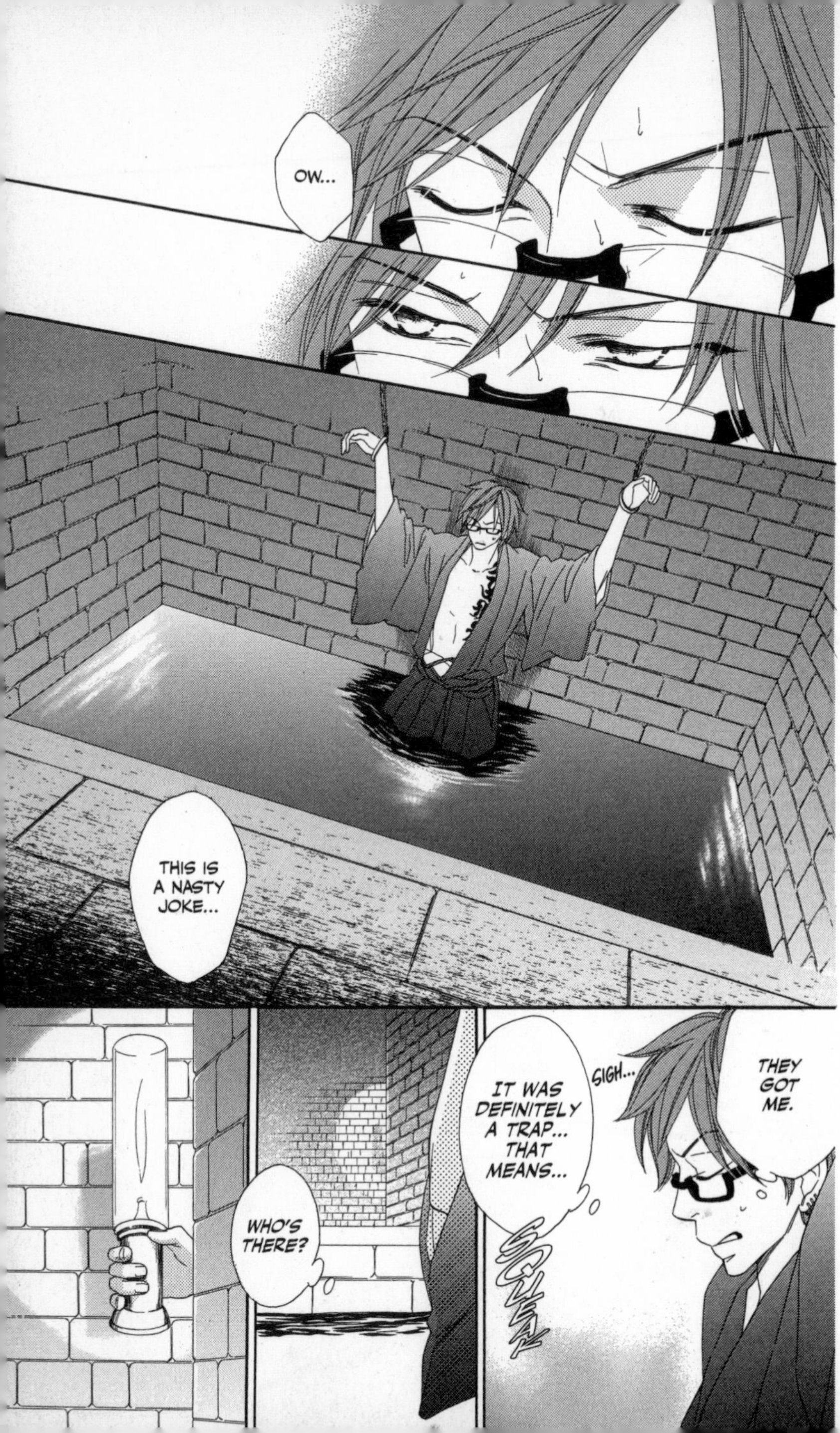
OW...
THIS IS A NASTY JOKE...
THEY GOT ME.
SIGH...
IT WAS DEFINITELY A TRAP... THAT MEANS...
SQUEAK
WHO'S THERE?

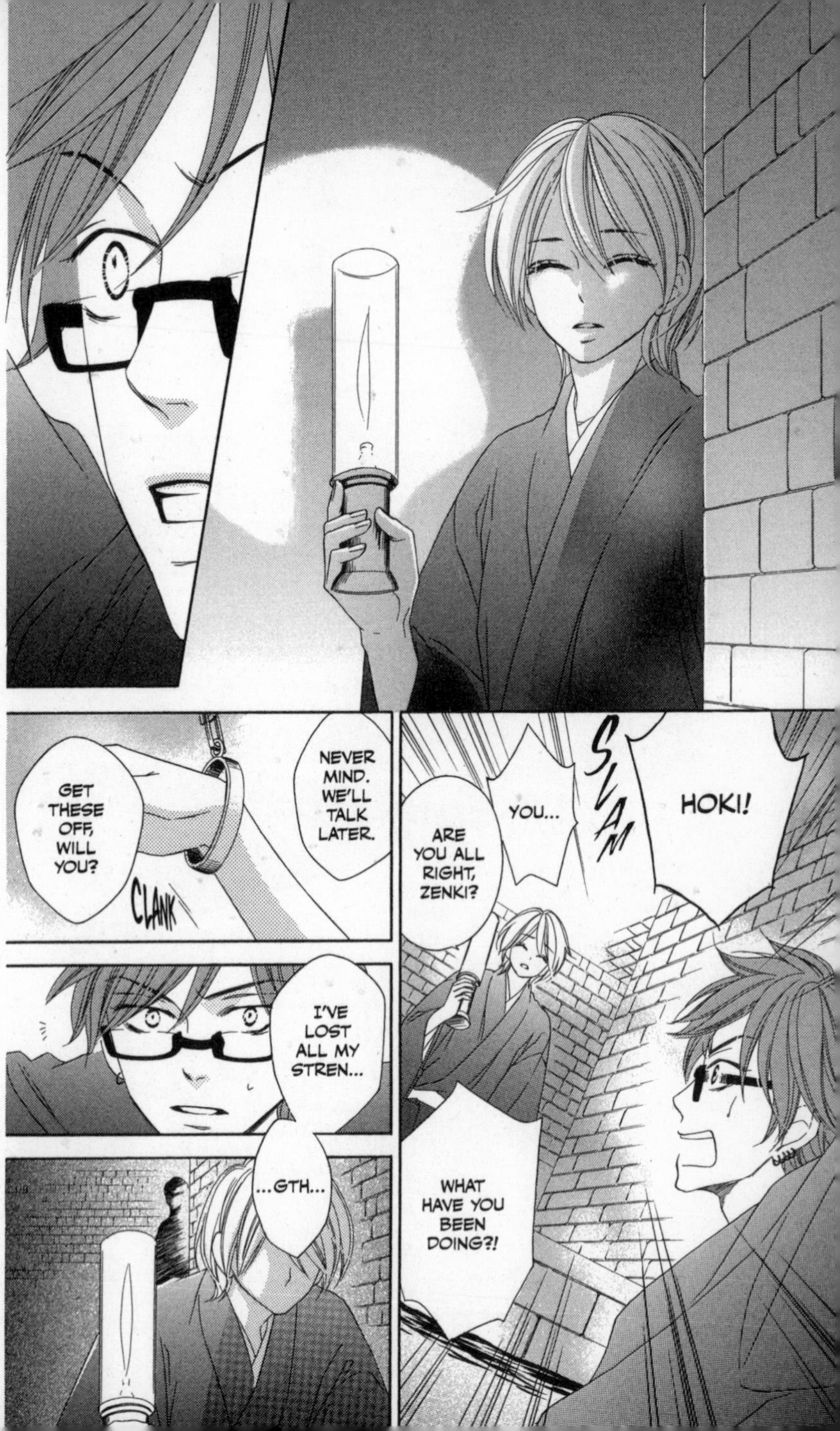
HOKI!
SLAM
YOU...
ARE YOU ALL RIGHT, ZENKI?
WHAT HAVE YOU BEEN DOING?!
NEVER MIND. WE'LL TALK LATER.
GET THESE OFF, WILL YOU?
CLANK
I'VE LOST ALL MY STREN...
...GTH...

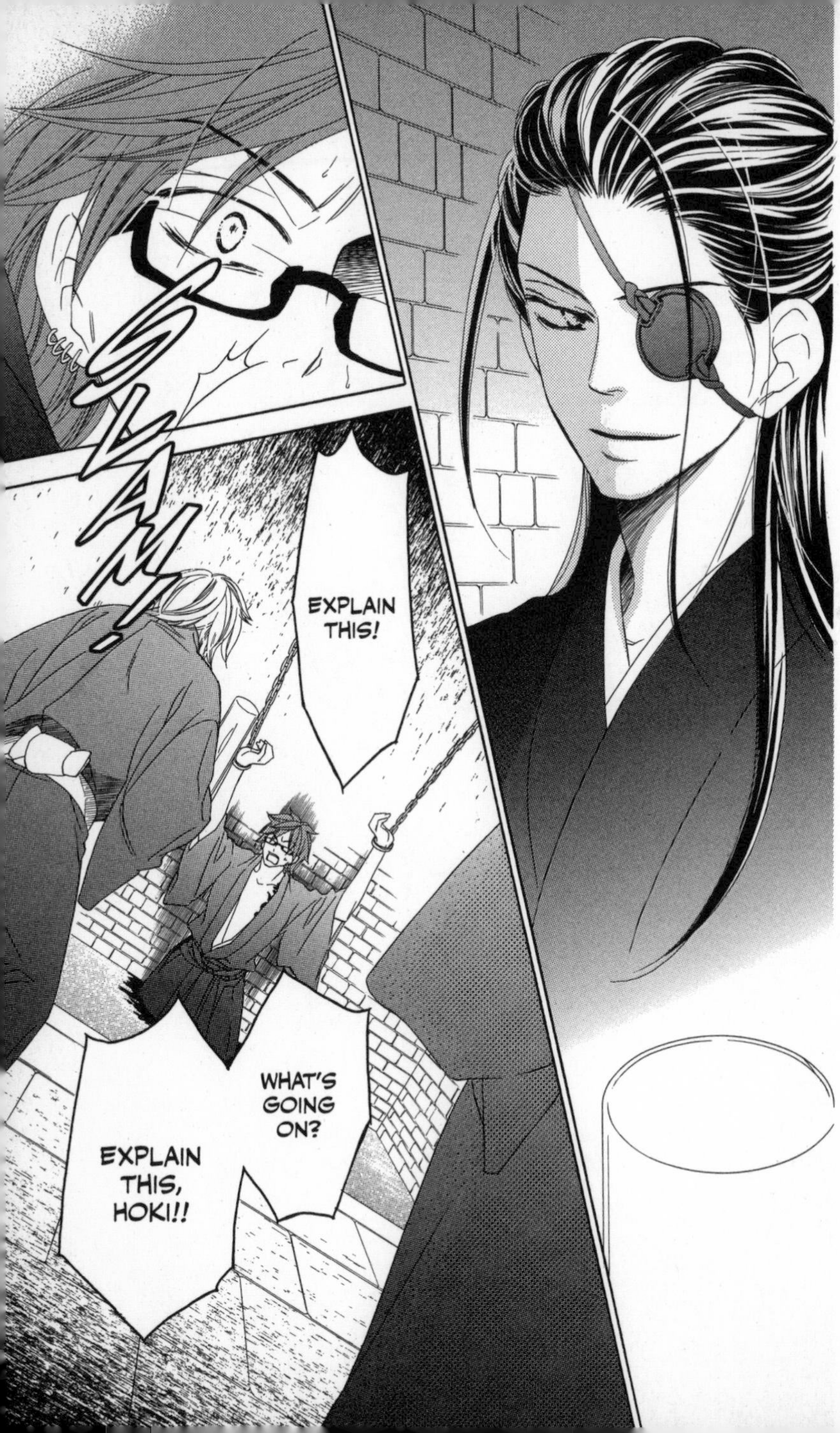
SWAM!
EXPLAIN THIS!
WHAT'S GOING ON?
EXPLAIN THIS, HOKI!!

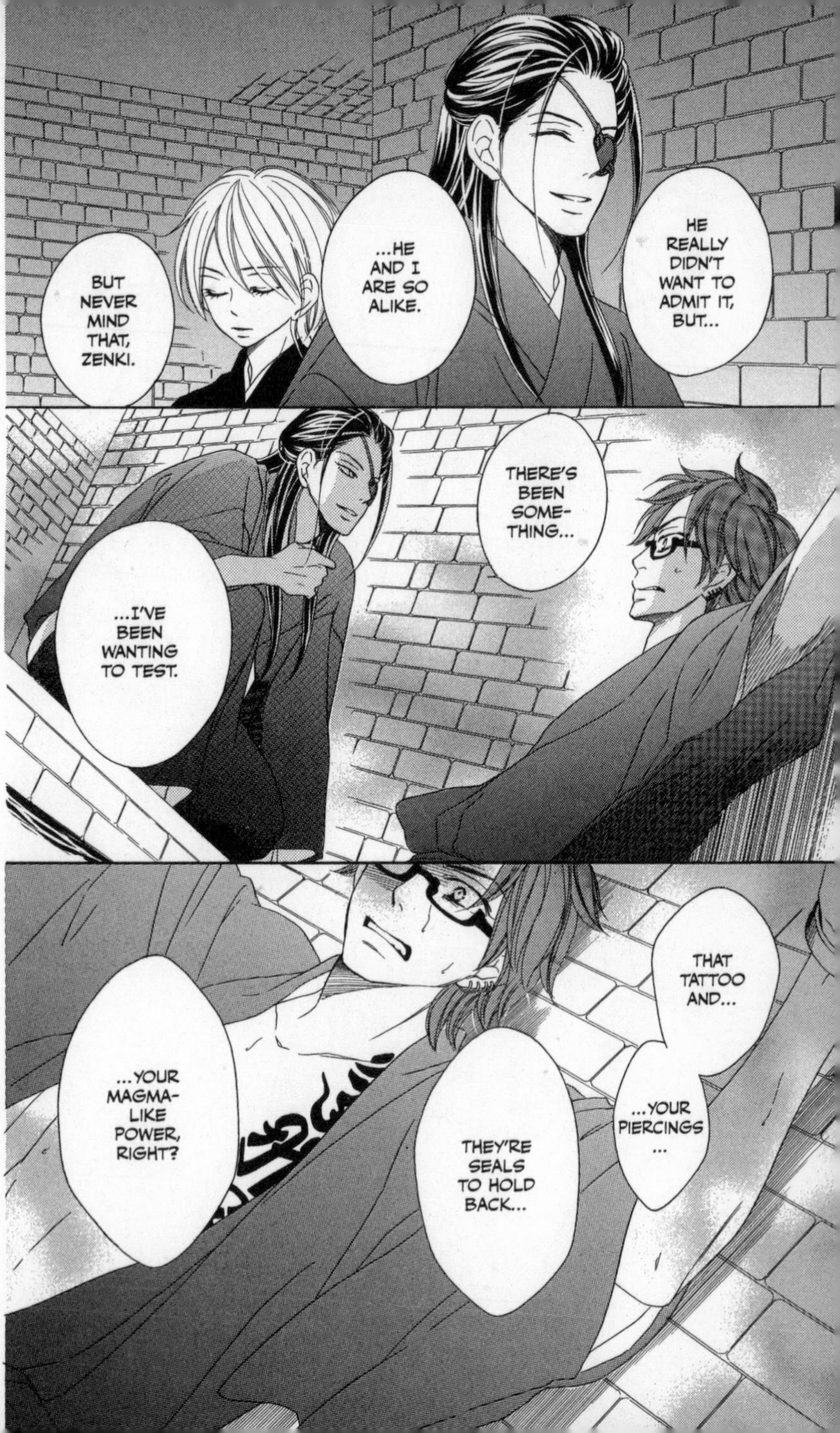
HE REALLY DIDN'T WANT TO ADMIT IT, BUT...
...HE AND I ARE SO ALIKE.
BUT NEVER MIND THAT, ZENKI.
THERE'S BEEN SOME-THING...
...I'VE BEEN WANTING TO TEST.
THAT TATTOO AND...
...YOUR PIERCINGS...
THEY'RE SEALS TO HOLD BACK...
...YOUR MAGMA-LIKE POWER, RIGHT?

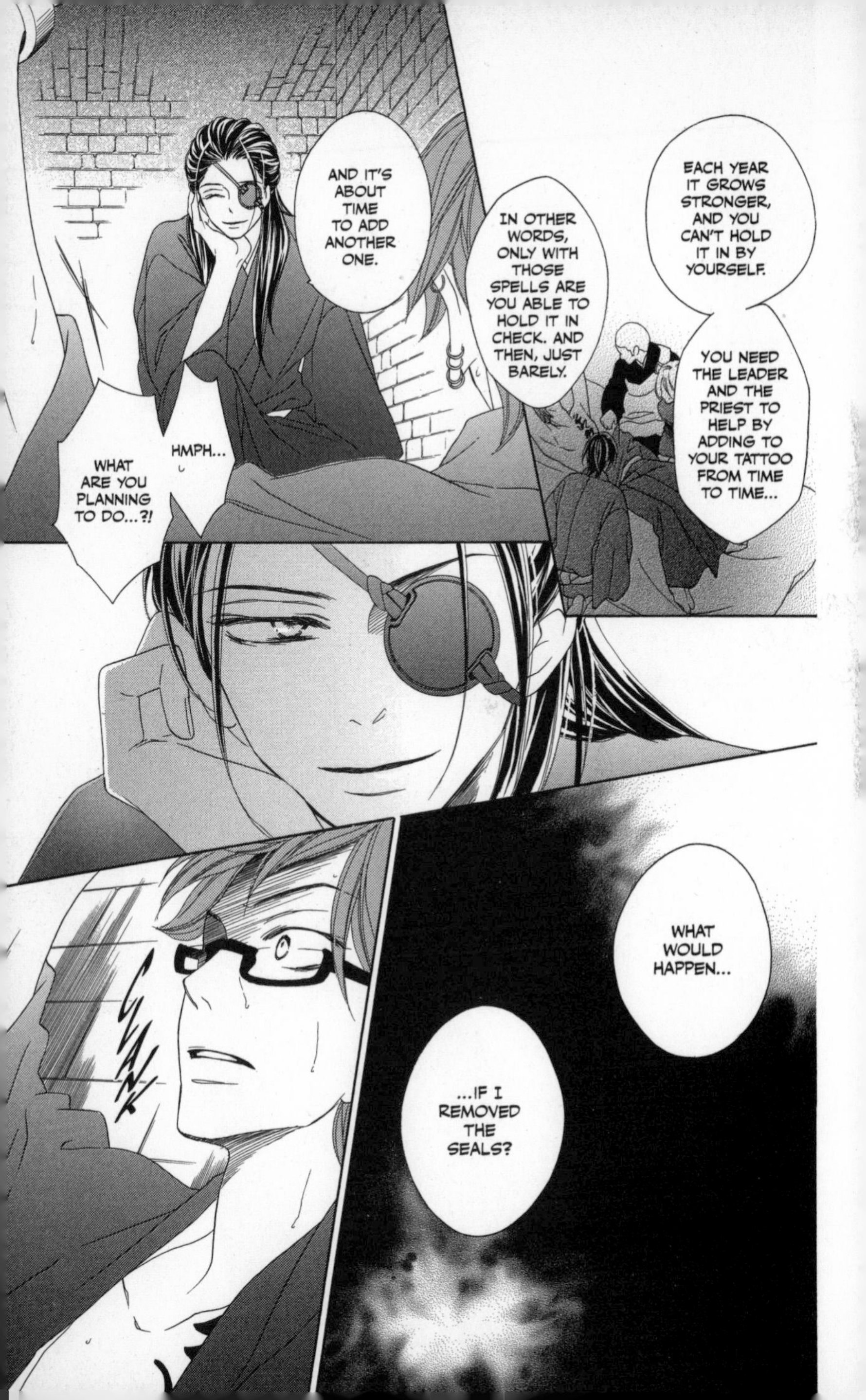
EACH YEAR IT GROWS STRONGER, AND YOU CAN'T HOLD IT IN BY YOURSELF.
YOU NEED THE LEADER AND THE PRIEST TO HELP BY ADDING TO YOUR TATTOO FROM TIME TO TIME...
IN OTHER WORDS, ONLY WITH THOSE SPELLS ARE YOU ABLE TO HOLD IT IN CHECK. AND THEN, JUST BARELY.
AND IT'S ABOUT TIME TO ADD ANOTHER ONE.
HMPH...
WHAT ARE YOU PLANNING TO DO...?!
WHAT WOULD HAPPEN...
...IF I REMOVED THE SEALS?
CLANK

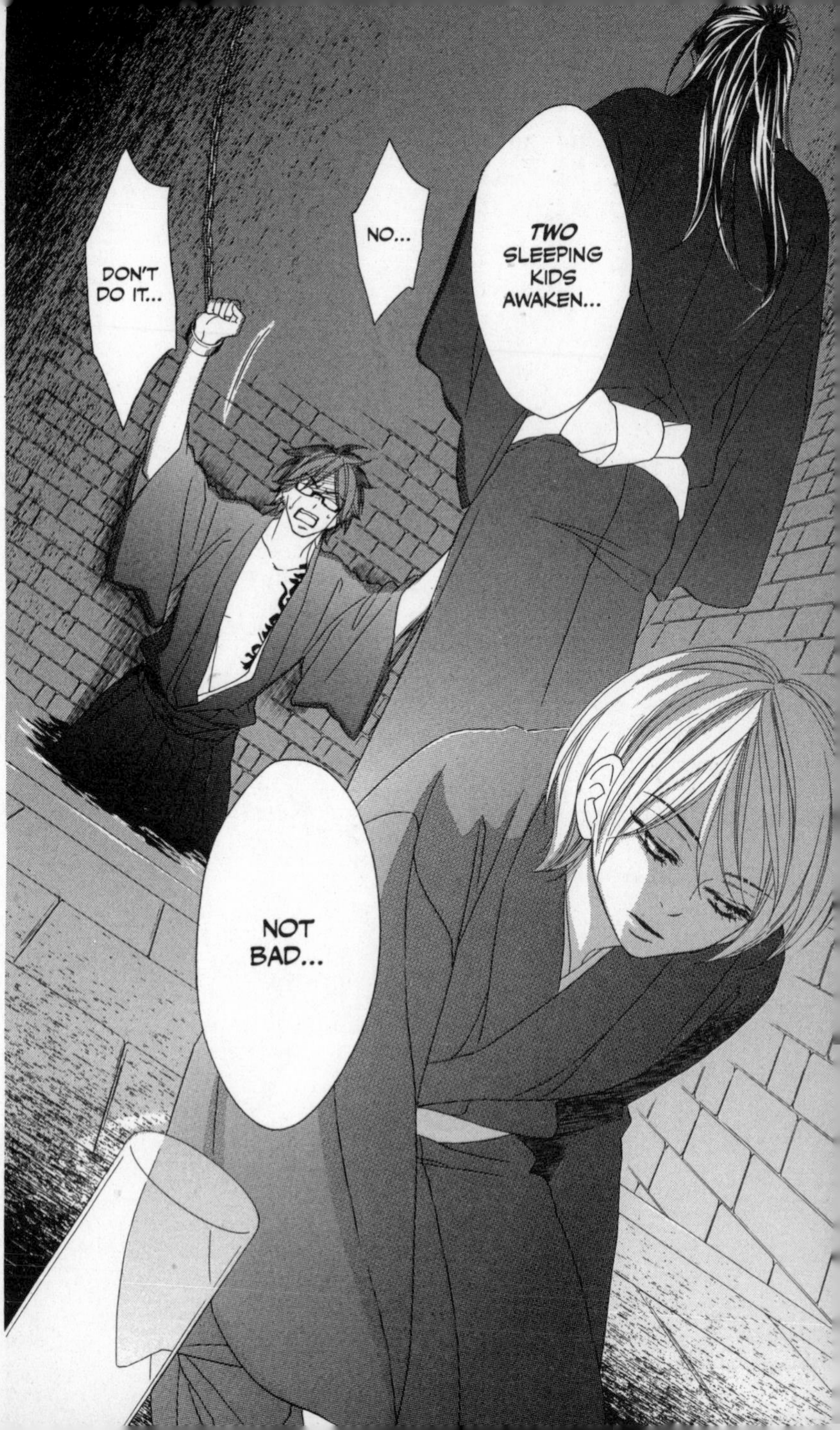
TWO SLEEPING KIDS AWAKEN...
NO...
DON'T DO IT...
NOT BAD...

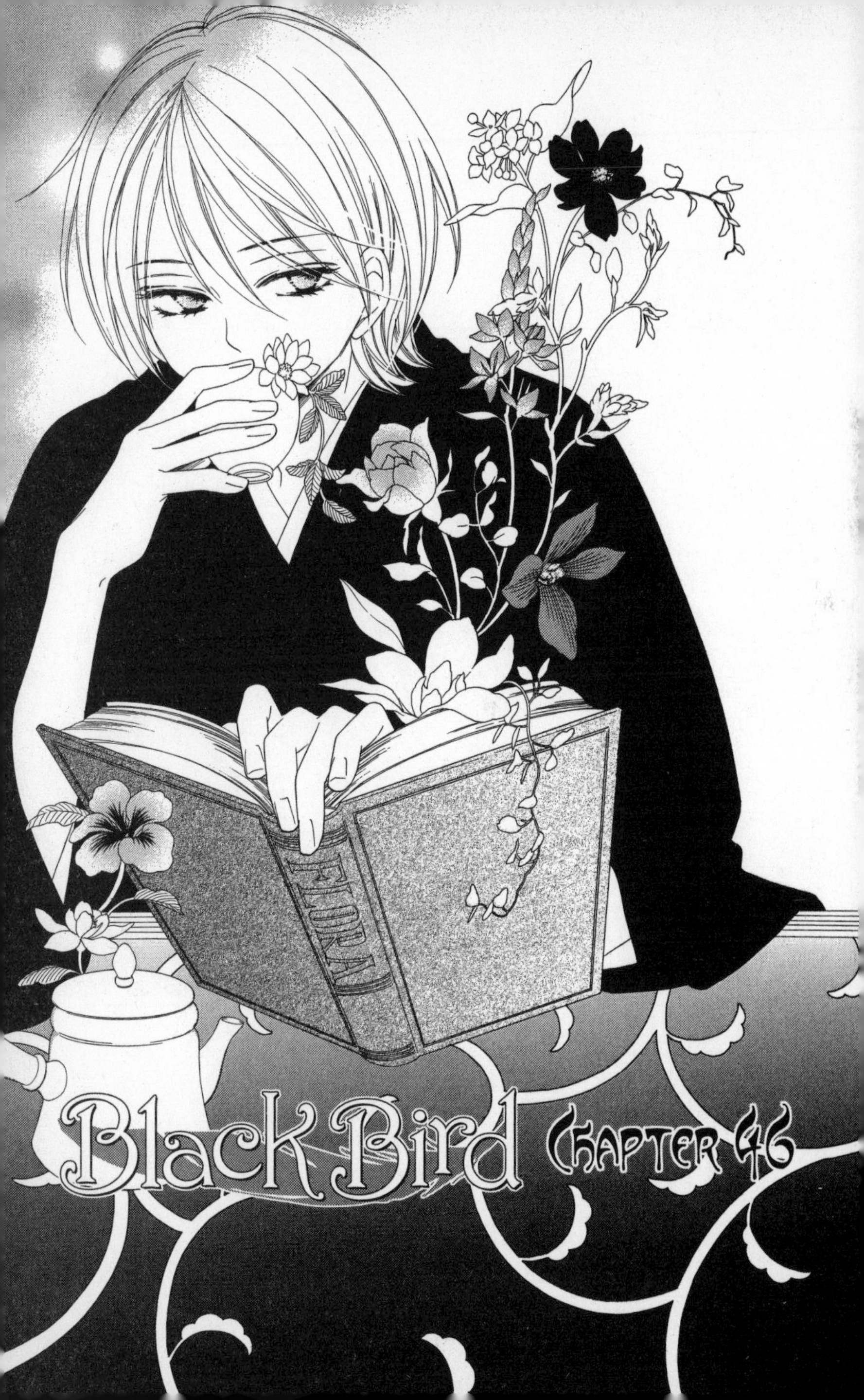
FLORA
Black Bird
Chapter 46

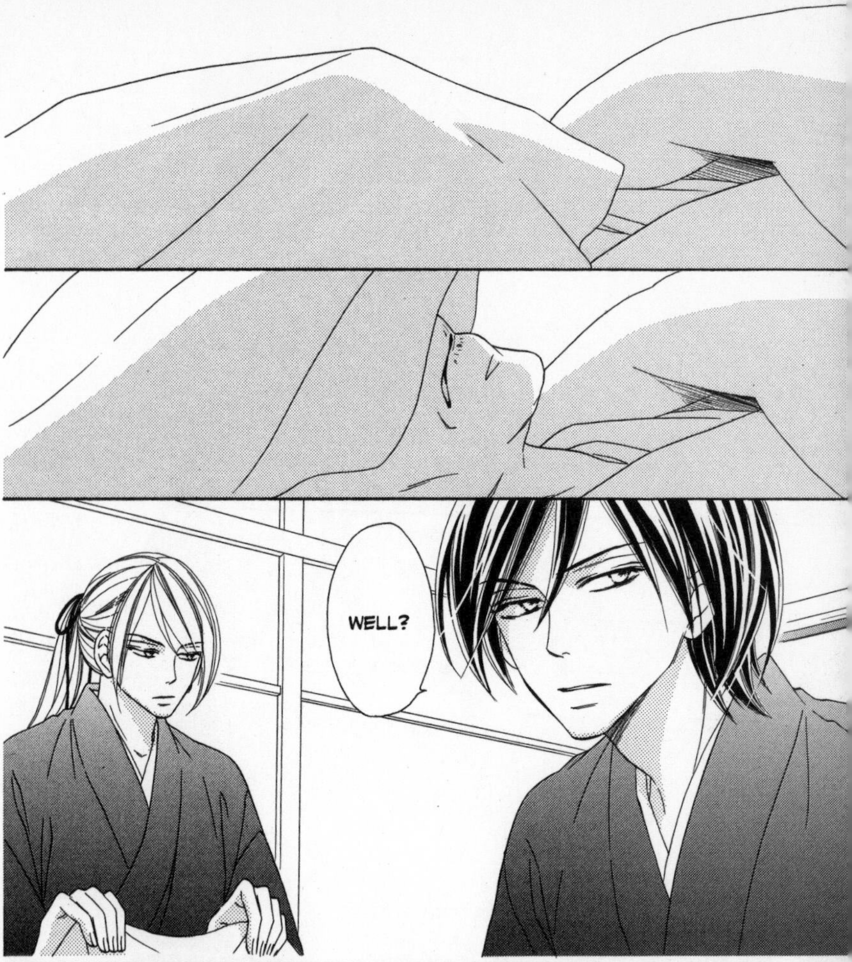
WELL?

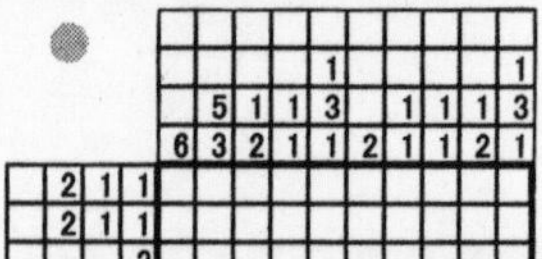
6 | 5 3 | 1 2 | 1 1 | 1 3 1 | 2 | 1 1 | 1 1 | 1 2 | 1 3 1
2 1 1
2 1 1
2
2 1 1
2 1 1
1 1 1 1
1
1 6
2 1 1
2 2

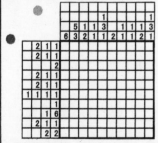

Picross Puzzle Number 3.♡

If you send me your answers,
I will randomly give selected
perfect-score winners a present...
Just kidding! It's no use! It's futile!

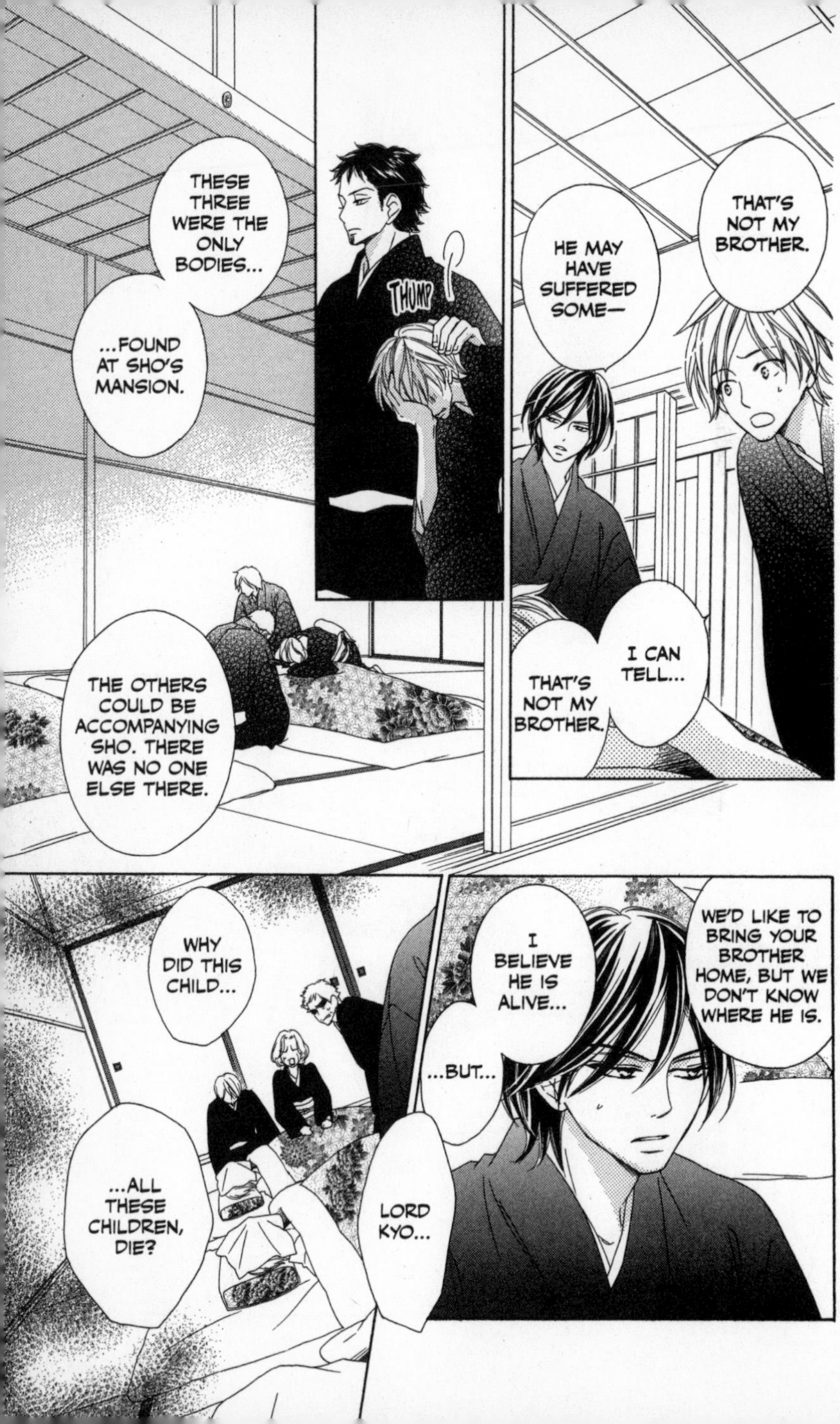
THAT'S NOT MY BROTHER.
HE MAY HAVE SUFFERED SOME—
I CAN TELL...
THAT'S NOT MY BROTHER.
THUMP
THESE THREE WERE THE ONLY BODIES...
...FOUND AT SHO'S MANSION.
THE OTHERS COULD BE ACCOMPANYING SHO. THERE WAS NO ONE ELSE THERE.
WE'D LIKE TO BRING YOUR BROTHER HOME, BUT WE DON'T KNOW WHERE HE IS.
I BELIEVE HE IS ALIVE...
...BUT...
LORD KYO...
WHY DID THIS CHILD...
...ALL THESE CHILDREN, DIE?

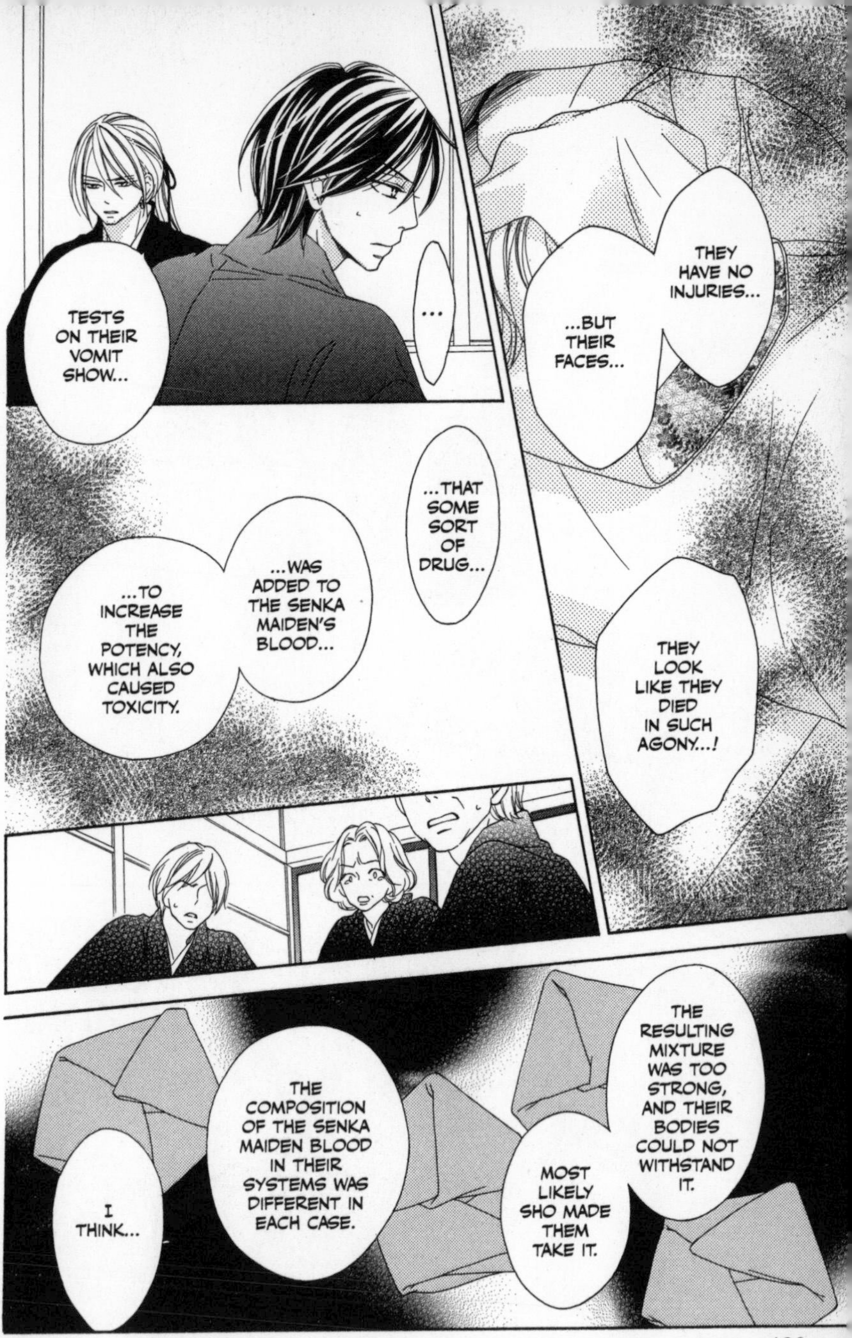
THEY HAVE NO INJURIES...
...BUT THEIR FACES...
THEY LOOK LIKE THEY DIED IN SUCH AGONY...!
...
TESTS ON THEIR VOMIT SHOW...
...THAT SOME SORT OF DRUG...
...WAS ADDED TO THE SENKA MAIDEN'S BLOOD...
...TO INCREASE THE POTENCY, WHICH ALSO CAUSED TOXICITY.
THE RESULTING MIXTURE WAS TOO STRONG, AND THEIR BODIES COULD NOT WITHSTAND IT.
MOST LIKELY SHO MADE THEM TAKE IT.
THE COMPOSITION OF THE SENKA MAIDEN BLOOD IN THEIR SYSTEMS WAS DIFFERENT IN EACH CASE.
I THINK...

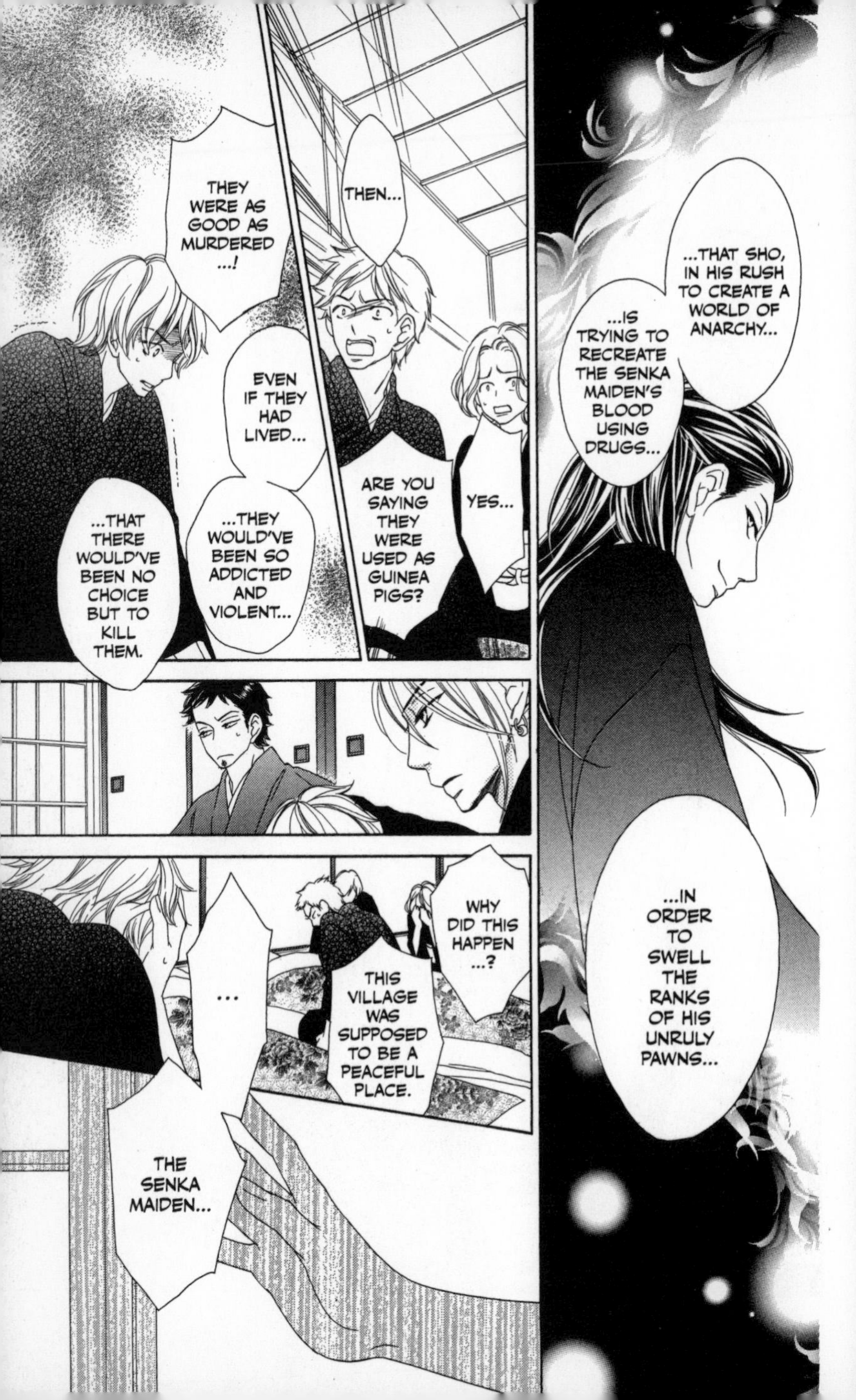
...THAT SHO, IN HIS RUSH TO CREATE A WORLD OF ANARCHY...
...IS TRYING TO RECREATE THE SENKA MAIDEN'S BLOOD USING DRUGS...
...IN ORDER TO SWELL THE RANKS OF HIS UNRULY PAWNS...
THEN...
ARE YOU SAYING THEY WERE USED AS GUINEA PIGS?
YES...
THEY WERE AS GOOD AS MURDERED ...!
EVEN IF THEY HAD LIVED...
...THEY WOULD'VE BEEN SO ADDICTED AND VIOLENT...
...THAT THERE WOULD'VE BEEN NO CHOICE BUT TO KILL THEM.
WHY DID THIS HAPPEN ...?
THIS VILLAGE WAS SUPPOSED TO BE A PEACEFUL PLACE.
...
THE SENKA MAIDEN...

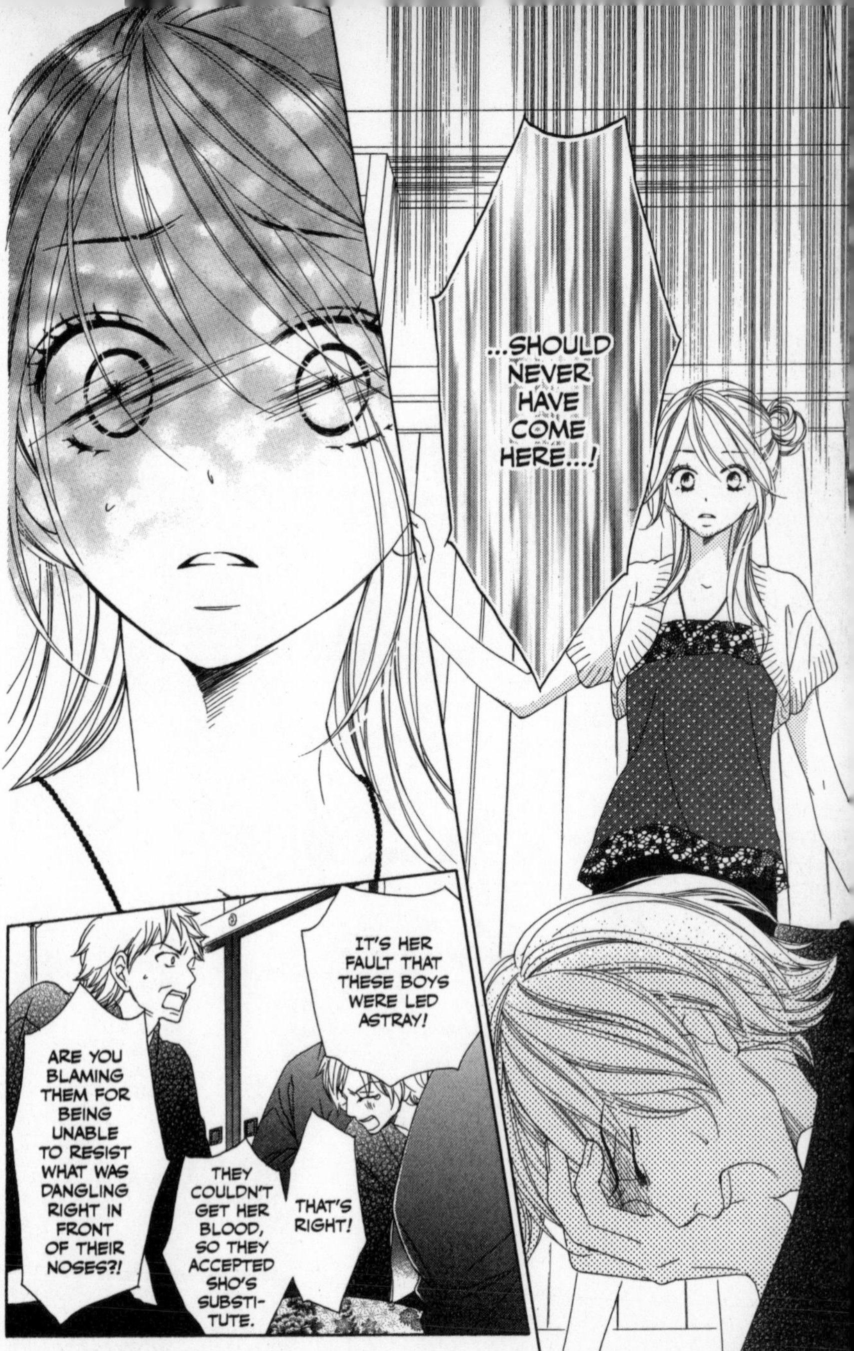
...SHOULD NEVER HAVE COME HERE...!
IT'S HER FAULT THAT THESE BOYS WERE LED ASTRAY!
THAT'S RIGHT!
THEY COULDN'T GET HER BLOOD, SO THEY ACCEPTED SHO'S SUBSTI-TUTE.
ARE YOU BLAMING THEM FOR BEING UNABLE TO RESIST WHAT WAS DANGLING RIGHT IN FRONT OF THEIR NOSES?!

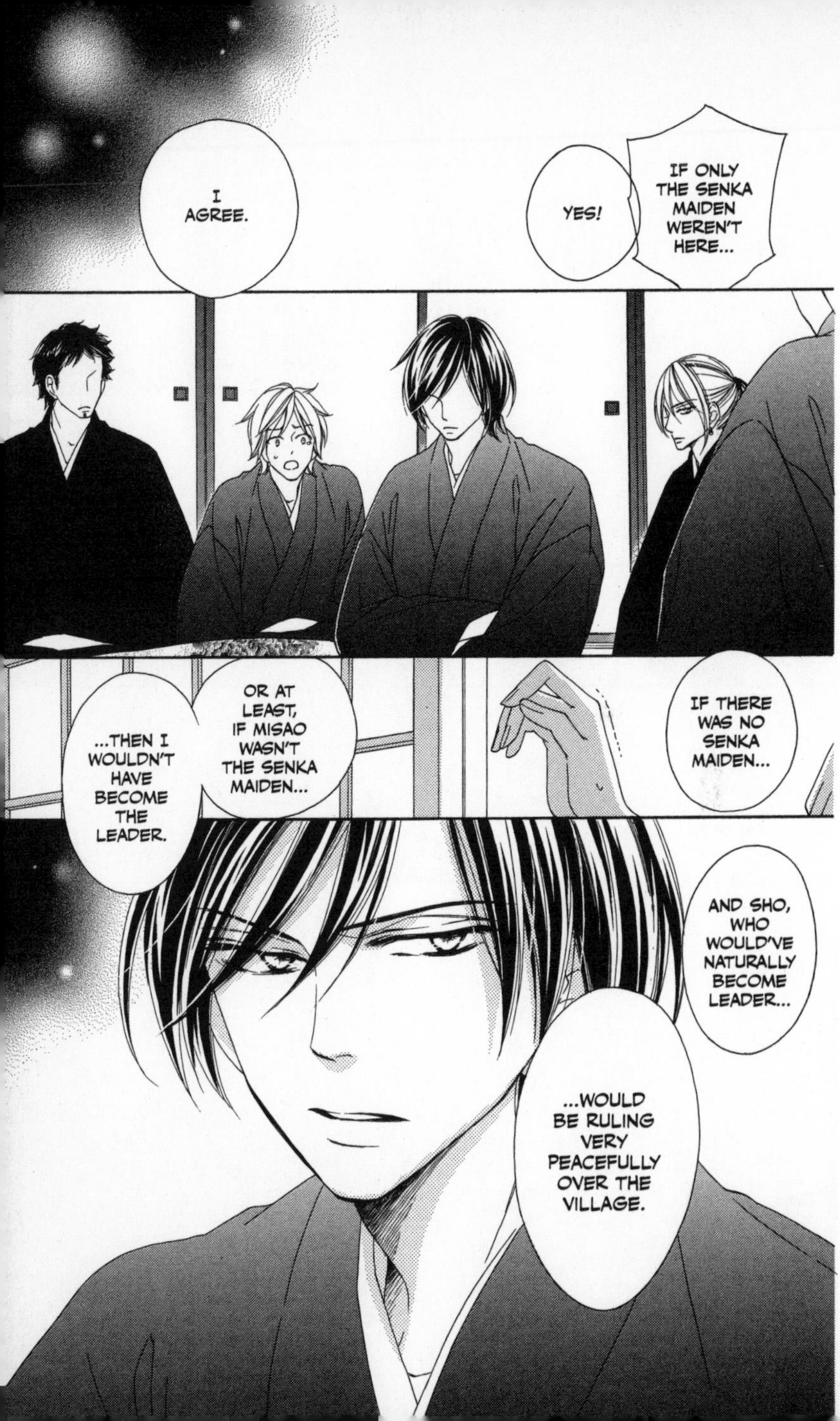
IF ONLY THE SENKA MAIDEN WEREN'T HERE...
YES!
I AGREE.
IF THERE WAS NO SENKA MAIDEN...
OR AT LEAST, IF MISAO WASN'T THE SENKA MAIDEN...
...THEN I WOULDN'T HAVE BECOME THE LEADER.
AND SHO, WHO WOULD'VE NATURALLY BECOME LEADER...
...WOULD BE RULING VERY PEACEFULLY OVER THE VILLAGE.

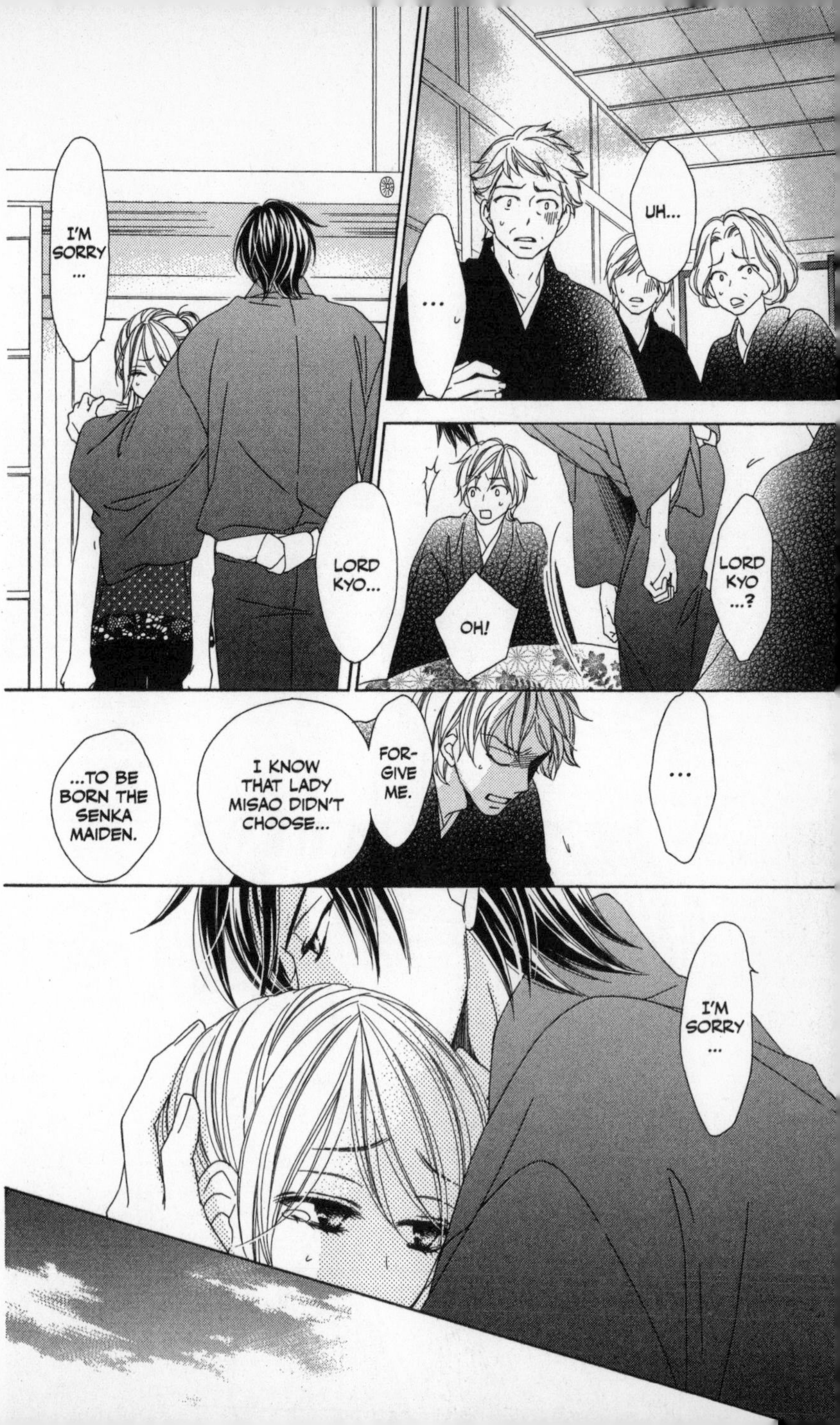
UH...
...
LORD KYO ...?
OH!
LORD KYO...
I'M SORRY ...
...
FOR-GIVE ME.
I KNOW THAT LADY MISAO DIDN'T CHOOSE...
...TO BE BORN THE SENKA MAIDEN.
I'M SORRY ...

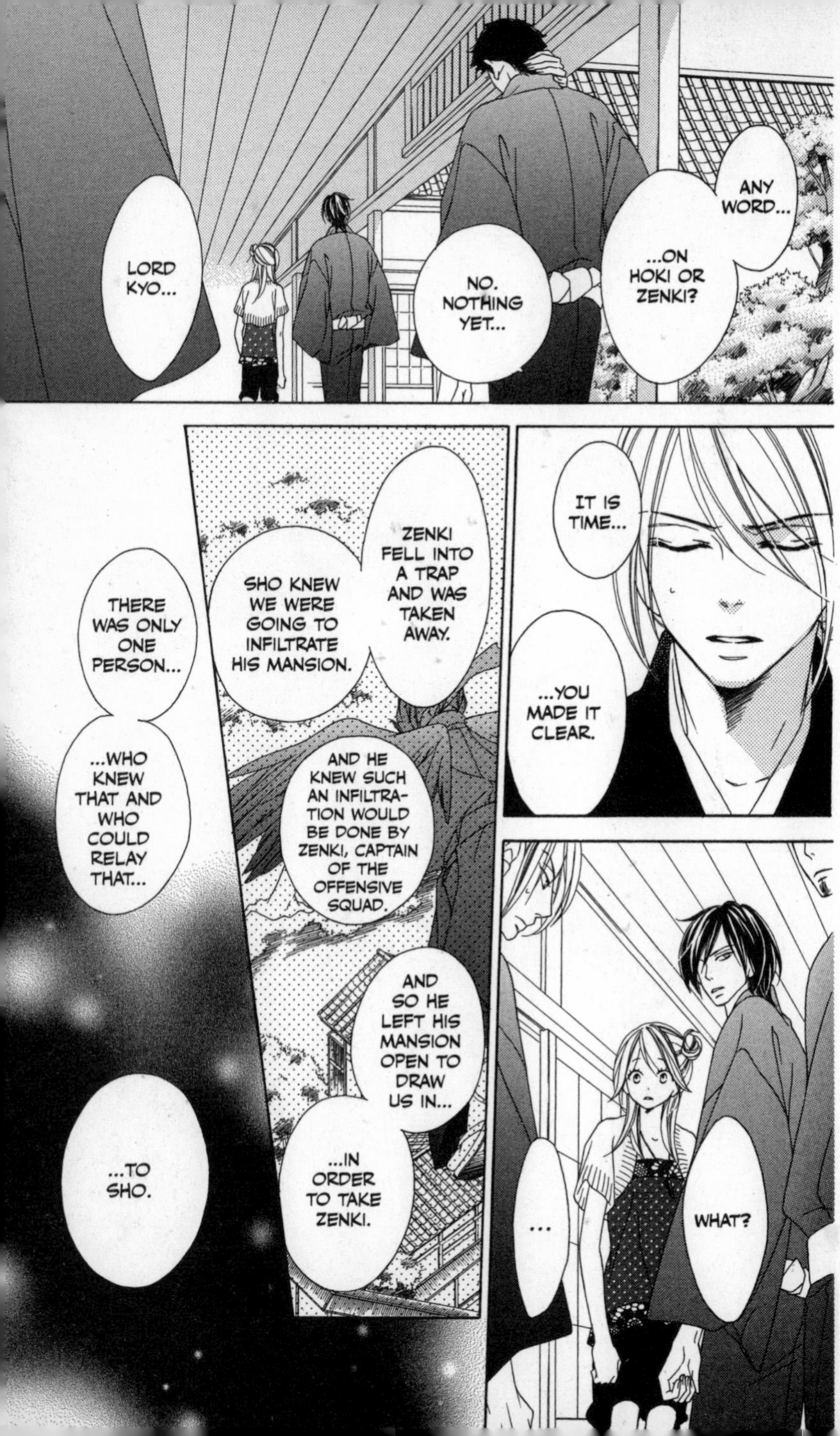
ANY WORD...
...ON HOKI OR ZENKI?
NO. NOTHING YET...
LORD KYO...
IT IS TIME...
...YOU MADE IT CLEAR.
WHAT?
...
ZENKI FELL INTO A TRAP AND WAS TAKEN AWAY.
SHO KNEW WE WERE GOING TO INFILTRATE HIS MANSION.
AND HE KNEW SUCH AN INFILTRA-TION WOULD BE DONE BY ZENKI, CAPTAIN OF THE OFFENSIVE SQUAD.
AND SO HE LEFT HIS MANSION OPEN TO DRAW US IN...
...IN ORDER TO TAKE ZENKI.
THERE WAS ONLY ONE PERSON...
...WHO KNEW THAT AND WHO COULD RELAY THAT...
...TO SHO.

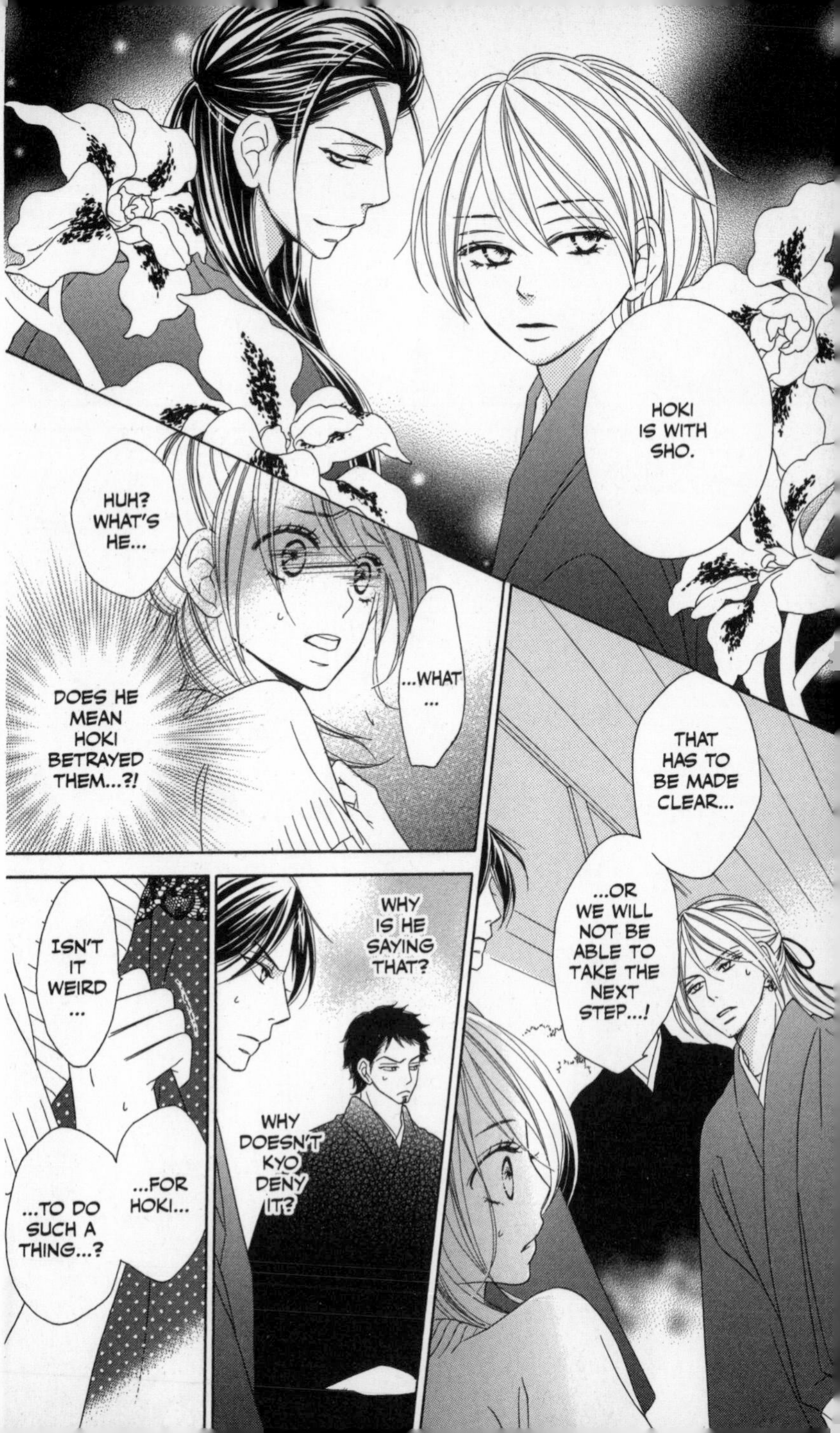
HOKI IS WITH SHO.
THAT HAS TO BE MADE CLEAR...
...OR WE WILL NOT BE ABLE TO TAKE THE NEXT STEP...!
...WHAT ...
HUH? WHAT'S HE...
DOES HE MEAN HOKI BETRAYED THEM...?!
WHY IS HE SAYING THAT?
WHY DOESN'T KYO DENY IT?
ISN'T IT WEIRD ...
...FOR HOKI...
...TO DO SUCH A THING...?

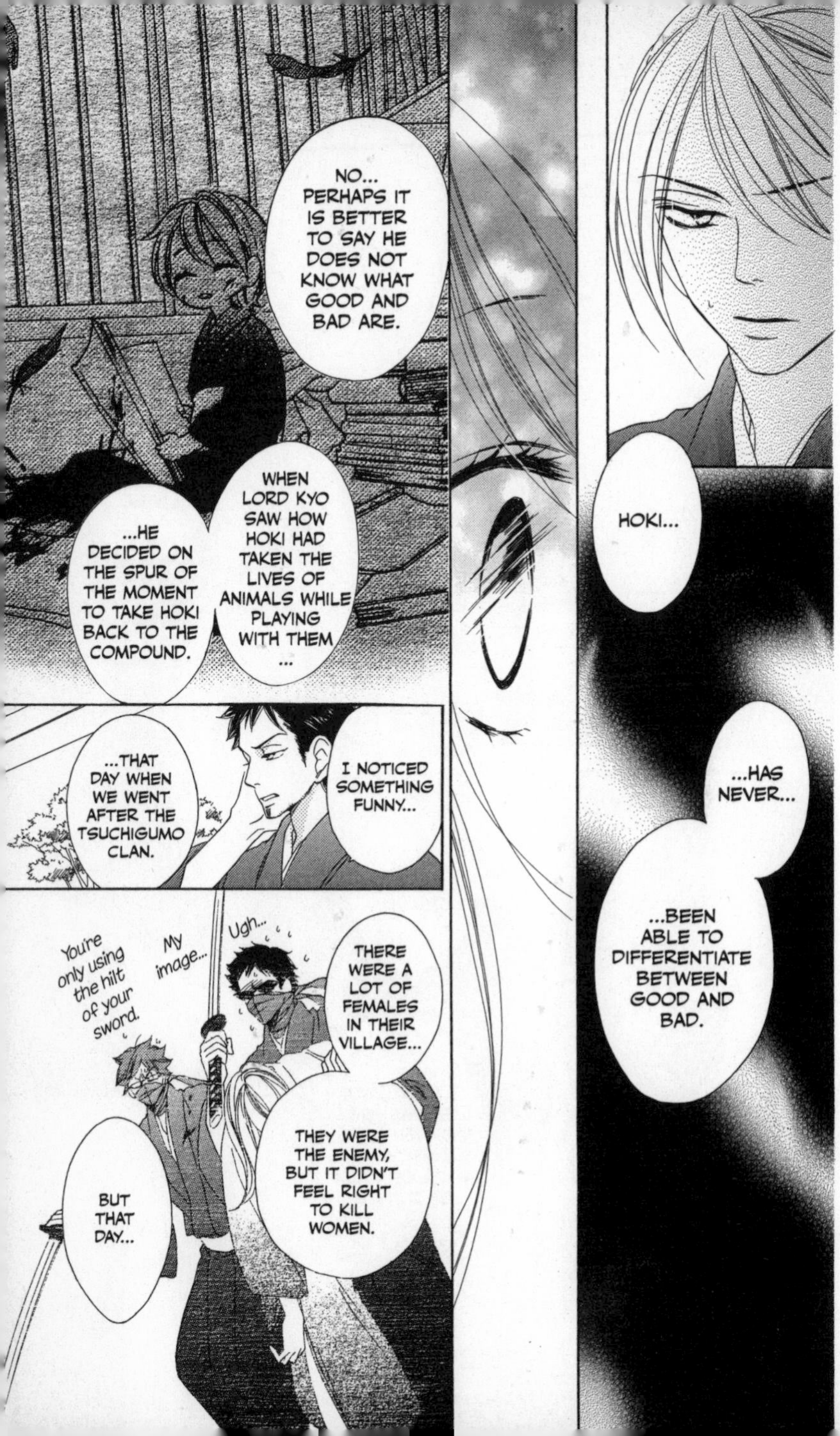
HOKI...
...HAS NEVER...
...BEEN ABLE TO DIFFERENTIATE BETWEEN GOOD AND BAD.
NO... PERHAPS IT IS BETTER TO SAY HE DOES NOT KNOW WHAT GOOD AND BAD ARE.
WHEN LORD KYO SAW HOW HOKI HAD TAKEN THE LIVES OF ANIMALS WHILE PLAYING WITH THEM...
...HE DECIDED ON THE SPUR OF THE MOMENT TO TAKE HOKI BACK TO THE COMPOUND.
I NOTICED SOMETHING FUNNY...
...THAT DAY WHEN WE WENT AFTER THE TSUCHIGUMO CLAN.
THERE WERE A LOT OF FEMALES IN THEIR VILLAGE...
Ugh...
My image...
You're only using the hilt of your sword.
THEY WERE THE ENEMY, BUT IT DIDN'T FEEL RIGHT TO KILL WOMEN.
BUT THAT DAY...

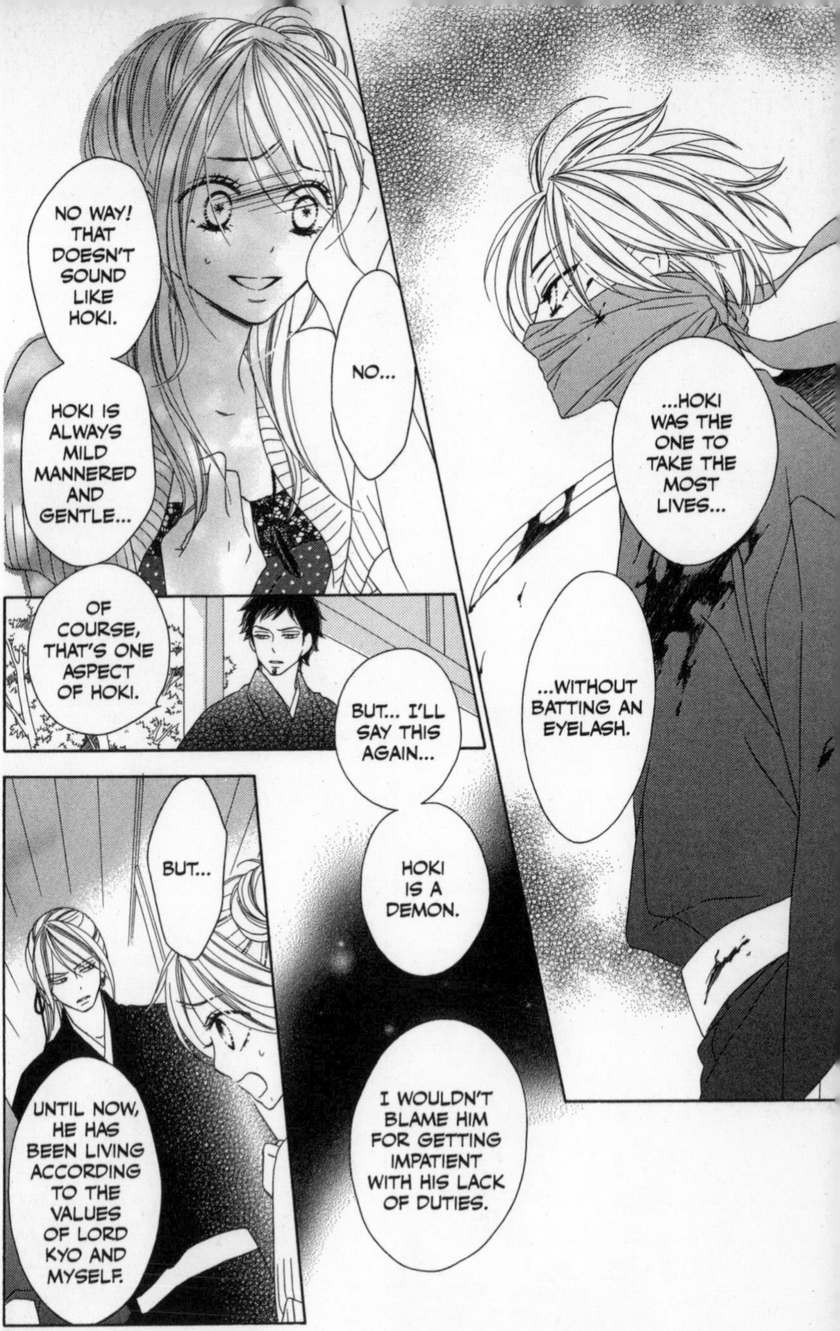
...HOKI WAS THE ONE TO TAKE THE MOST LIVES...
...WITHOUT BATTING AN EYELASH.
NO WAY! THAT DOESN'T SOUND LIKE HOKI.
HOKI IS ALWAYS MILD MANNERED AND GENTLE...
NO...
OF COURSE, THAT'S ONE ASPECT OF HOKI.
BUT... I'LL SAY THIS AGAIN...
HOKI IS A DEMON.
BUT...
UNTIL NOW, HE HAS BEEN LIVING ACCORDING TO THE VALUES OF LORD KYO AND MYSELF.
I WOULDN'T BLAME HIM FOR GETTING IMPATIENT WITH HIS LACK OF DUTIES.

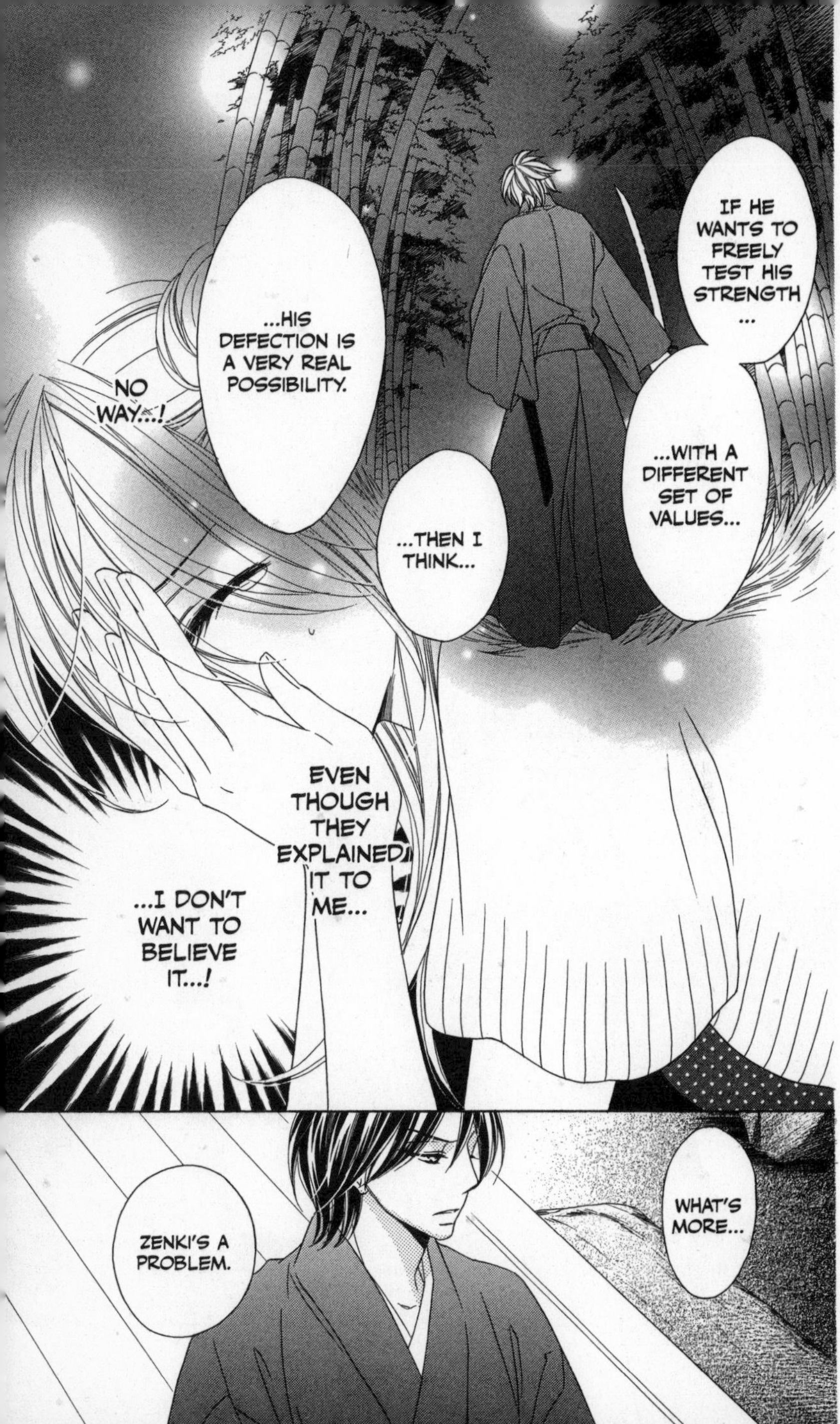
IF HE WANTS TO FREELY TEST HIS STRENGTH...
...WITH A DIFFERENT SET OF VALUES...
...THEN I THINK...
...HIS DEFECTION IS A VERY REAL POSSIBILITY.
NO WAY...!
EVEN THOUGH THEY EXPLAINED IT TO ME...
...I DON'T WANT TO BELIEVE IT...!
WHAT'S MORE...
ZENKI'S A PROBLEM.

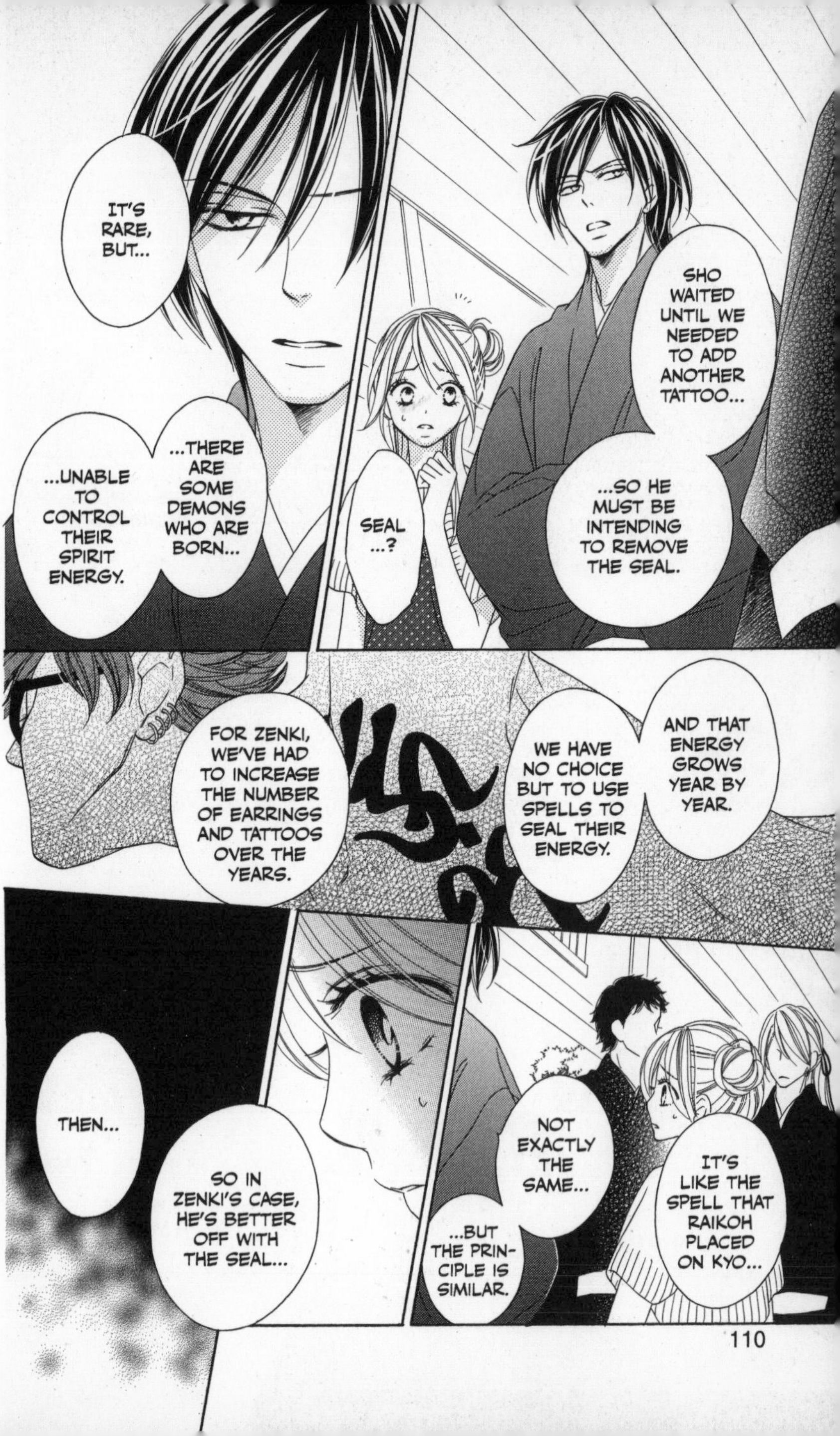
SHO WAITED UNTIL WE NEEDED TO ADD ANOTHER TATTOO...
...SO HE MUST BE INTENDING TO REMOVE THE SEAL.
SEAL ...?
IT'S RARE, BUT...
...THERE ARE SOME DEMONS WHO ARE BORN...
...UNABLE TO CONTROL THEIR SPIRIT ENERGY.
AND THAT ENERGY GROWS YEAR BY YEAR.
WE HAVE NO CHOICE BUT TO USE SPELLS TO SEAL THEIR ENERGY.
FOR ZENKI, WE'VE HAD TO INCREASE THE NUMBER OF EARRINGS AND TATTOOS OVER THE YEARS.
IT'S LIKE THE SPELL THAT RAIKOH PLACED ON KYO...
NOT EXACTLY THE SAME...
...BUT THE PRIN-CIPLE IS SIMILAR.
SO IN ZENKI'S CASE, HE'S BETTER OFF WITH THE SEAL...
THEN...

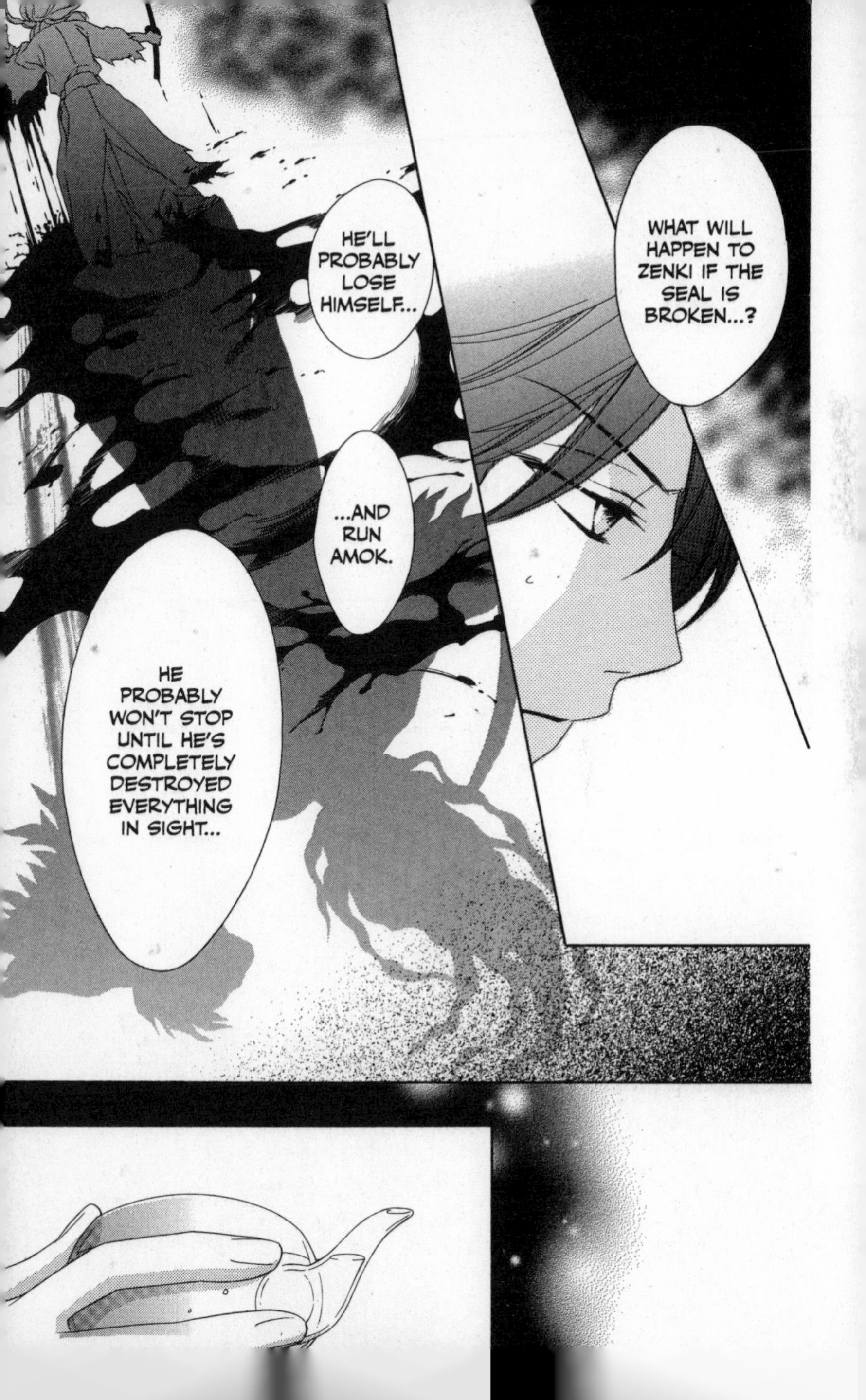
WHAT WILL HAPPEN TO ZENKI IF THE SEAL IS BROKEN...?
HE'LL PROBABLY LOSE HIMSELF...
...AND RUN AMOK.
HE PROBABLY WON'T STOP UNTIL HE'S COMPLETELY DESTROYED EVERYTHING IN SIGHT...

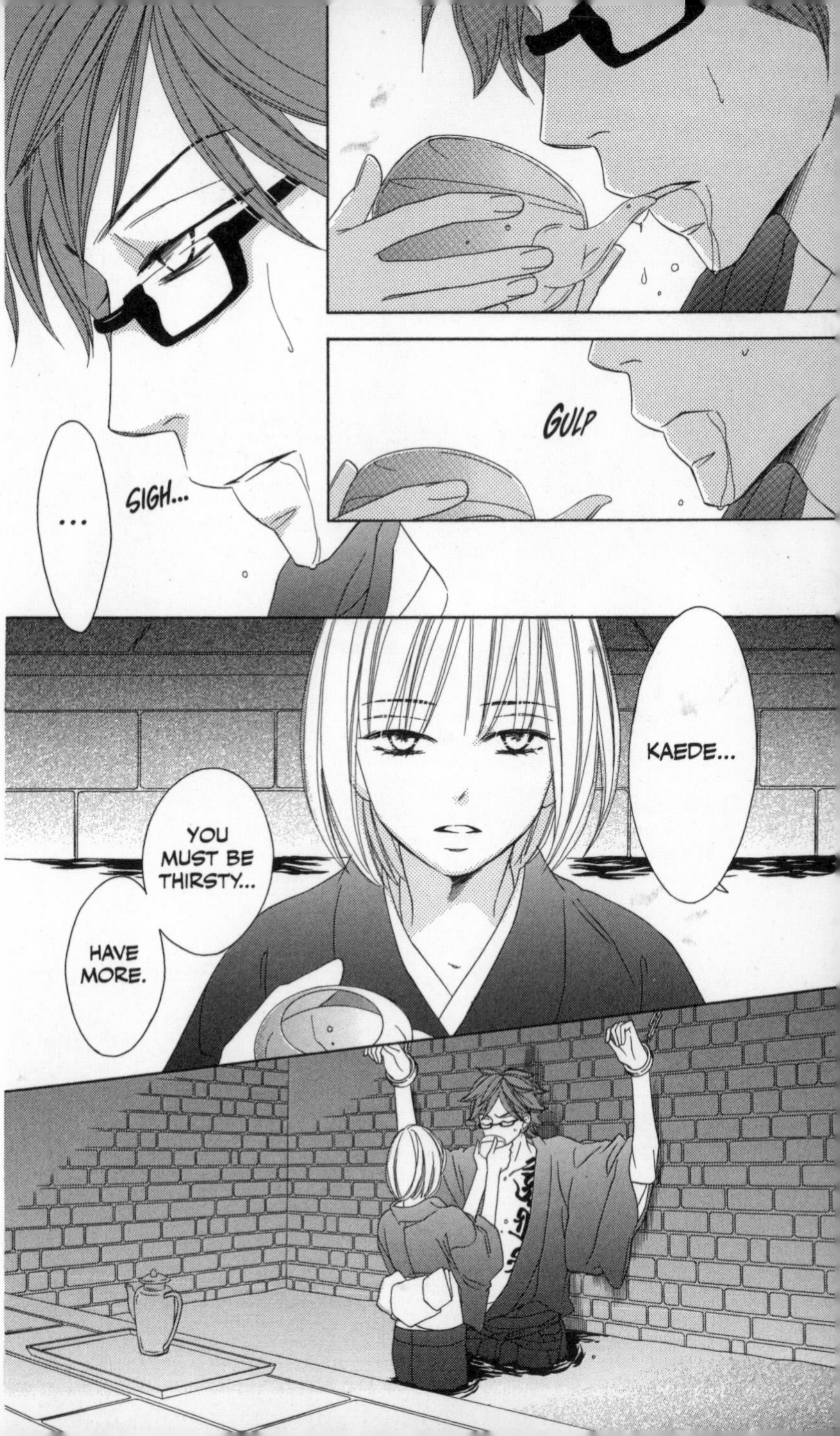
GULP
SIGH...
...
KAEDE...
YOU MUST BE THIRSTY...
HAVE MORE.

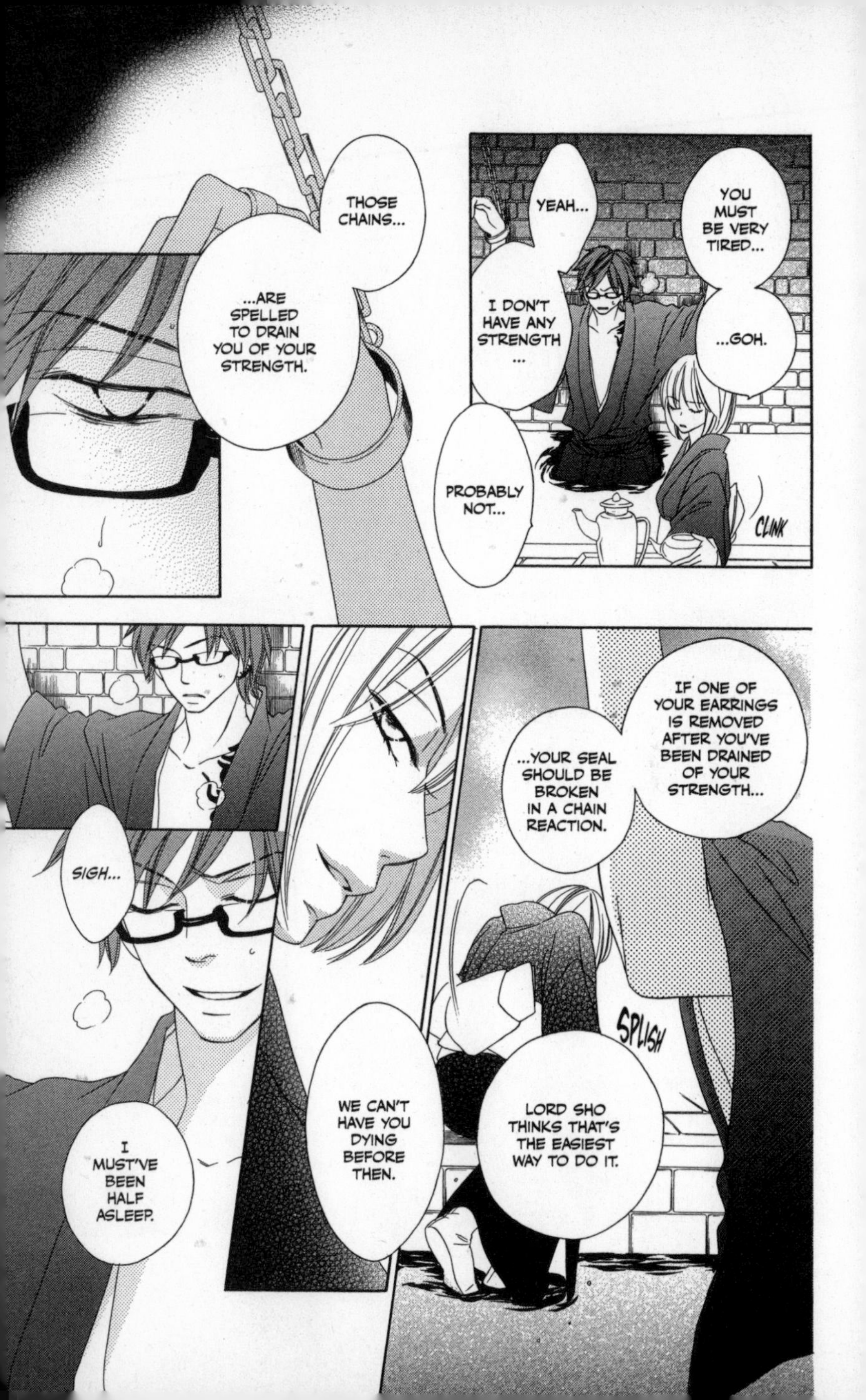
YOU MUST BE VERY TIRED...
...GOH.
YEAH...
I DON'T HAVE ANY STRENGTH ...
PROBABLY NOT...
CLINK
THOSE CHAINS...
...ARE SPELLED TO DRAIN YOU OF YOUR STRENGTH.
IF ONE OF YOUR EARRINGS IS REMOVED AFTER YOU'VE BEEN DRAINED OF YOUR STRENGTH...
...YOUR SEAL SHOULD BE BROKEN IN A CHAIN REACTION.
SPLISH
LORD SHO THINKS THAT'S THE EASIEST WAY TO DO IT.
WE CAN'T HAVE YOU DYING BEFORE THEN.
SIGH...
I MUST'VE BEEN HALF ASLEEP.

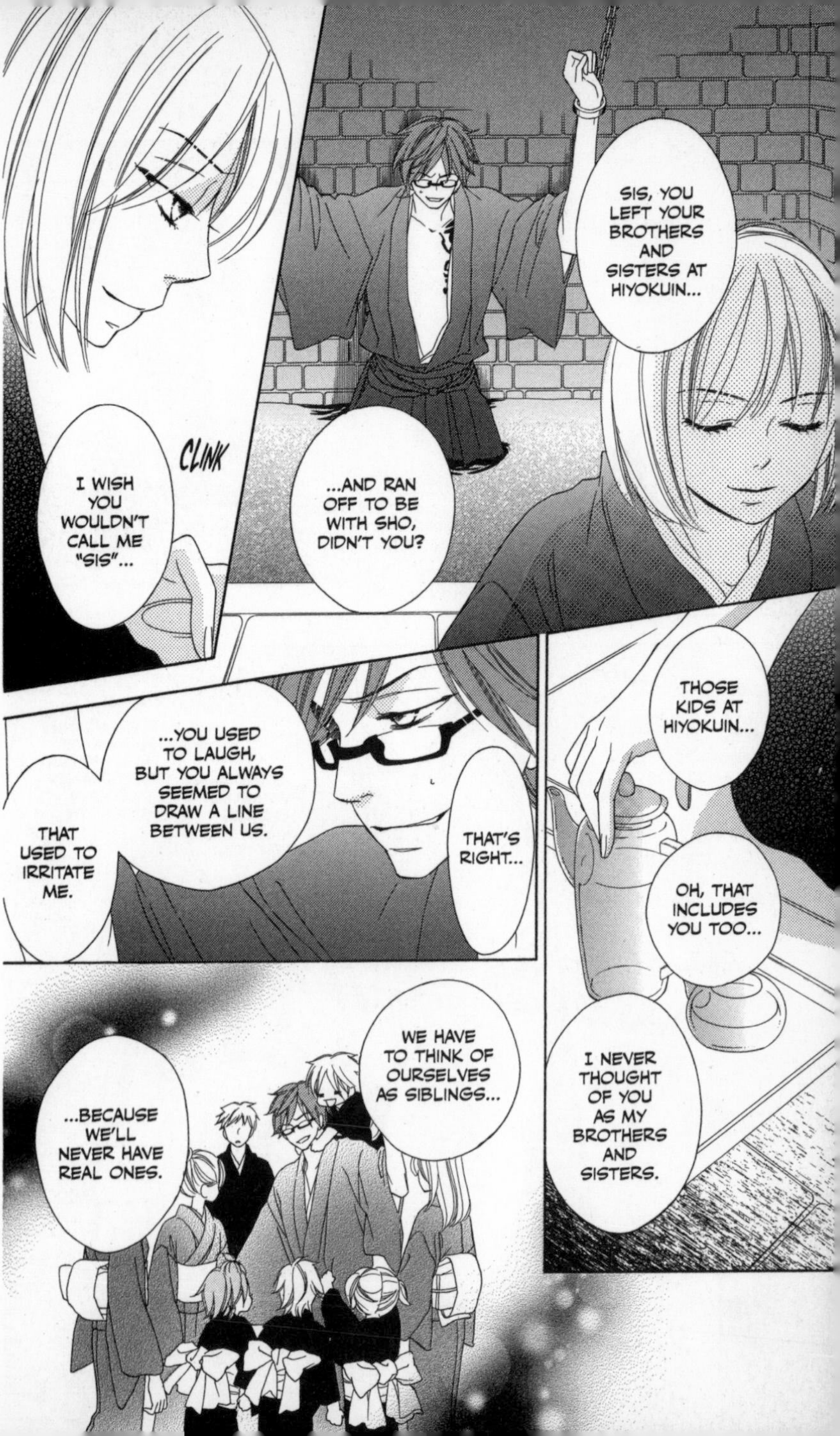
SIS, YOU LEFT YOUR BROTHERS AND SISTERS AT HIYOKUIN...
...AND RAN OFF TO BE WITH SHO, DIDN'T YOU?
CLINK
I WISH YOU WOULDN'T CALL ME "SIS"...
THOSE KIDS AT HIYOKUIN...
OH, THAT INCLUDES YOU TOO...
I NEVER THOUGHT OF YOU AS MY BROTHERS AND SISTERS.
THAT'S RIGHT...
...YOU USED TO LAUGH, BUT YOU ALWAYS SEEMED TO DRAW A LINE BETWEEN US.
THAT USED TO IRRITATE ME.
WE HAVE TO THINK OF OURSELVES AS SIBLINGS...
...BECAUSE WE'LL NEVER HAVE REAL ONES.

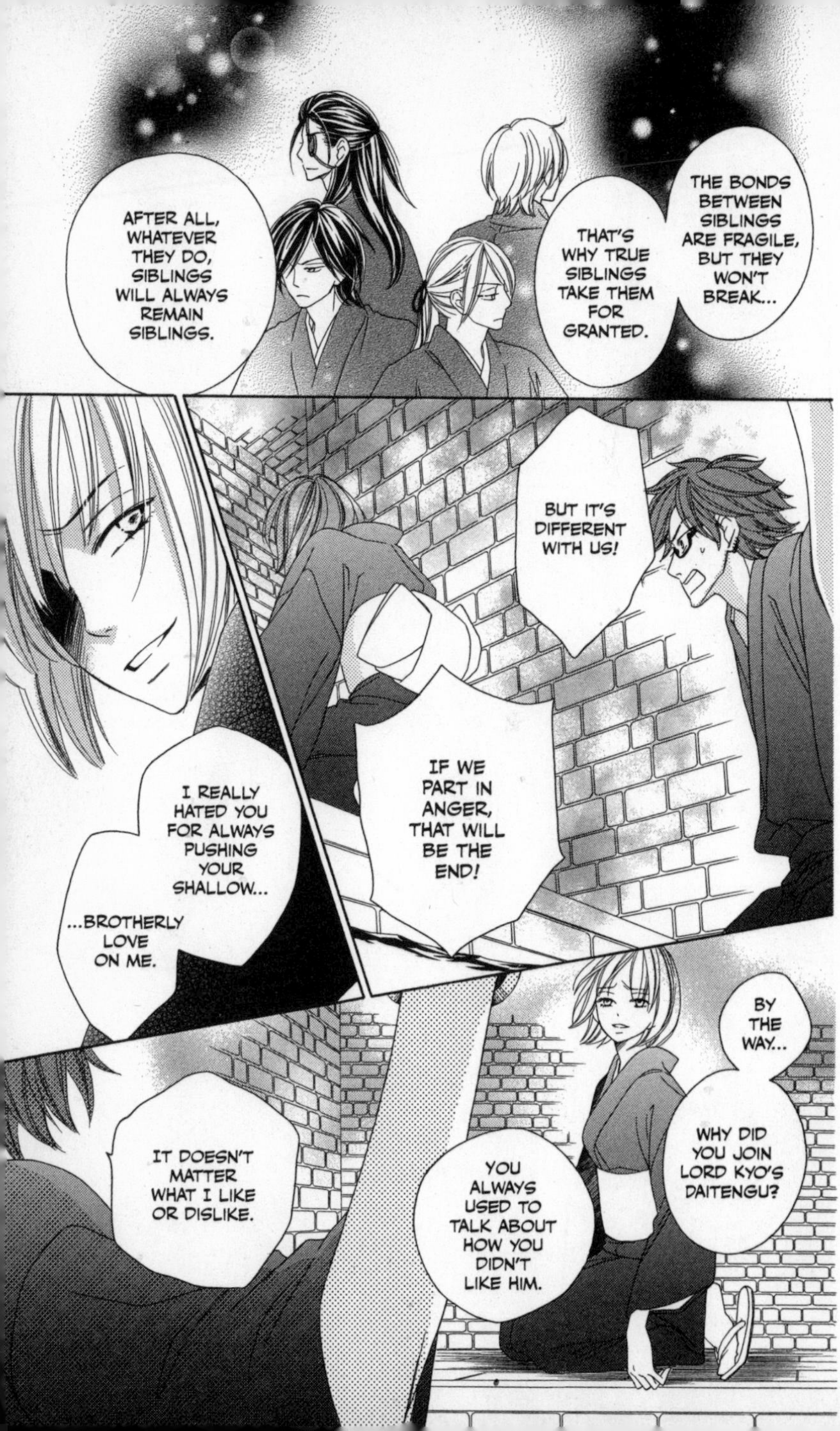
THE BONDS BETWEEN SIBLINGS ARE FRAGILE, BUT THEY WON'T BREAK...
THAT'S WHY TRUE SIBLINGS TAKE THEM FOR GRANTED.
AFTER ALL, WHATEVER THEY DO, SIBLINGS WILL ALWAYS REMAIN SIBLINGS.
BUT IT'S DIFFERENT WITH US!
IF WE PART IN ANGER, THAT WILL BE THE END!
I REALLY HATED YOU FOR ALWAYS PUSHING YOUR SHALLOW...
...BROTHERLY LOVE ON ME.
BY THE WAY...
WHY DID YOU JOIN LORD KYO'S DAITENGU?
YOU ALWAYS USED TO TALK ABOUT HOW YOU DIDN'T LIKE HIM.
IT DOESN'T MATTER WHAT I LIKE OR DISLIKE.

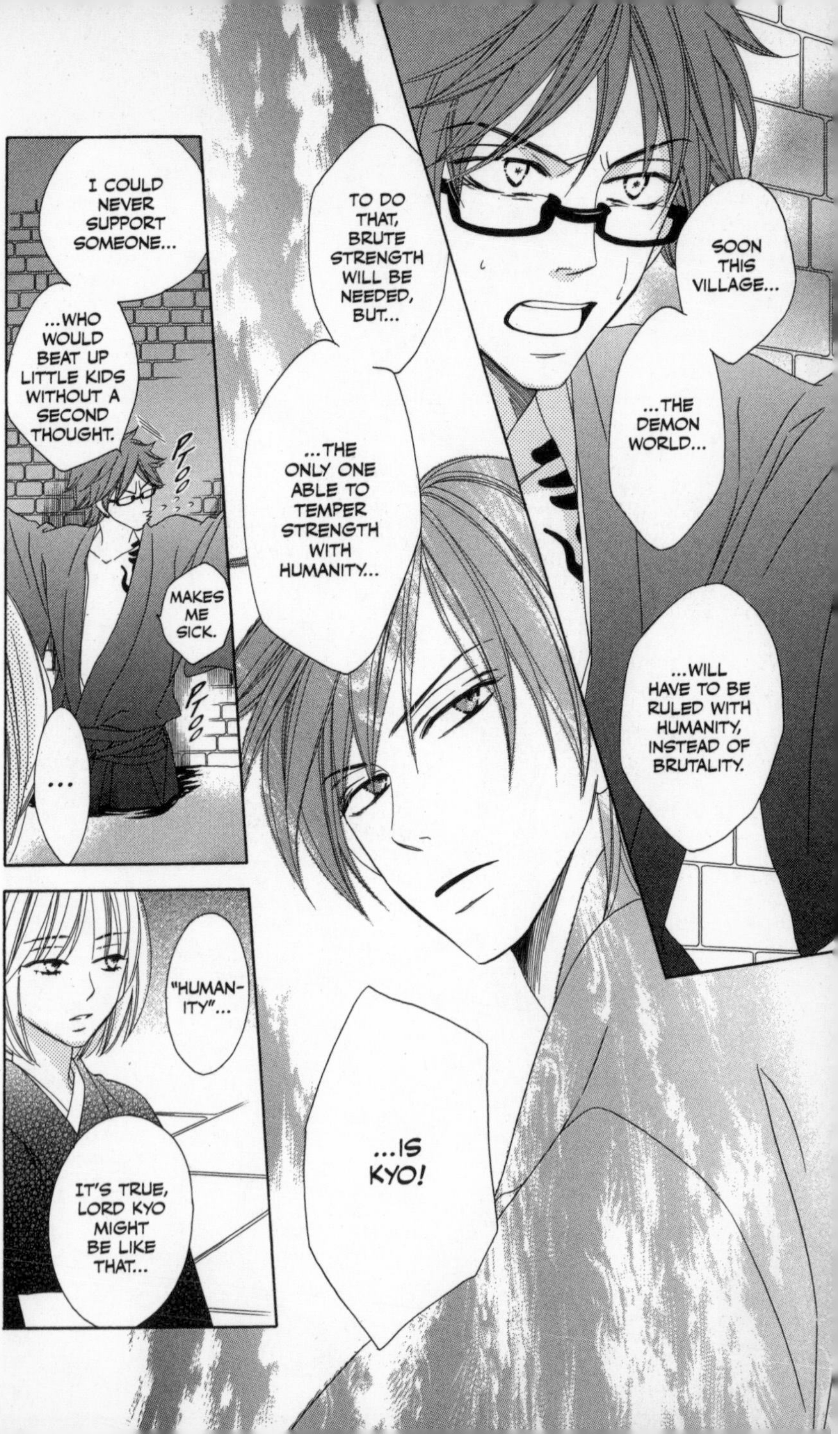
SOON THIS VILLAGE...
...THE DEMON WORLD...
...WILL HAVE TO BE RULED WITH HUMANITY, INSTEAD OF BRUTALITY.
TO DO THAT, BRUTE STRENGTH WILL BE NEEDED, BUT...
...THE ONLY ONE ABLE TO TEMPER STRENGTH WITH HUMANITY...
...IS KYO!
I COULD NEVER SUPPORT SOMEONE...
...WHO WOULD BEAT UP LITTLE KIDS WITHOUT A SECOND THOUGHT.
PTOO
MAKES ME SICK.
PTOO
...
"HUMAN-ITY"...
IT'S TRUE, LORD KYO MIGHT BE LIKE THAT...

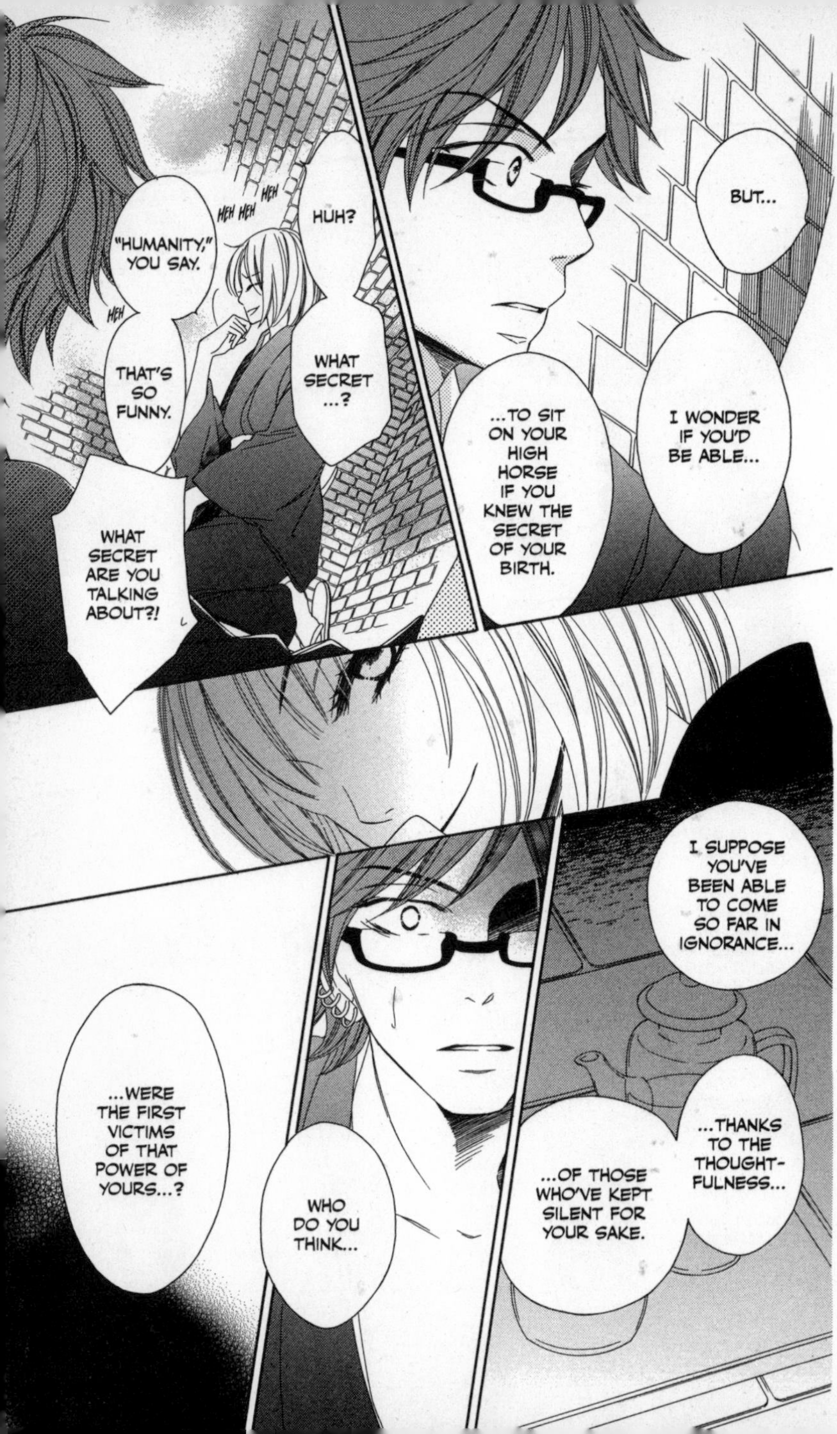
BUT...
I WONDER IF YOU'D BE ABLE...
...TO SIT ON YOUR HIGH HORSE IF YOU KNEW THE SECRET OF YOUR BIRTH.
HUH?
WHAT SECRET ...?
HEH HEH HEH
"HUMANITY," YOU SAY.
HEH
THAT'S SO FUNNY.
WHAT SECRET ARE YOU TALKING ABOUT?!
I SUPPOSE YOU'VE BEEN ABLE TO COME SO FAR IN IGNORANCE...
...THANKS TO THE THOUGHT-FULNESS...
...OF THOSE WHO'VE KEPT SILENT FOR YOUR SAKE.
WHO DO YOU THINK...
...WERE THE FIRST VICTIMS OF THAT POWER OF YOURS...?

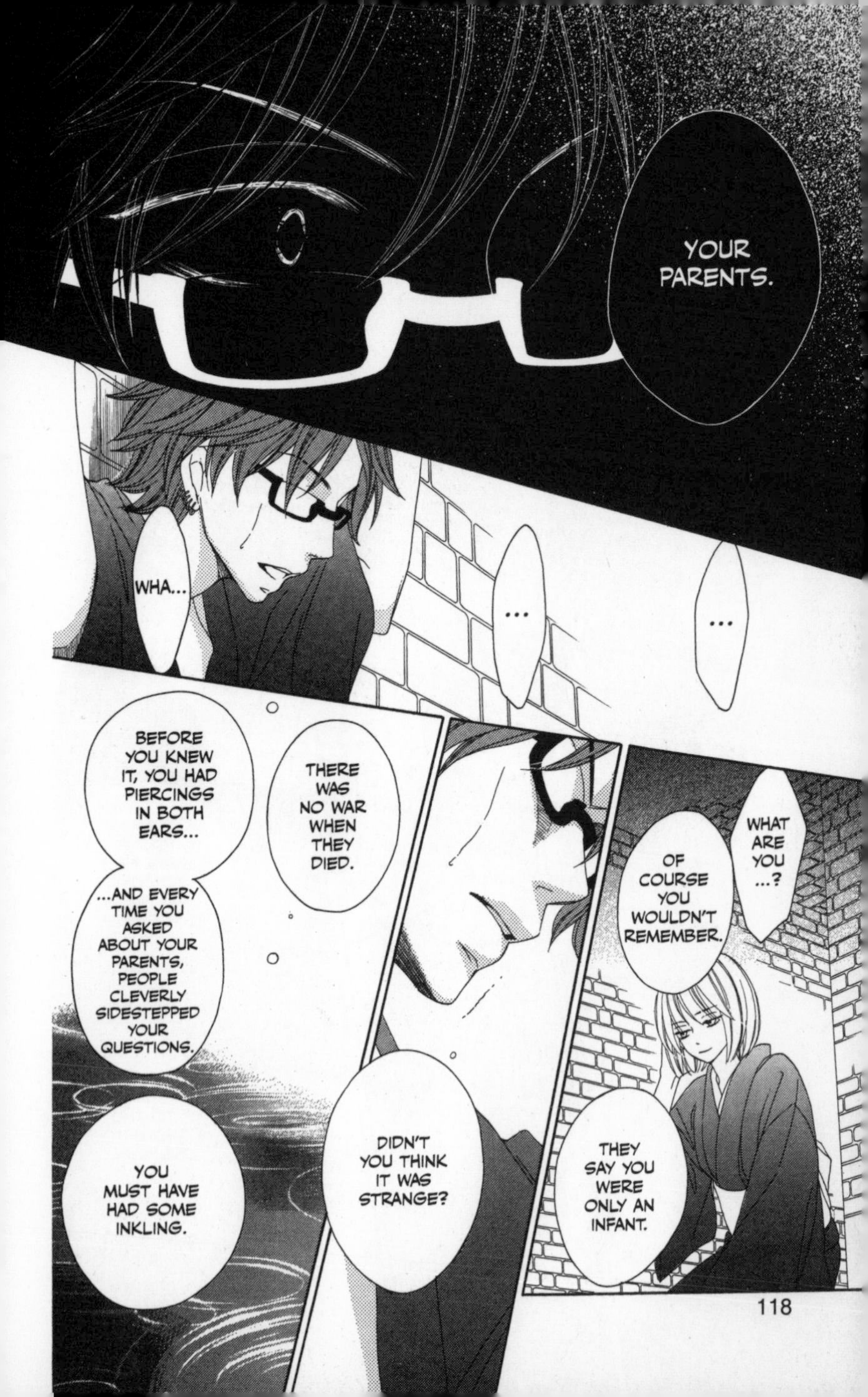
YOUR PARENTS.
...
...
WHA...
WHAT ARE YOU ...?
OF COURSE YOU WOULDN'T REMEMBER.
THEY SAY YOU WERE ONLY AN INFANT.
DIDN'T YOU THINK IT WAS STRANGE?
THERE WAS NO WAR WHEN THEY DIED.
BEFORE YOU KNEW IT, YOU HAD PIERCINGS IN BOTH EARS...
...AND EVERY TIME YOU ASKED ABOUT YOUR PARENTS, PEOPLE CLEVERLY SIDESTEPPED YOUR QUESTIONS.
YOU MUST HAVE HAD SOME INKLING.

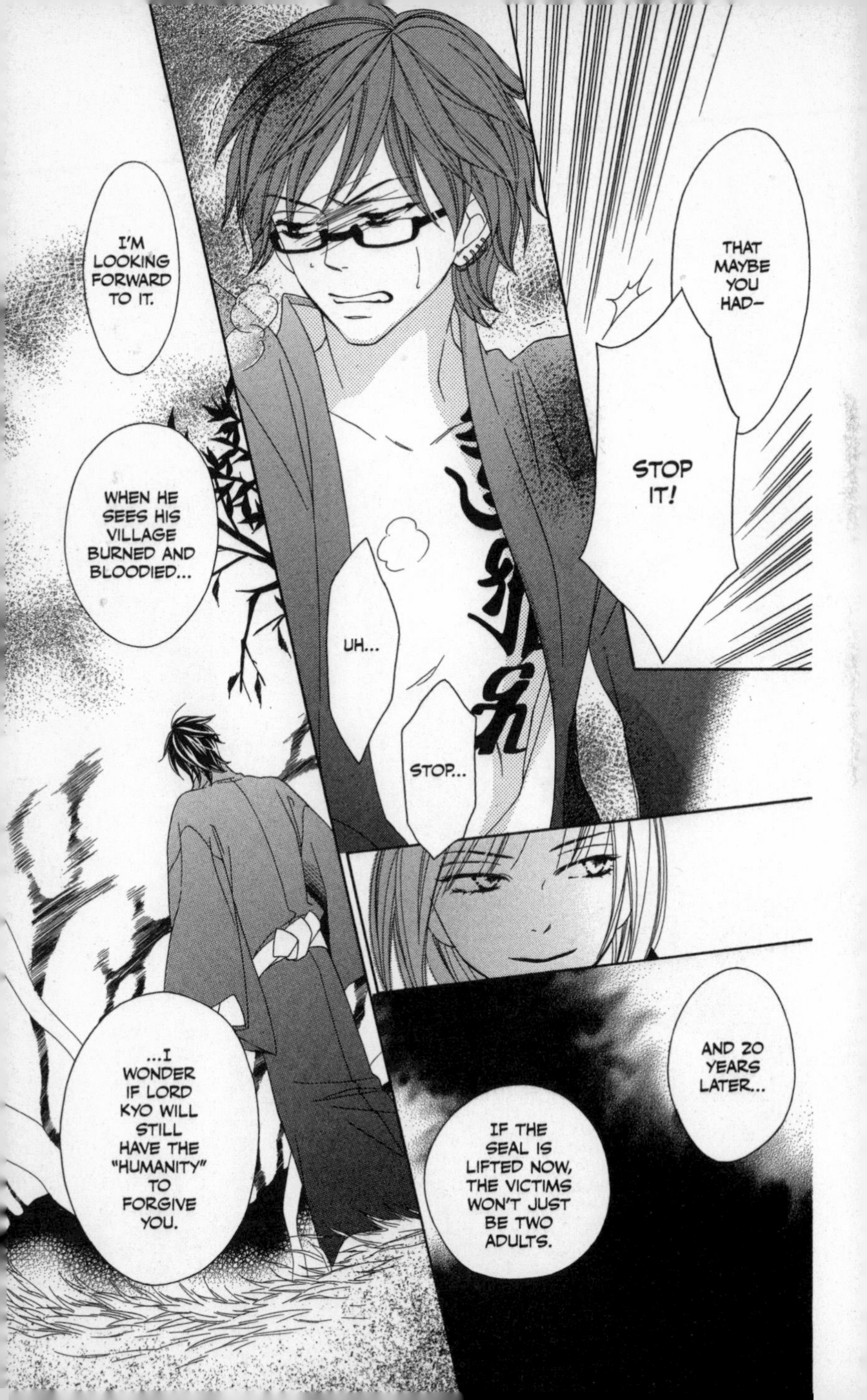
THAT MAYBE YOU HAD—
STOP IT!
UH...
STOP...
AND 20 YEARS LATER...
IF THE SEAL IS LIFTED NOW, THE VICTIMS WON'T JUST BE TWO ADULTS.
I'M LOOKING FORWARD TO IT.
WHEN HE SEES HIS VILLAGE BURNED AND BLOODIED...
...I WONDER IF LORD KYO WILL STILL HAVE THE "HUMANITY" TO FORGIVE YOU.

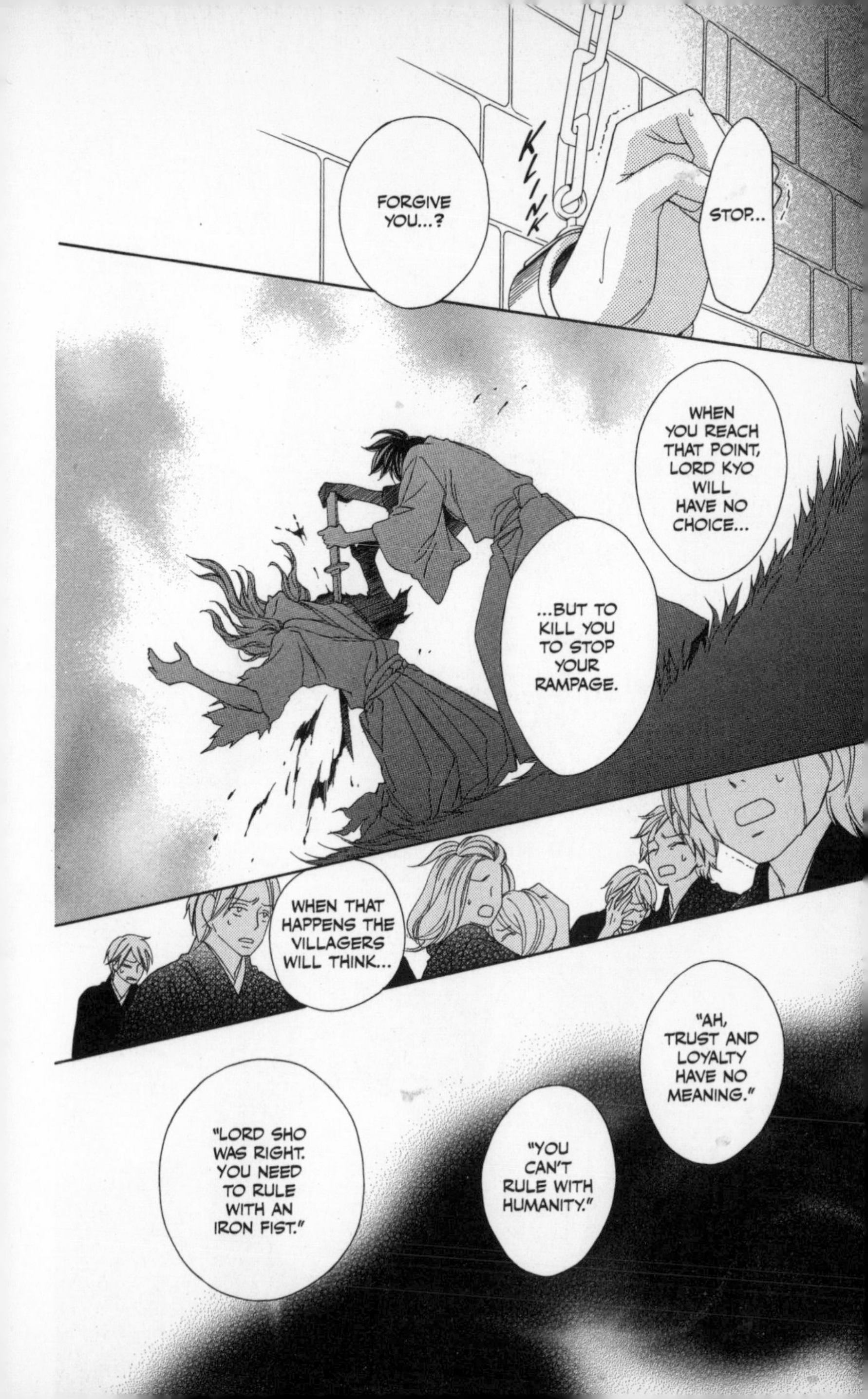

STOP...
KLINK
FORGIVE YOU...?
WHEN YOU REACH THAT POINT, LORD KYO WILL HAVE NO CHOICE...
...BUT TO KILL YOU TO STOP YOUR RAMPAGE.
WHEN THAT HAPPENS THE VILLAGERS WILL THINK...
"AH, TRUST AND LOYALTY HAVE NO MEANING."
"YOU CAN'T RULE WITH HUMANITY."
"LORD SHO WAS RIGHT. YOU NEED TO RULE WITH AN IRON FIST."

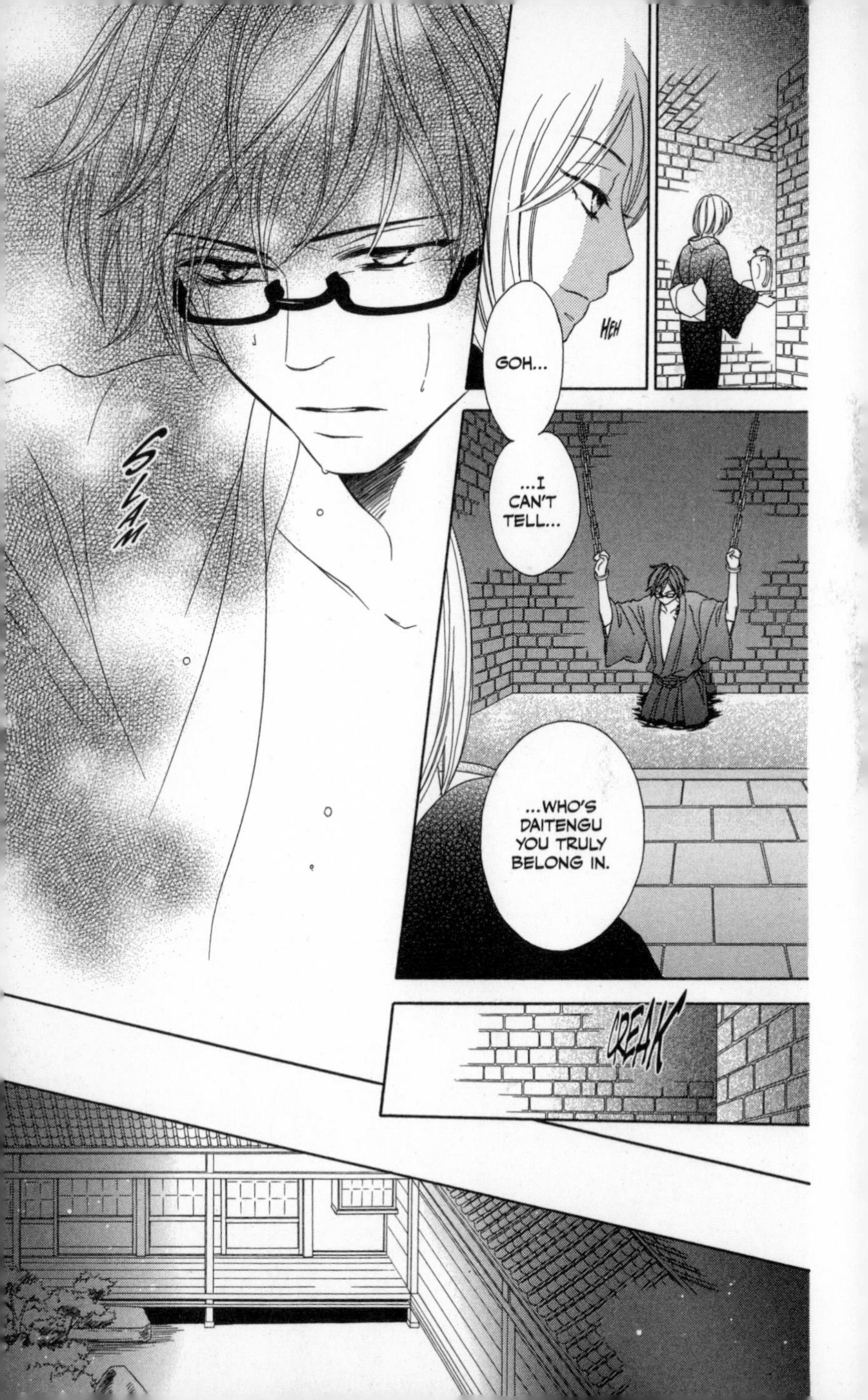
HEH
GOH...
...I CAN'T TELL...
...WHO'S DAITENGU YOU TRULY BELONG IN.
CREAK
SLAM

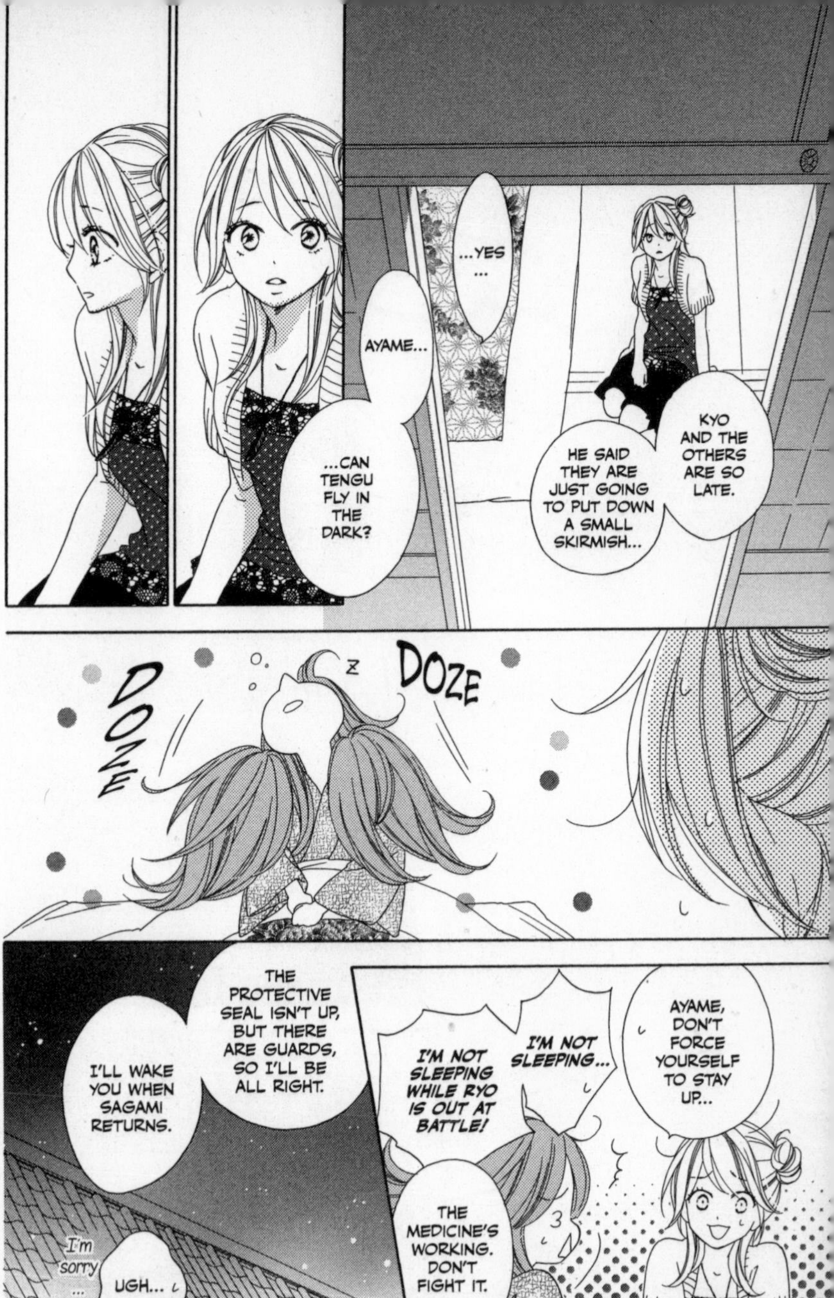
KYO AND THE OTHERS ARE SO LATE.
HE SAID THEY ARE JUST GOING TO PUT DOWN A SMALL SKIRMISH...
...YES ...
AYAME...
...CAN TENGU FLY IN THE DARK?
DOZE
DOZE
AYAME, DON'T FORCE YOURSELF TO STAY UP...
I'M NOT SLEEPING...
I'M NOT SLEEPING WHILE RYO IS OUT AT BATTLE!
THE MEDICINE'S WORKING. DON'T FIGHT IT.
THE PROTECTIVE SEAL ISN'T UP, BUT THERE ARE GUARDS, SO I'LL BE ALL RIGHT.
I'LL WAKE YOU WHEN SAGAMI RETURNS.
UGH...
I'm sorry ...

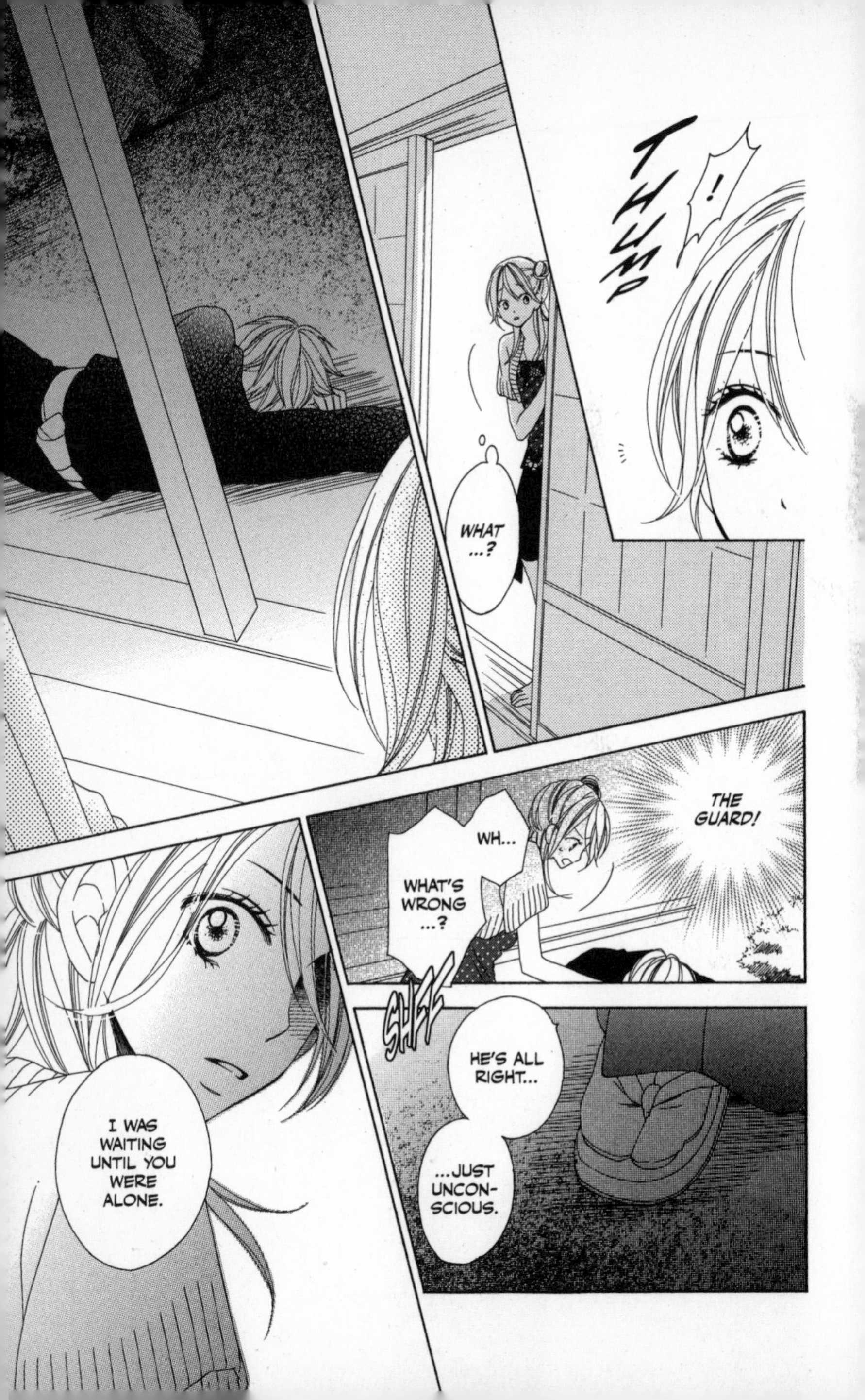
THUMP
!
WHAT ...?
THE GUARD!
WH...
WHAT'S WRONG ...?
SHFF
HE'S ALL RIGHT...
...JUST UNCON-SCIOUS.
I WAS WAITING UNTIL YOU WERE ALONE.

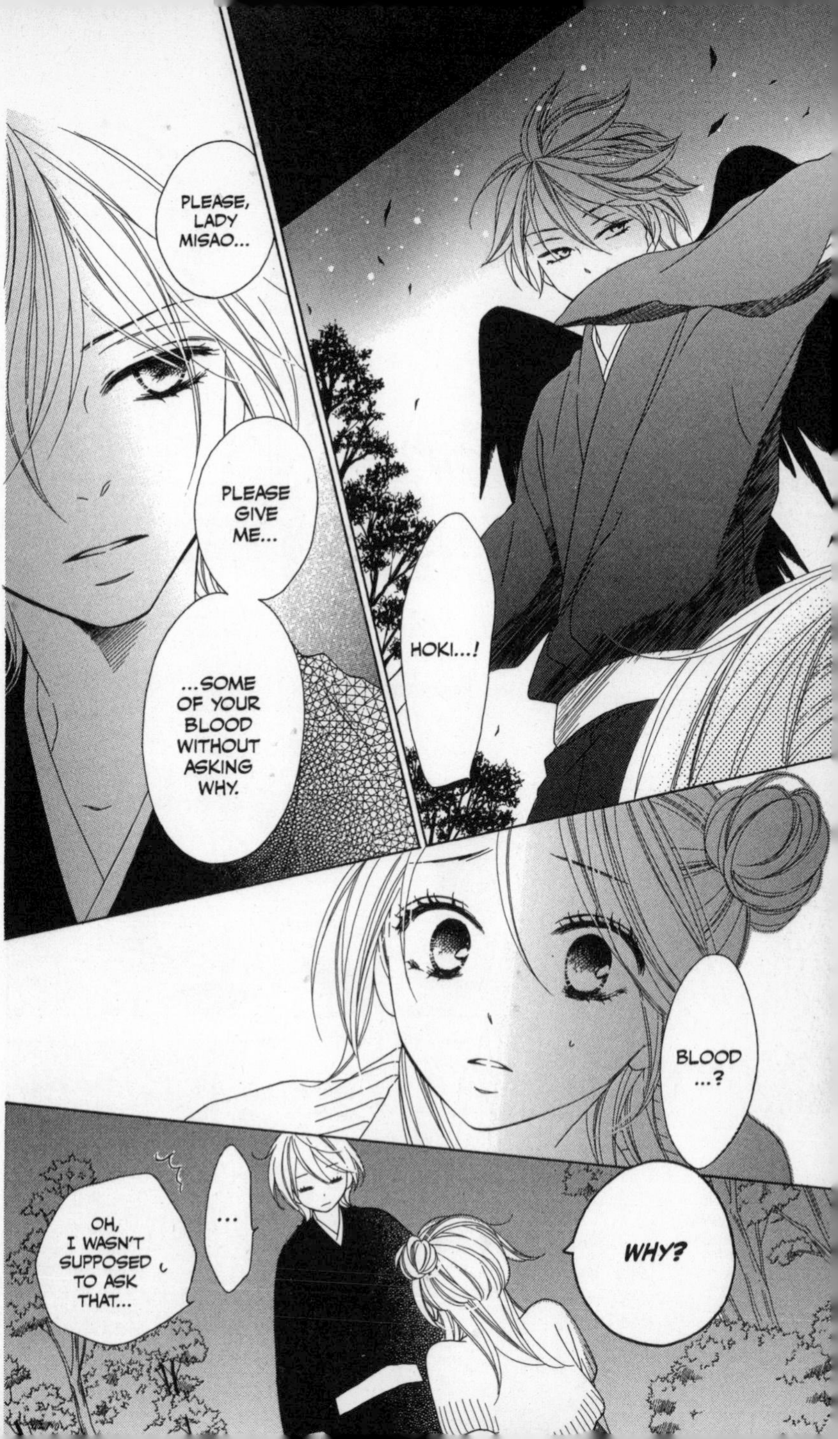
HOKI...!
PLEASE, LADY MISAO...
PLEASE GIVE ME...
...SOME OF YOUR BLOOD WITHOUT ASKING WHY.
BLOOD ...?
WHY?
...
OH, I WASN'T SUPPOSED TO ASK THAT...

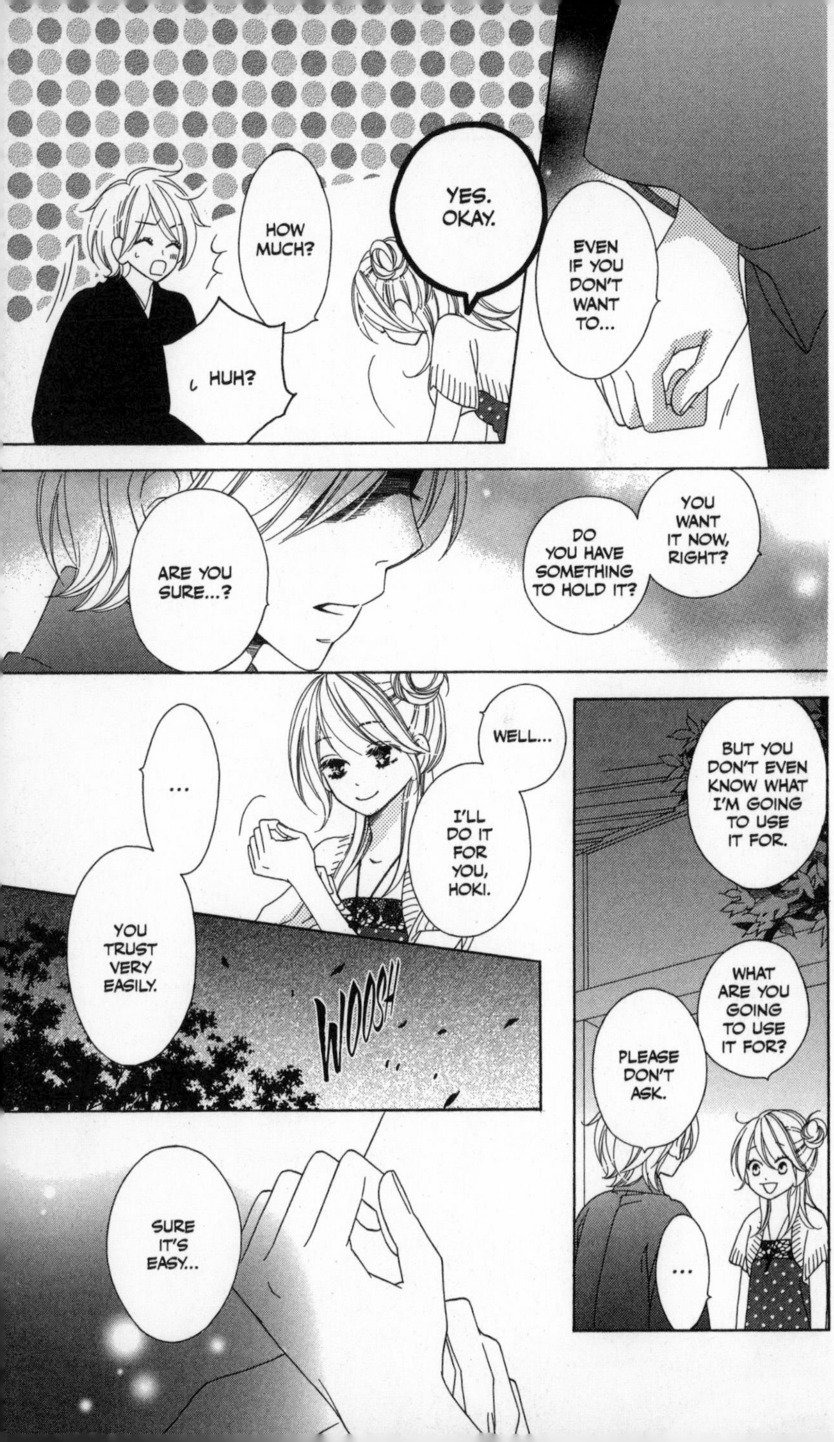
EVEN IF YOU DON'T WANT TO...
YES. OKAY.
HOW MUCH?
HUH?
YOU WANT IT NOW, RIGHT?
DO YOU HAVE SOMETHING TO HOLD IT?
ARE YOU SURE...?
BUT YOU DON'T EVEN KNOW WHAT I'M GOING TO USE IT FOR.
WHAT ARE YOU GOING TO USE IT FOR?
PLEASE DON'T ASK.
...
WELL...
I'LL DO IT FOR YOU, HOKI.
...
YOU TRUST VERY EASILY.
WOOSH
SURE IT'S EASY...

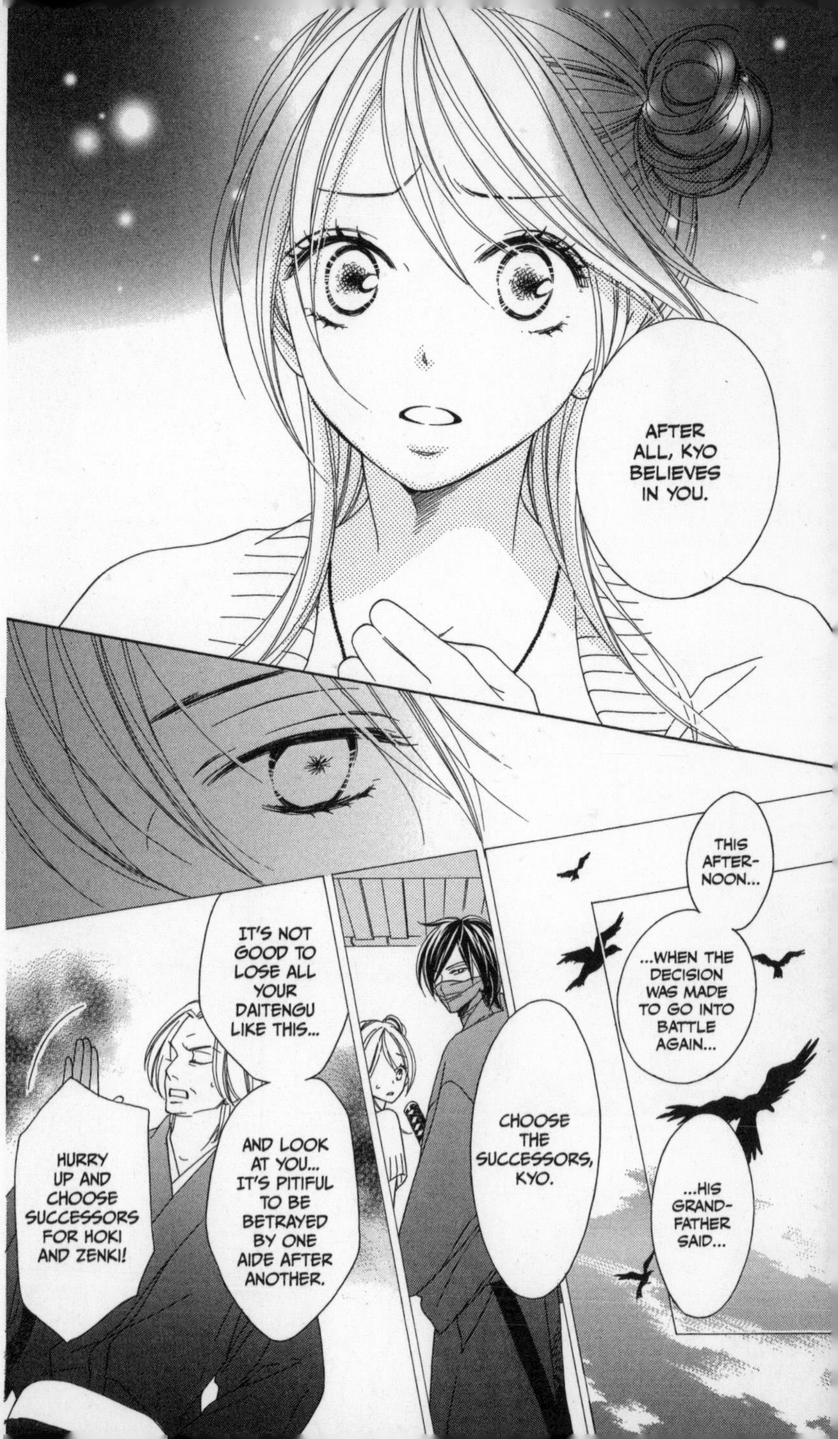
AFTER ALL, KYO BELIEVES IN YOU.
THIS AFTER-NOON...
...WHEN THE DECISION WAS MADE TO GO INTO BATTLE AGAIN...
...HIS GRAND-FATHER SAID...
CHOOSE THE SUCCESSORS, KYO.
IT'S NOT GOOD TO LOSE ALL YOUR DAITENGU LIKE THIS...
AND LOOK AT YOU... IT'S PITIFUL TO BE BETRAYED BY ONE AIDE AFTER ANOTHER.
HURRY UP AND CHOOSE SUCCESSORS FOR HOKI AND ZENKI!

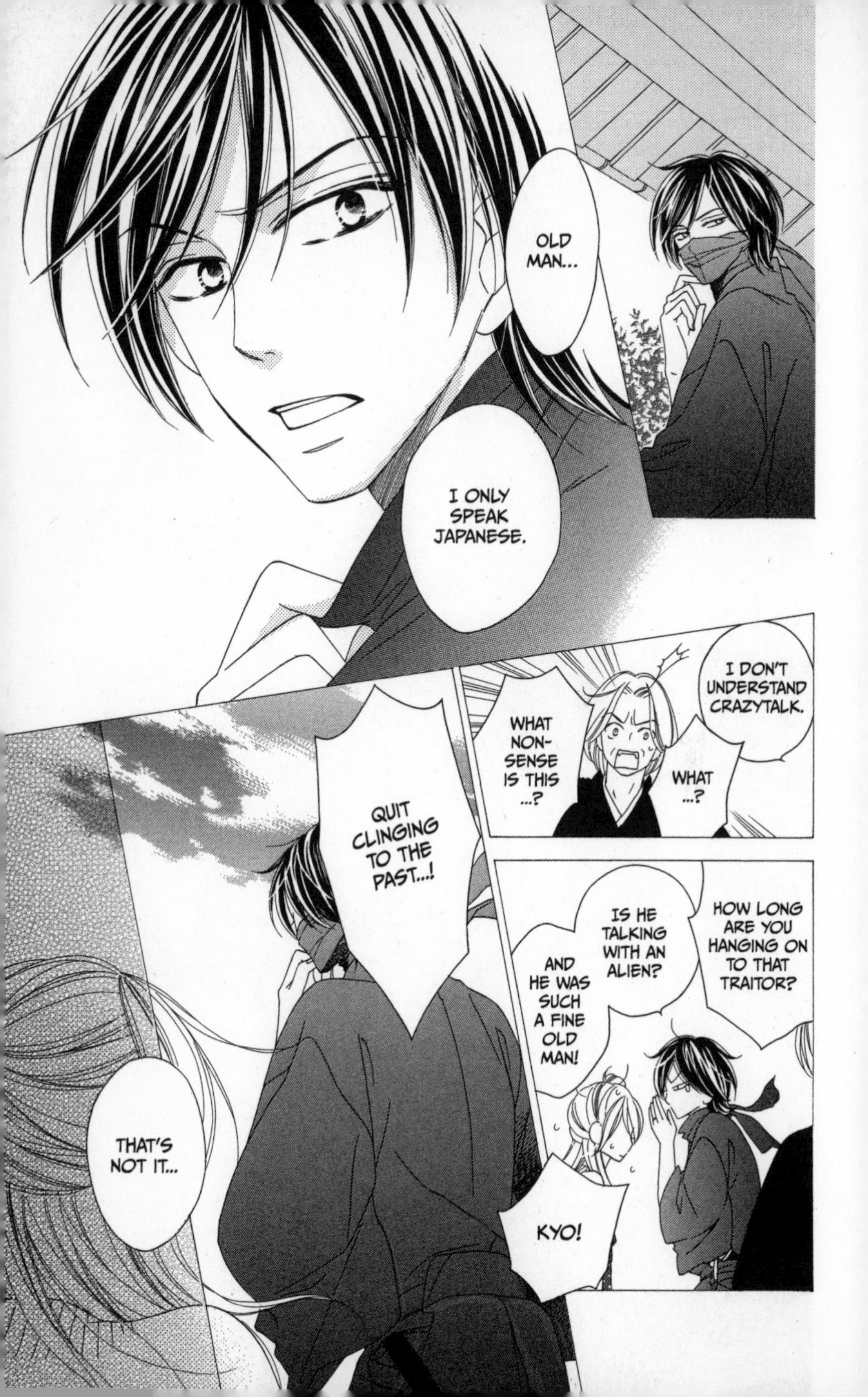
OLD MAN...
I ONLY SPEAK JAPANESE.
I DON'T UNDERSTAND CRAZYTALK.
WHAT ...?
WHAT NON-SENSE IS THIS ...?
HOW LONG ARE YOU HANGING ON TO THAT TRAITOR?
IS HE TALKING WITH AN ALIEN?
AND HE WAS SUCH A FINE OLD MAN!
KYO!
QUIT CLINGING TO THE PAST...!
THAT'S NOT IT...

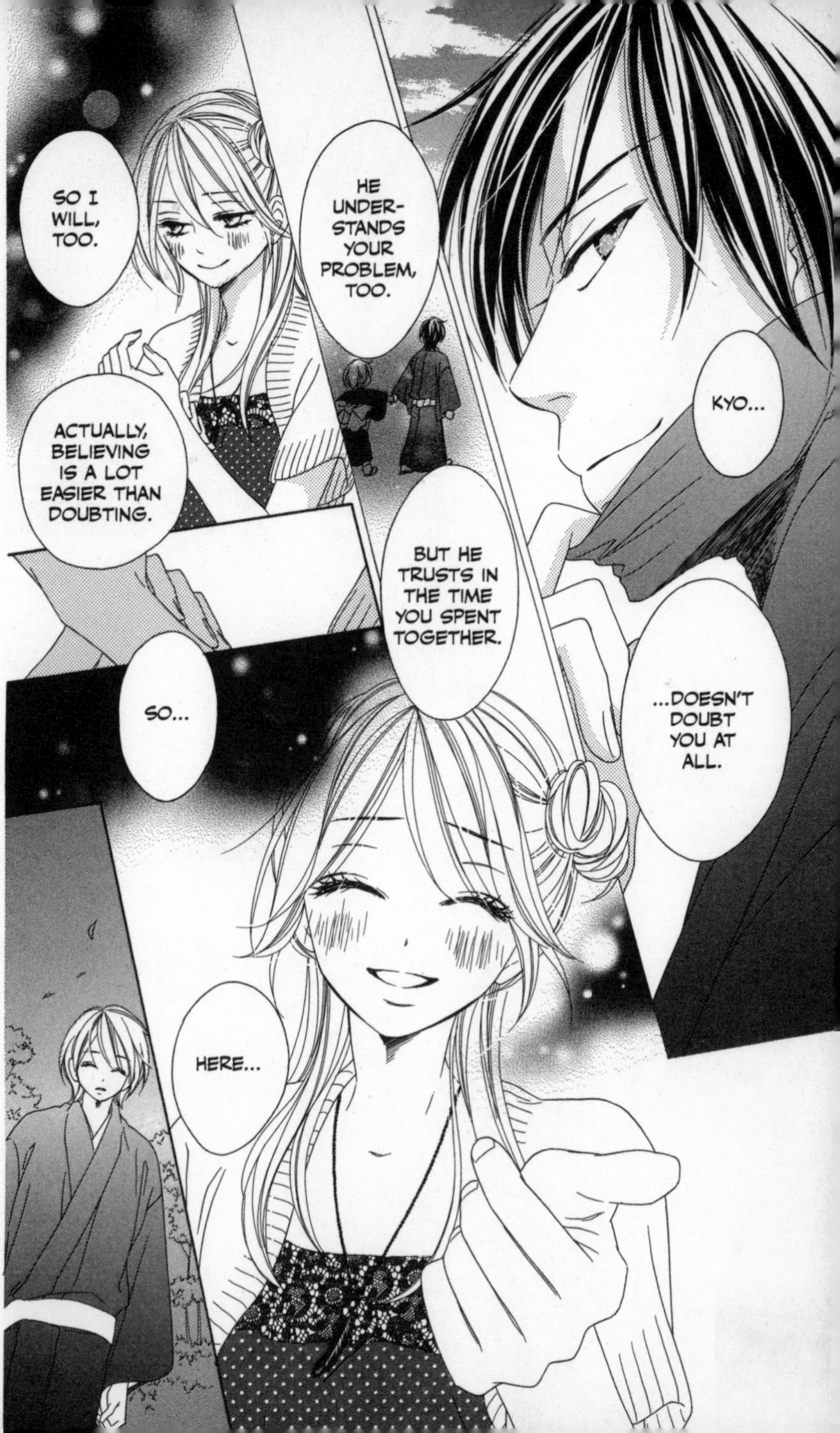
KYO...
...DOESN'T DOUBT YOU AT ALL.
HE UNDER-STANDS YOUR PROBLEM, TOO.
BUT HE TRUSTS IN THE TIME YOU SPENT TOGETHER.
SO I WILL, TOO.
ACTUALLY, BELIEVING IS A LOT EASIER THAN DOUBTING.
SO...
HERE...

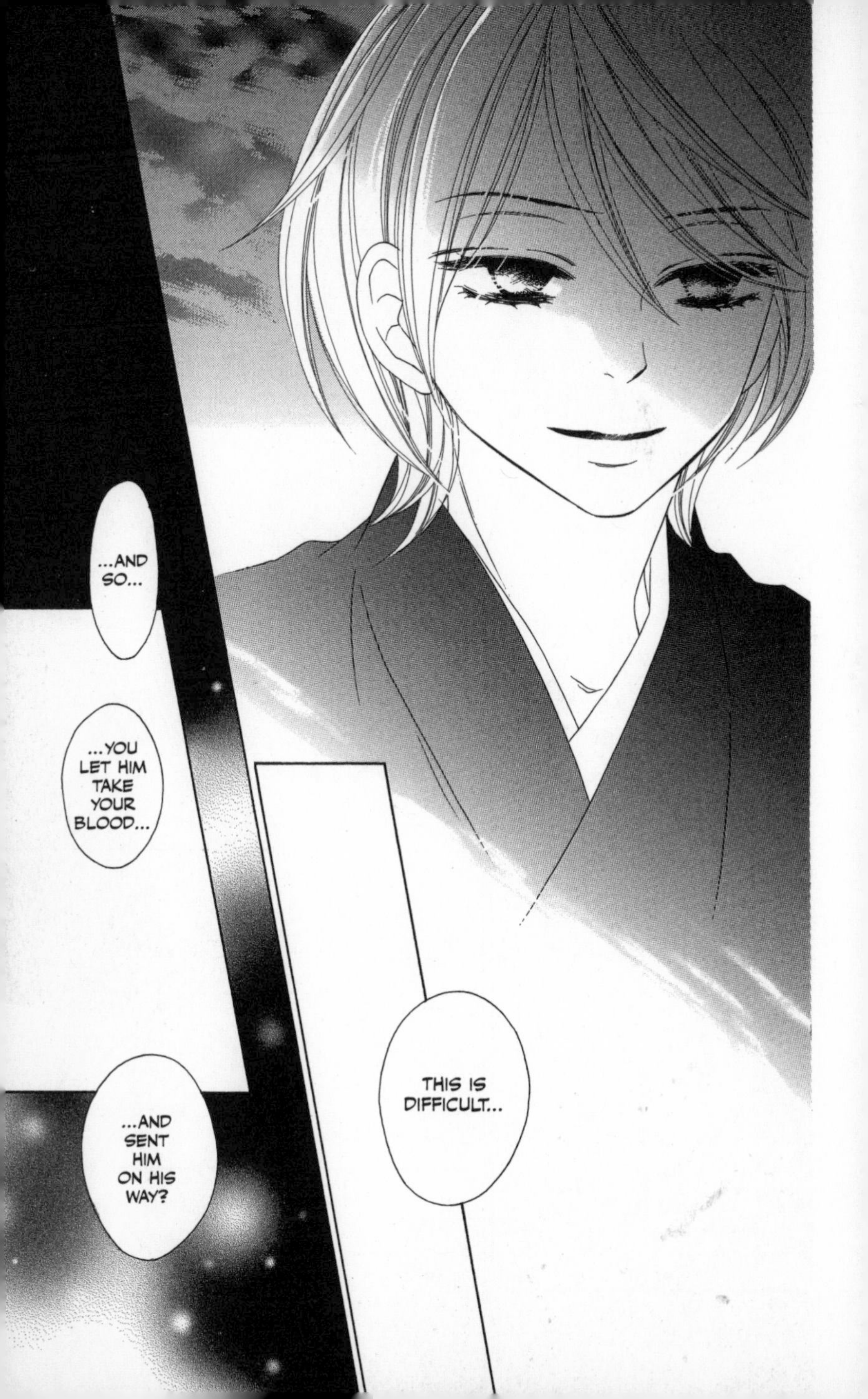
THIS IS DIFFICULT...
...AND SO...
...YOU LET HIM TAKE YOUR BLOOD...
...AND SENT HIM ON HIS WAY?

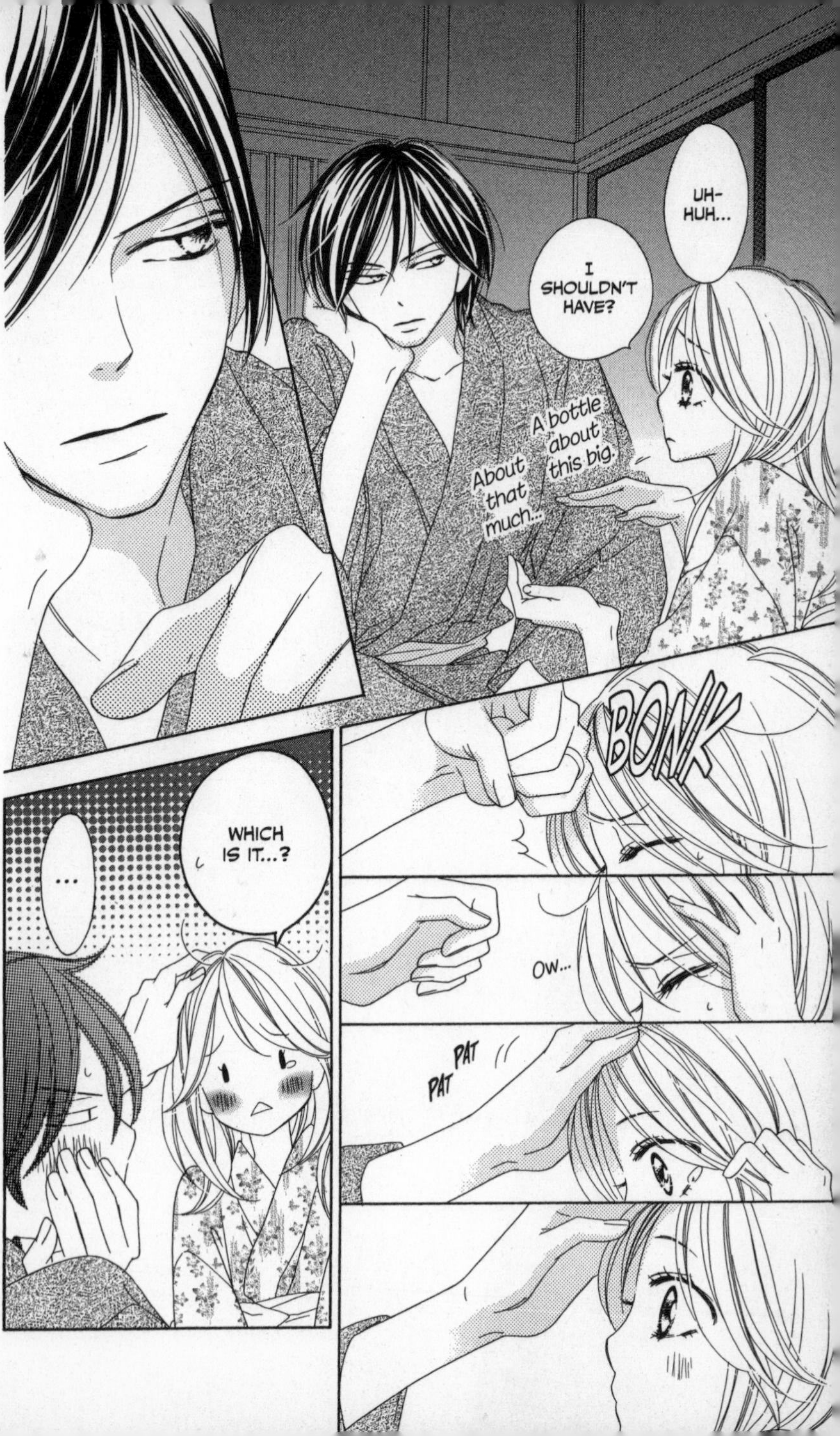
UH-HUH...
I SHOULDN'T HAVE?
A bottle about this big.
About that much...
BONK
OW...
PAT PAT
WHICH IS IT...?
...

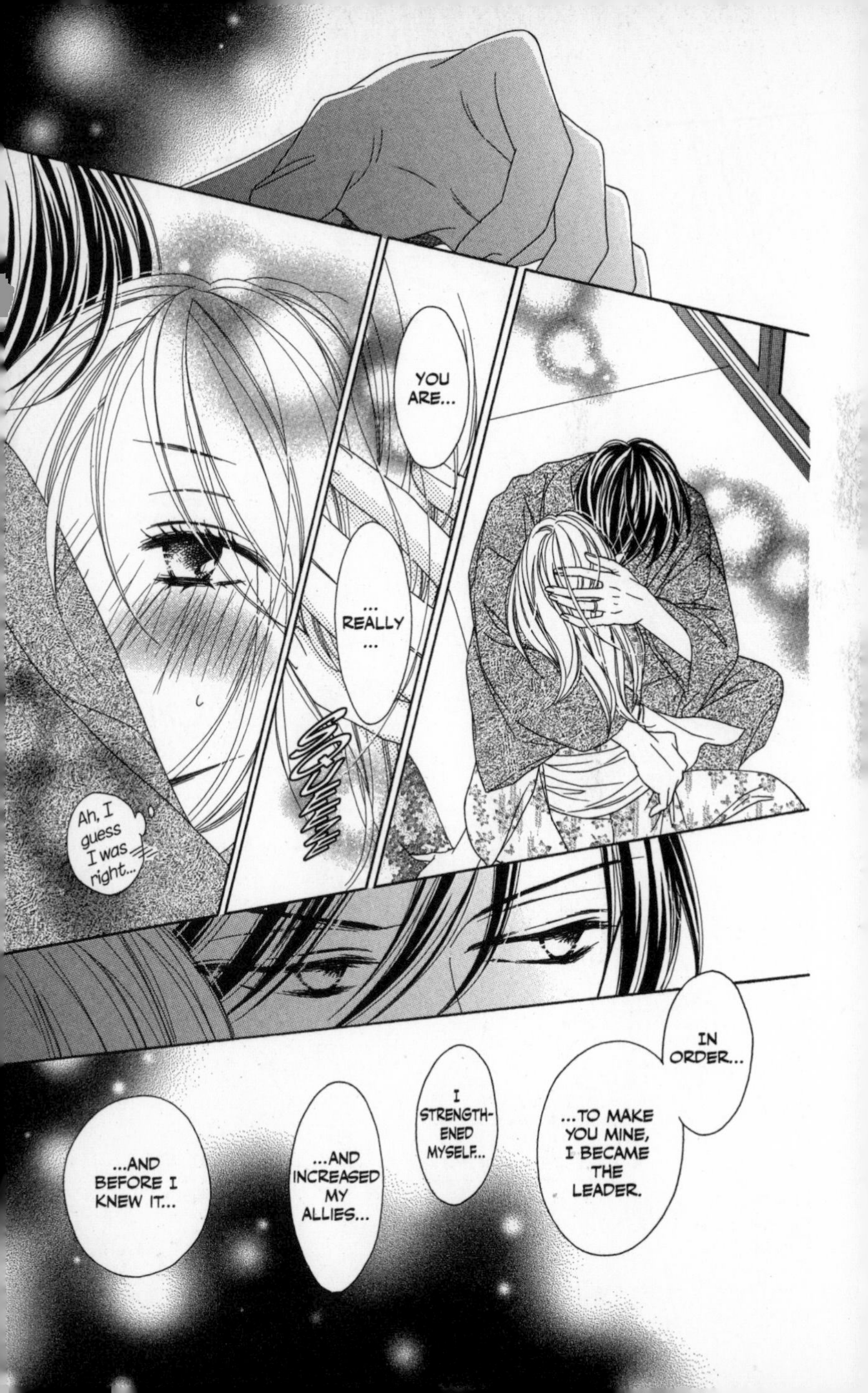
YOU ARE...
...REALLY...
Ah, I guess I was right...
IN ORDER...
...TO MAKE YOU MINE, I BECAME THE LEADER.
I STRENGTH-ENED MYSELF...
...AND INCREASED MY ALLIES...
...AND BEFORE I KNEW IT...

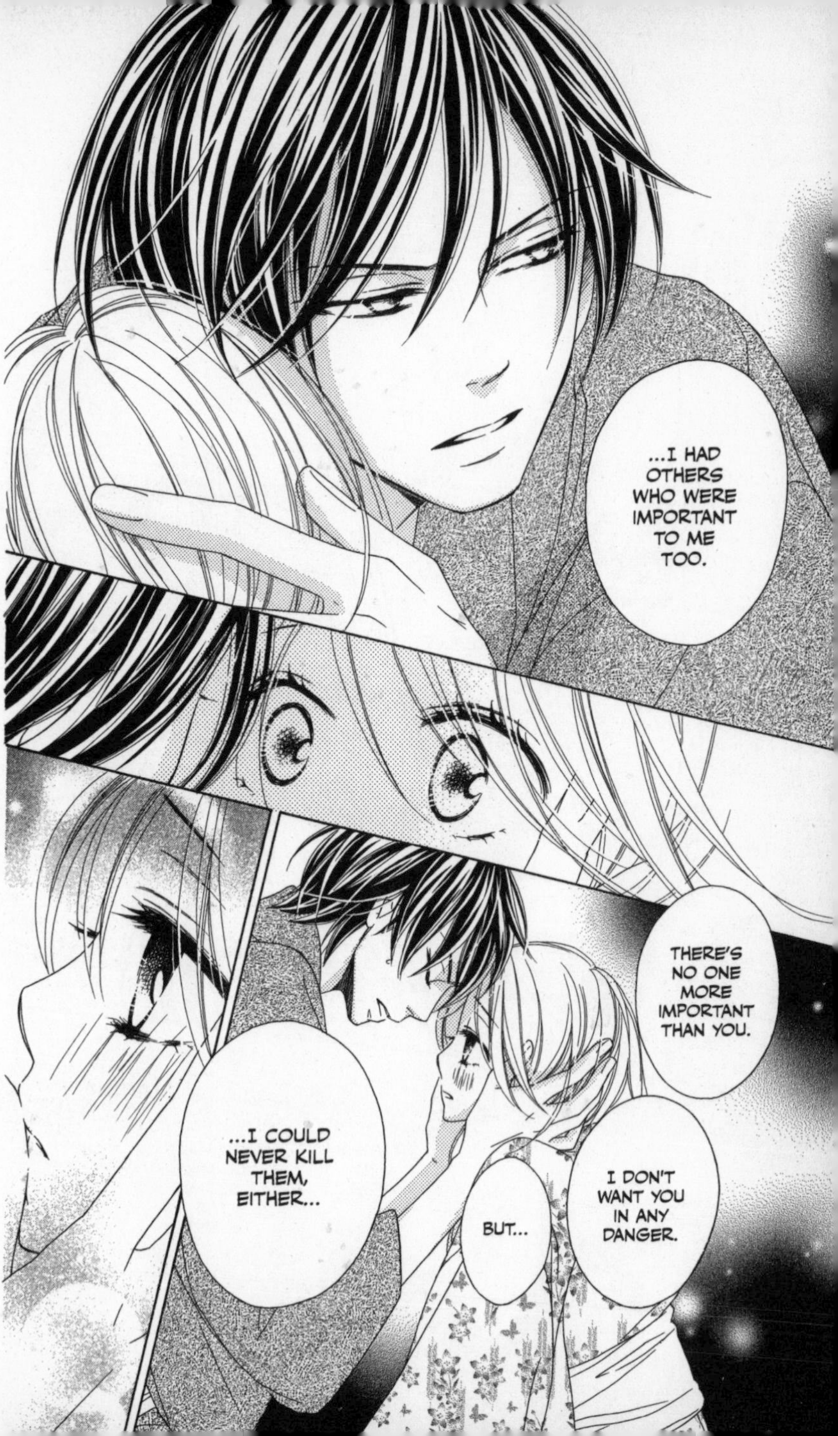
...I HAD OTHERS WHO WERE IMPORTANT TO ME TOO.
THERE'S NO ONE MORE IMPORTANT THAN YOU.
I DON'T WANT YOU IN ANY DANGER.
BUT...
...I COULD NEVER KILL THEM, EITHER...

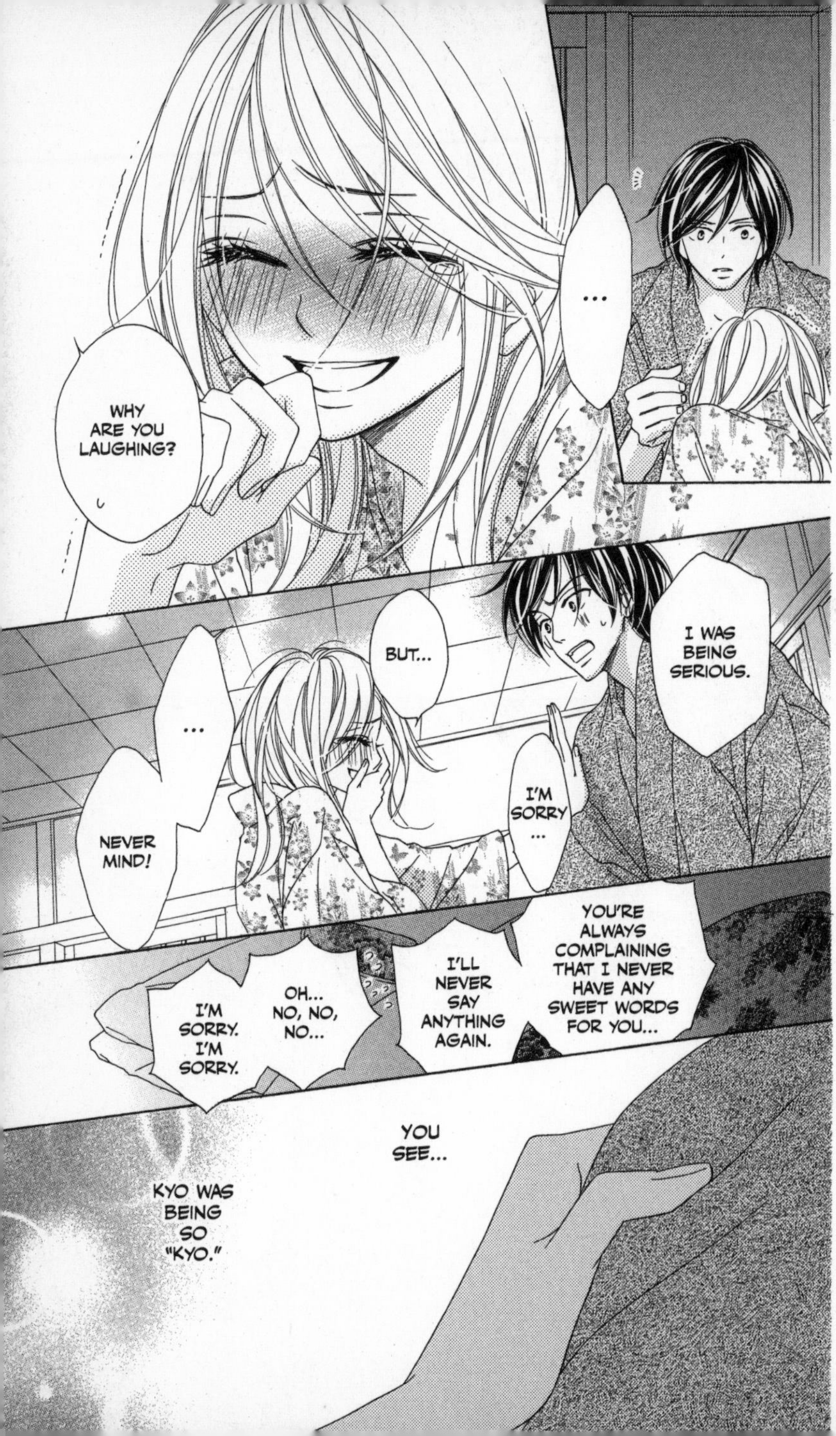
...
WHY ARE YOU LAUGHING?
I WAS BEING SERIOUS.
BUT...
I'M SORRY...
...
NEVER MIND!
YOU'RE ALWAYS COMPLAINING THAT I NEVER HAVE ANY SWEET WORDS FOR YOU...
I'LL NEVER SAY ANYTHING AGAIN.
OH... NO, NO, NO...
I'M SORRY. I'M SORRY.
YOU SEE...
KYO WAS BEING SO "KYO."

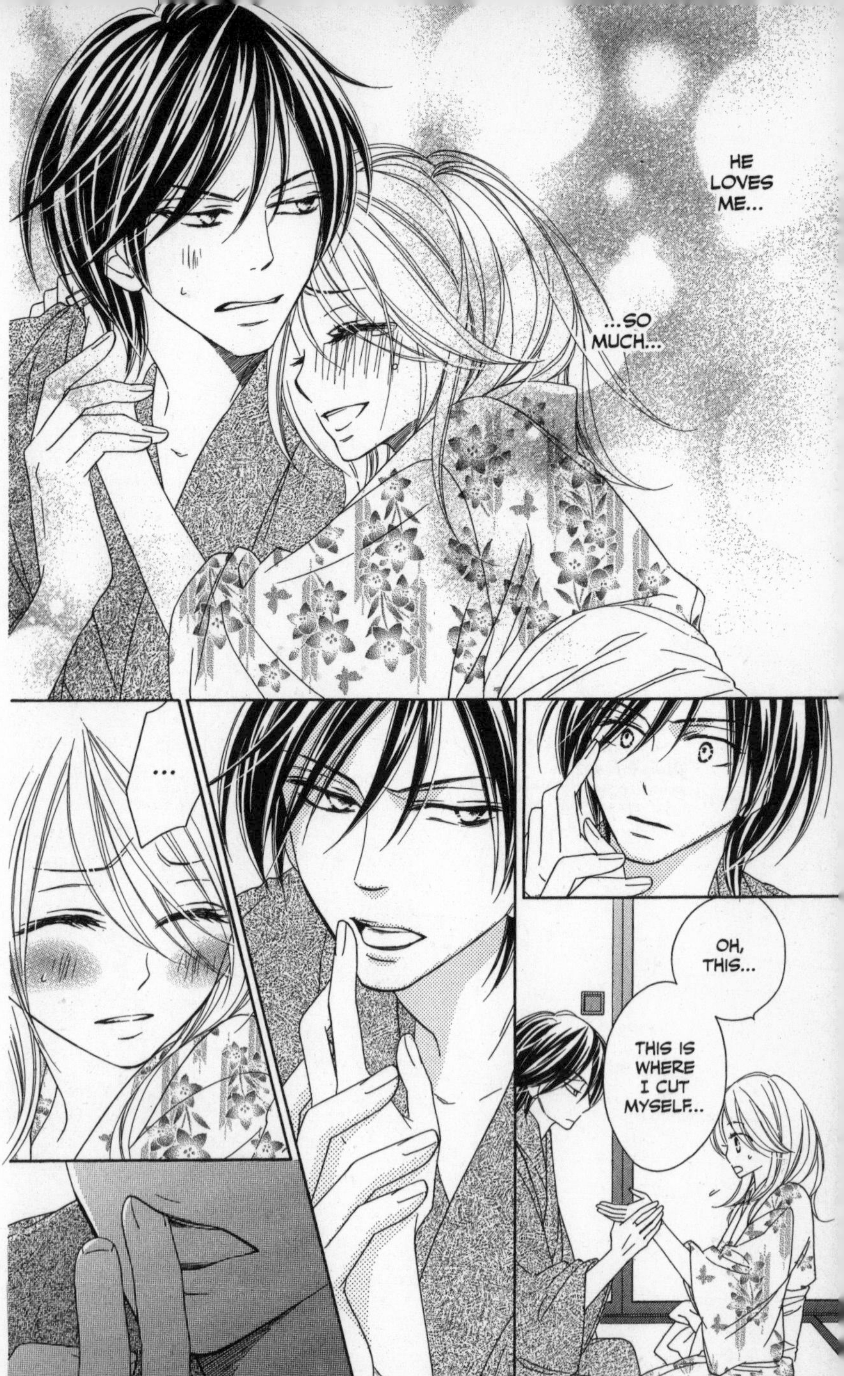
HE LOVES ME...
...SO MUCH...
OH, THIS...
THIS IS WHERE I CUT MYSELF...
...

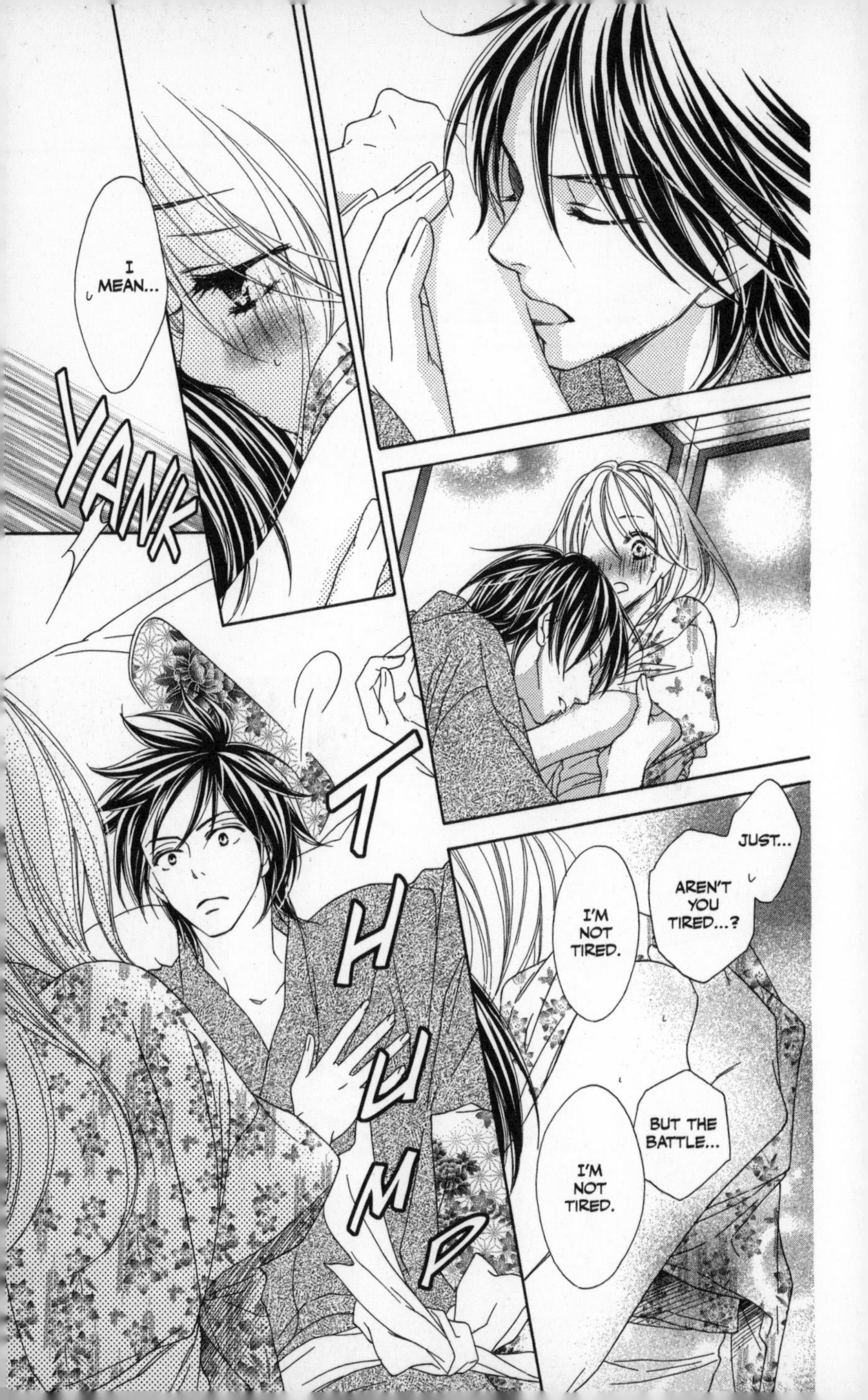
I MEAN...
YANK
JUST... AREN'T YOU TIRED...?
I'M NOT TIRED.
BUT THE BATTLE...
I'M NOT TIRED.
THUMP

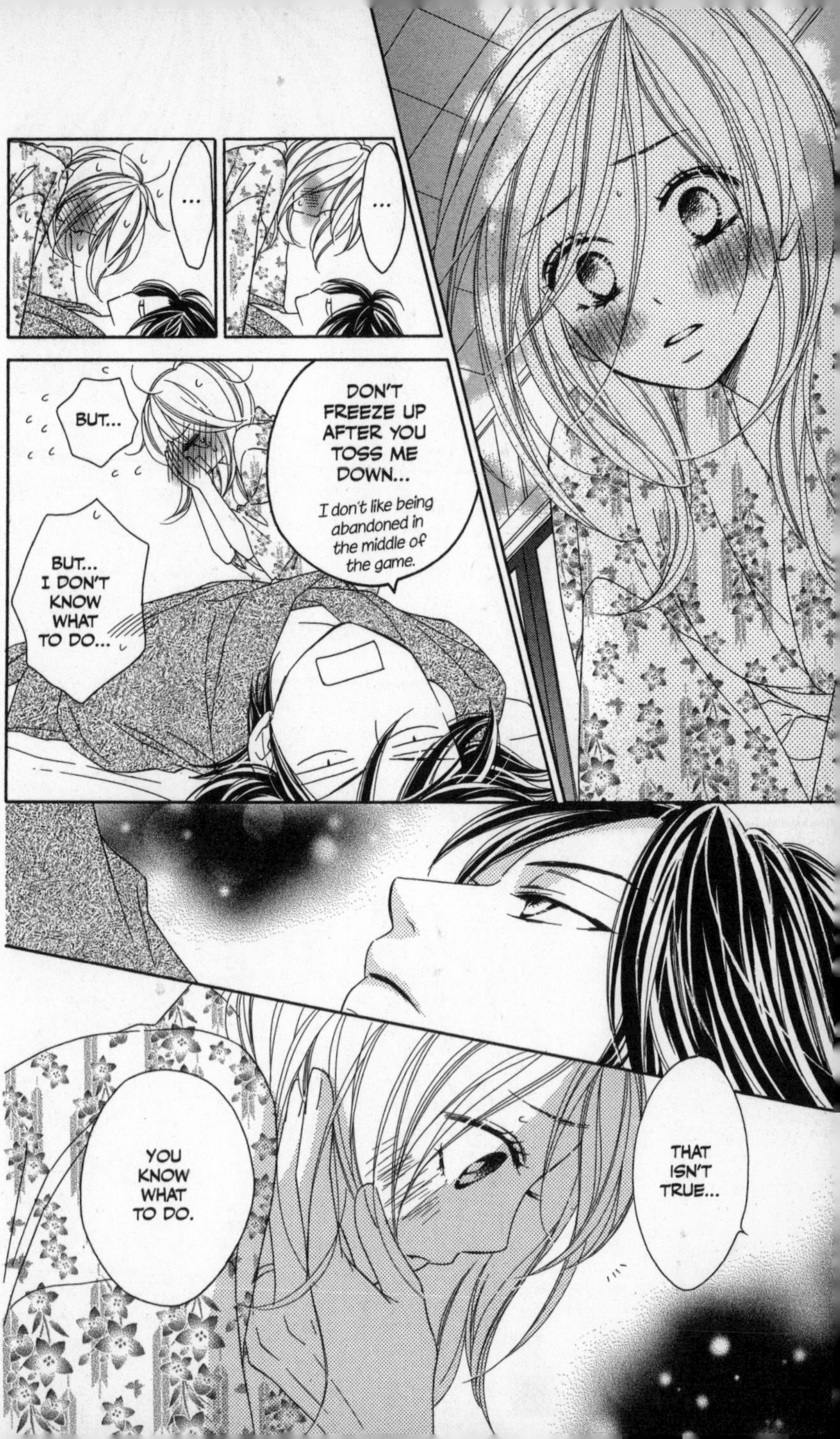
...
...
DON'T FREEZE UP AFTER YOU TOSS ME DOWN...
I don't like being abandoned in the middle of the game.
BUT...
BUT... I DON'T KNOW WHAT TO DO...
THAT ISN'T TRUE...
YOU KNOW WHAT TO DO.

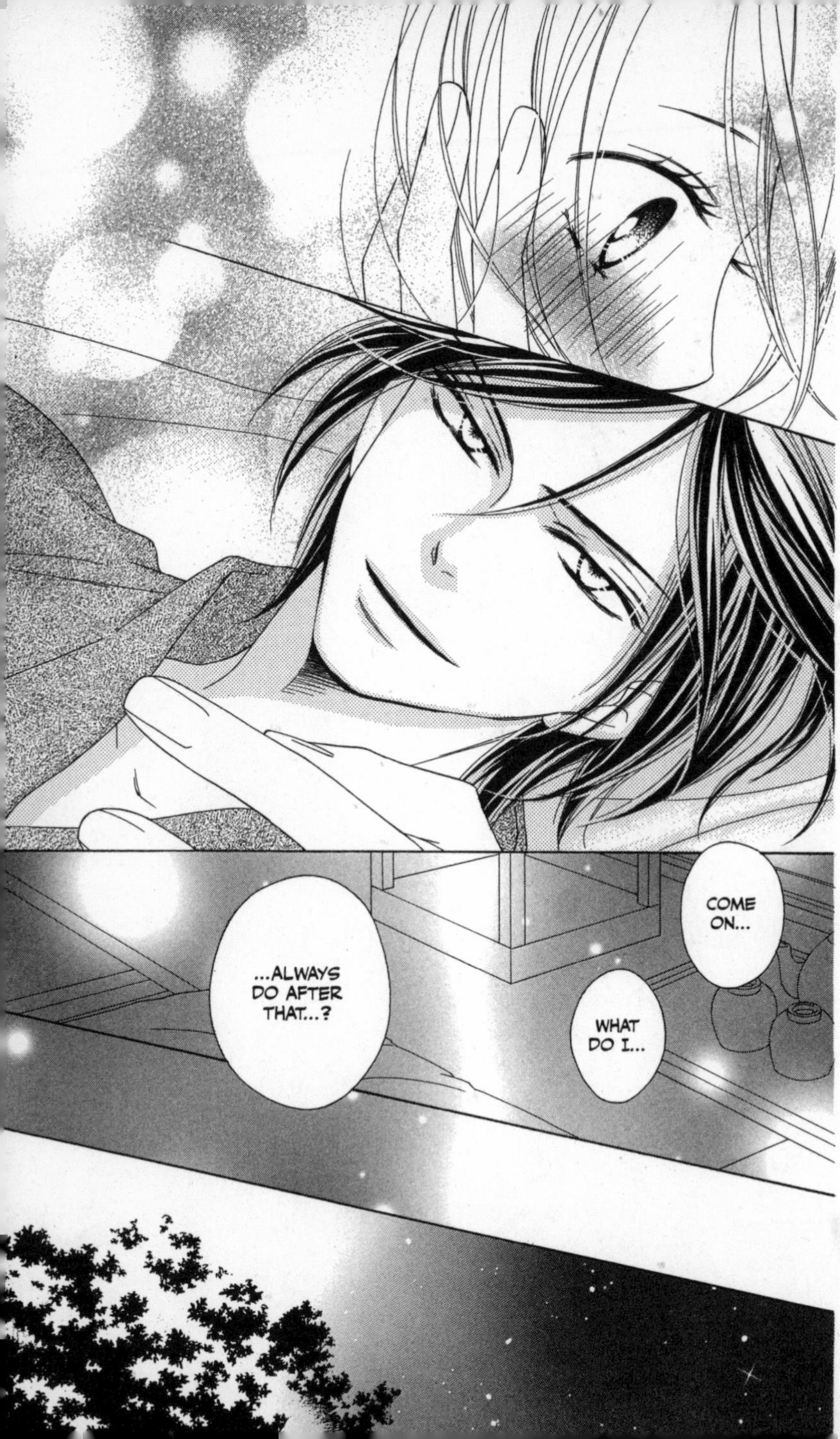
COME ON...
WHAT DO I...
...ALWAYS DO AFTER THAT...?

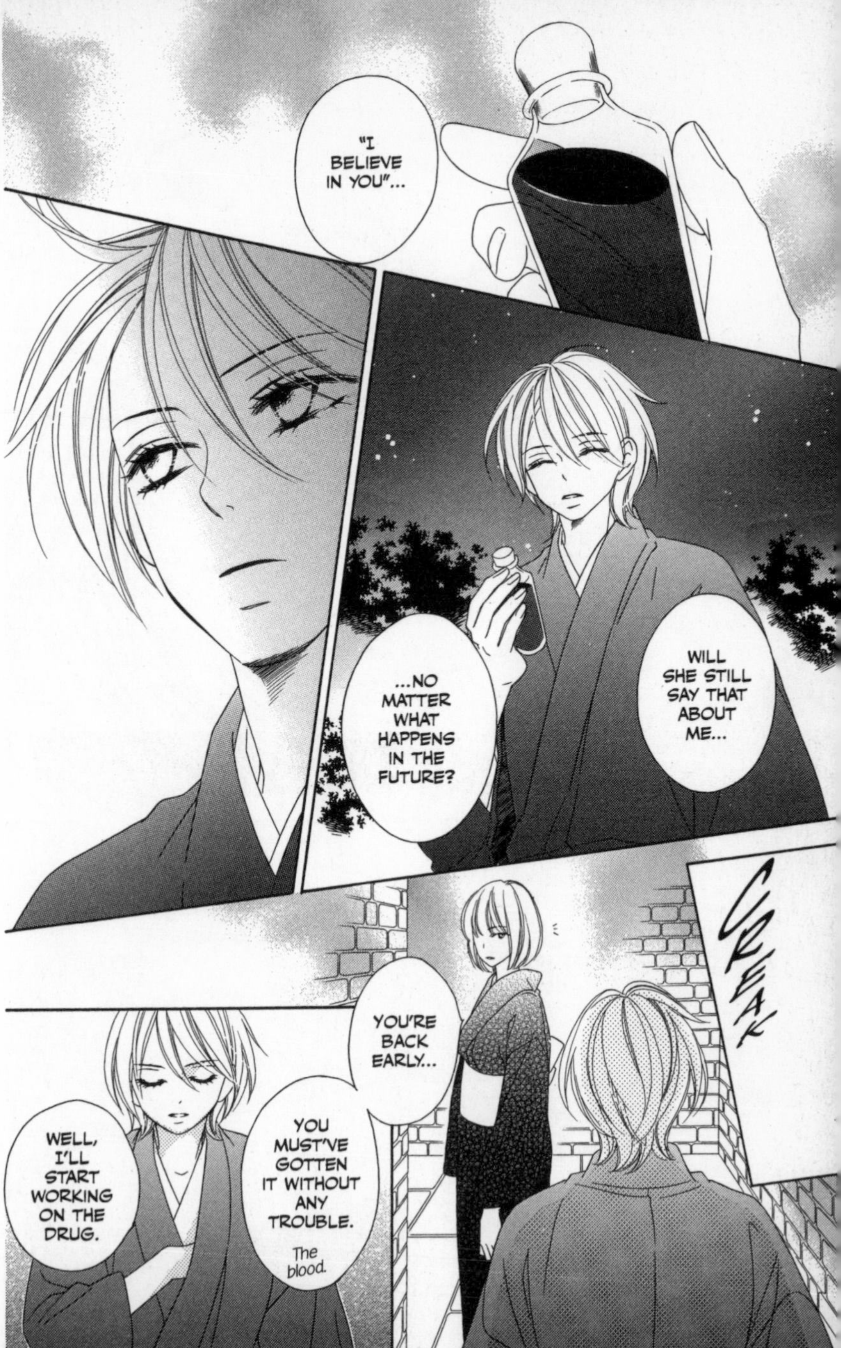
"I BELIEVE IN YOU"...
WILL SHE STILL SAY THAT ABOUT ME...
...NO MATTER WHAT HAPPENS IN THE FUTURE?
CREAK
YOU'RE BACK EARLY...
YOU MUST'VE GOTTEN IT WITHOUT ANY TROUBLE.
The blood.
WELL, I'LL START WORKING ON THE DRUG.

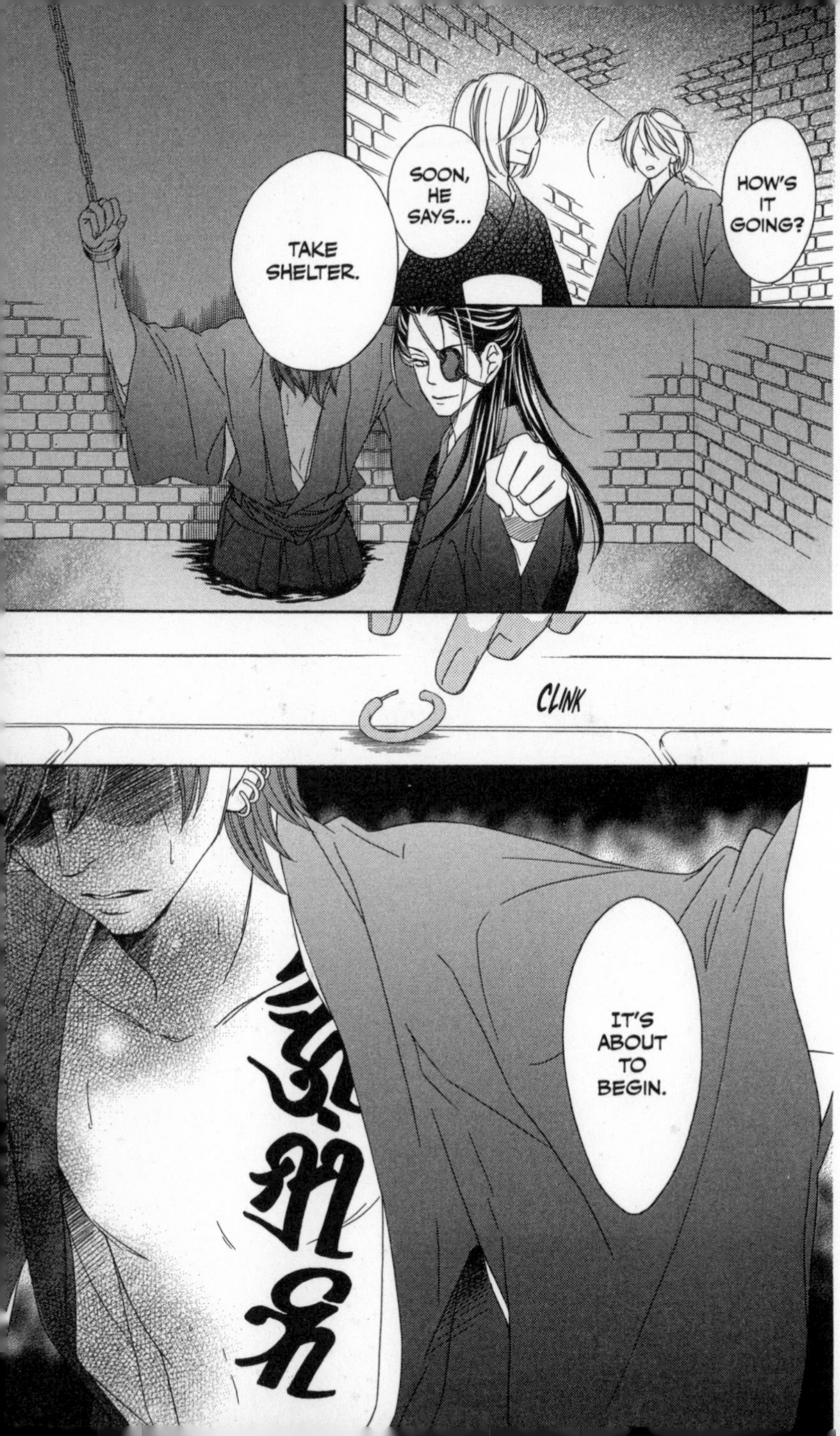
HOW'S IT GOING?
SOON, HE SAYS...
TAKE SHELTER.
CLINK
IT'S ABOUT TO BEGIN.

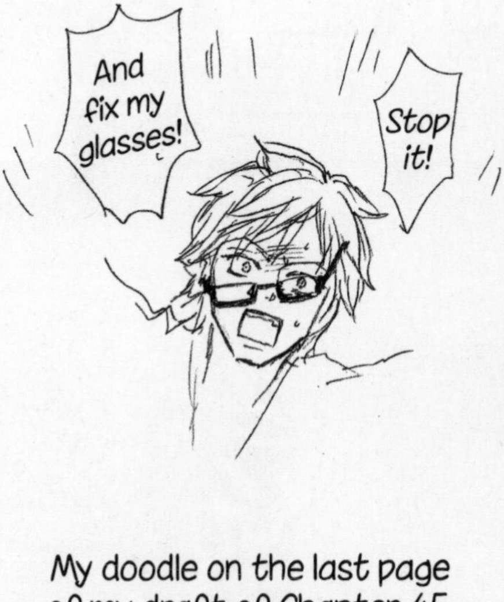
And fix my glasses!
Stop it!

My doodle on the last page
of my draft of Chapter 45.

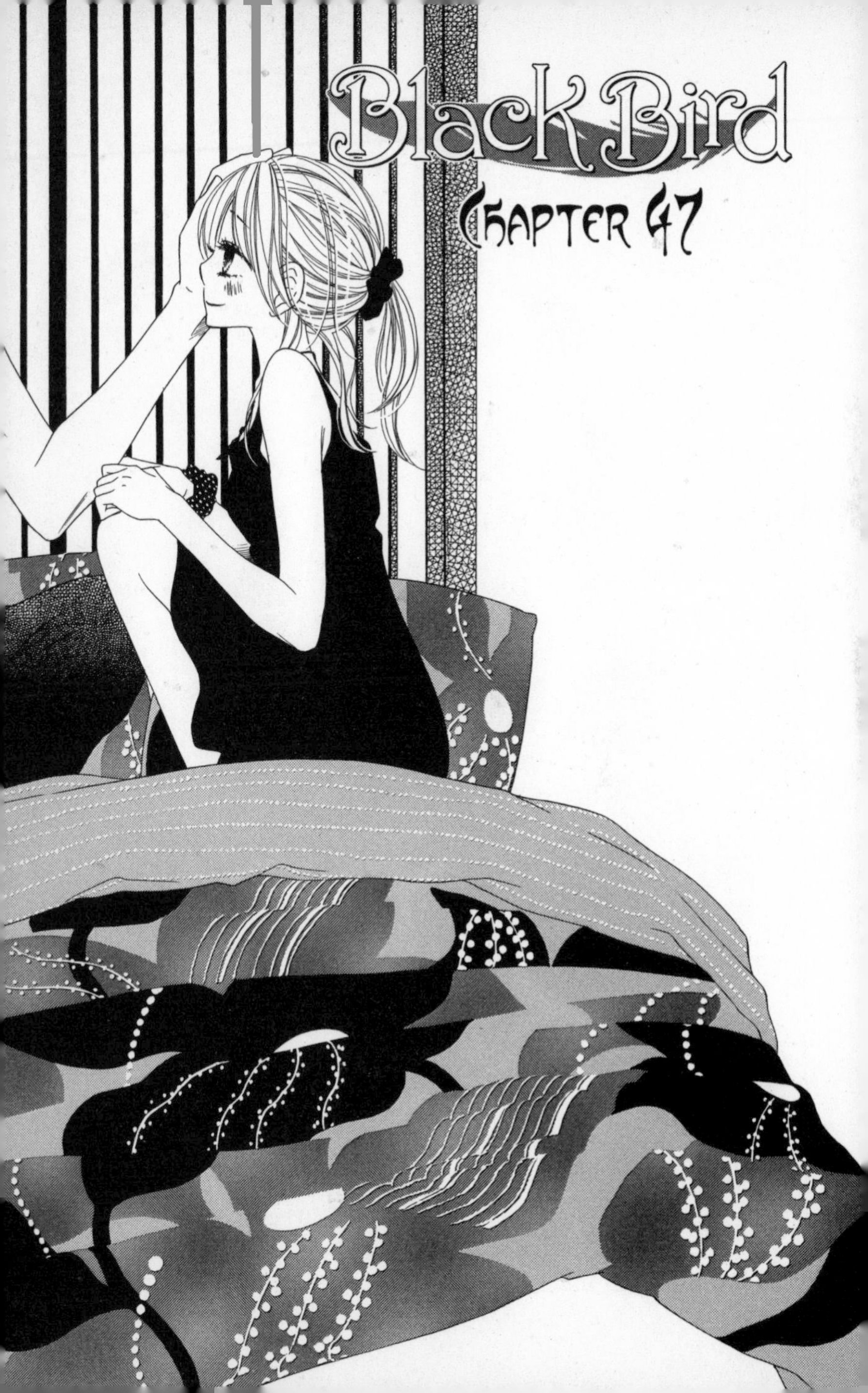
Black Bird
Chapter 47

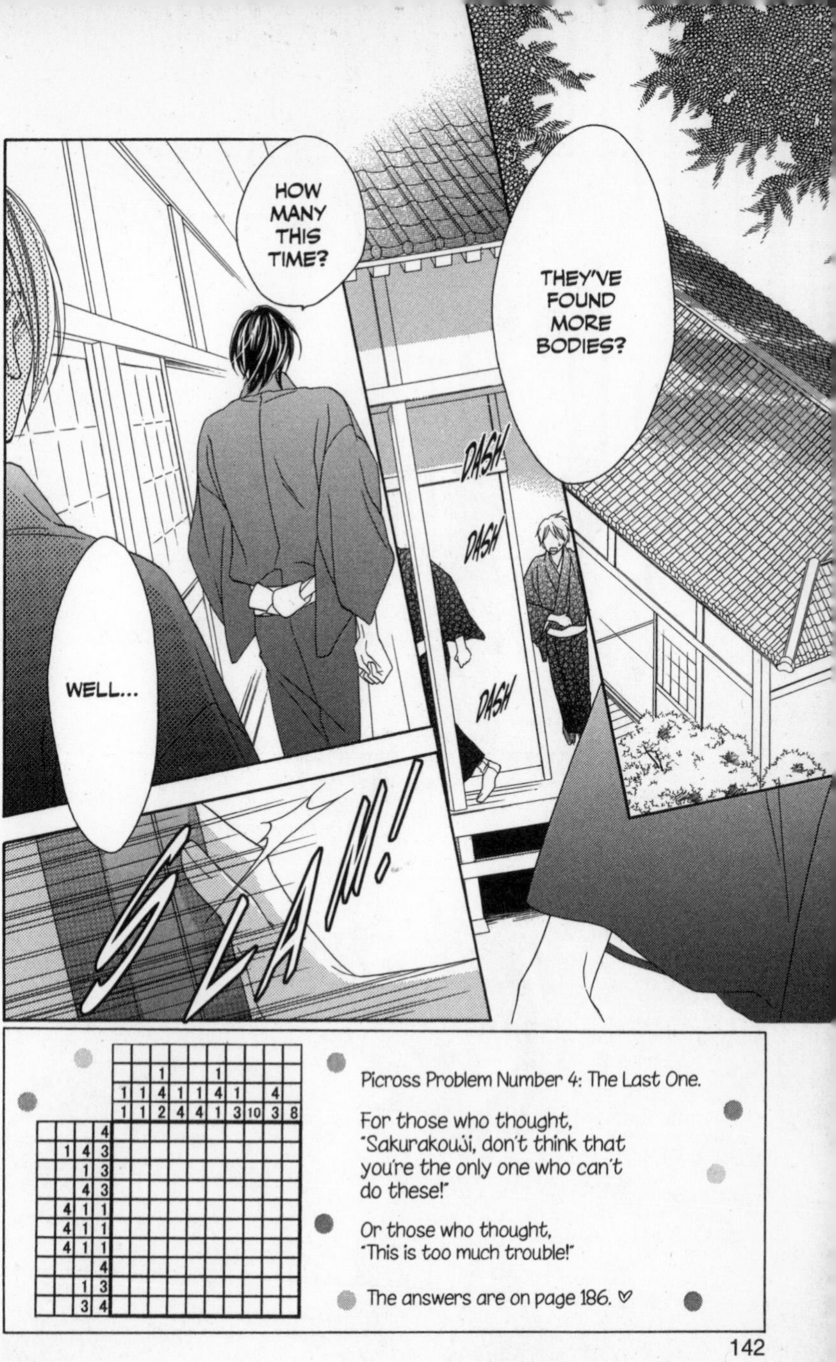
THEY'VE FOUND MORE BODIES?
HOW MANY THIS TIME?
DASH
DASH
DASH
WELL...
SLAM!

						1			1				
				1	1	4	1	1	4	1		4	
				1	1	2	4	4	1	3	10	3	8
			4										
1	4	3											
	1	3											
	4	3											
4	1	1											
4	1	1											
4	1	1											
		4											
	1	3											
	3	4											

Picross Problem Number 4: The Last One.

For those who thought, "Sakurakouji, don't think that you're the only one who can't do these!"

Or those who thought, "This is too much trouble!"

The answers are on page 186. ♡

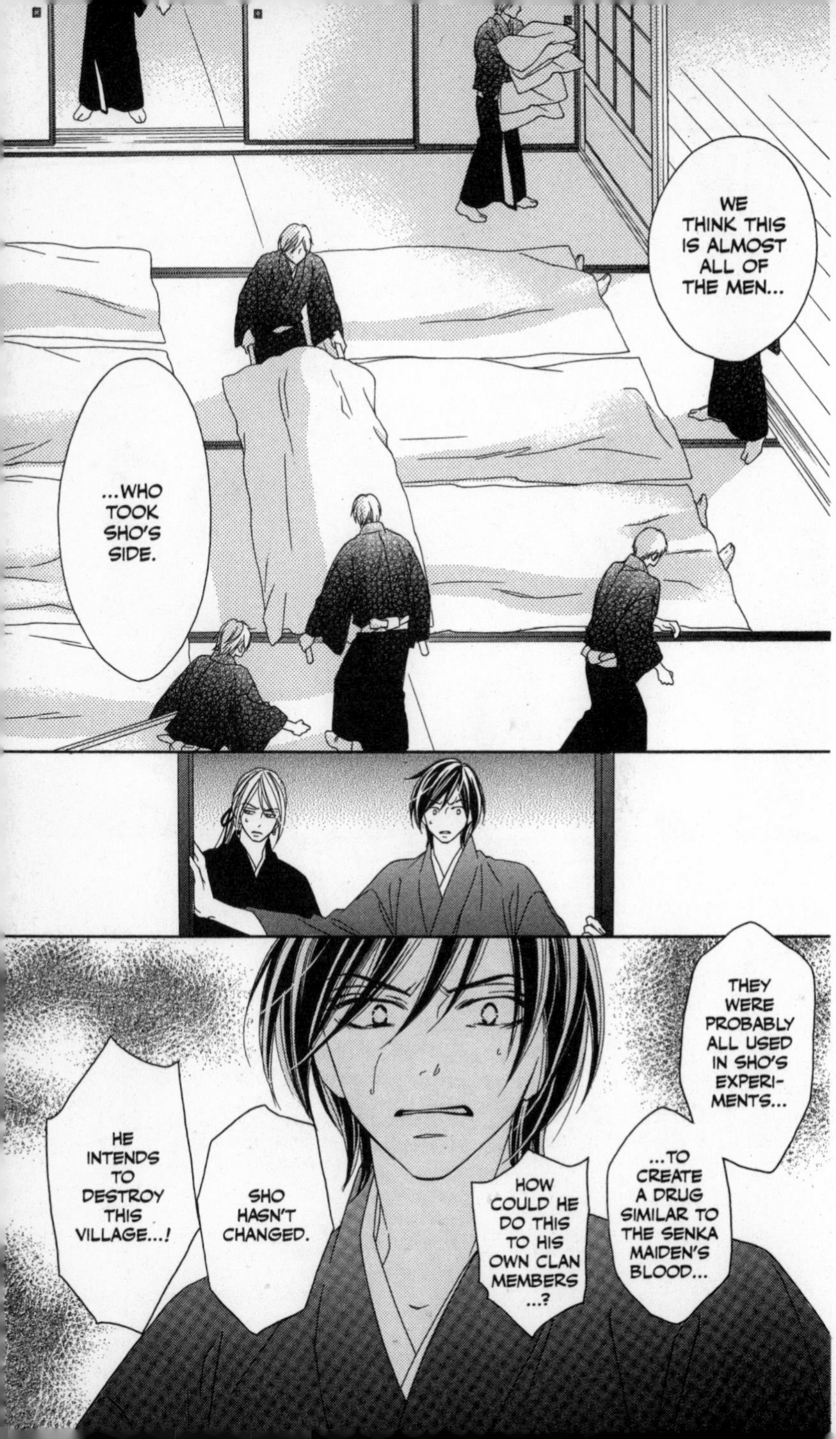
WE THINK THIS IS ALMOST ALL OF THE MEN...
...WHO TOOK SHO'S SIDE.
THEY WERE PROBABLY ALL USED IN SHO'S EXPERI- MENTS...
...TO CREATE A DRUG SIMILAR TO THE SENKA MAIDEN'S BLOOD...
HOW COULD HE DO THIS TO HIS OWN CLAN MEMBERS ...?
SHO HASN'T CHANGED.
HE INTENDS TO DESTROY THIS VILLAGE...!

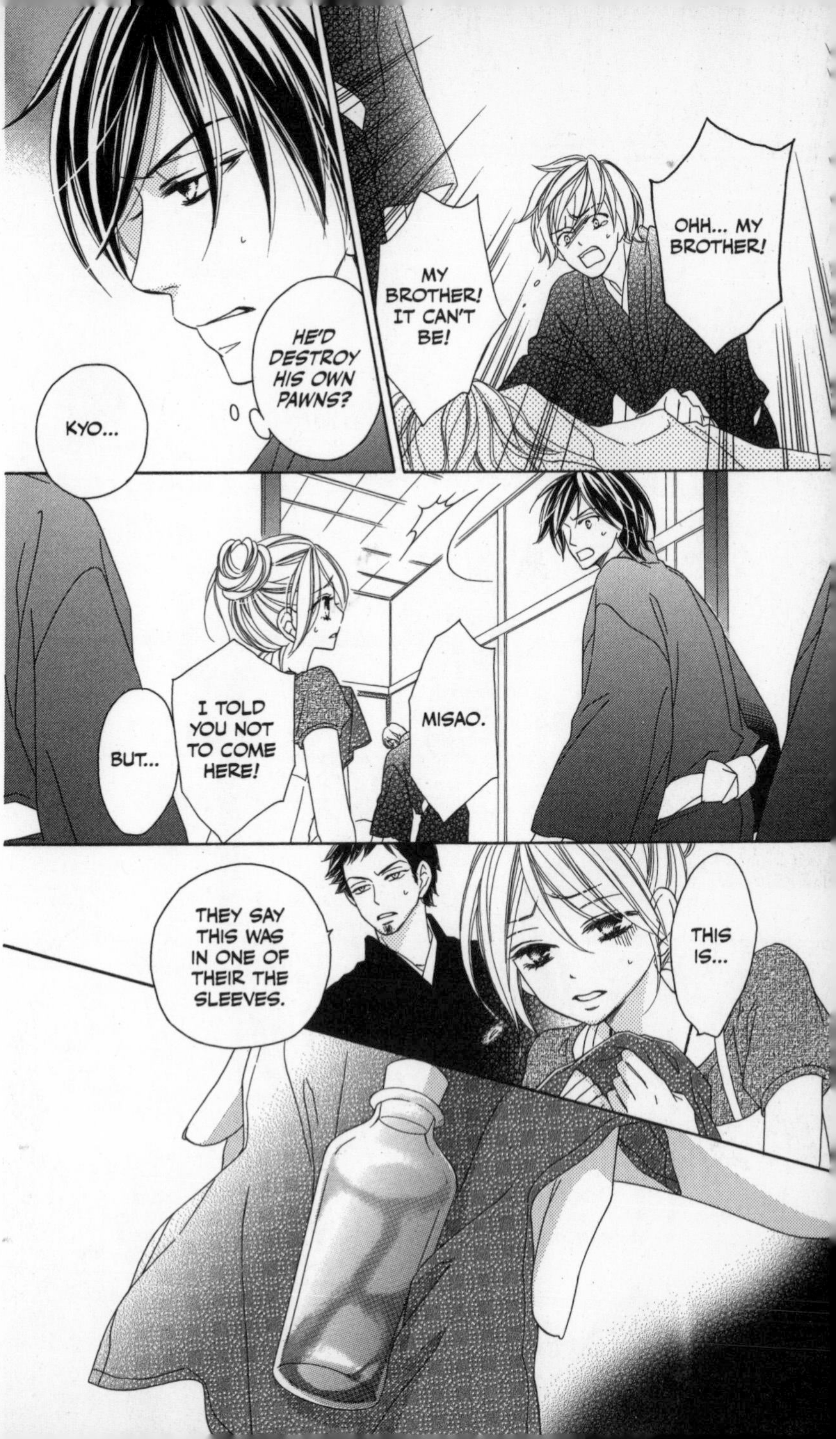
OHH... MY BROTHER!
MY BROTHER! IT CAN'T BE!
HE'D DESTROY HIS OWN PAWNS?
KYO...
MISAO.
I TOLD YOU NOT TO COME HERE!
BUT...
THIS IS...
THEY SAY THIS WAS IN ONE OF THEIR THE SLEEVES.

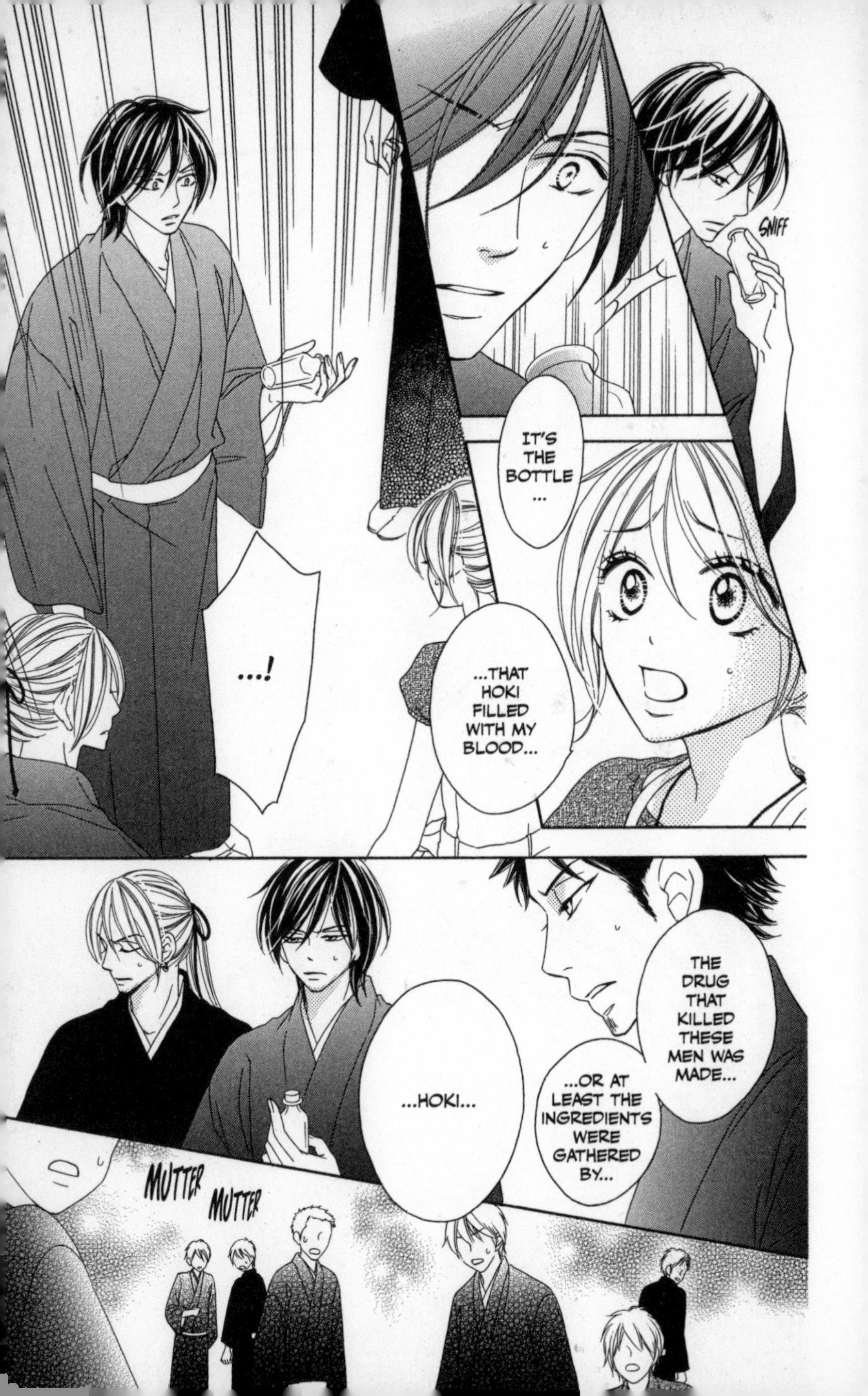
SNIFF
IT'S THE BOTTLE...
...THAT HOKI FILLED WITH MY BLOOD...
...!
THE DRUG THAT KILLED THESE MEN WAS MADE...
...OR AT LEAST THE INGREDIENTS WERE GATHERED BY...
...HOKI...
MUTTER
MUTTER

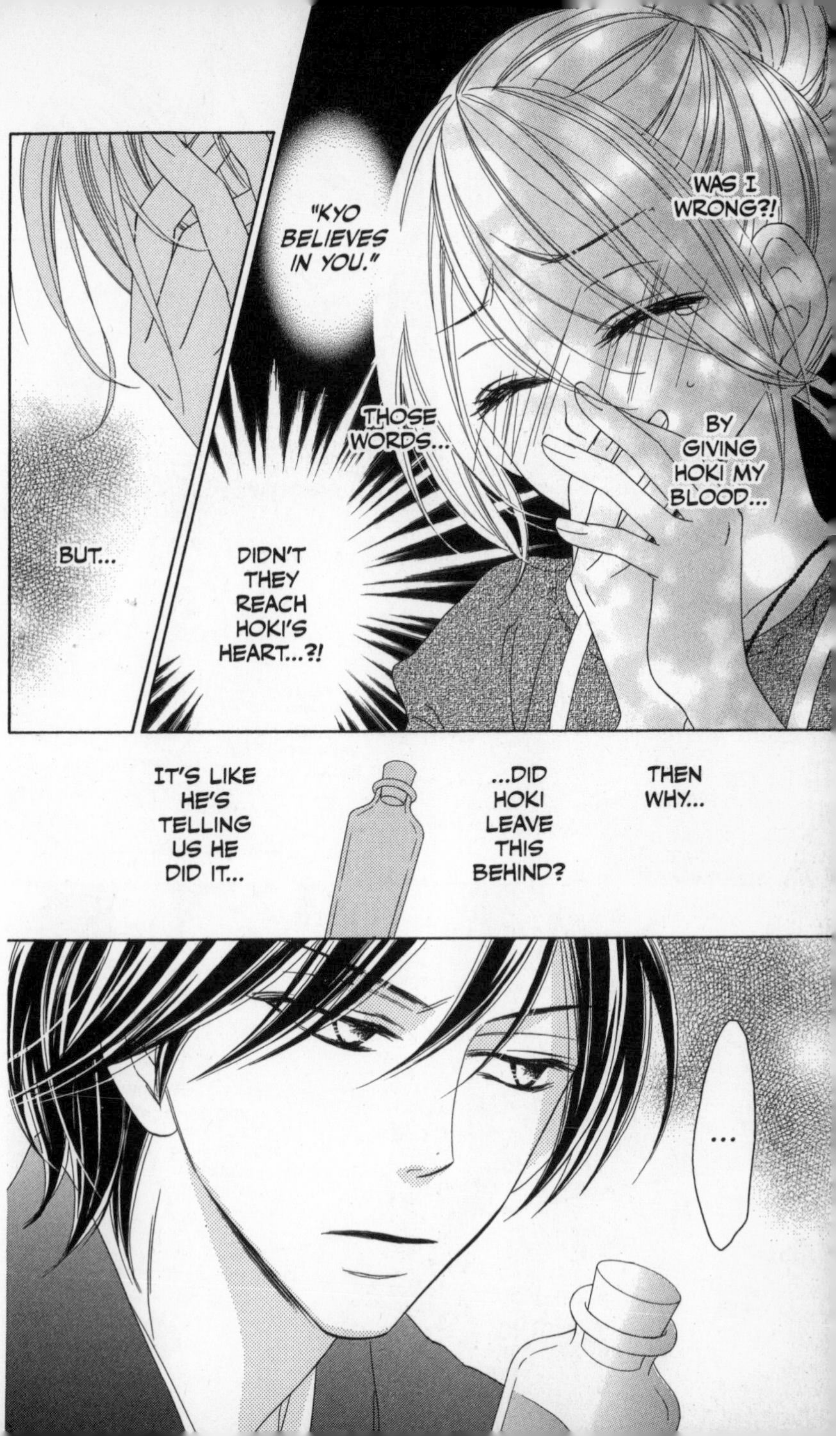
WAS I WRONG?!
BY GIVING HOKI MY BLOOD...
"KYO BELIEVES IN YOU."
THOSE WORDS...
DIDN'T THEY REACH HOKI'S HEART...?!
BUT...
THEN WHY...
...DID HOKI LEAVE THIS BEHIND?
IT'S LIKE HE'S TELLING US HE DID IT...
...

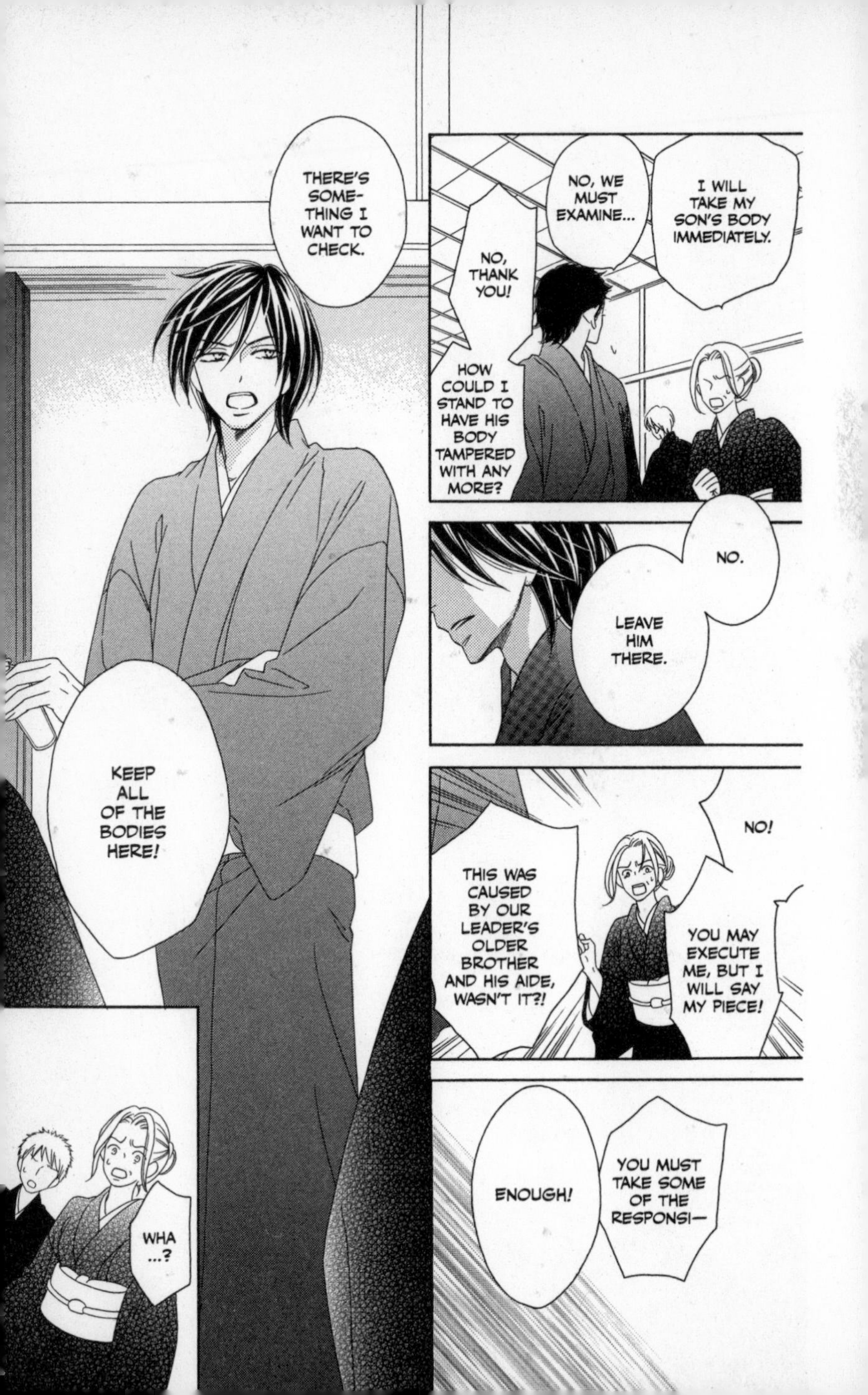
I WILL TAKE MY SON'S BODY IMMEDIATELY.
NO, WE MUST EXAMINE...
NO, THANK YOU!
HOW COULD I STAND TO HAVE HIS BODY TAMPERED WITH ANY MORE?
NO.
LEAVE HIM THERE.
NO!
YOU MAY EXECUTE ME, BUT I WILL SAY MY PIECE!
THIS WAS CAUSED BY OUR LEADER'S OLDER BROTHER AND HIS AIDE, WASN'T IT?!
YOU MUST TAKE SOME OF THE RESPONSI—
ENOUGH!
THERE'S SOME-THING I WANT TO CHECK.
KEEP ALL OF THE BODIES HERE!
WHA ...?

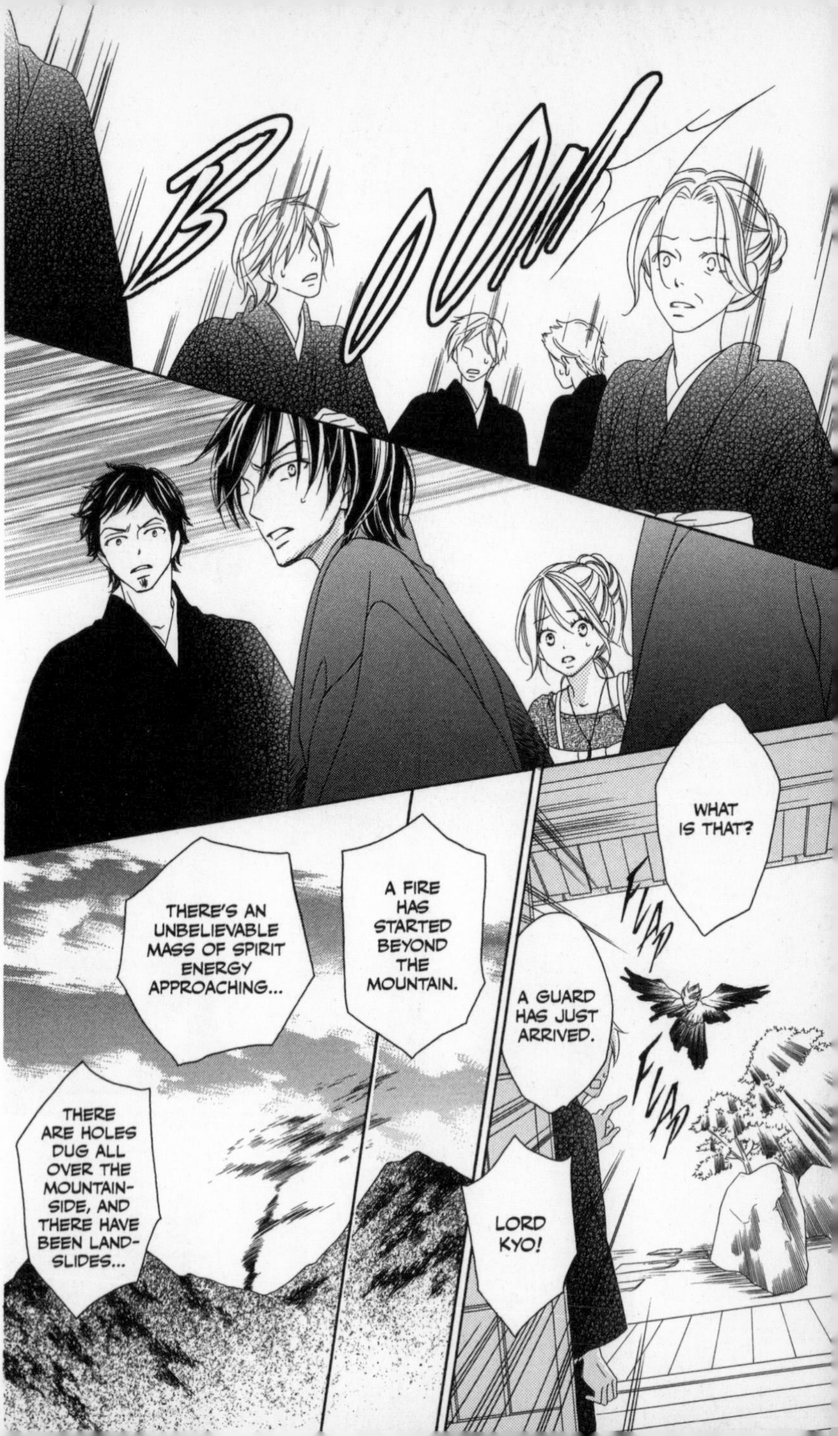
BOOM
WHAT IS THAT?
A GUARD HAS JUST ARRIVED.
LORD KYO!
A FIRE HAS STARTED BEYOND THE MOUNTAIN.
THERE'S AN UNBELIEVABLE MASS OF SPIRIT ENERGY APPROACHING...
THERE ARE HOLES DUG ALL OVER THE MOUNTAIN-SIDE, AND THERE HAVE BEEN LAND-SLIDES...

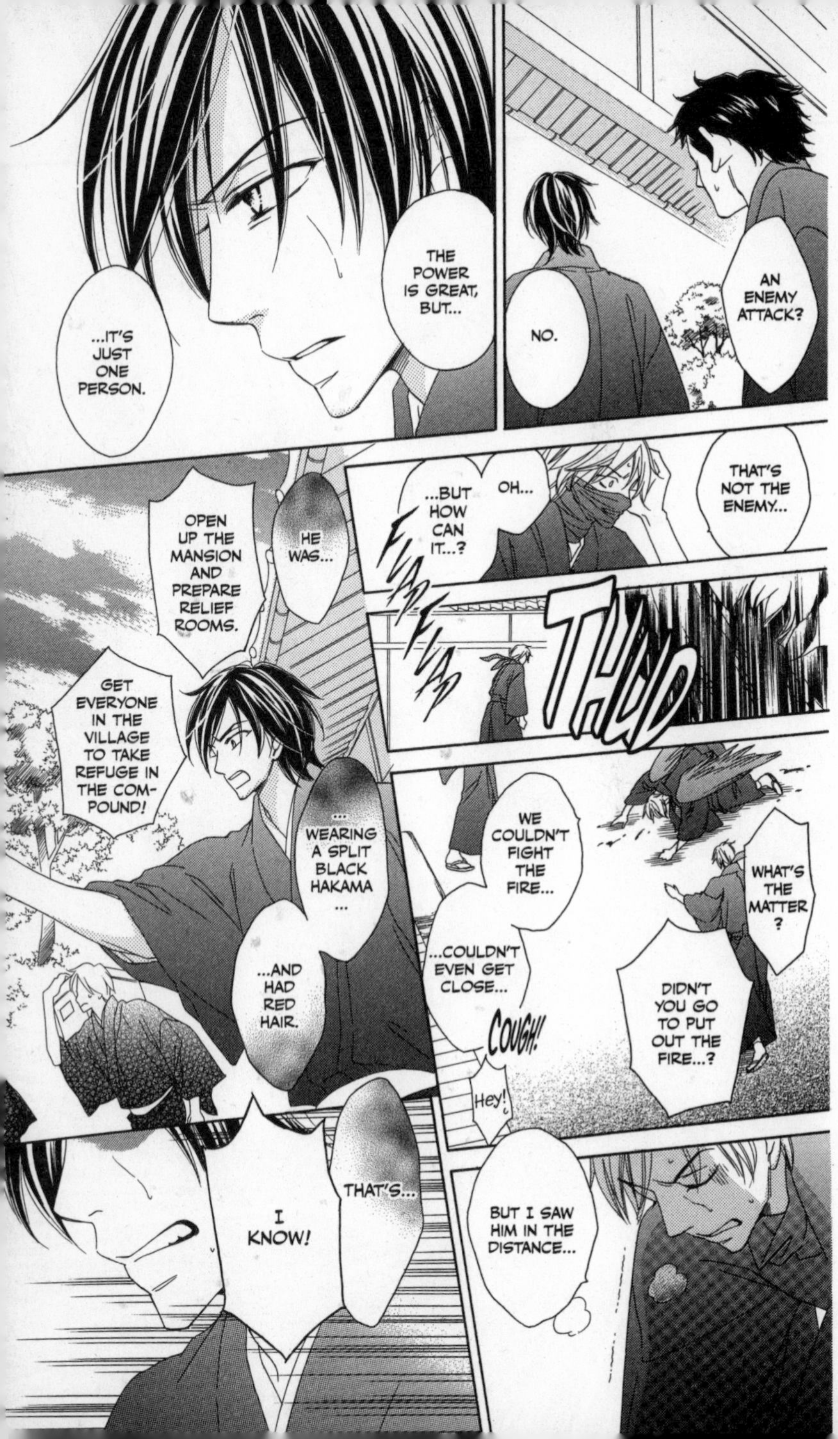
AN ENEMY ATTACK?
NO.
THE POWER IS GREAT, BUT...
...IT'S JUST ONE PERSON.
THAT'S NOT THE ENEMY...
OH...
...BUT HOW CAN IT...?
THUD
FUMP FUMP
WHAT'S THE MATTER?
WE COULDN'T FIGHT THE FIRE...
DIDN'T YOU GO TO PUT OUT THE FIRE...?
...COULDN'T EVEN GET CLOSE...
COUGH!
Hey!
HE WAS...
OPEN UP THE MANSION AND PREPARE RELIEF ROOMS.
GET EVERYONE IN THE VILLAGE TO TAKE REFUGE IN THE COM- POUND!
...WEARING A SPLIT BLACK HAKAMA...
...AND HAD RED HAIR.
BUT I SAW HIM IN THE DISTANCE...
THAT'S...
I KNOW!

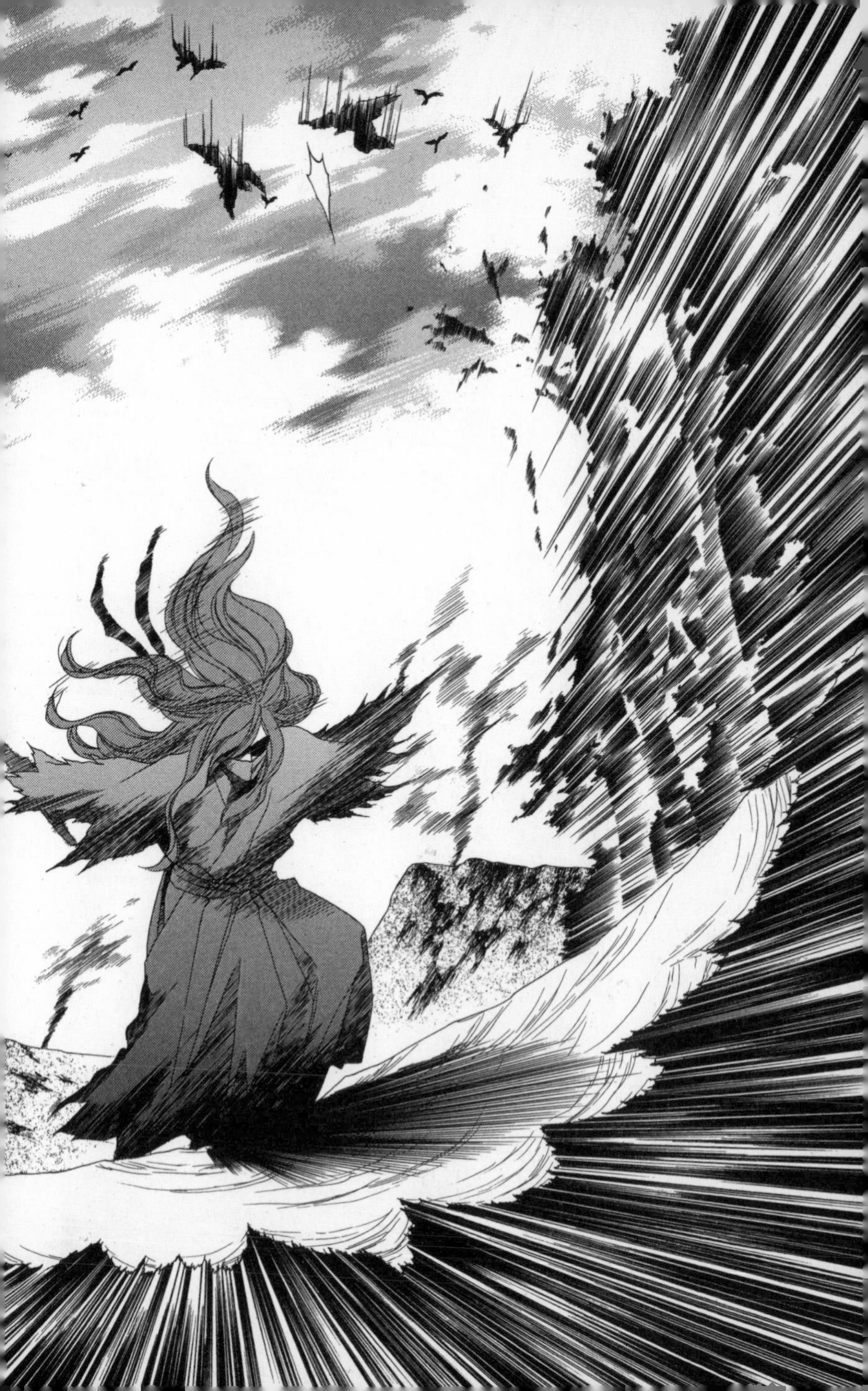

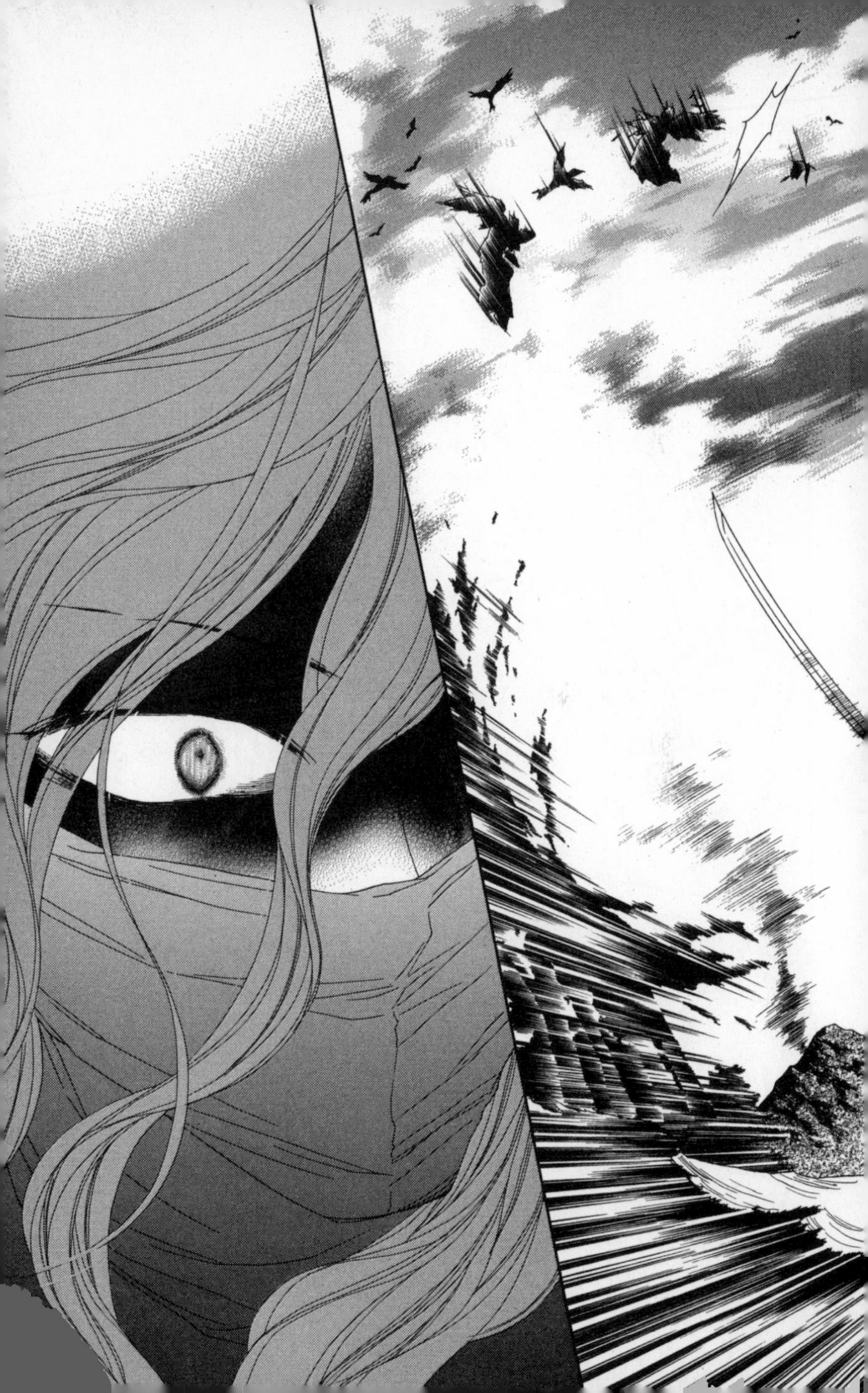

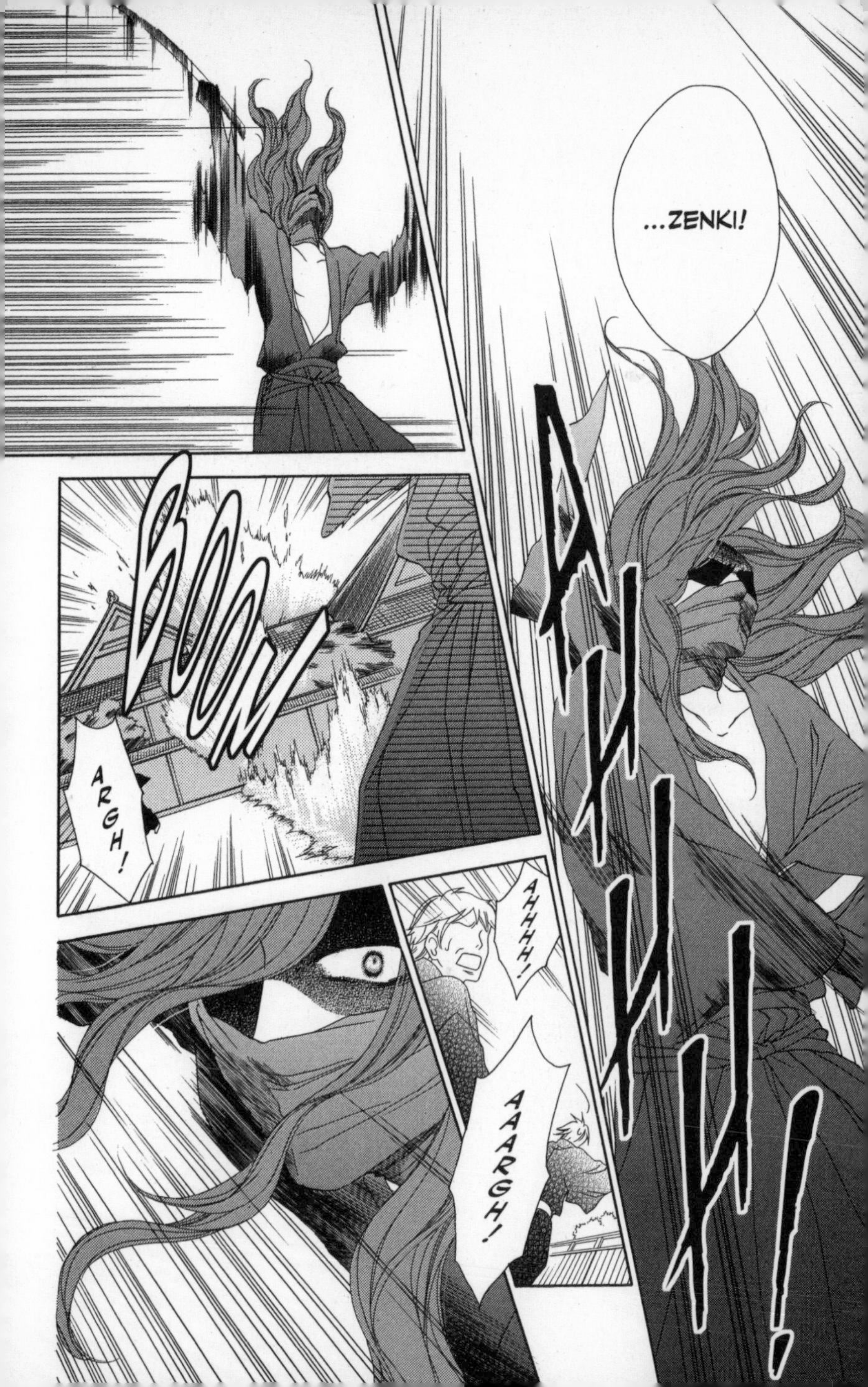
...ZENKI!
AHHHH!
BOOM
ARGH!
AHHHH!
AAAARGH!

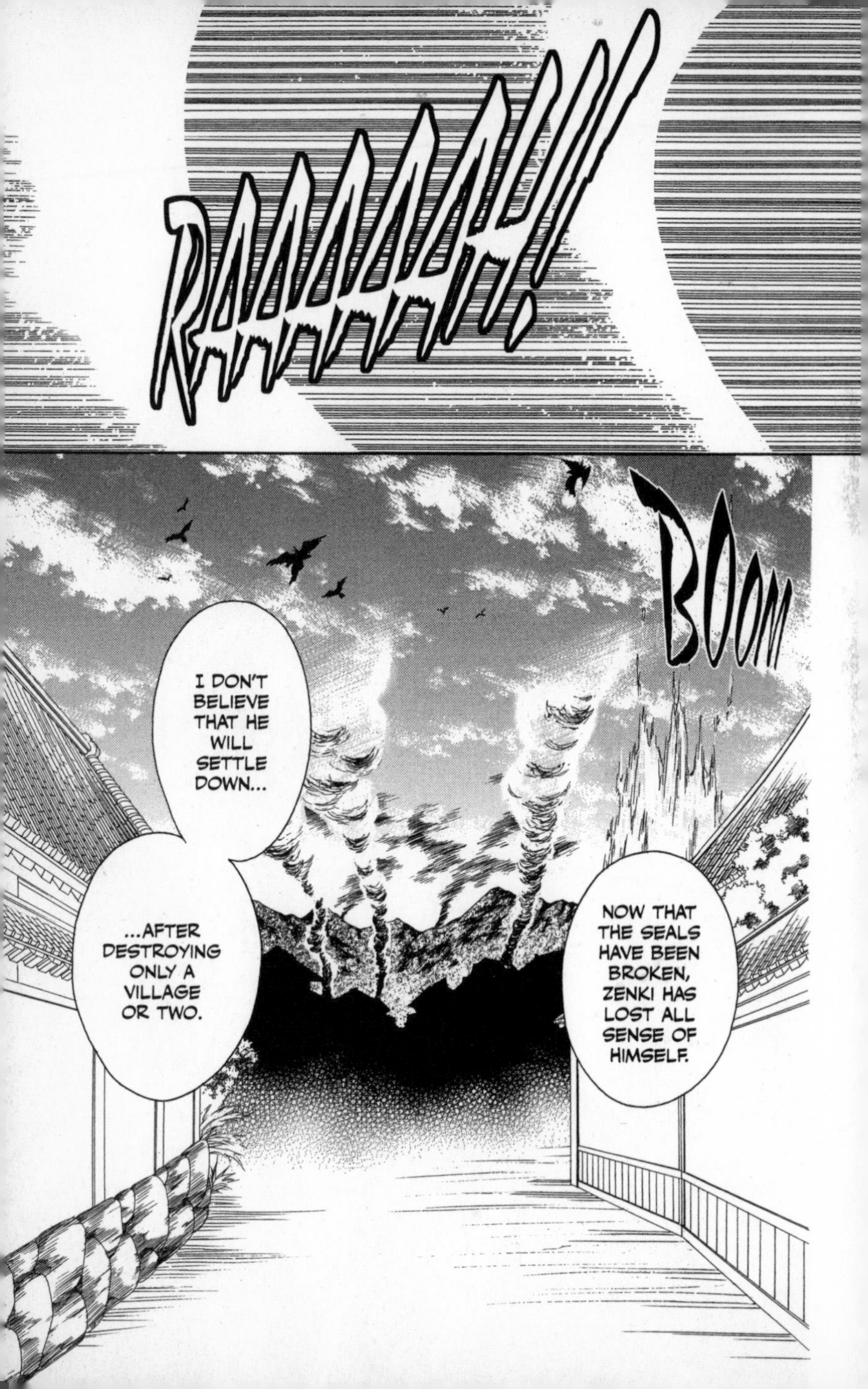
RAAAAAAH!!
BOOM
NOW THAT THE SEALS HAVE BEEN BROKEN, ZENKI HAS LOST ALL SENSE OF HIMSELF.
I DON'T BELIEVE THAT HE WILL SETTLE DOWN...
...AFTER DESTROYING ONLY A VILLAGE OR TWO.

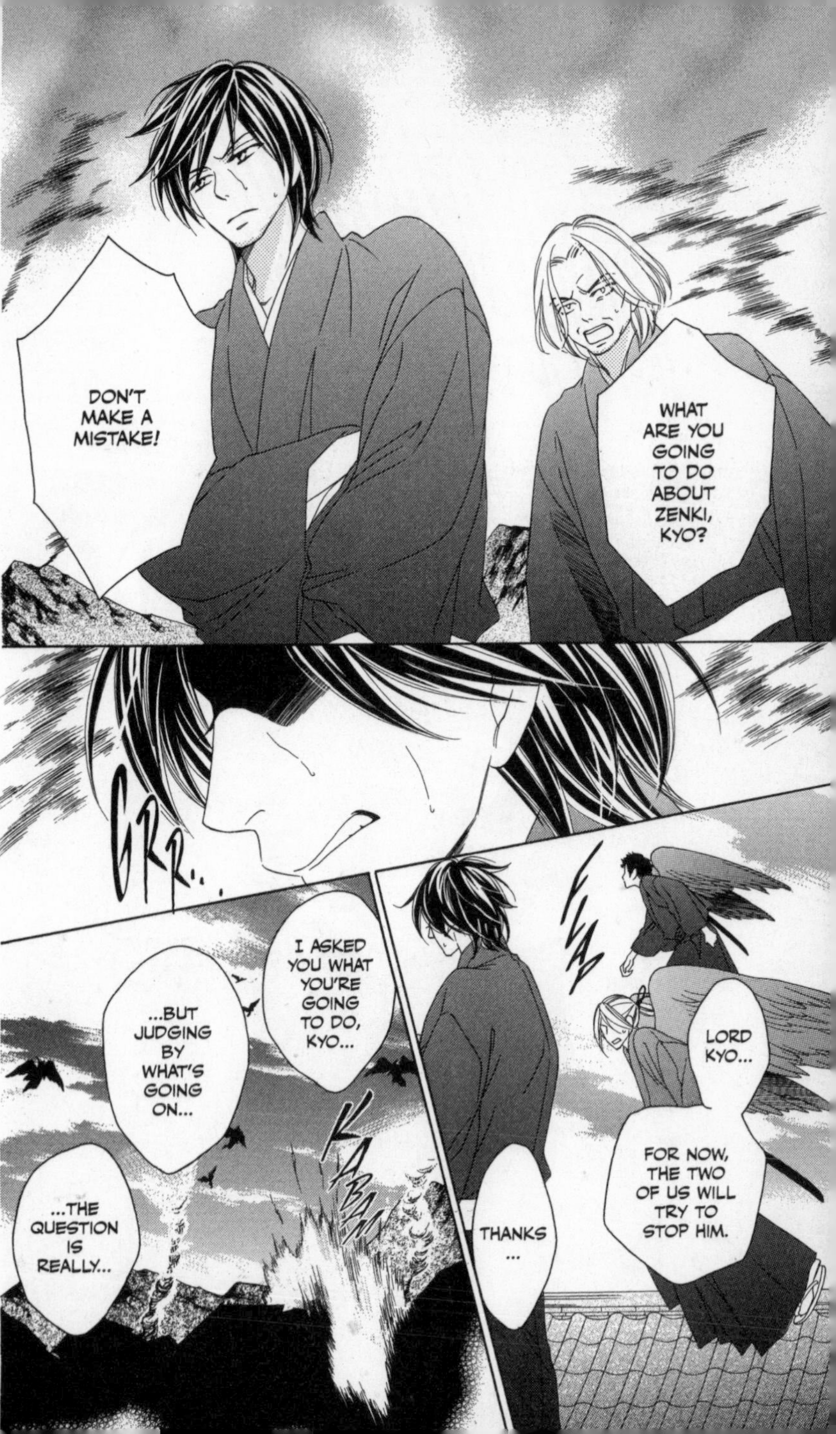
WHAT ARE YOU GOING TO DO ABOUT ZENKI, KYO?
DON'T MAKE A MISTAKE!
GRR...
LORD KYO...
FOR NOW, THE TWO OF US WILL TRY TO STOP HIM.
THANKS...
I ASKED YOU WHAT YOU'RE GOING TO DO, KYO...
...BUT JUDGING BY WHAT'S GOING ON...
KABAM
...THE QUESTION IS REALLY...

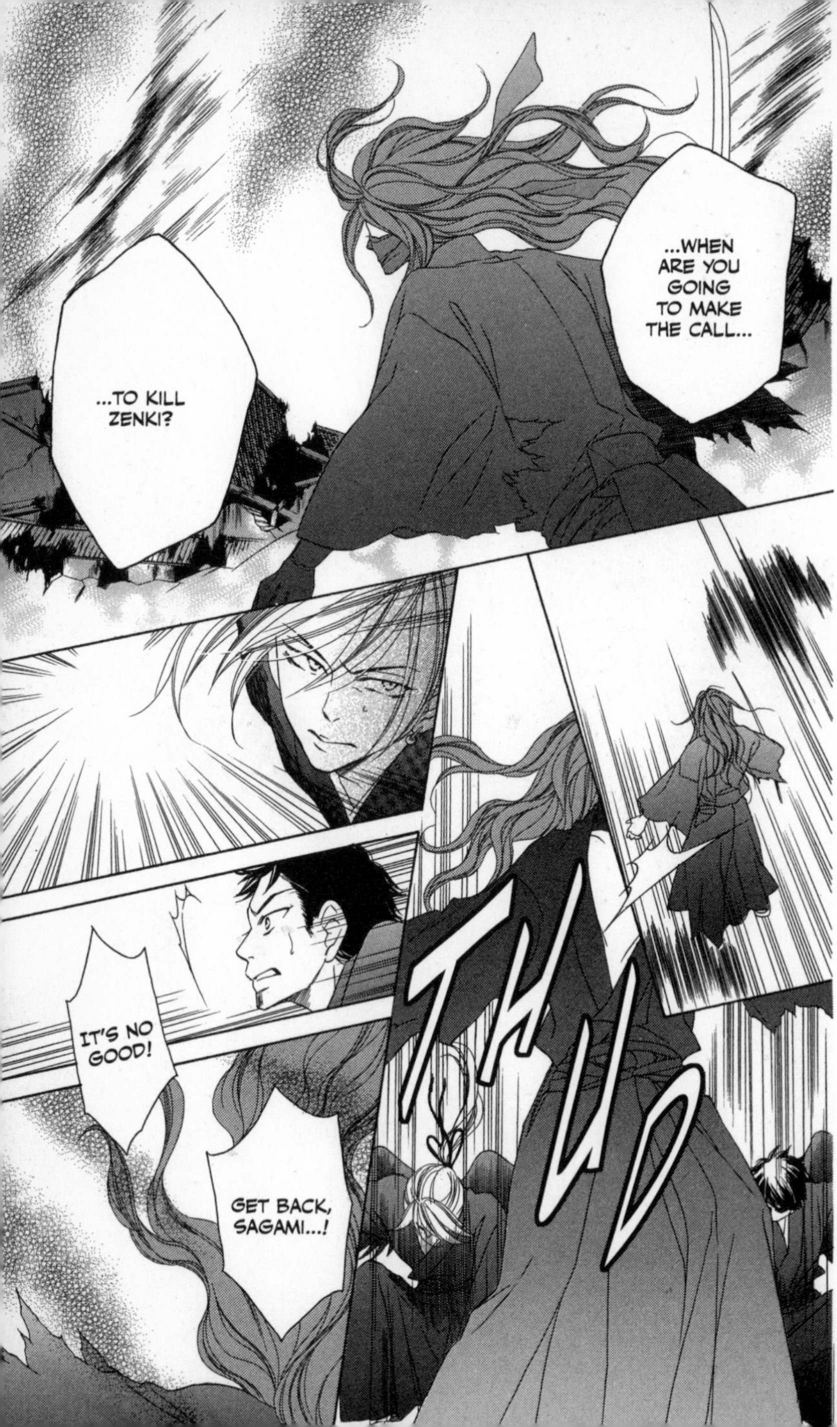
...WHEN ARE YOU GOING TO MAKE THE CALL...
...TO KILL ZENKI?
THUD
IT'S NO GOOD!
GET BACK, SAGAMI...!

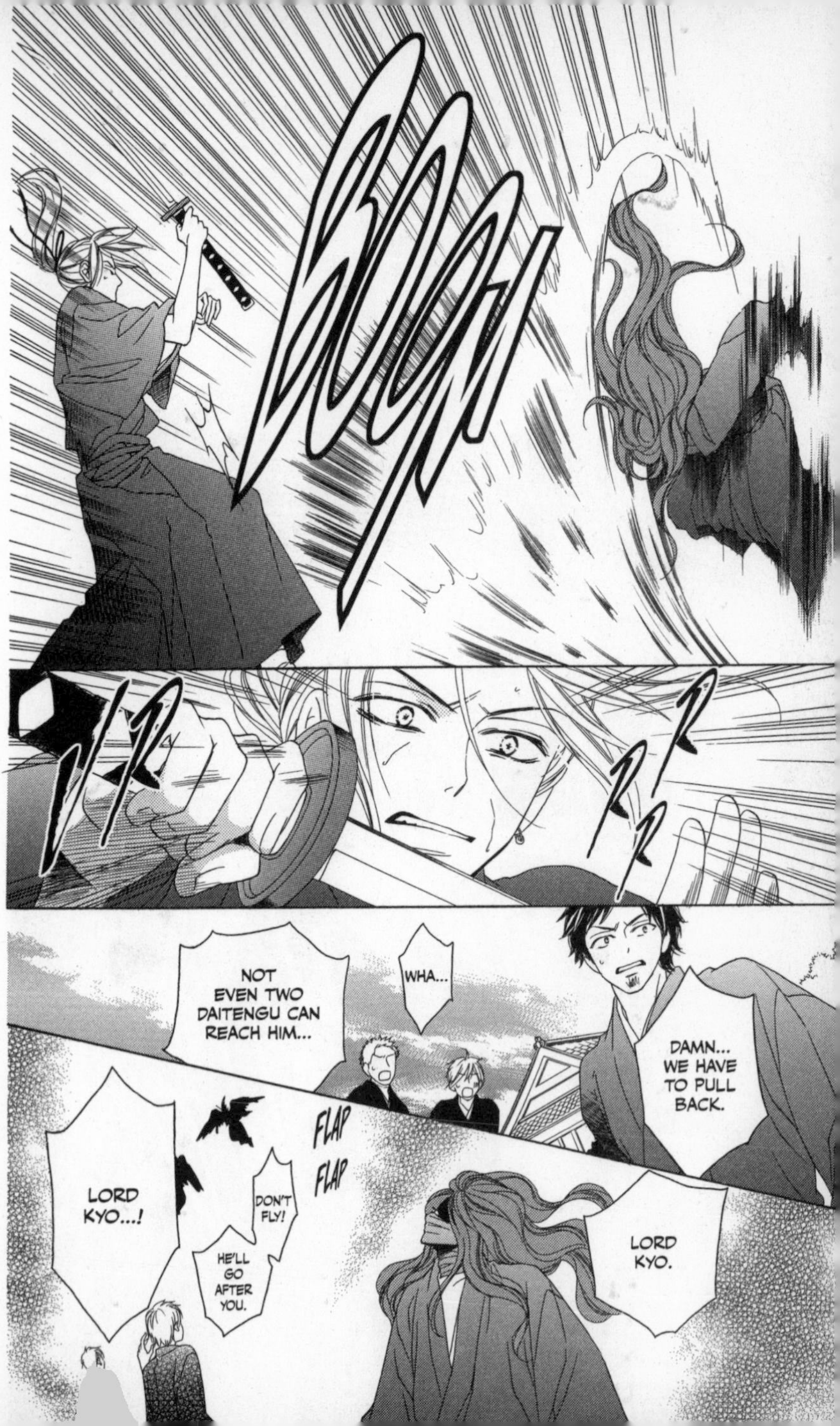
WHA...
NOT EVEN TWO DAITENGU CAN REACH HIM...
DAMN... WE HAVE TO PULL BACK.
LORD KYO.
FLAP
FLAP
DON'T FLY!
HE'LL GO AFTER YOU.
LORD KYO...!

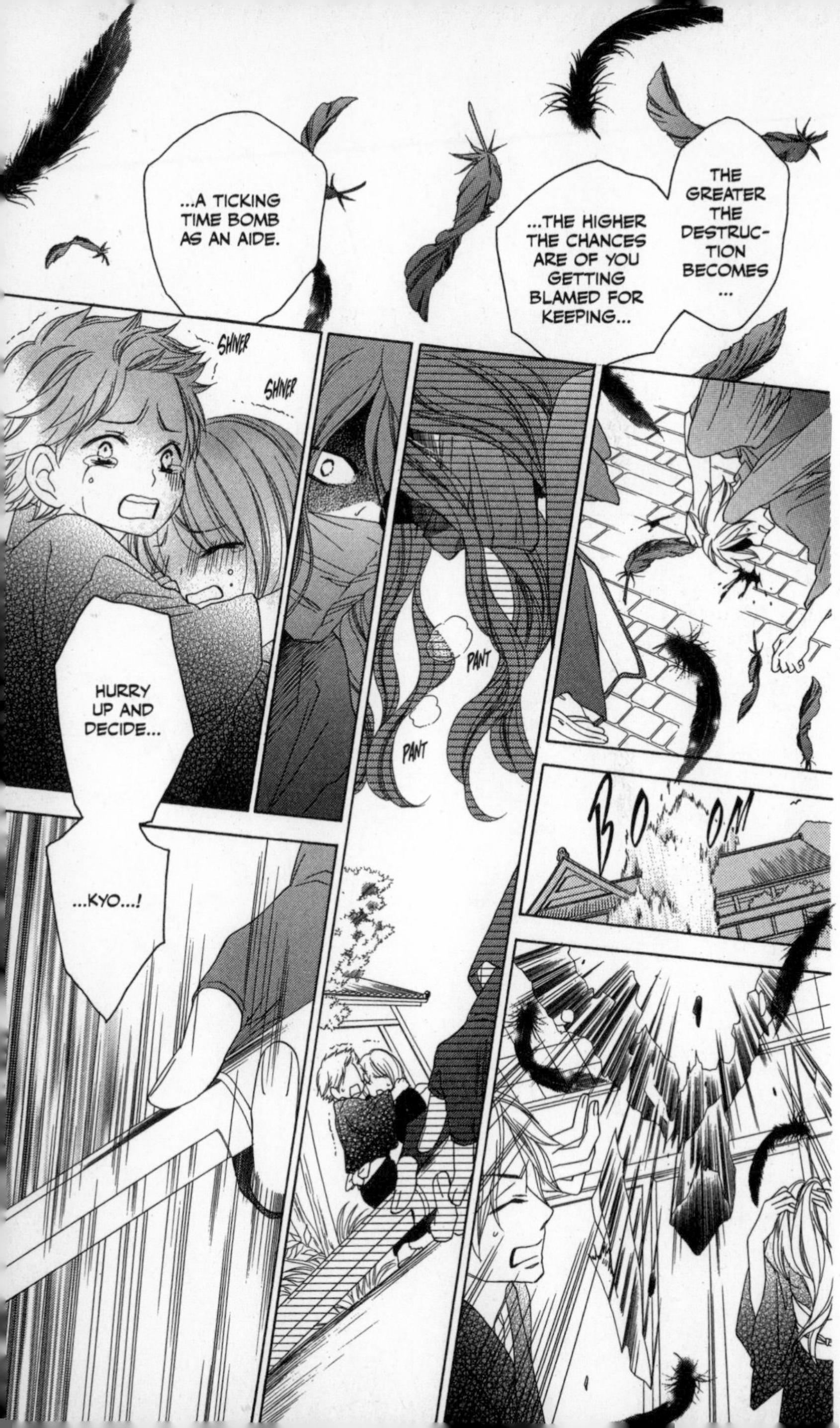
THE GREATER THE DESTRUCTION BECOMES...
...THE HIGHER THE CHANCES ARE OF YOU GETTING BLAMED FOR KEEPING...
...A TICKING TIME BOMB AS AN AIDE.
PANT
PANT
SHIVER
SHIVER
HURRY UP AND DECIDE...
BOOM
...KYO...!

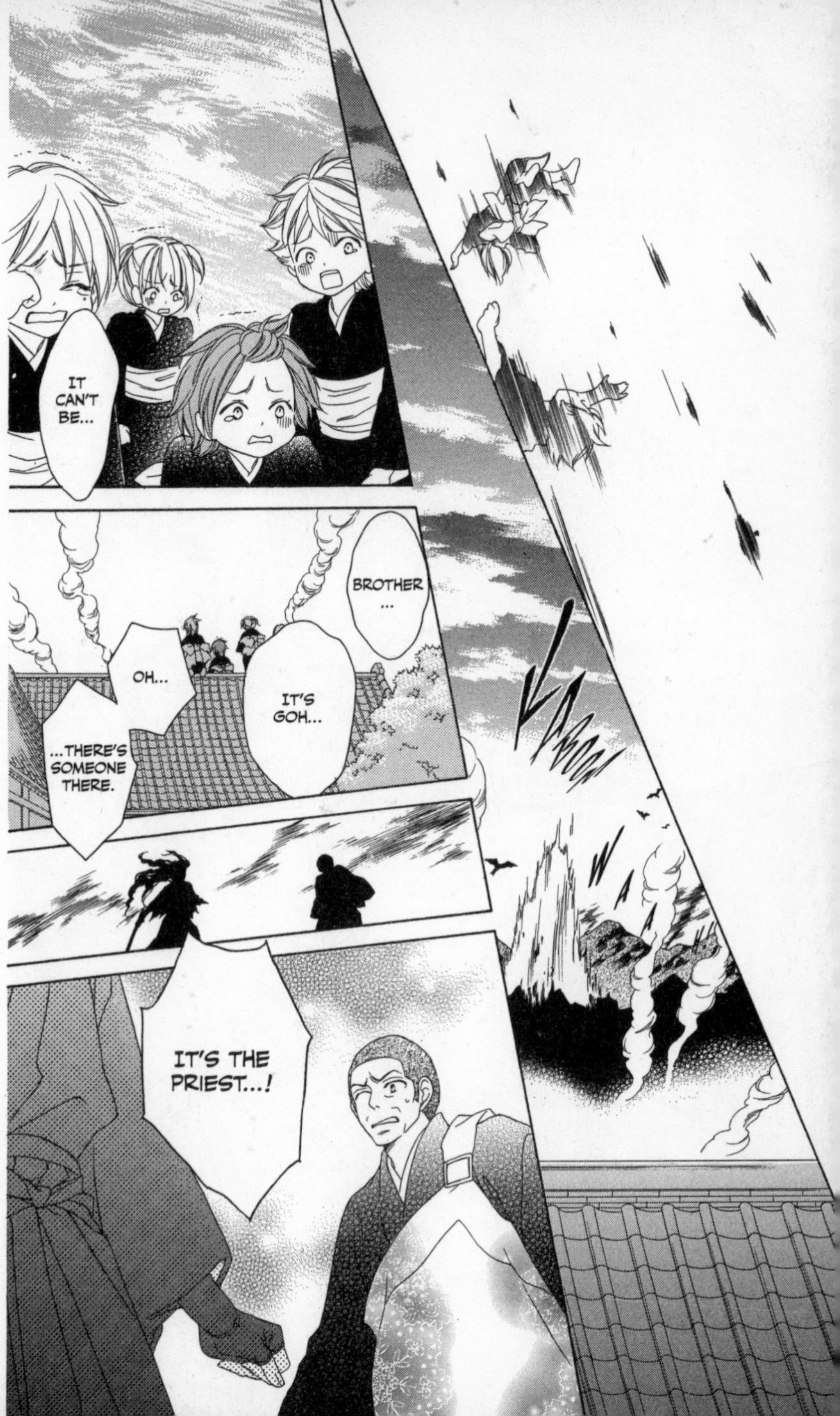
WAAH
IT CAN'T BE...
BROTHER ...
IT'S GOH...
OH...
...THERE'S SOMEONE THERE.
IT'S THE PRIEST...!

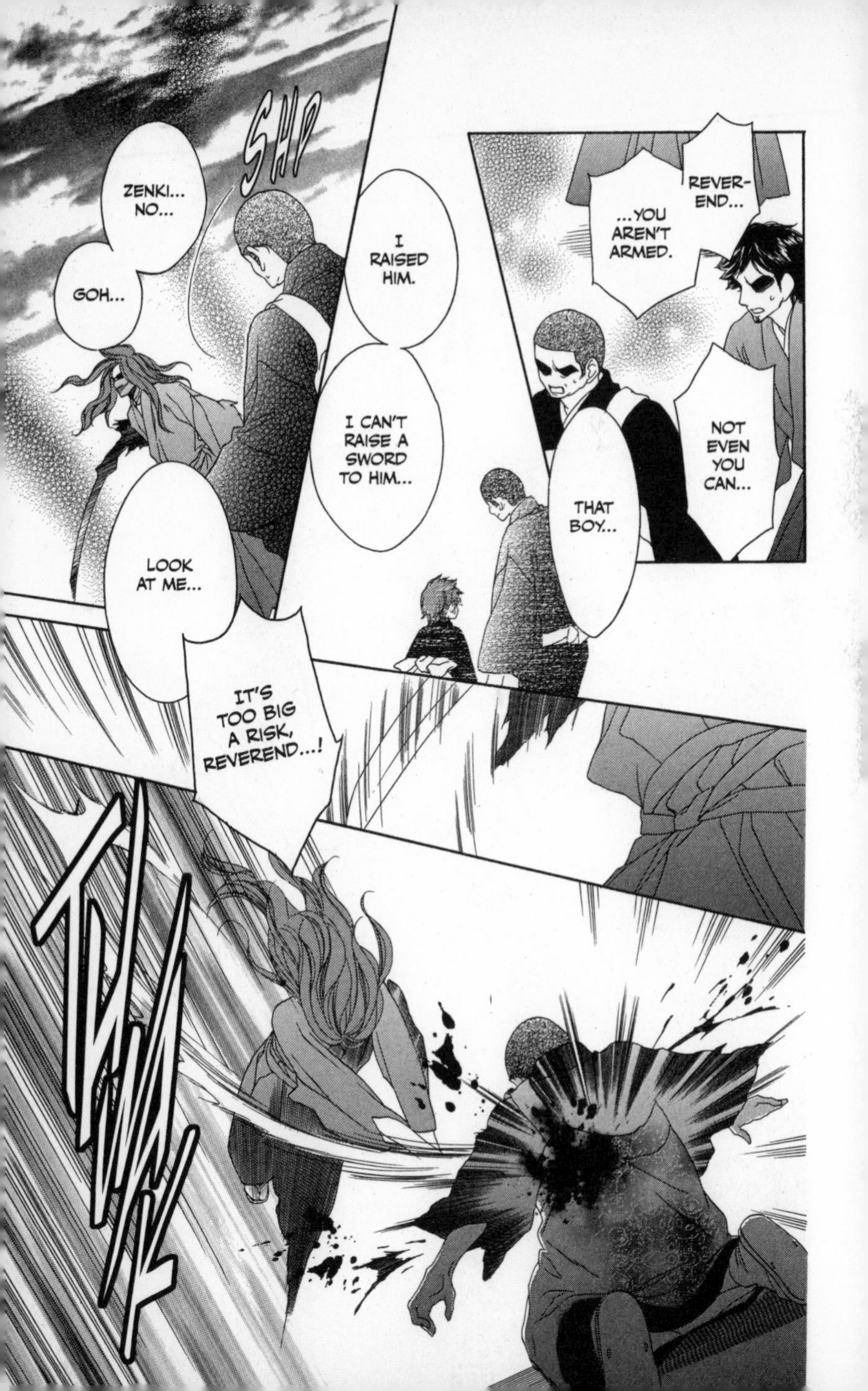

REVER-END...
...YOU AREN'T ARMED.
NOT EVEN YOU CAN...
THAT BOY...
I RAISED HIM.
I CAN'T RAISE A SWORD TO HIM...
SHP
ZENKI... NO...
GOH...
LOOK AT ME...
IT'S TOO BIG A RISK, REVEREND...!
TWAK

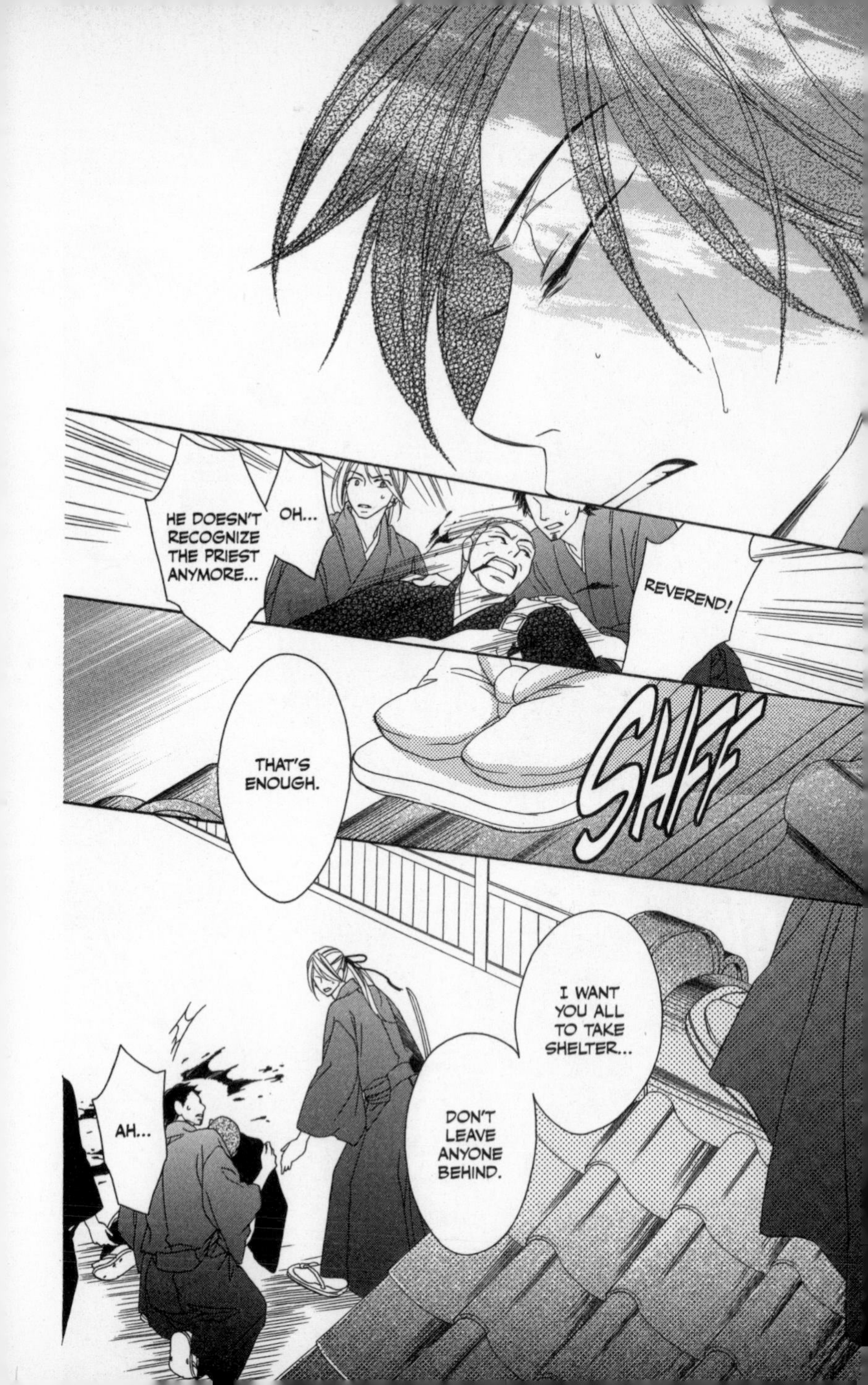
REVEREND!
OH...
HE DOESN'T RECOGNIZE THE PRIEST ANYMORE...
SHFF
THAT'S ENOUGH.
I WANT YOU ALL TO TAKE SHELTER...
DON'T LEAVE ANYONE BEHIND.
AH...

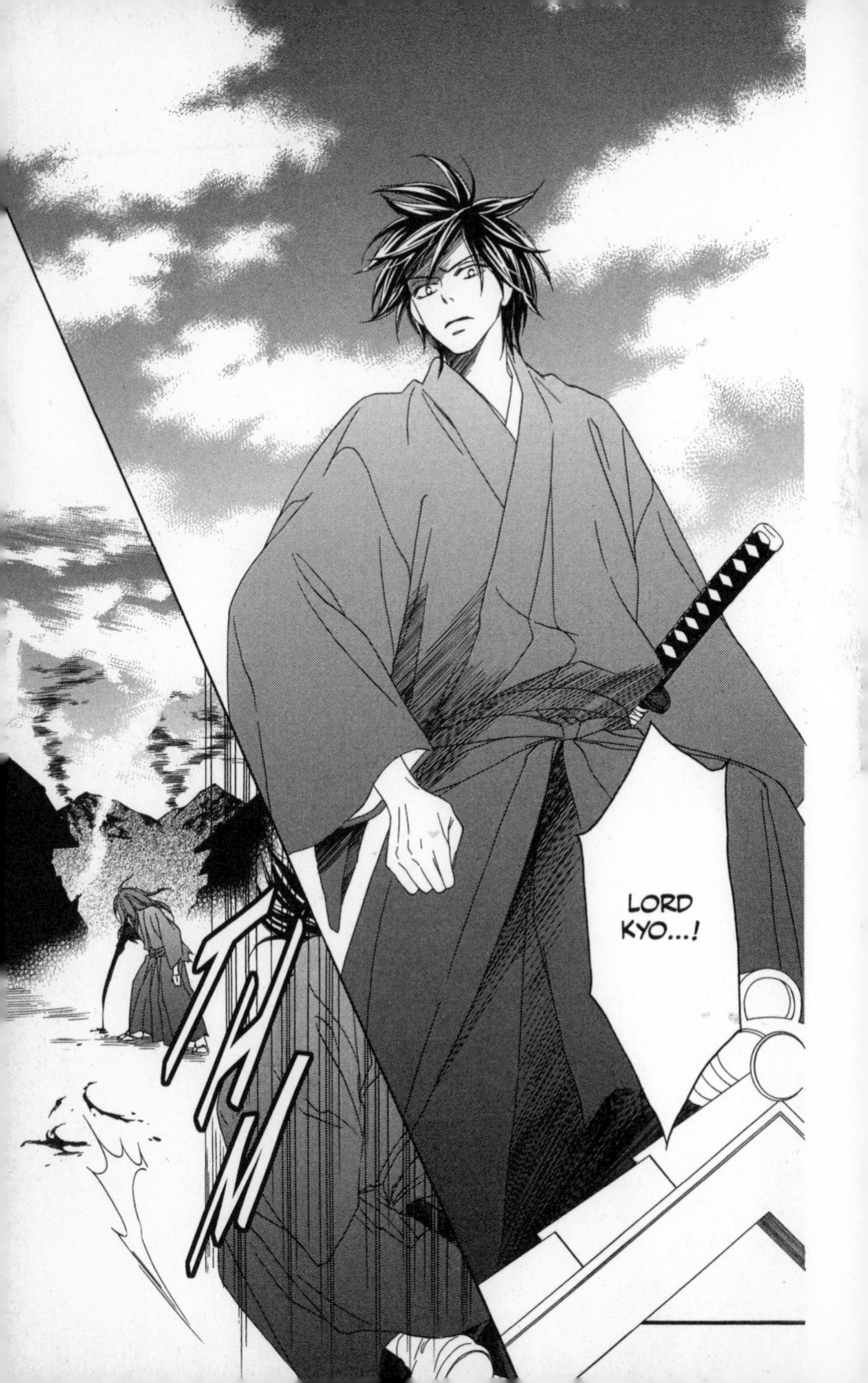
LORD KYO...!

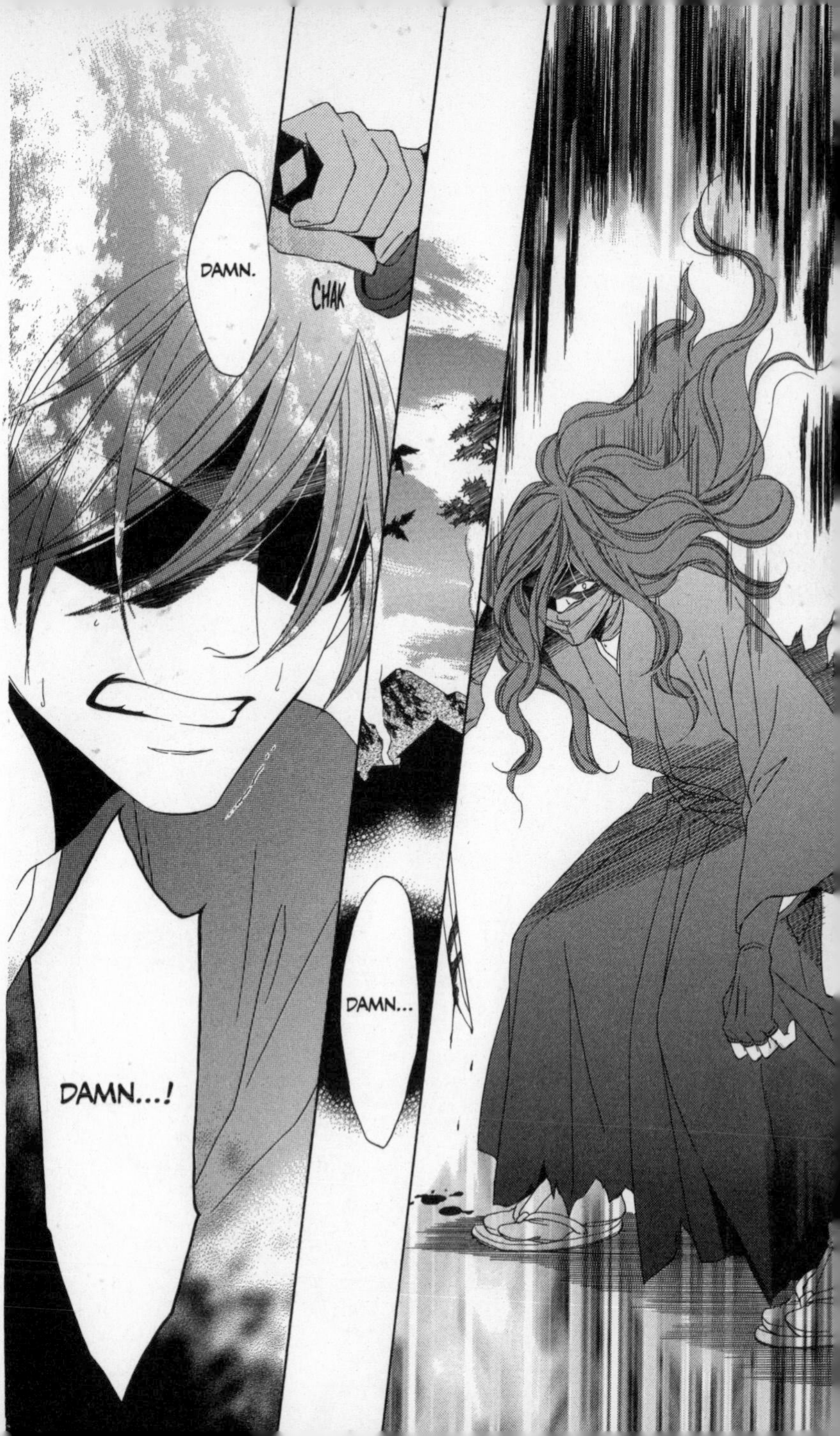
CHAK
DAMN...
DAMN.
DAMN...!

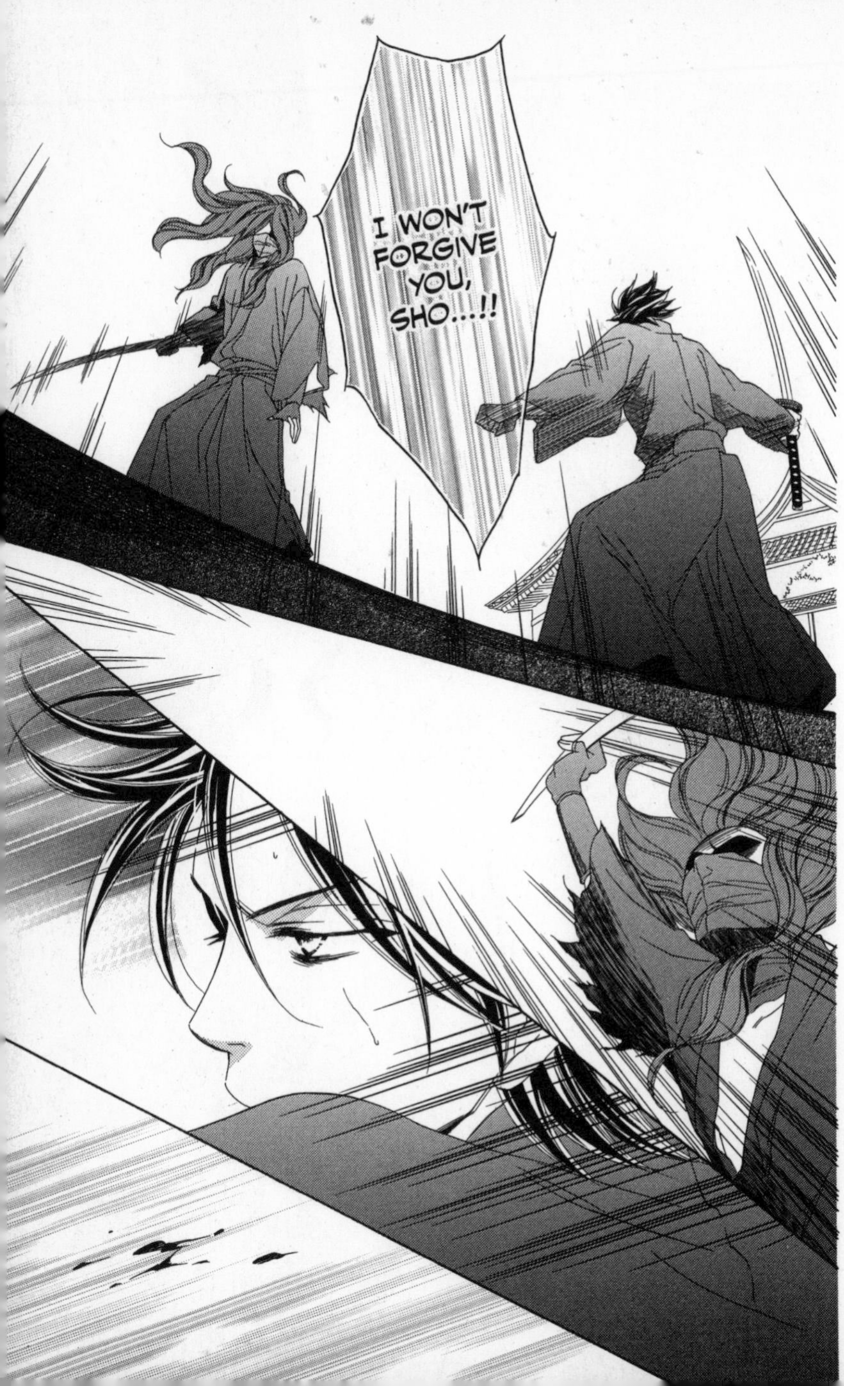
I WON'T FORGIVE YOU, SHO...!!

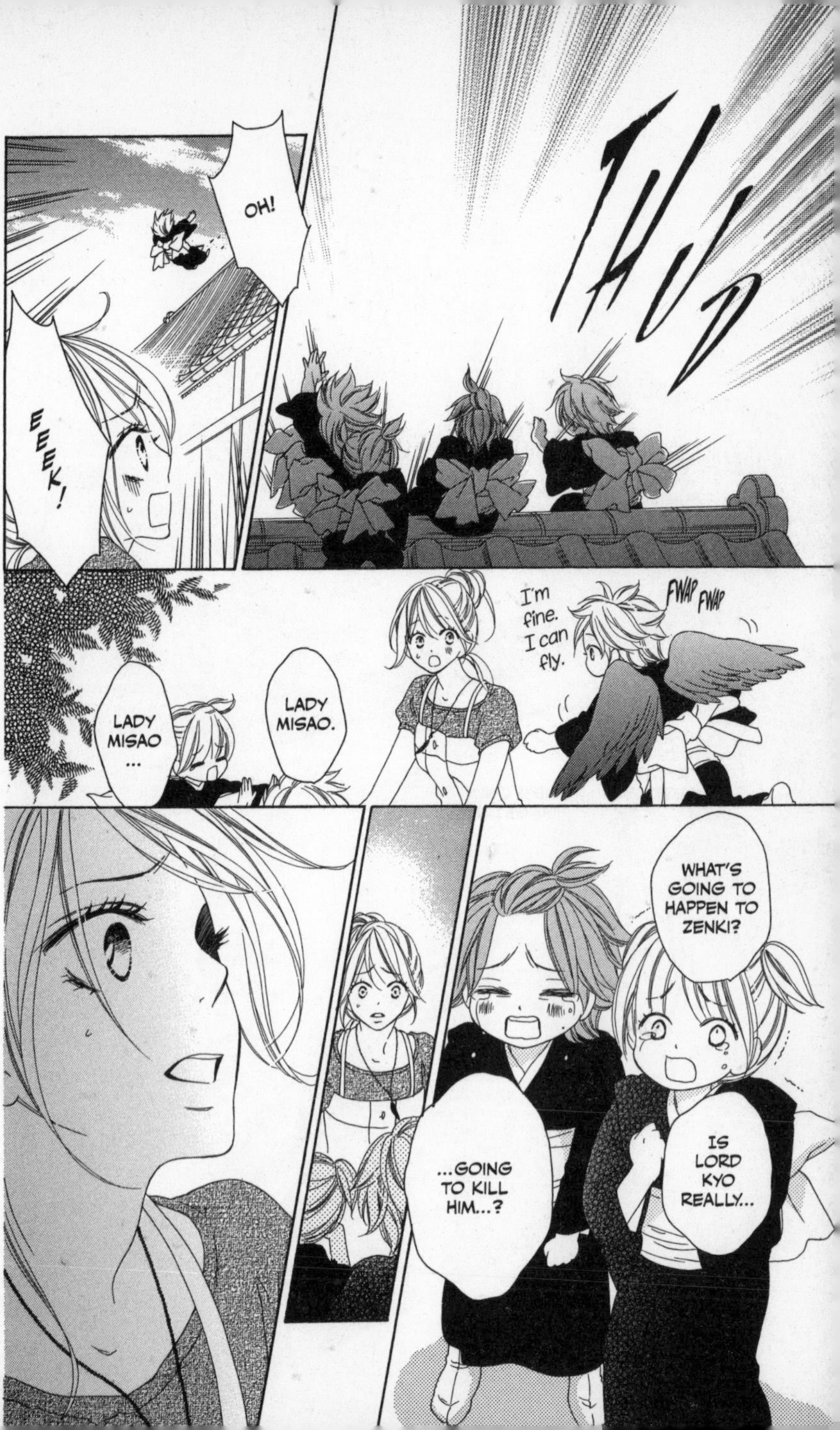
THUD
OH!
EEEK!
FWAP FWAP
I'm fine. I can fly.
LADY MISAO.
LADY MISAO...
WHAT'S GOING TO HAPPEN TO ZENKI?
IS LORD KYO REALLY...
...GOING TO KILL HIM...?

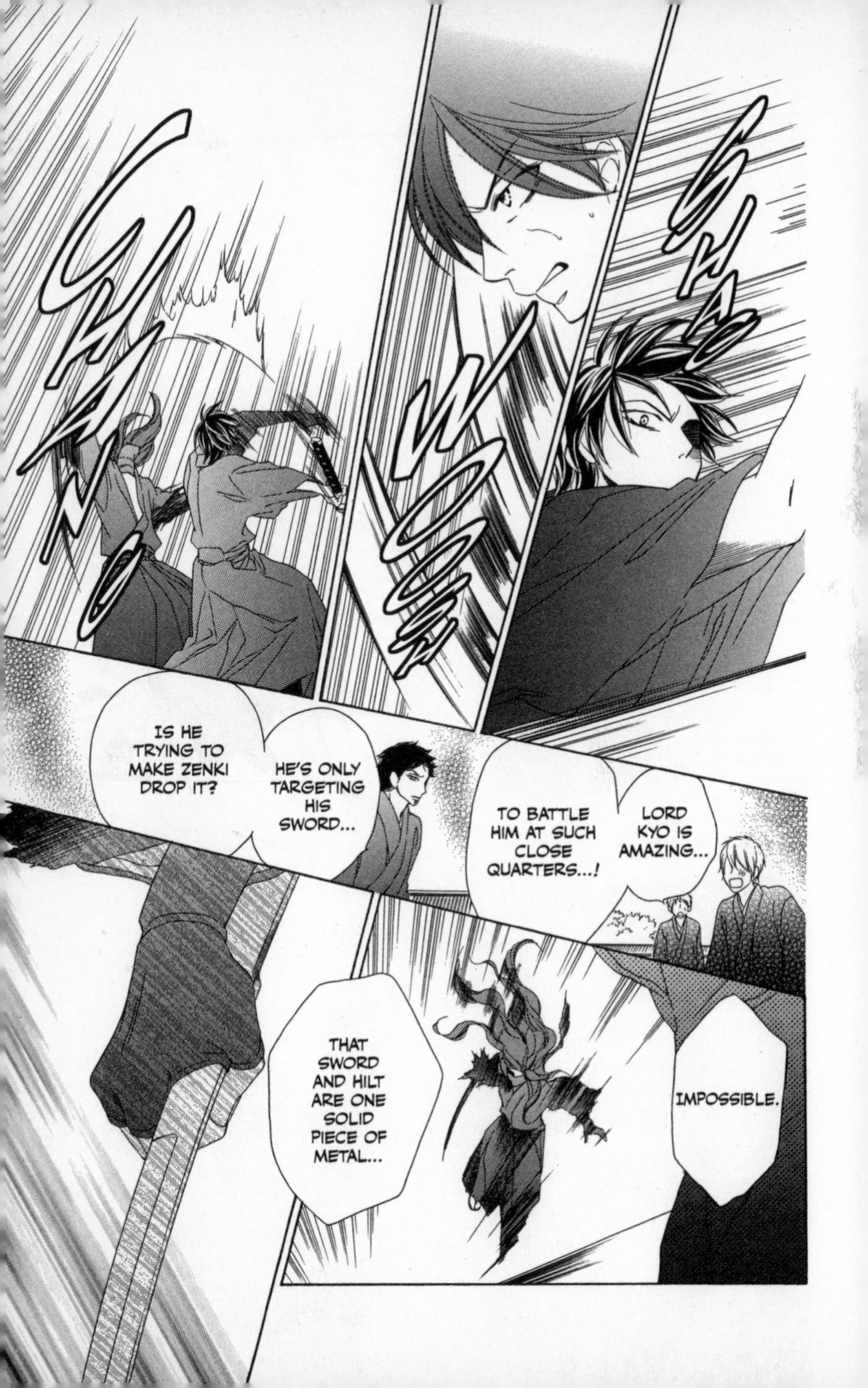
CHING
LORD KYO IS AMAZING...
TO BATTLE HIM AT SUCH CLOSE QUARTERS...!
HE'S ONLY TARGETING HIS SWORD...
IS HE TRYING TO MAKE ZENKI DROP IT?
IMPOSSIBLE.
THAT SWORD AND HILT ARE ONE SOLID PIECE OF METAL...

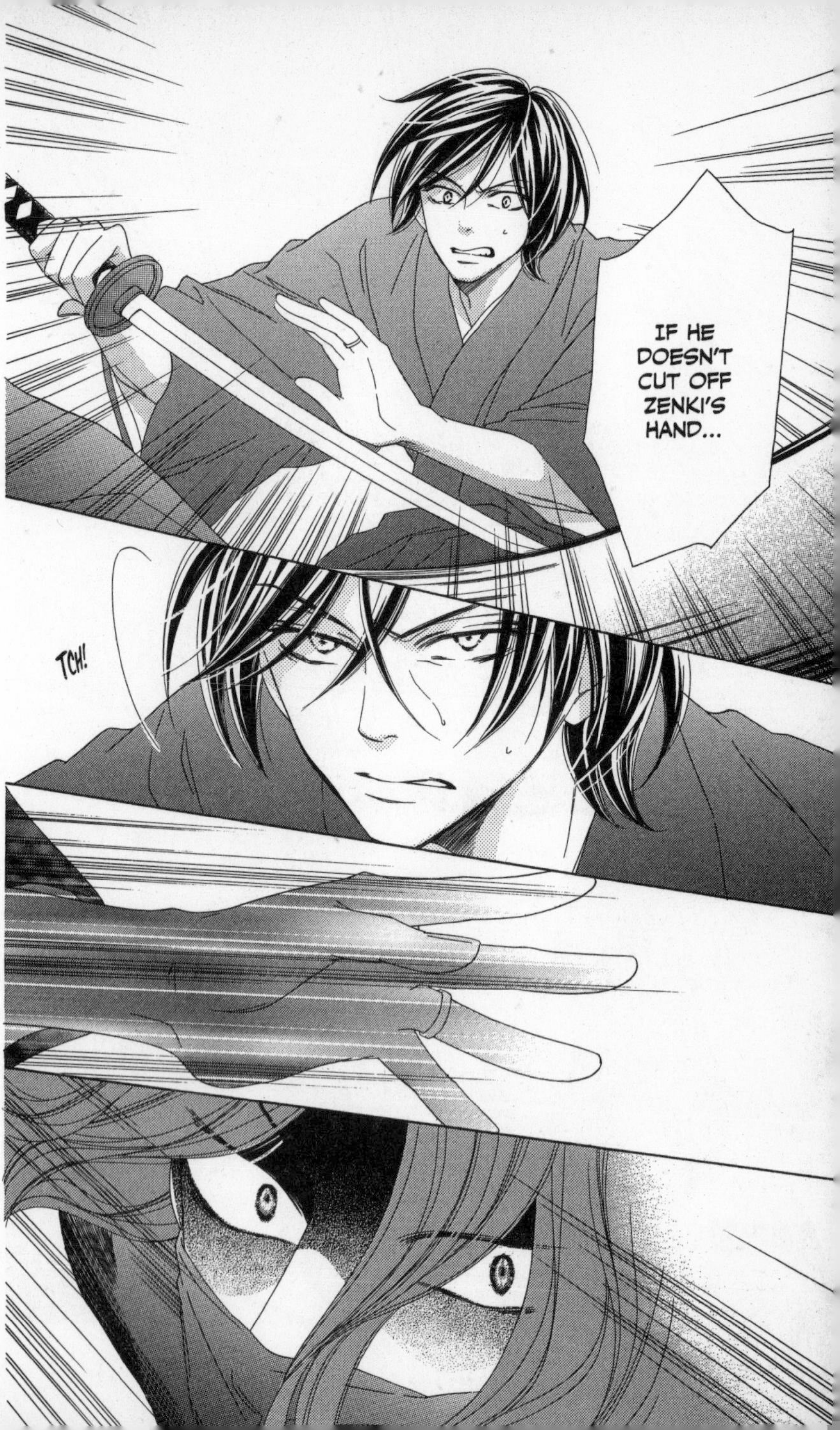
IF HE DOESN'T CUT OFF ZENKI'S HAND...
TCH!

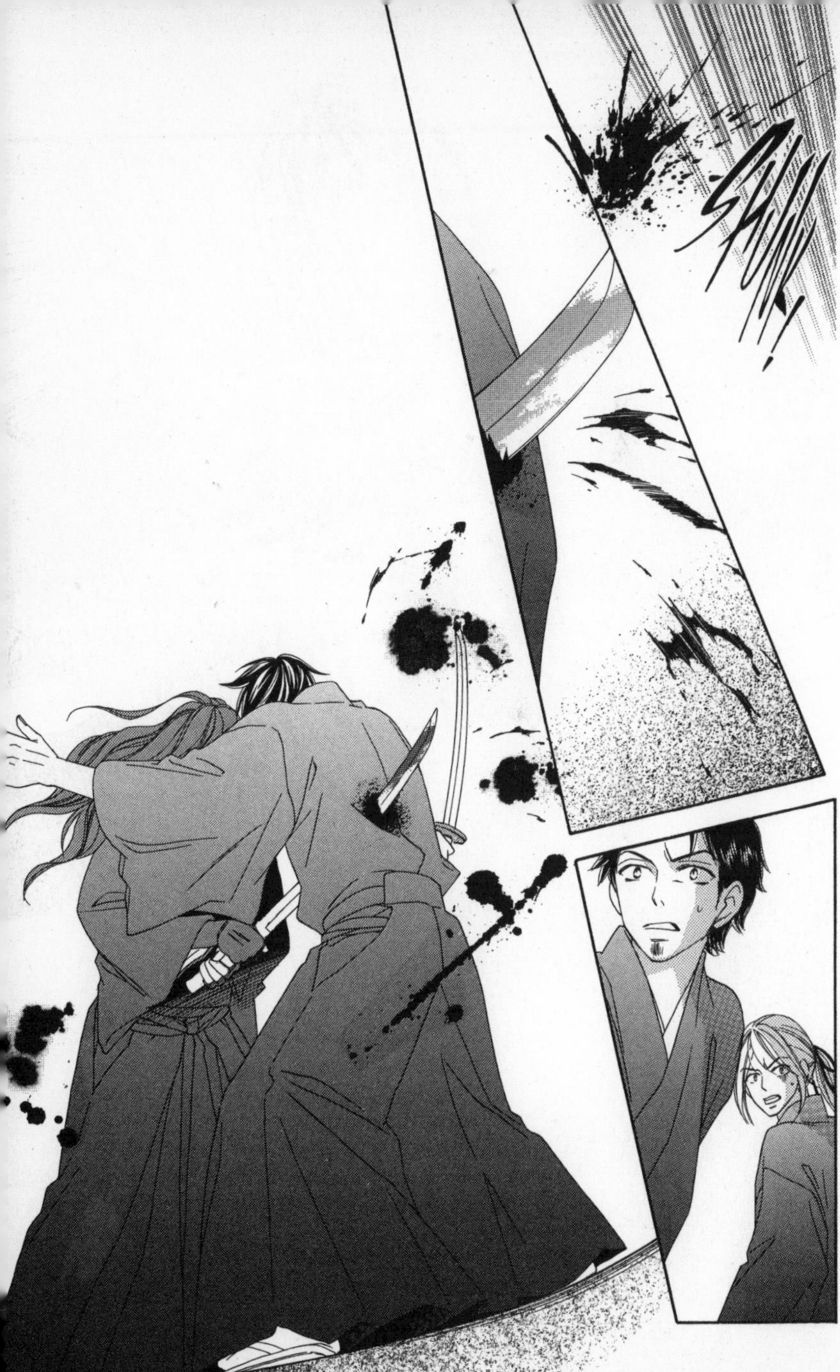

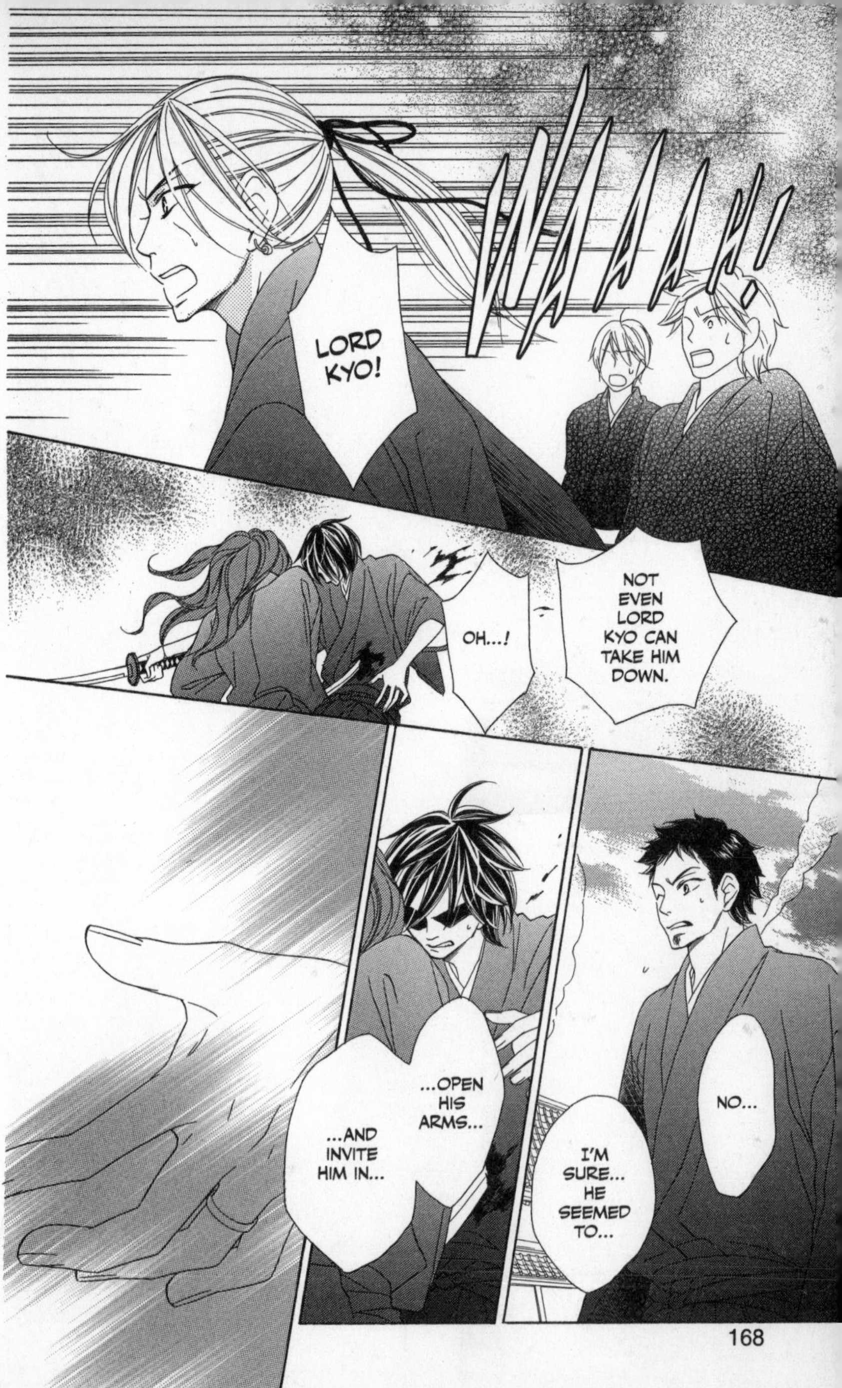

WAAAAH!
LORD KYO!
NOT EVEN LORD KYO CAN TAKE HIM DOWN.
OH...!
NO...
I'M SURE... HE SEEMED TO...
...OPEN HIS ARMS...
...AND INVITE HIM IN...

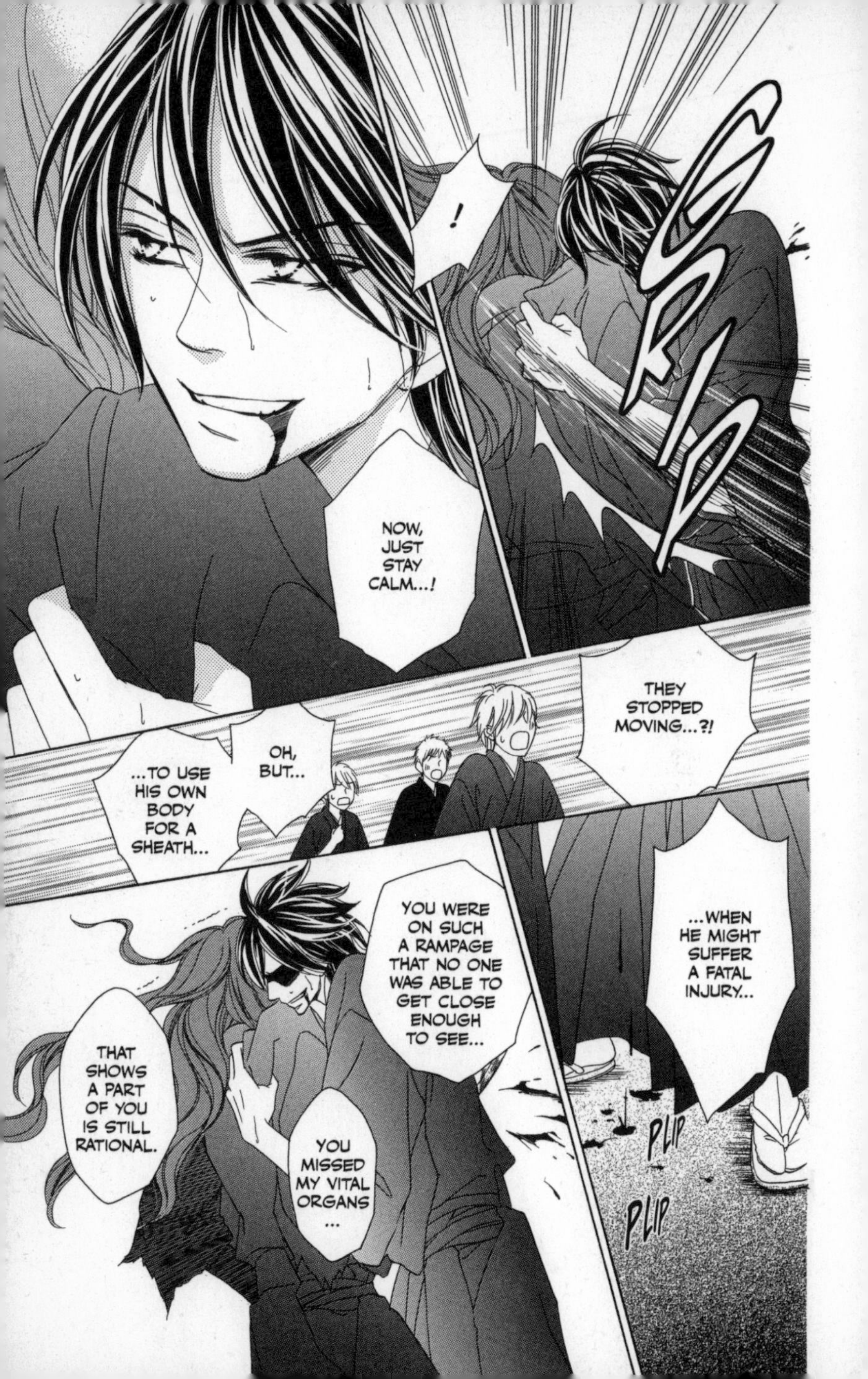
!
NOW, JUST STAY CALM...!
THEY STOPPED MOVING...?!
OH, BUT...
...TO USE HIS OWN BODY FOR A SHEATH...
...WHEN HE MIGHT SUFFER A FATAL INJURY...
PLIP
PLIP
YOU WERE ON SUCH A RAMPAGE THAT NO ONE WAS ABLE TO GET CLOSE ENOUGH TO SEE...
YOU MISSED MY VITAL ORGANS...
THAT SHOWS A PART OF YOU IS STILL RATIONAL.

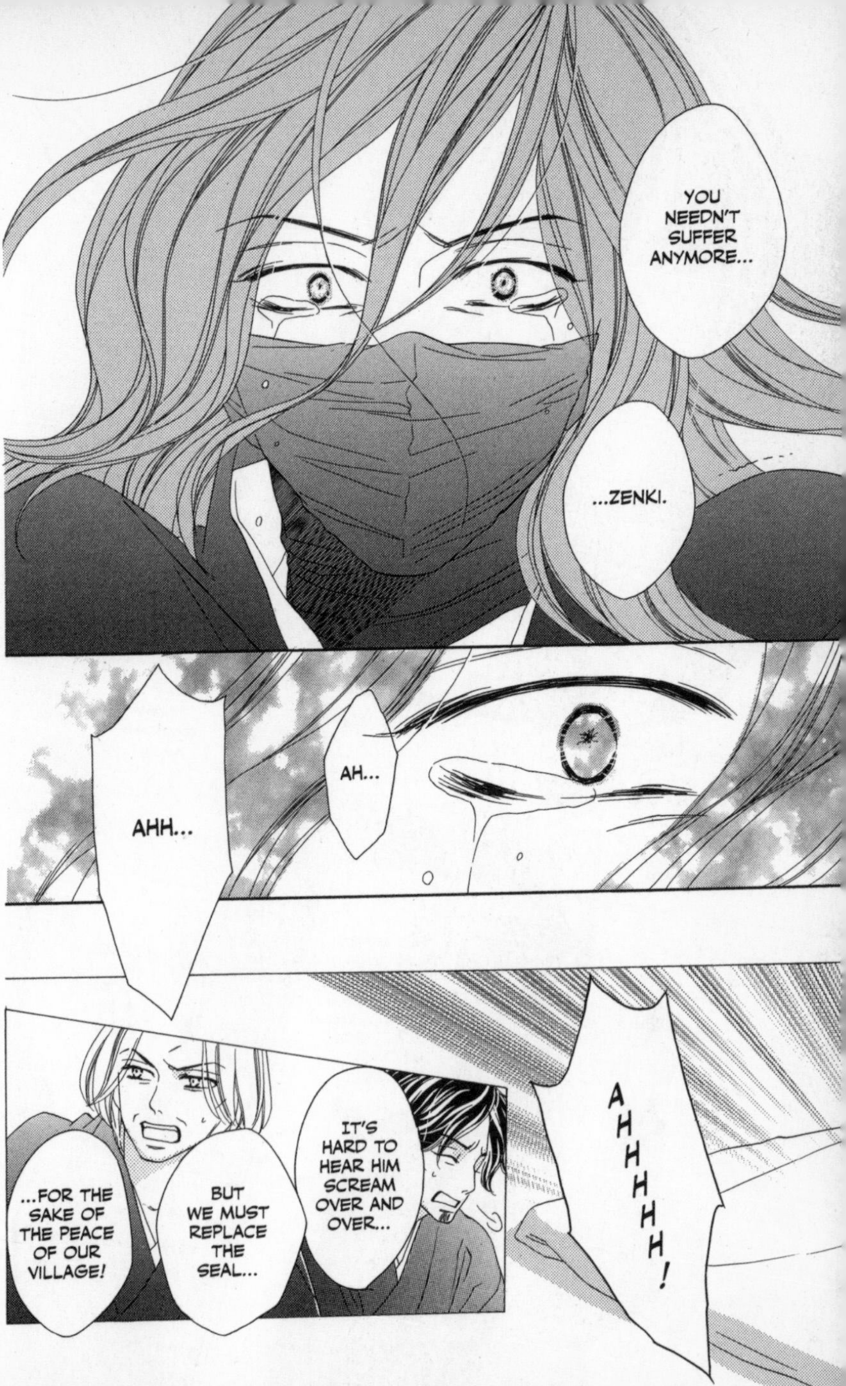
YOU NEEDN'T SUFFER ANYMORE...
...ZENKI.
AH...
AHH...
AHHHHH!
IT'S HARD TO HEAR HIM SCREAM OVER AND OVER...
BUT WE MUST REPLACE THE SEAL...
...FOR THE SAKE OF THE PEACE OF OUR VILLAGE!

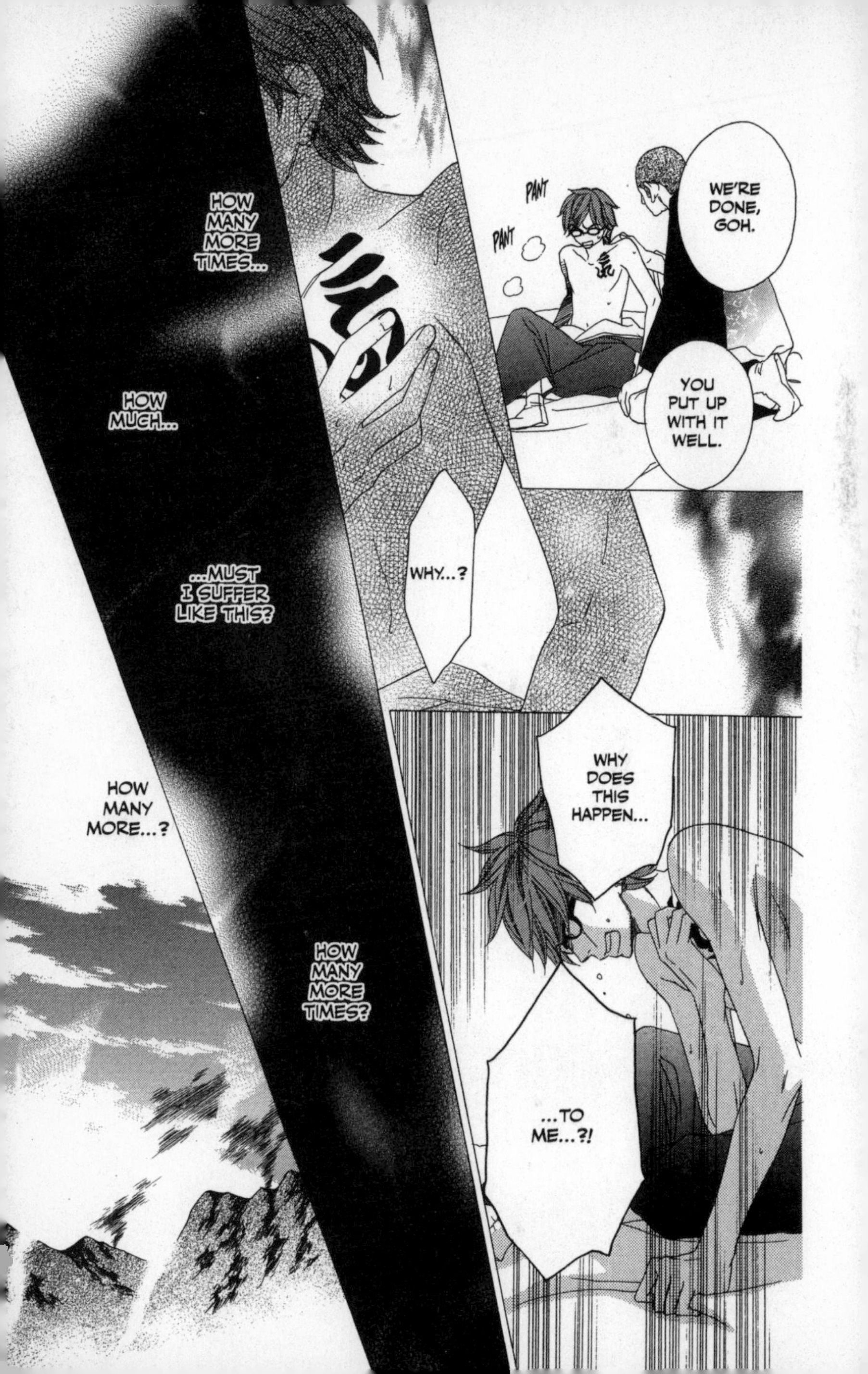
PANT
PANT
WE'RE DONE, GOH.
YOU PUT UP WITH IT WELL.
WHY...?
HOW MANY MORE TIMES...
HOW MUCH...
...MUST I SUFFER LIKE THIS?
WHY DOES THIS HAPPEN...
...TO ME...?!
HOW MANY MORE...?
HOW MANY MORE TIMES?

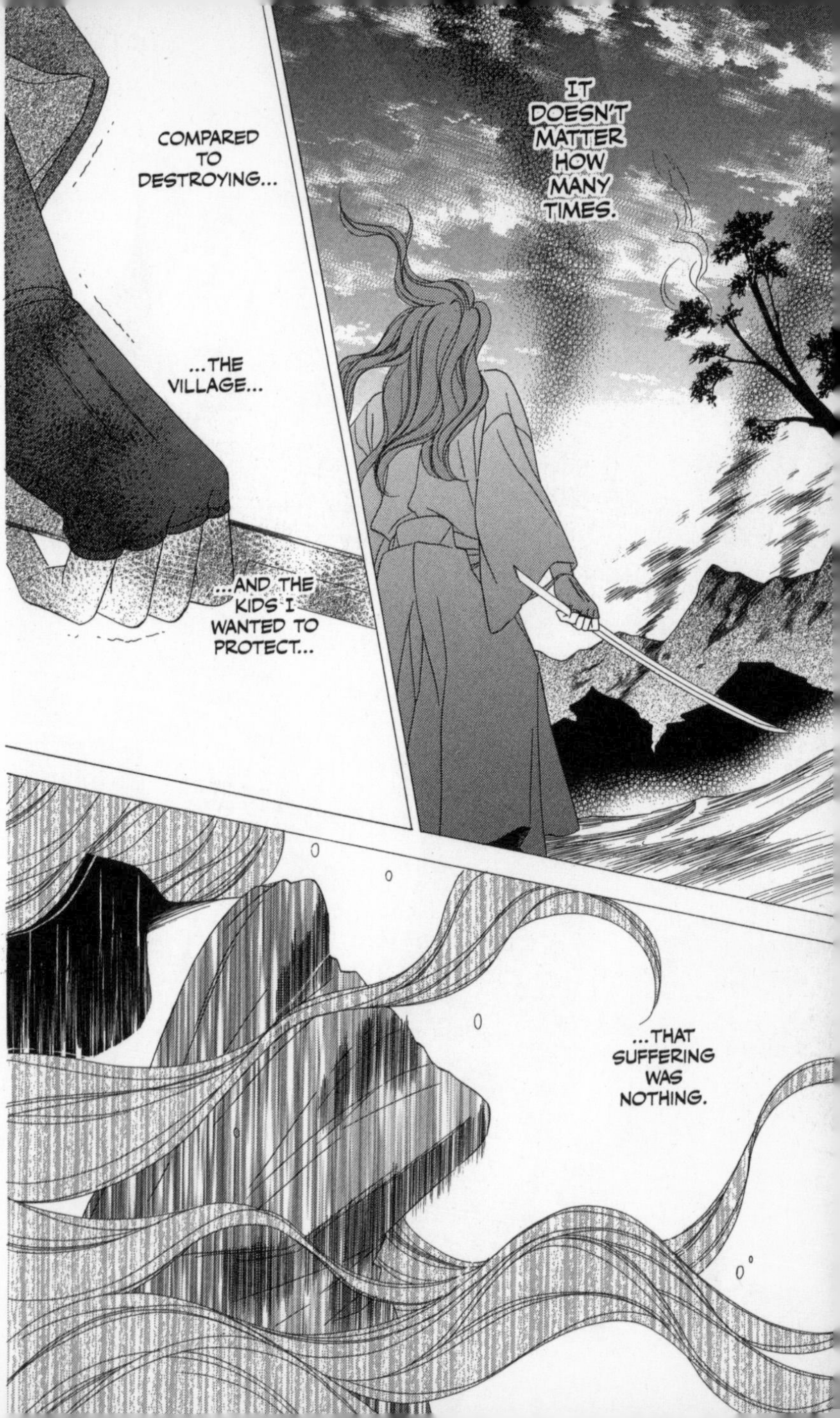
IT DOESN'T MATTER HOW MANY TIMES.
COMPARED TO DESTROYING...
...THE VILLAGE...
...AND THE KIDS I WANTED TO PROTECT...
...THAT SUFFERING WAS NOTHING.

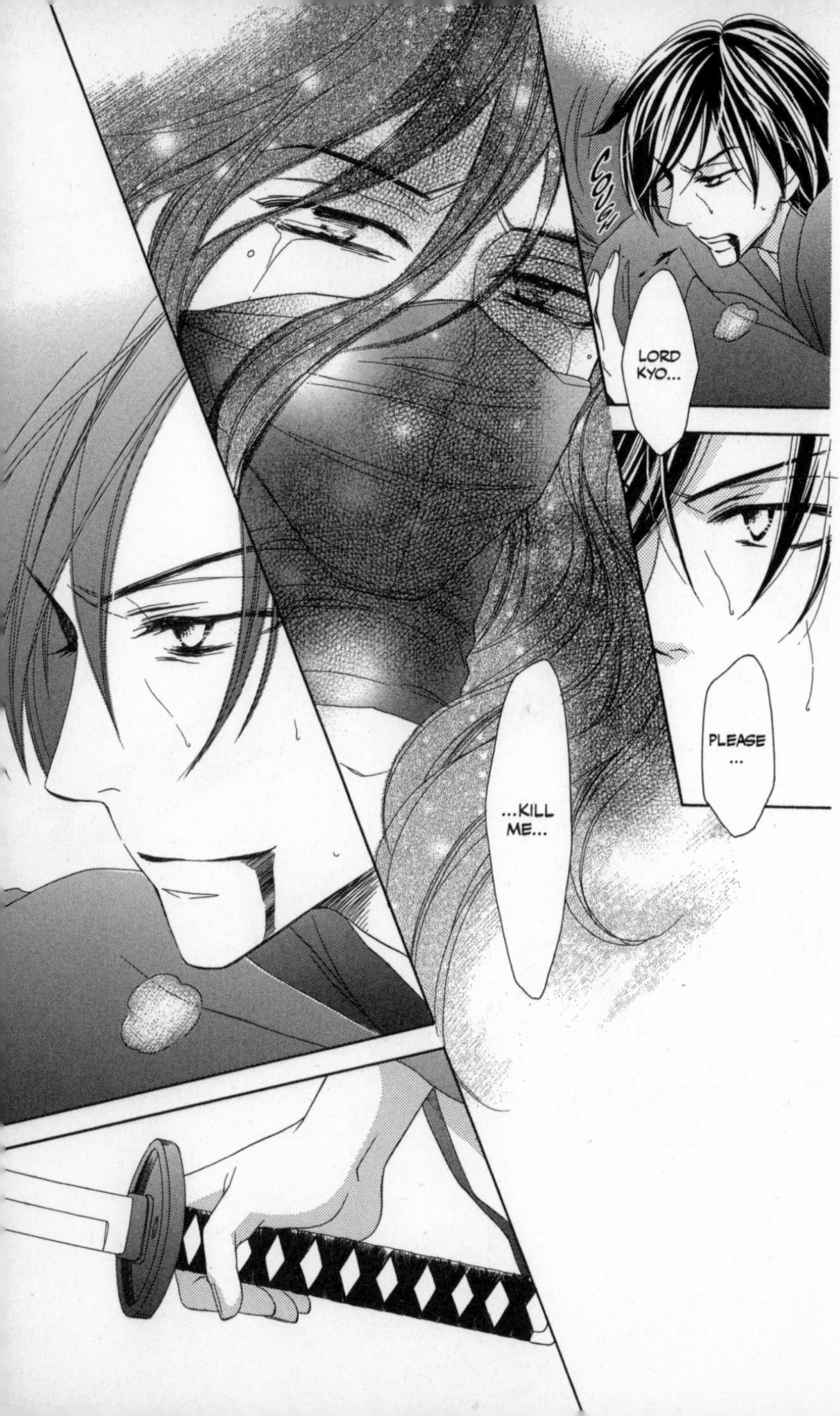
COUGH
LORD KYO...
PLEASE ...
...KILL ME...

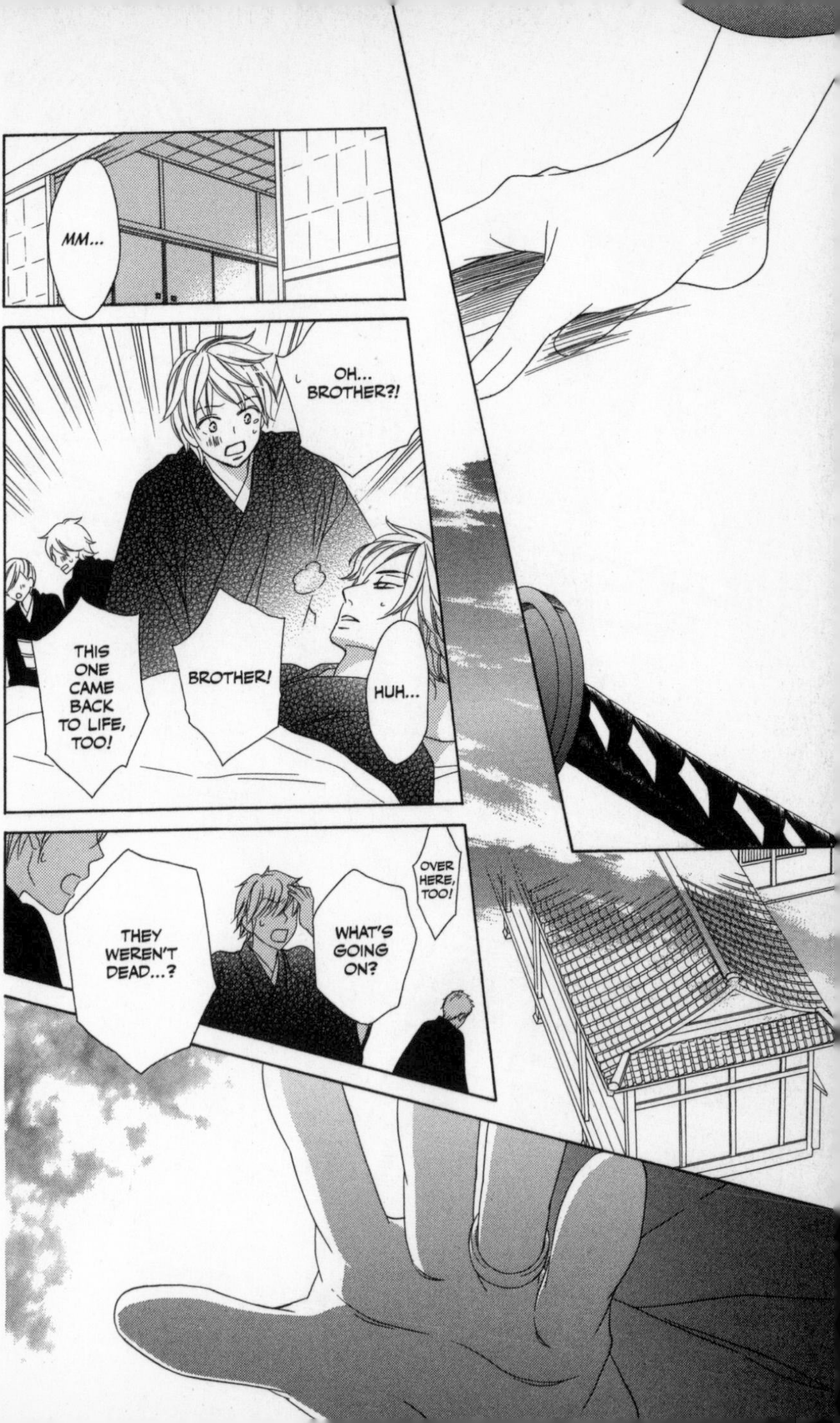
MM...
OH... BROTHER?!
HUH...
BROTHER!
THIS ONE CAME BACK TO LIFE, TOO!
OVER HERE, TOO!
WHAT'S GOING ON?
THEY WEREN'T DEAD...?

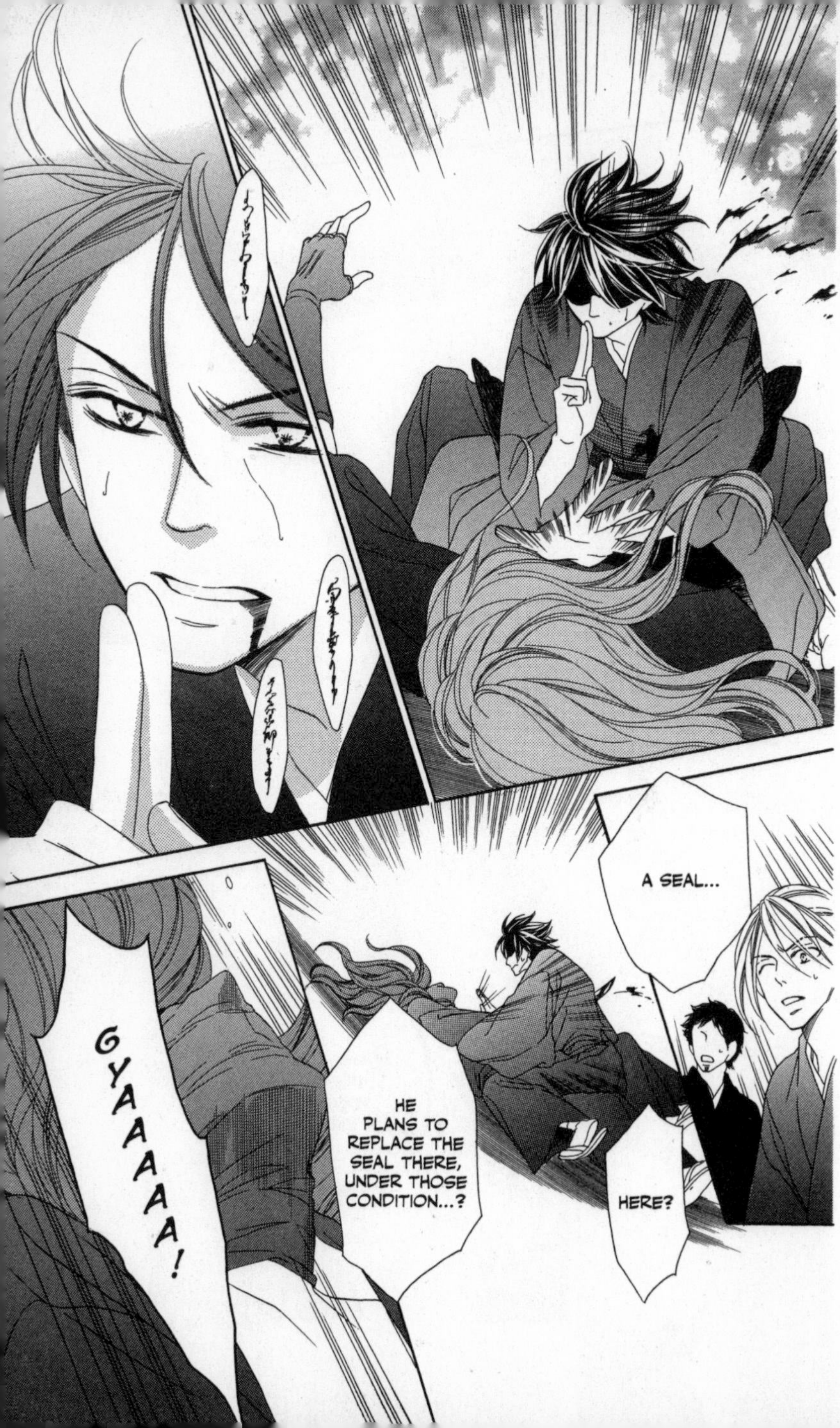
A SEAL...
HERE?
HE PLANS TO REPLACE THE SEAL THERE, UNDER THOSE CONDITION...?
GYAAAAAA!

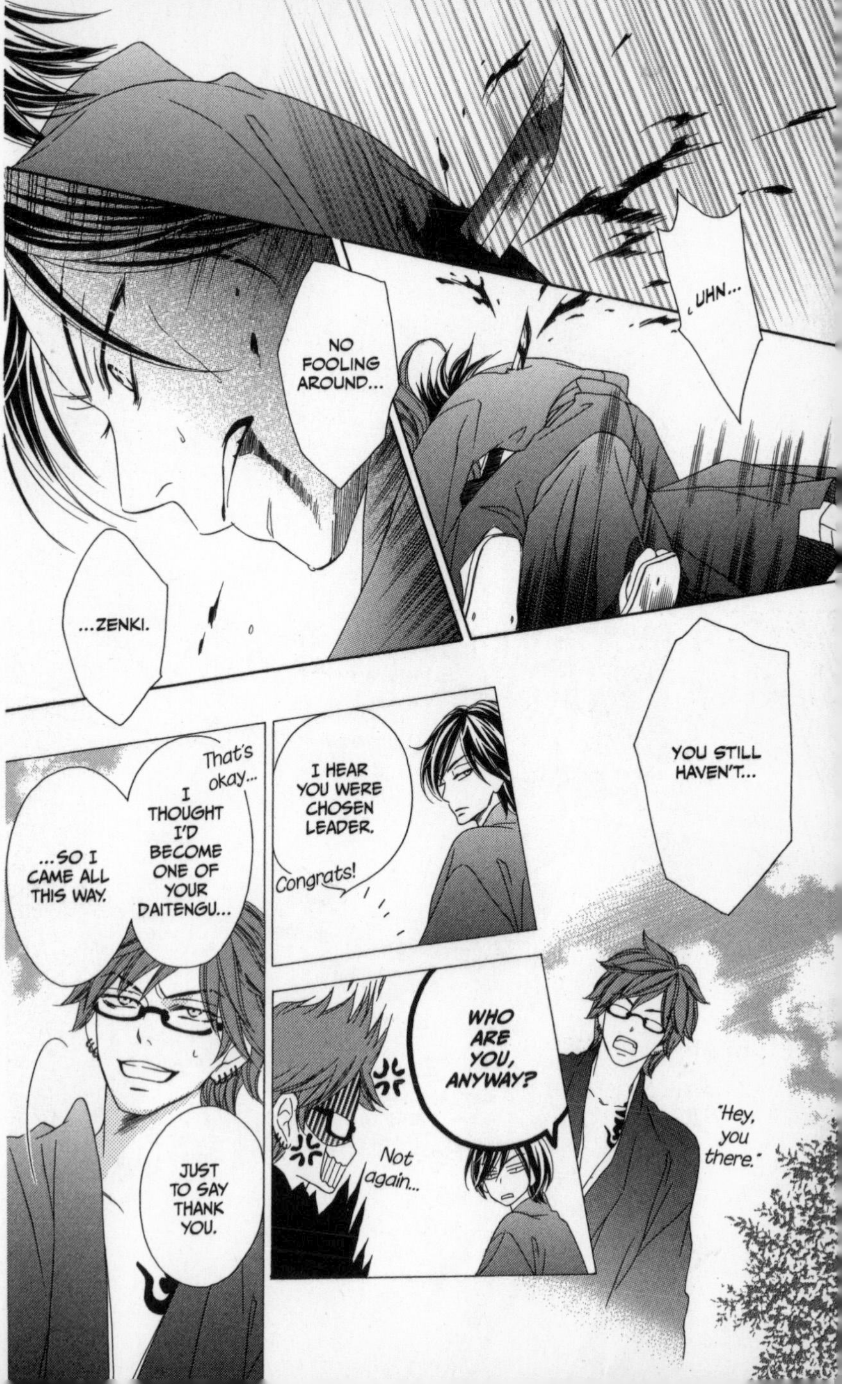
UHN...
NO FOOLING AROUND...
...ZENKI.
YOU STILL HAVEN'T...
"Hey, you there."
I HEAR YOU WERE CHOSEN LEADER.
Congrats!
WHO ARE YOU, ANYWAY?
Not again...
That's okay...
I THOUGHT I'D BECOME ONE OF YOUR DAITENGU...
...SO I CAME ALL THIS WAY.
JUST TO SAY THANK YOU.

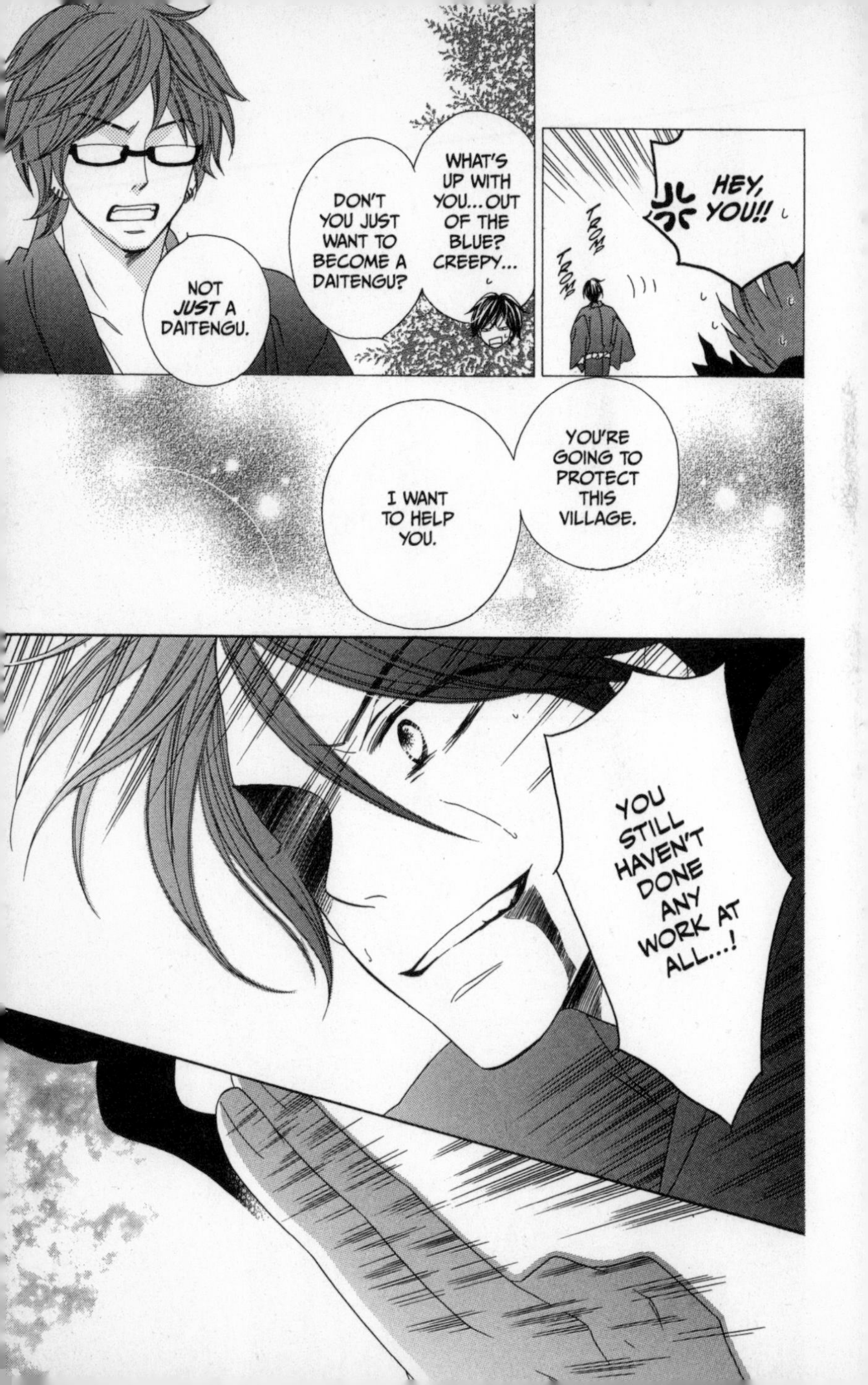
HEY, YOU!!
TROMP TROMP
WHAT'S UP WITH YOU...OUT OF THE BLUE? CREEPY...
DON'T YOU JUST WANT TO BECOME A DAITENGU?
NOT *JUST* A DAITENGU.
YOU'RE GOING TO PROTECT THIS VILLAGE.
I WANT TO HELP YOU.
YOU STILL HAVEN'T DONE ANY WORK AT ALL...!

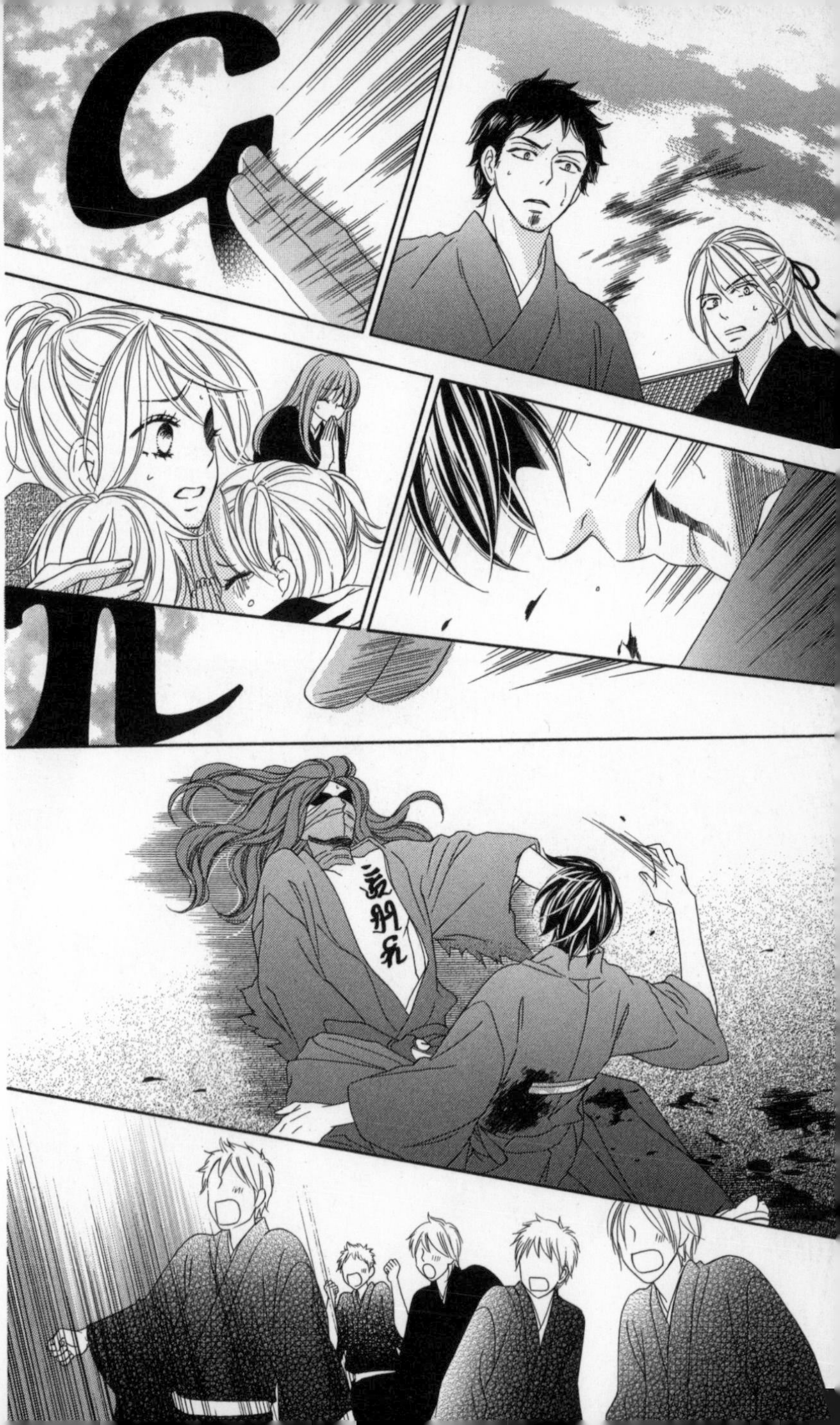

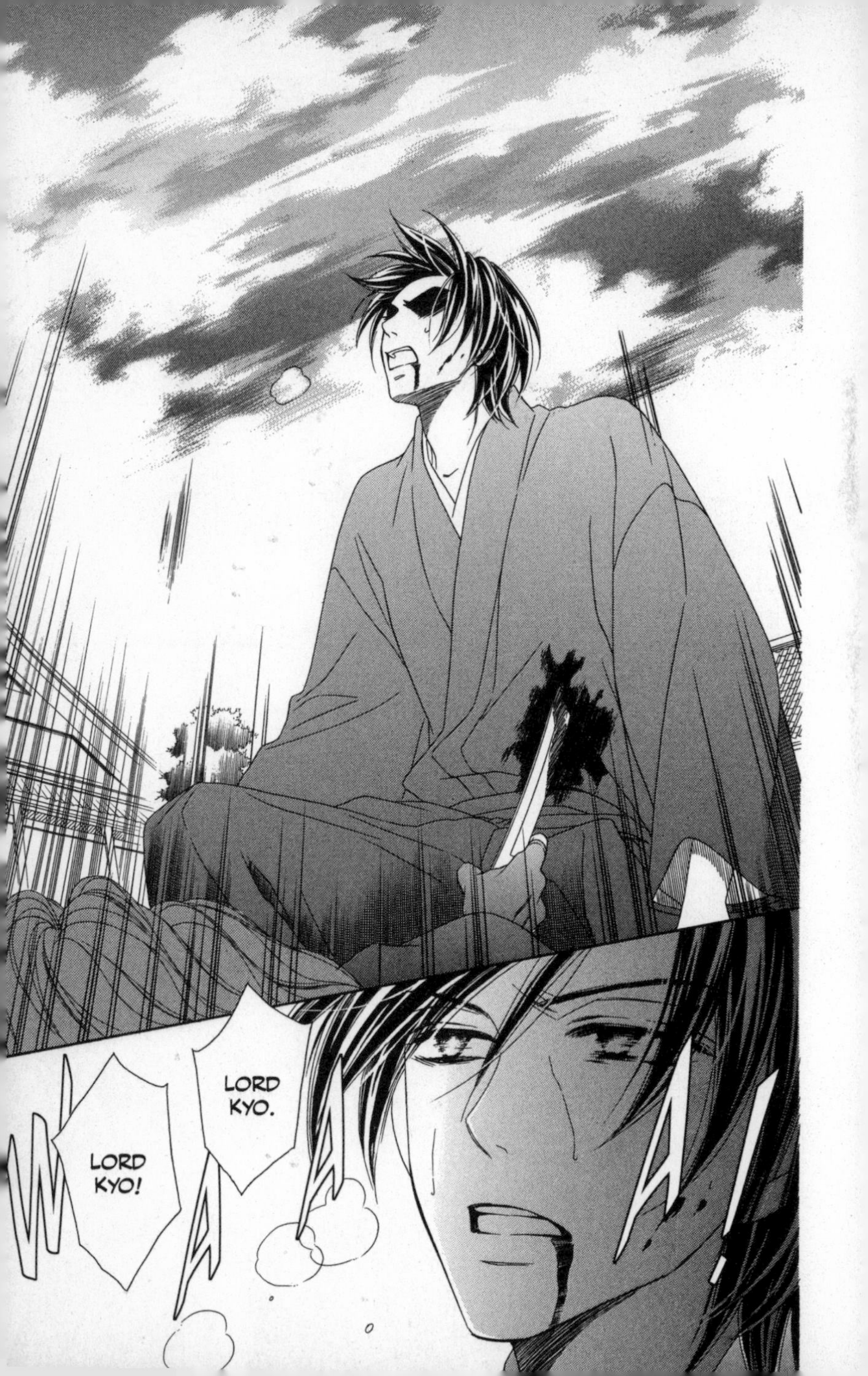
LORD KYO.
LORD KYO!

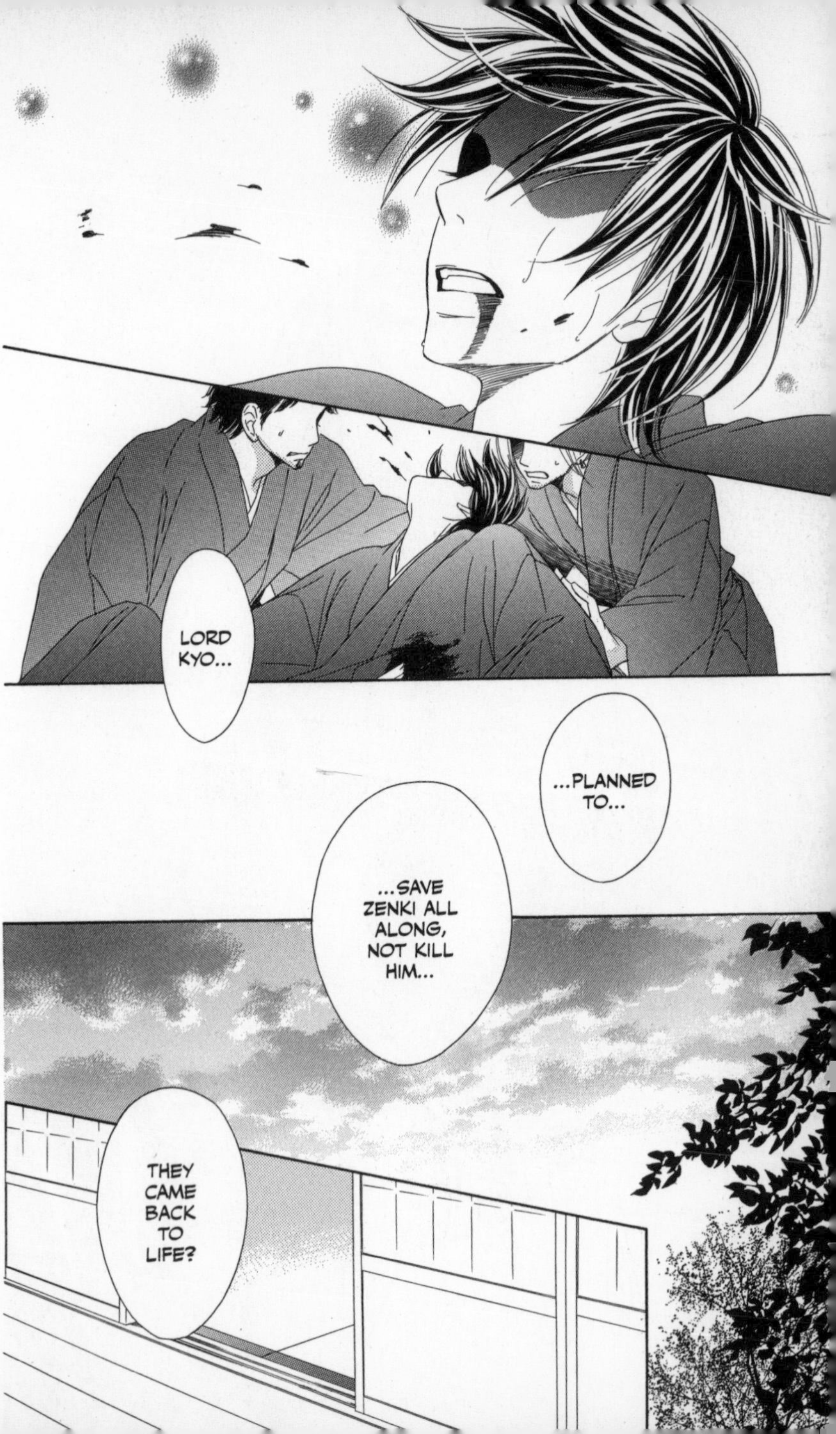
LORD KYO...
...PLANNED TO...
...SAVE ZENKI ALL ALONG, NOT KILL HIM...
THEY CAME BACK TO LIFE?

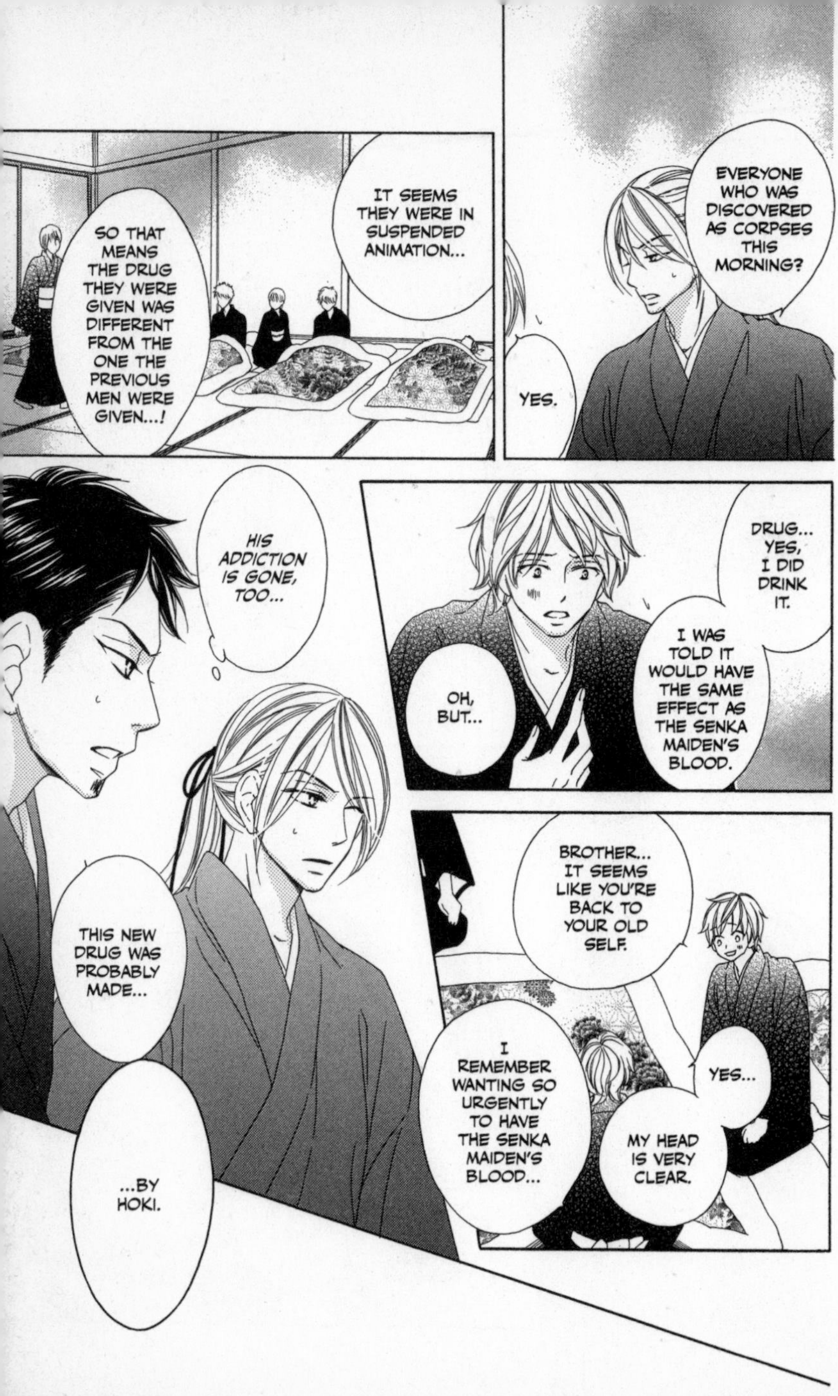
EVERYONE WHO WAS DISCOVERED AS CORPSES THIS MORNING?
YES.
IT SEEMS THEY WERE IN SUSPENDED ANIMATION...
SO THAT MEANS THE DRUG THEY WERE GIVEN WAS DIFFERENT FROM THE ONE THE PREVIOUS MEN WERE GIVEN...!
DRUG... YES, I DID DRINK IT.
I WAS TOLD IT WOULD HAVE THE SAME EFFECT AS THE SENKA MAIDEN'S BLOOD.
OH, BUT...
BROTHER... IT SEEMS LIKE YOU'RE BACK TO YOUR OLD SELF.
YES...
MY HEAD IS VERY CLEAR.
I REMEMBER WANTING SO URGENTLY TO HAVE THE SENKA MAIDEN'S BLOOD...
HIS ADDICTION IS GONE, TOO...
THIS NEW DRUG WAS PROBABLY MADE...
...BY HOKI.

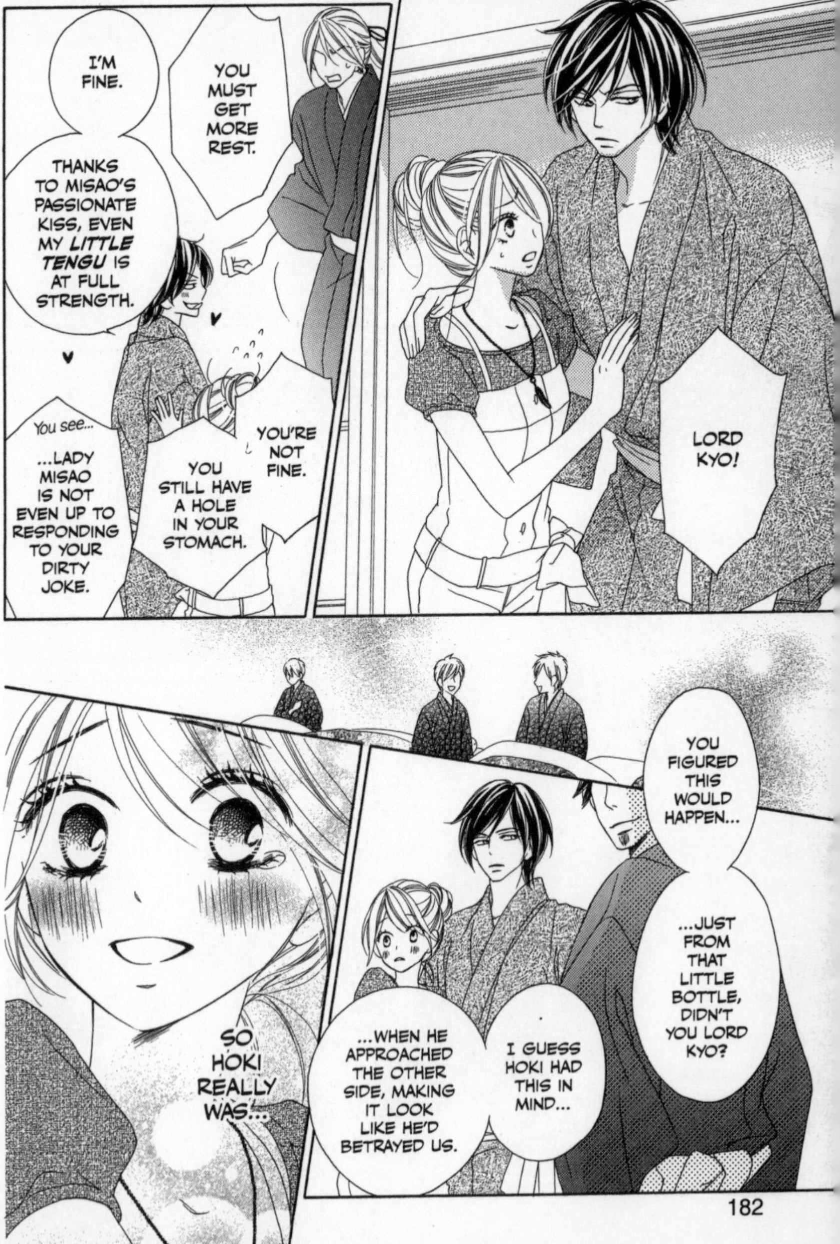
LORD KYO!
YOU MUST GET MORE REST.
I'M FINE.
THANKS TO MISAO'S PASSIONATE KISS, EVEN MY *LITTLE TENGU* IS AT FULL STRENGTH.
YOU'RE NOT FINE.
YOU STILL HAVE A HOLE IN YOUR STOMACH.
You see...
...LADY MISAO IS NOT EVEN UP TO RESPONDING TO YOUR DIRTY JOKE.
YOU FIGURED THIS WOULD HAPPEN...
...JUST FROM THAT LITTLE BOTTLE, DIDN'T YOU LORD KYO?
I GUESS HOKI HAD THIS IN MIND...
...WHEN HE APPROACHED THE OTHER SIDE, MAKING IT LOOK LIKE HE'D BETRAYED US.
SO HOKI REALLY WAS...

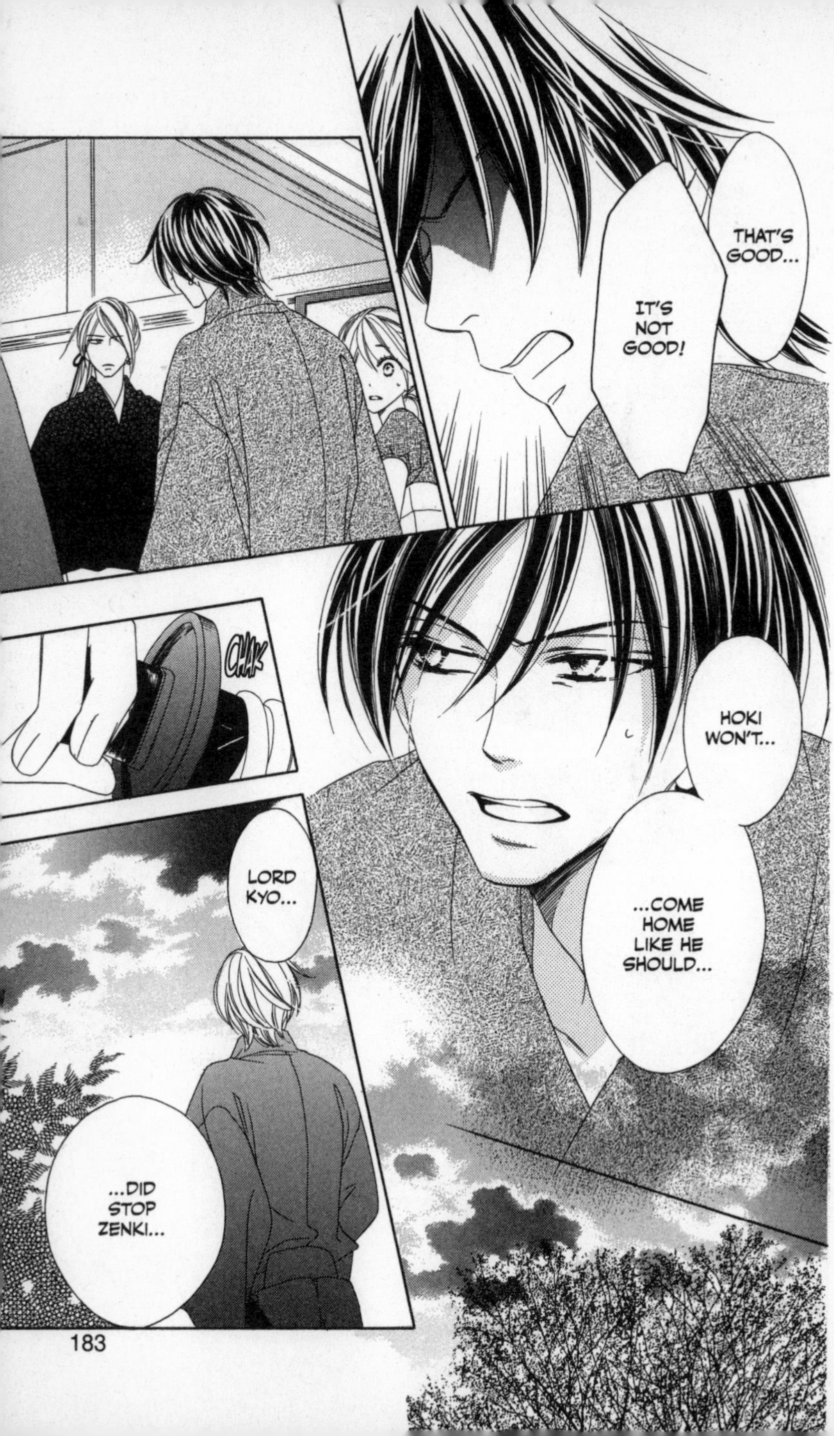
THAT'S GOOD...
IT'S NOT GOOD!
HOKI WON'T...
...COME HOME LIKE HE SHOULD...
CHAK
LORD KYO...
...DID STOP ZENKI...

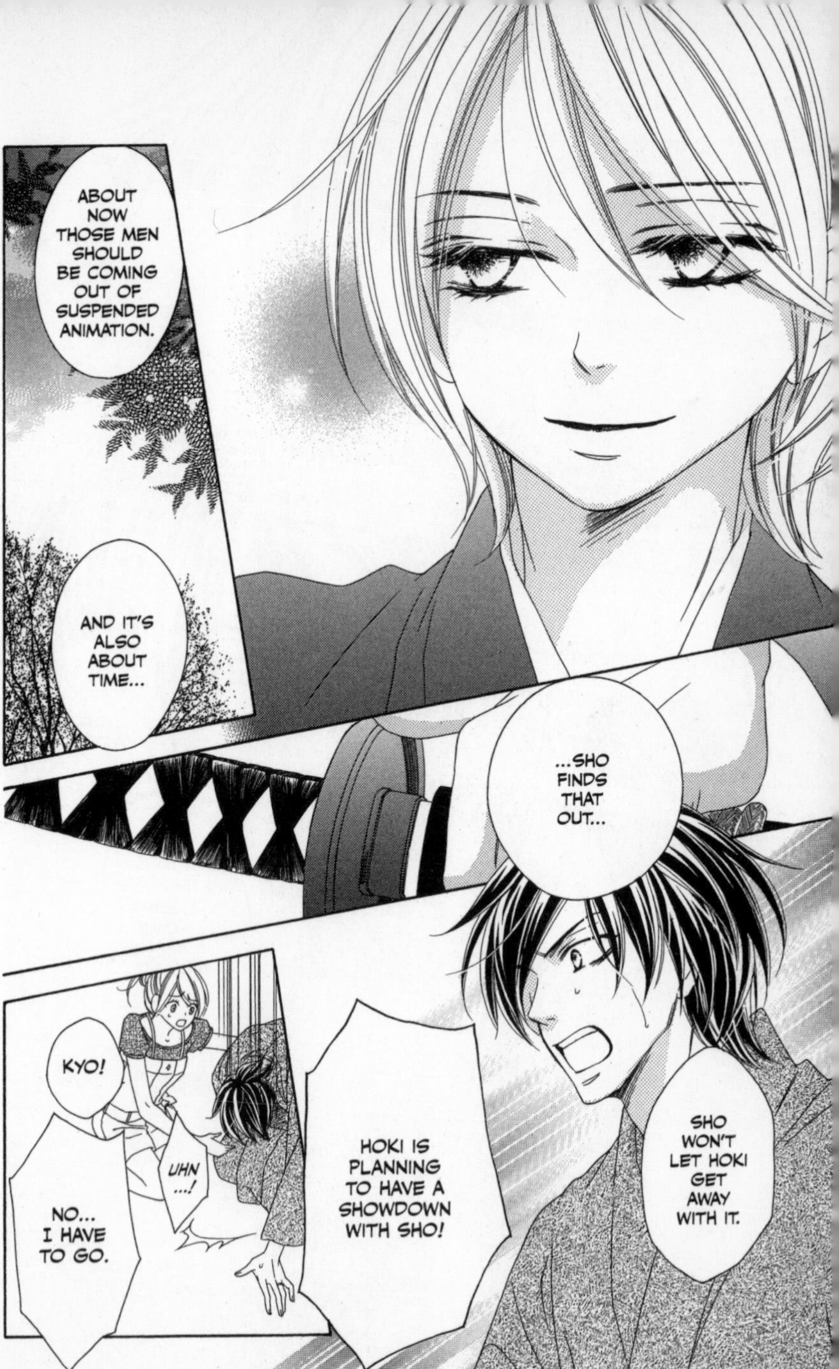
ABOUT NOW THOSE MEN SHOULD BE COMING OUT OF SUSPENDED ANIMATION.
AND IT'S ALSO ABOUT TIME...
...SHO FINDS THAT OUT...
SHO WON'T LET HOKI GET AWAY WITH IT.
HOKI IS PLANNING TO HAVE A SHOWDOWN WITH SHO!
KYO!
UHN ...!
NO... I HAVE TO GO.

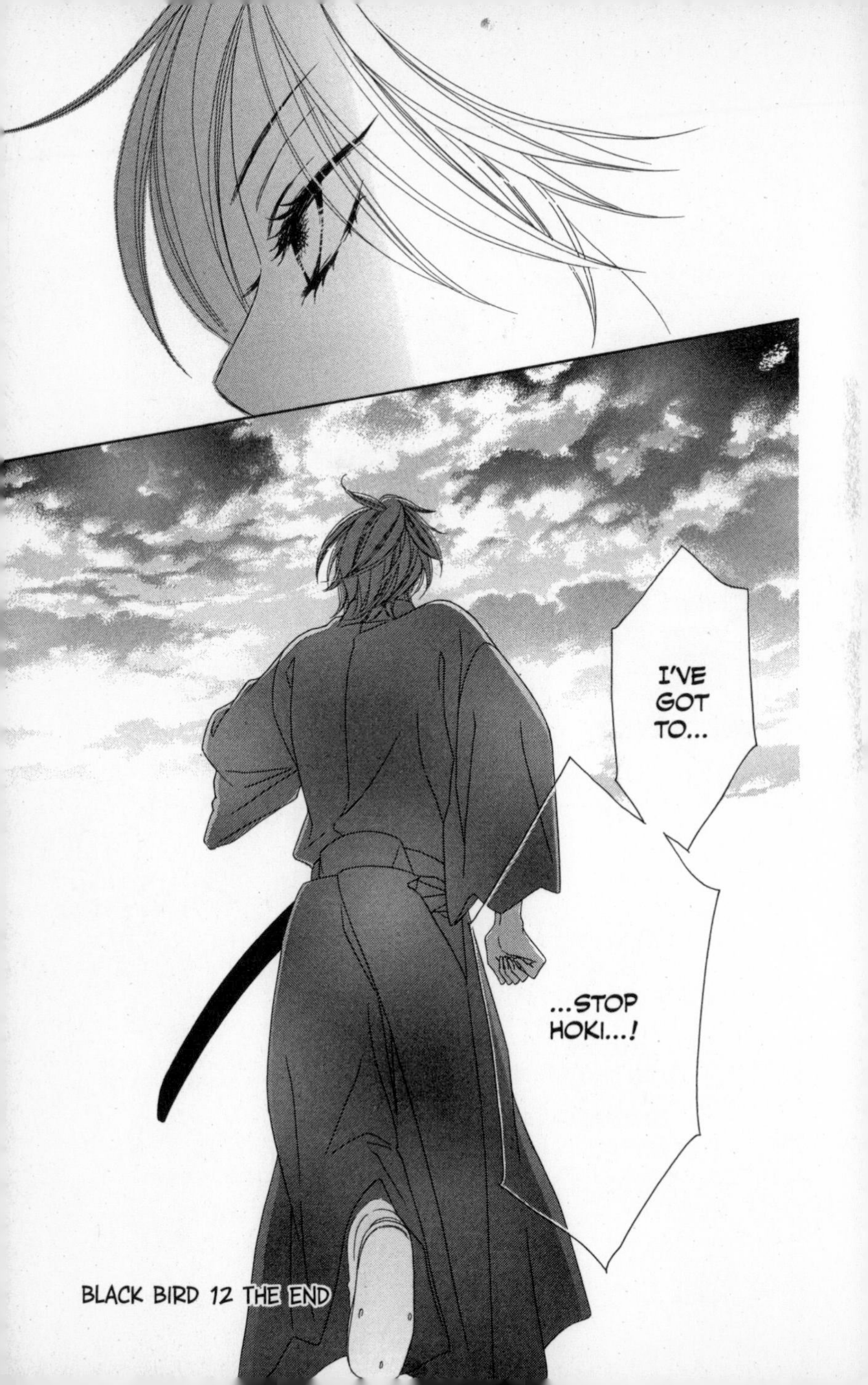

I'VE GOT TO...
...STOP HOKI...!
BLACK BIRD 12 THE END

Picross Answers ♡

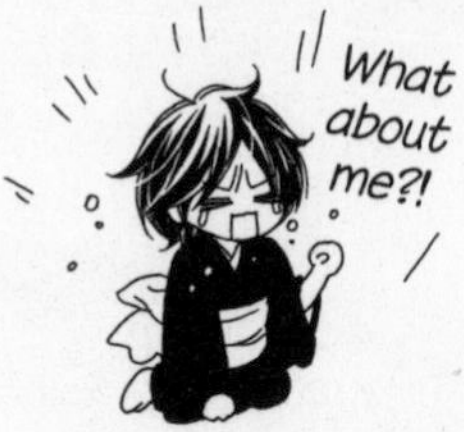
What about me?!

Q1. Saburo

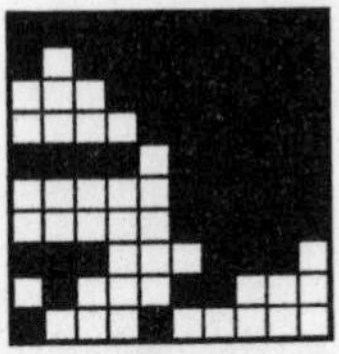

Q2. Kyo

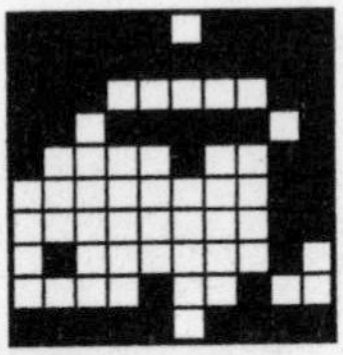

Q3. Taro

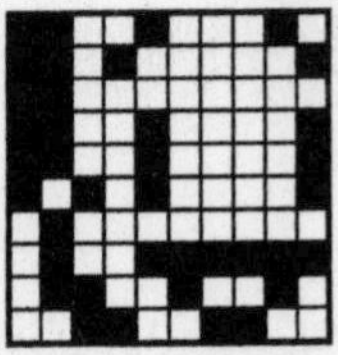

Q4. Sho

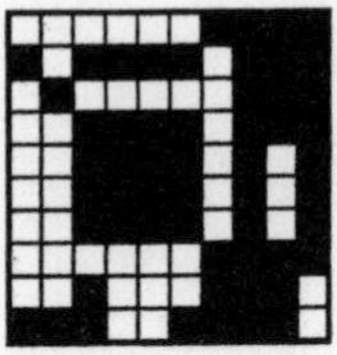

I had considered these ones as well...

Misao

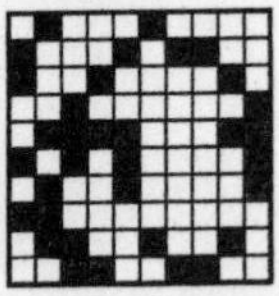

Sagami

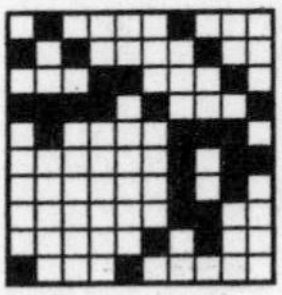

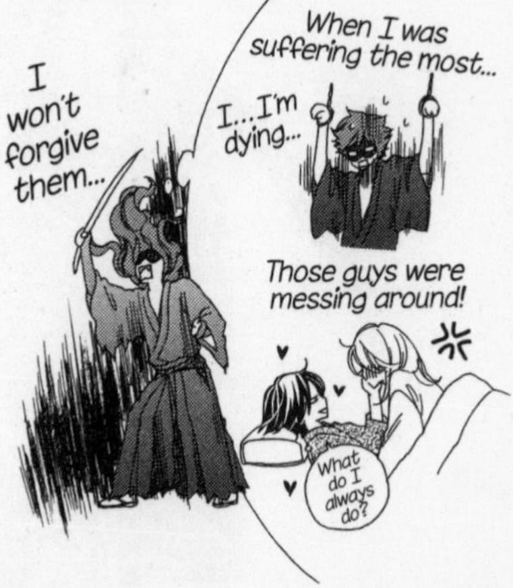
When I was suffering the most...
I...I'm dying...
I won't forgive them...
Those guys were messing around!
What do I always do?

I will leave the rest of the pages for my Special Feature(←).

I hope to see you again in my next volume...♡

An auspicious day,
September 2010
Kanako Sakurakouji
桜小路 かのこ

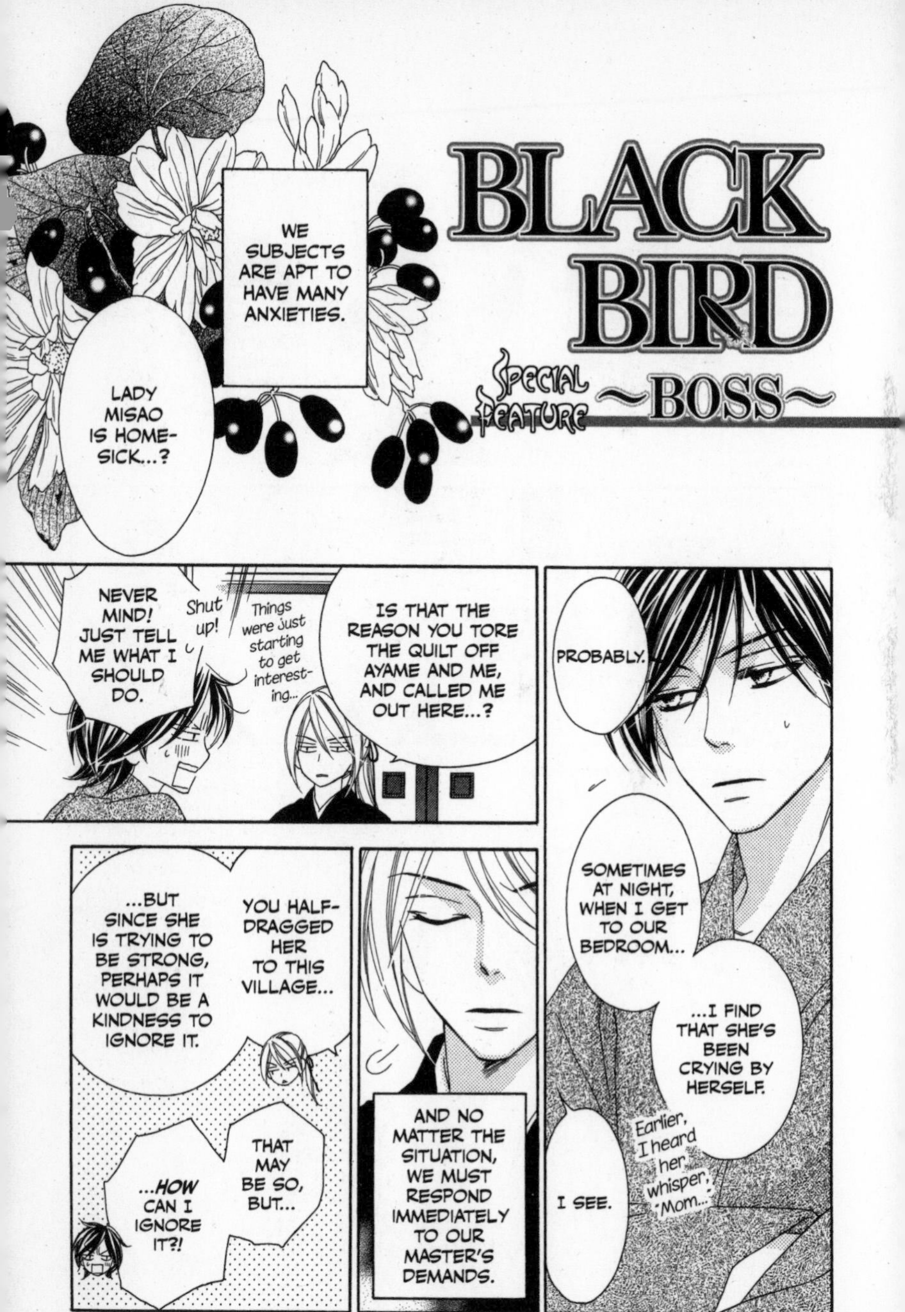
BLACK BIRD
Special Feature
~BOSS~
WE SUBJECTS ARE APT TO HAVE MANY ANXIETIES.
LADY MISAO IS HOME-SICK...?
PROBABLY.
SOMETIMES AT NIGHT, WHEN I GET TO OUR BEDROOM...
...I FIND THAT SHE'S BEEN CRYING BY HERSELF.
Earlier, I heard her whisper, "Mom..."
I SEE.
IS THAT THE REASON YOU TORE THE QUILT OFF AYAME AND ME, AND CALLED ME OUT HERE...?
Things were just starting to get interest-ing...
Shut up!
NEVER MIND! JUST TELL ME WHAT I SHOULD DO.
AND NO MATTER THE SITUATION, WE MUST RESPOND IMMEDIATELY TO OUR MASTER'S DEMANDS.
YOU HALF-DRAGGED HER TO THIS VILLAGE...
...BUT SINCE SHE IS TRYING TO BE STRONG, PERHAPS IT WOULD BE A KINDNESS TO IGNORE IT.
THAT MAY BE SO, BUT...
...HOW CAN I IGNORE IT?!

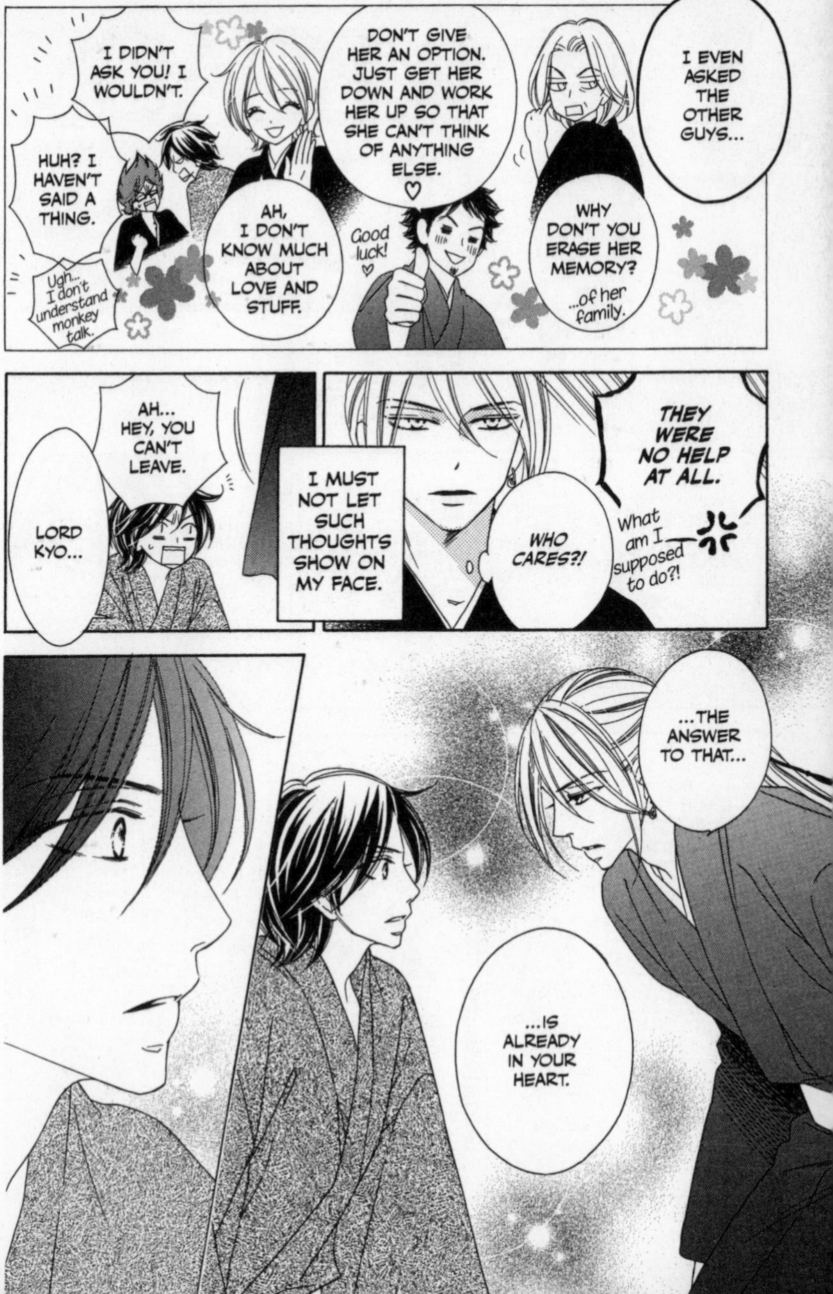
I EVEN ASKED THE OTHER GUYS...
WHY DON'T YOU ERASE HER MEMORY?
...of her family.
DON'T GIVE HER AN OPTION. JUST GET HER DOWN AND WORK HER UP SO THAT SHE CAN'T THINK OF ANYTHING ELSE. ♡
Good luck! ♡
AH, I DON'T KNOW MUCH ABOUT LOVE AND STUFF.
I DIDN'T ASK YOU! I WOULDN'T.
HUH? I HAVEN'T SAID A THING.
Ugh... I don't understand monkey talk.
THEY WERE NO HELP AT ALL.
What am I supposed to do?!
WHO CARES?!
I MUST NOT LET SUCH THOUGHTS SHOW ON MY FACE.
AH... HEY, YOU CAN'T LEAVE.
LORD KYO...
...THE ANSWER TO THAT...
...IS ALREADY IN YOUR HEART.

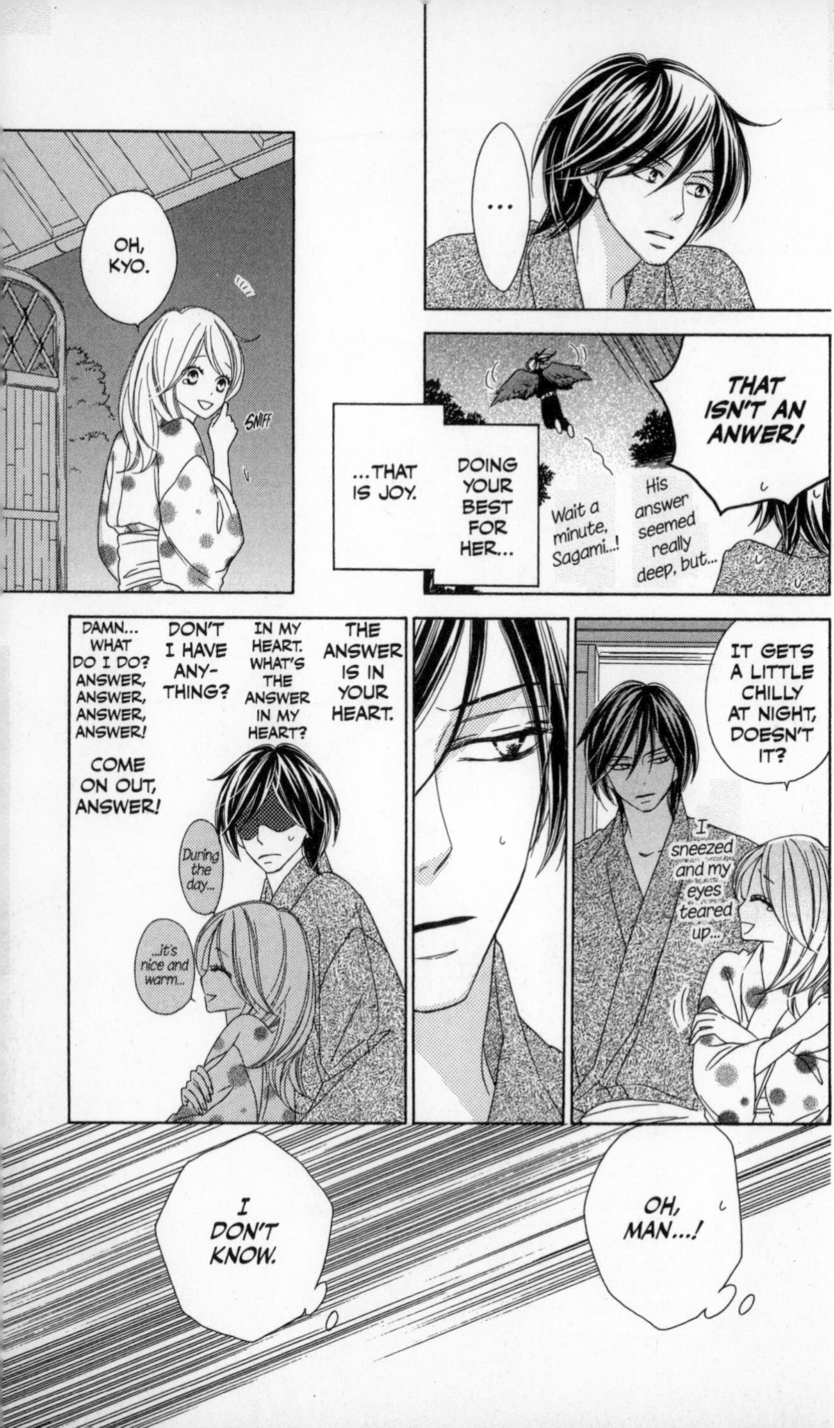
...
THAT ISN'T AN ANWER!
His answer seemed really deep, but...
Wait a minute, Sagami...!
DOING YOUR BEST FOR HER...
...THAT IS JOY.
OH, KYO.
SNIFF
IT GETS A LITTLE CHILLY AT NIGHT, DOESN'T IT?
I sneezed and my eyes teared up...
THE ANSWER IS IN YOUR HEART.
IN MY HEART. WHAT'S THE ANSWER IN MY HEART?
DON'T I HAVE ANY-THING?
DAMN... WHAT DO I DO? ANSWER, ANSWER, ANSWER, ANSWER!
COME ON OUT, ANSWER!
During the day...
...it's nice and warm...
OH, MAN...!
I DON'T KNOW.

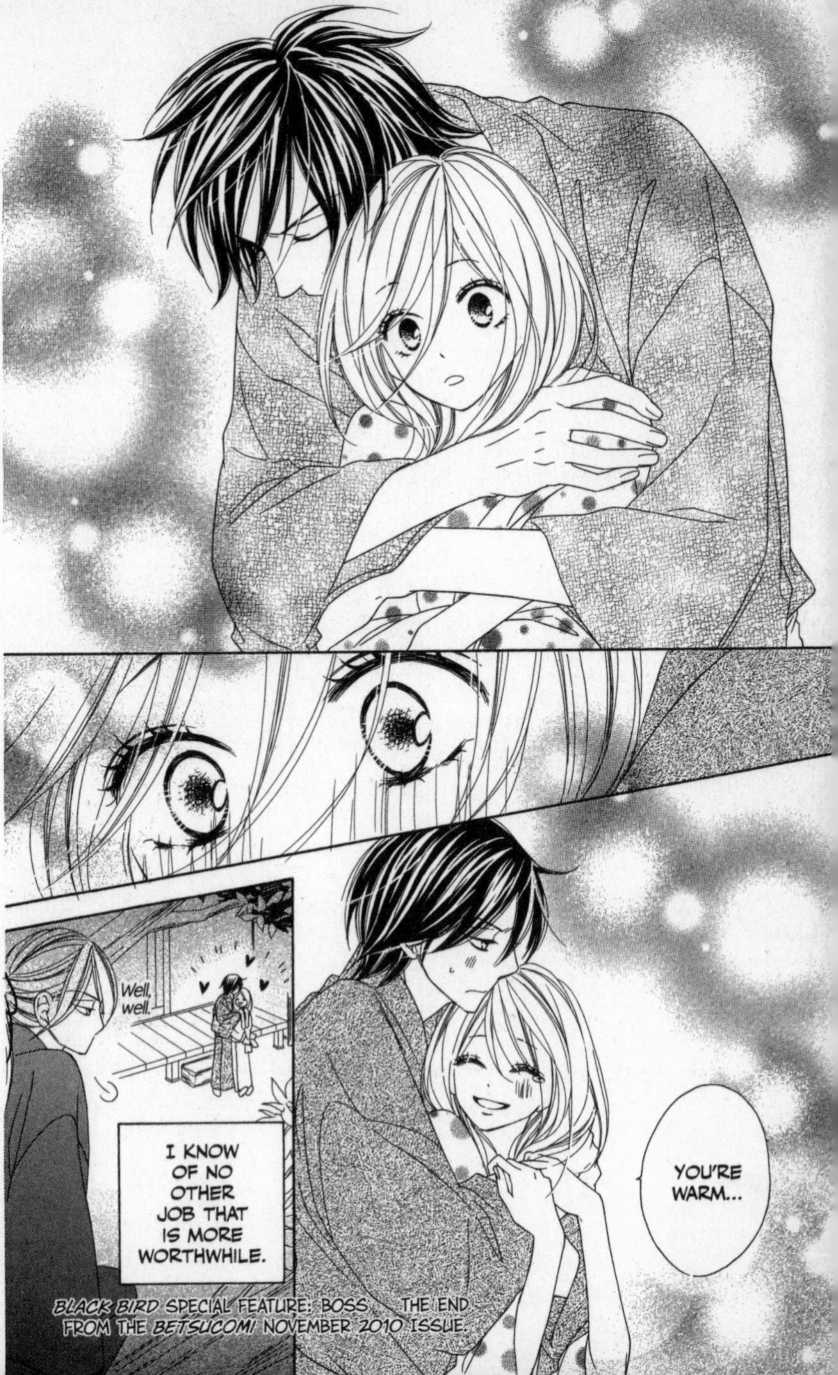
YOU'RE WARM...
Well, well.
I KNOW OF NO OTHER JOB THAT IS MORE WORTHWHILE.

BLACK BIRD SPECIAL FEATURE: BOSS THE END
FROM THE *BETSUCOMI* NOVEMBER 2010 ISSUE.

GLOSSARY

PAGE 6, AUTHOR NOTE: Picross Puzzle
A puzzle game from Nintendo. The
name is a combination of Picture and
Crossword. It is similar to a Nonogram
(also known as Hanjie, Paint by Numbers,
or Griddlers) in which cells in a
grid have to be colored or left blank
according to numbers given at the side
of the grid to reveal a hidden picture.

PAGE 35, PANEL 2: Obi
The wide panel of fabric used to
belt kimono. Depending on the
fabric, it can be quite thick.

Kanoko Sakurakouji was born in downtown
Tokyo, and her hobbies include reading,
watching plays, traveling and shopping. Her
debut title, *Raibu ga Hanetara*, ran in *Bessatsu
Shojo Comic* (currently called *Bestucomi*) in
2000, and her 2004 *Bestucomi* title *Backstage
Prince* was serialized in VIZ Media's
Shojo Beat magazine. She won the 54th
Shogakukan Manga Award for *Black Bird*.

BLACK BIRD
VOL. 12
Shojo Beat Edition

Story and Art by KANOKO SAKURAKOUJI

© 2007 Kanoko SAKURAKOUJI/Shogakukan
All rights reserved.
Original Japanese edition "BLACK BIRD" published by SHOGAKUKAN Inc.

TRANSLATION JN Productions
TOUCH-UP ART & LETTERING Gia Cam Luc
DESIGN Amy Martin
EDITOR Pancha Diaz

The rights of the author(s) of the work(s) in this publication
to be so identified have been asserted in accordance with
the Copyright, Designs and Patents Act 1988. A CIP catalogue
record for this book is available from the British Library.

The stories, characters and incidents mentioned
in this publication are entirely fictional.

Printed in the U.S.A.

Published by VIZ Media, LLC
P.O. Box 77010
San Francisco, CA 94107

10 9 8 7 6 5 4 3 2 1
First printing, January 2012

www.shojobeat.com www.viz.com

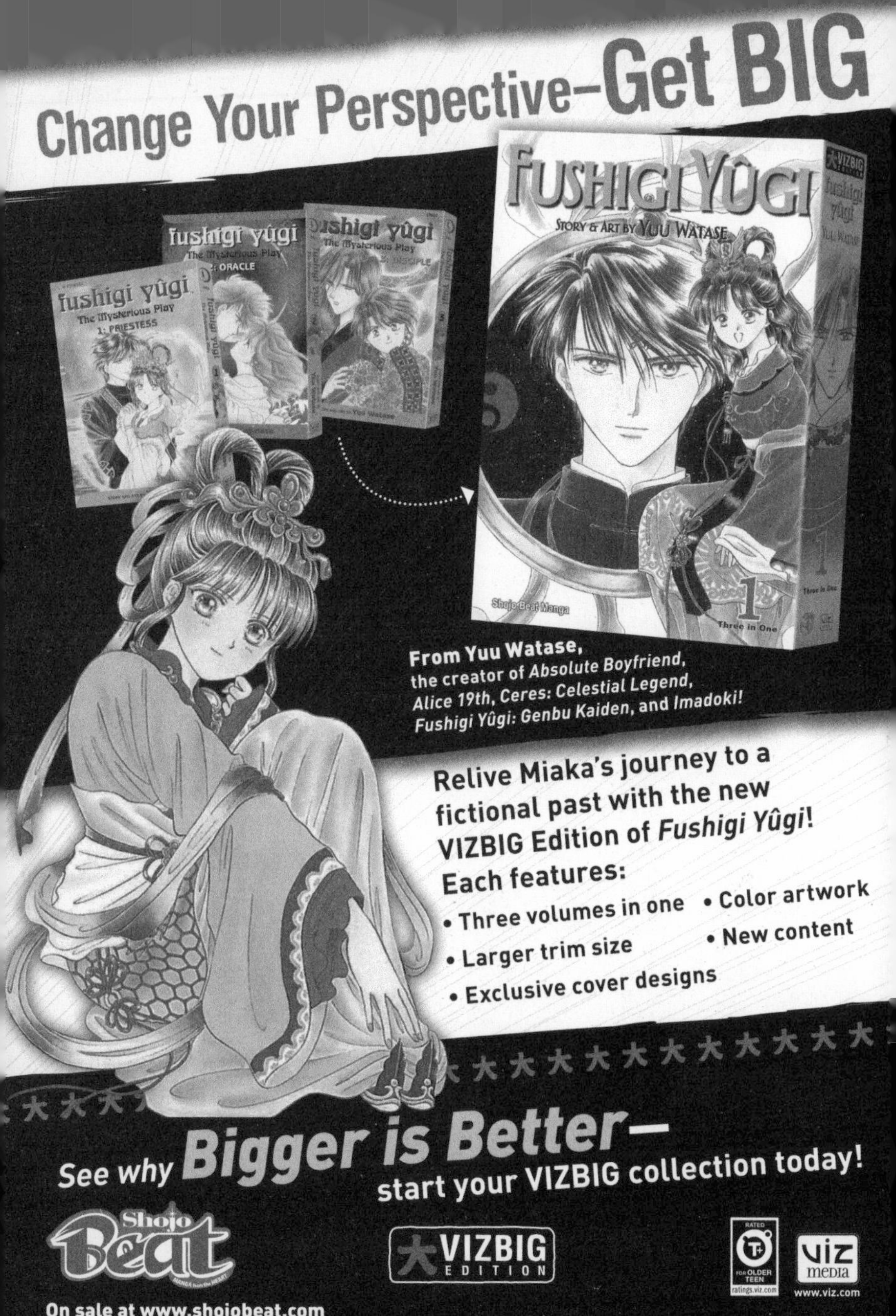
Change Your Perspective–Get BIG
FUSHIGI YÛGI
STORY & ART BY YUU WATASE
Shojo Beat Manga
1
Three in One
fushigi yûgi
The Mysterious Play
1: PRIESTESS
2: ORACLE
From Yuu Watase,
the creator of Absolute Boyfriend, Alice 19th, Ceres: Celestial Legend, Fushigi Yûgi: Genbu Kaiden, and Imadoki!
Relive Miaka's journey to a fictional past with the new VIZBIG Edition of Fushigi Yûgi!
Each features:
• Three volumes in one
• Color artwork
• Larger trim size
• New content
• Exclusive cover designs
See why Bigger is Better—
start your VIZBIG collection today!
Shojo Beat
VIZBIG EDITION
RATED T+ FOR OLDER TEEN
ratings.viz.com
viz media
www.viz.com
On sale at www.shojobeat.com
Also available at your local bookstore and comic store.
FUSHIGI YUGI © Yuu WATASE/Shogakukan Inc.

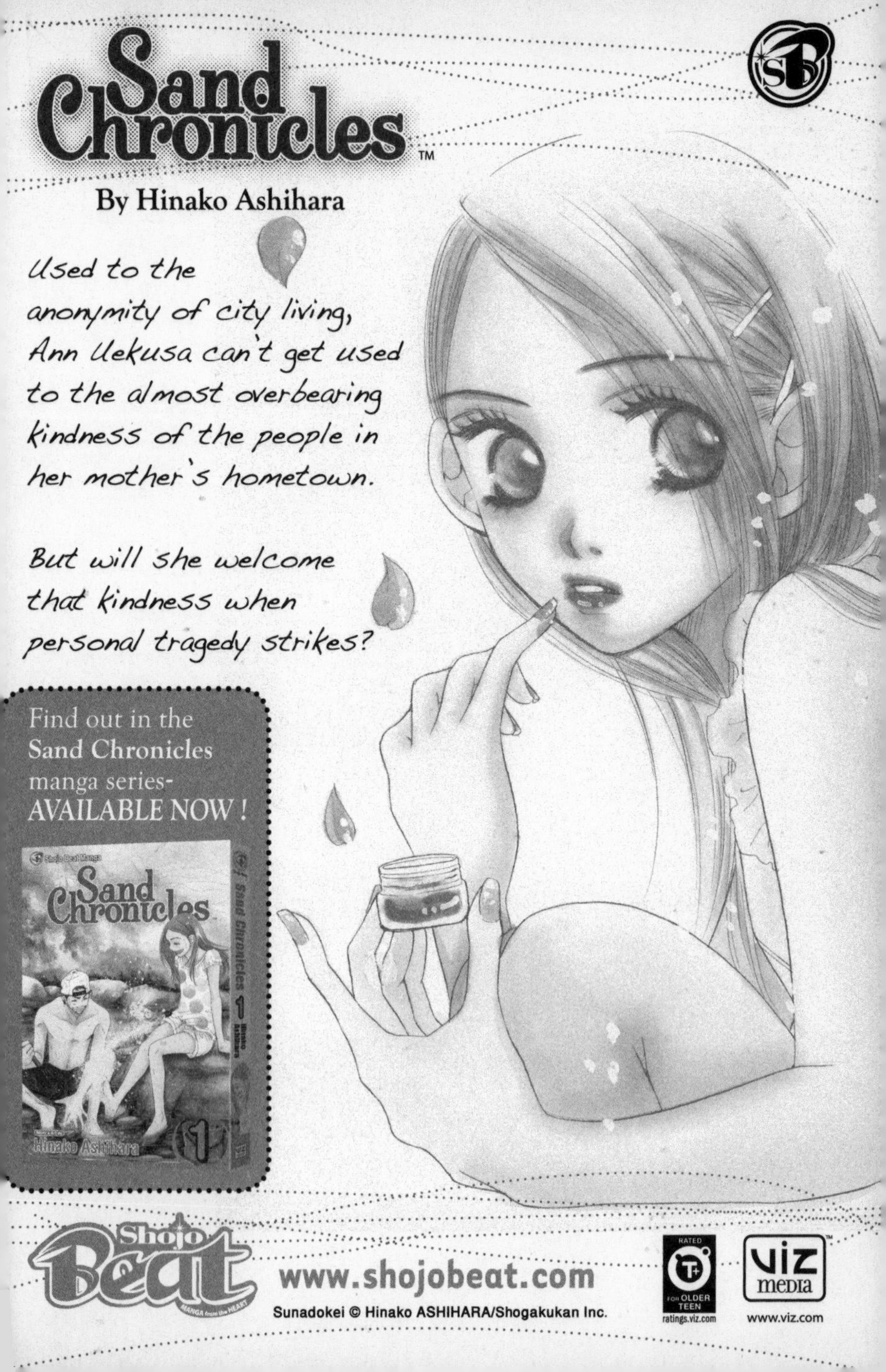

Sand Chronicles™
By Hinako Ashihara
Used to the anonymity of city living, Ann Uekusa can't get used to the almost overbearing kindness of the people in her mother's hometown.
But will she welcome that kindness when personal tragedy strikes?
Find out in the Sand Chronicles manga series- AVAILABLE NOW!
Shojo Beat Manga
Sand Chronicles
Sand Chronicles 1
Hinako Ashihara
Shojo Beat
www.shojobeat.com
Sunadokei © Hinako ASHIHARA/Shogakukan Inc.
RATED T+ FOR OLDER TEEN
ratings.viz.com
VIZ MEDIA
www.viz.com

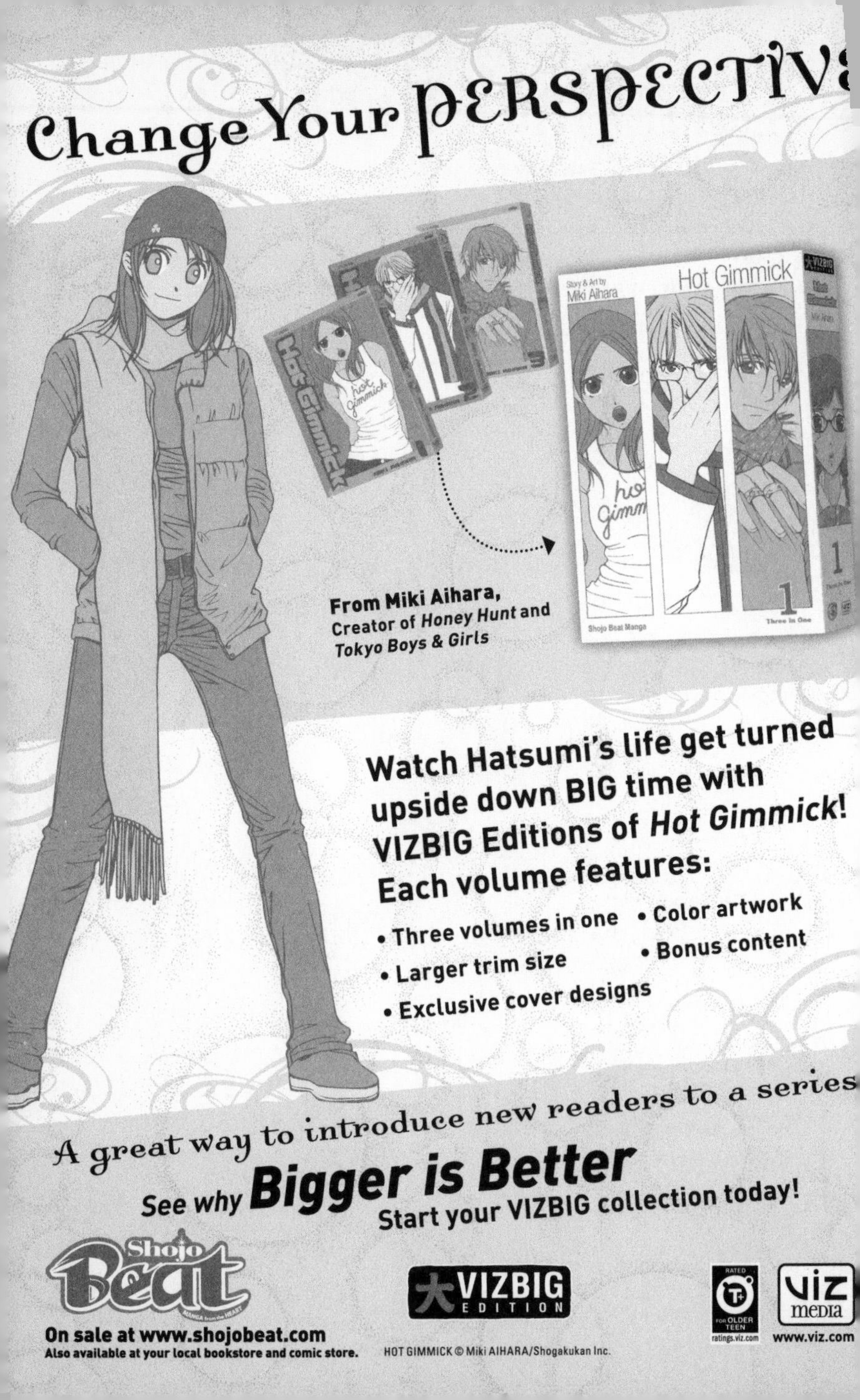
Change Your PERSPECTIVE
Story & Art by Miki Aihara
Hot Gimmick
Shojo Beat Manga
1
Three in One
From Miki Aihara, Creator of Honey Hunt and Tokyo Boys & Girls
Watch Hatsumi's life get turned upside down BIG time with VIZBIG Editions of Hot Gimmick!
Each volume features:
• Three volumes in one
• Larger trim size
• Exclusive cover designs
• Color artwork
• Bonus content
A great way to introduce new readers to a series
See why Bigger is Better
Start your VIZBIG collection today!
Shojo Beat
VIZBIG EDITION
RATED T+ FOR OLDER TEEN
ratings.viz.com
VIZ media
www.viz.com
On sale at www.shojobeat.com
Also available at your local bookstore and comic store.
HOT GIMMICK © Miki AIHARA/Shogakukan Inc.